CONTENTS

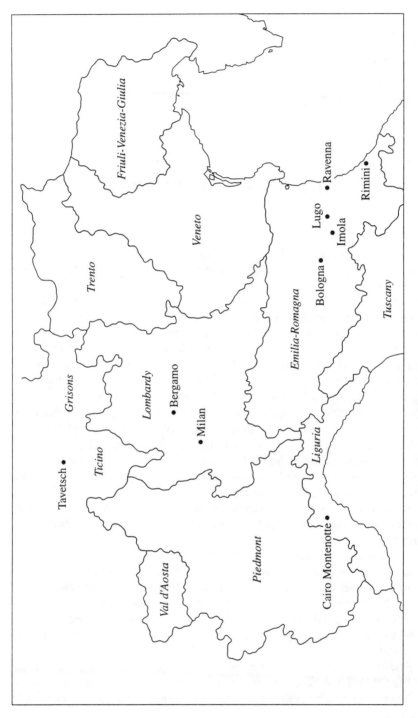

Map of Northern Italy with Location of Sample Dialects

ACKNOWLEDGEMENTS

It is difficult to predict where one's university studies will lead. I had little idea when first coming to Oxford in 1986 that I would eventually complete my D.Phil. dissertation on questions relating to distinctive nasalization and universals of sound change. I have had the great fortune along the way of having worked extensively on the magnificent dialects of Northern Italy – a relatively rare phenomenon in the English-speaking world. First thanks go to my supervisors, Rebecca Posner and Ian Watson, for all their help, advice and support. My gratitude goes also to the examiners, Nigel Vincent and Stephen Parkinson. Of course there are many others, too numerous to mention, who are to be thanked for their invaluable assistance. I take the liberty nevertheless of singling out Jane Warren and my wife, Sandra, for their help and encouragement, during those last heady days in Oxford, and John Bowden for all his help with editing this time around. Heartfelt thanks also go to the Philological Society of Great Britain for very kindly offering to publish this volume. I would like also to acknowledge the extremely generous encouragement given by the anonymous reviewers, as well as by additional readers, Tom Cravens, and Helen Fraser. I have tried to respond to all suggested revisions, but of course responsibility for any defects rests solely with me.

The dissertation remains essentially the same in content as when submitted. The major change wrought by revision primarily involves formatting and the elimination of copious footnoting – the result of my earlier legal training. This monograph is of course not the final word on any of the issues raised, but should, I hope, encourage more work on the substantive basis of language universals, and in particular on distinctive nasalization.

Finally, both apologies and a special expression of gratitude are directed to Max Wheeler, a beacon of patience in Great Britain during what seemed to be an interminable wait for editing to be completed 13,000 miles away in Australia.

Copyright © The Philological Society 1997

ISBN 0–631–20456–3

First published 1997

Blackwell Publishers
108 Cowley Road, Oxford, OX4 1JF, UK

and
350 Main Street,
Malden, MA 02148, USA.

British Library Cataloguing in Publication Data
Applied for

Library of Congress Cataloging-in-Publication Data
Applied for

Printed in Great Britain by
Whitstable Litho Printers Ltd., Whitstable, Kent

Universals of Sound Change in Nasalization

John Hajek

Publications of the Philological Society, 31

Oxford UK & Boston USA

LIST OF FIGURES

LIST OF TABLES

NOTE ON TRANSCRIPTION

Wherever possible examples are transcribed according to IPA convention. However, where examples are taken from secondary sources and phonetic detail is not complete, e.g. vowel length is not marked, examples are given in italics. Some Northern Italian examples are occasionally given in italics, where the point under discussion is clear from the traditional orthographic representation, e.g. N-loss in Bergamese *bu* 'good' (m.) from Latin BONU.

ABBREVIATIONS

Symbols

C	consonant	Ṽ	nasalized vowel
Σ	stress foot	'V(σ)	stressed vowel (syllable)
F(ric)	fricative	⁺V(σ)	pretonic vowel (syllable)
G	glide	⁻V(σ)	post-tonic vowel (syllable)
N	nasal consonant	^V(σ)	atonic vowel (syllable)
$	syllable boundary	w	phonological word
σ	syllable	X	skeletal slot
T	time	≫	e.g. A ≫ B = A before B
V	vowel		

Abbreviations

Bg.	Bergamese
Bo.	Bolognese
Ca.	Cairese
Cat.	Catalan
CL	Compensatory Lengthening
Co	Coda
Cors.	Corsican
CS	Continuous Speech
DENAS	Denasalization
ESP	Extended Stress Parameter

f.   feminine
Fr.   French
Gal.   Galician
Gasc.   Gascon
Gmc   Germanic
Gmn   German
GP   Generative Phonology
Im.   Imolese
It.   Italian
Lat.   Latin
LC   Lexical Component
Lg.   Lughese
LP   Lexical Phonology
LS   Laboratory Speech
m.   masculine
Mi.   Milanese
N-DEL   N-Deletion
N.It.   Northern Italian
NTM   New Ternary Model
Nu   Nucleus
Occ.   Occitan
OE.   Old English
OFr.   Old French
OIr.   Old Irish
On   Onset
OPt.   Old Portuguese
oxy.   oxytonic
par.   paroxytonic
Piac.   Piacentino
P-L   Post-Lexical
PN   Place Node
prop.   proparoxytonic
Pt.   Portuguese
Ra.   Ravennate
Rh   Rhyme
Ri.   Riminese
RN   Root Node
s.   singular
Sal.   Salodiano
Sard.   Sardinian
SC   Surface Contrastive
SL   Supralaryngeal Node
SP   Structure Preservation
SR   Surface Representation

ST	Skeletal Tier
St. 1	Stage 1
St. 2	Stage 2
Ta.	Tavetschan
Tusc.	Tuscan
UR	Underlying Representation
VHP	Vowel-Height Parameter
VLP	Vowel-Length Parameter

INTRODUCTION

The historical development of distinctive nasalization, traditionally formalized as VN > Ṽ, represented in the 1970s an area of major activity in the
search for phonological universals of sound change.[1] As the inadequacy of
formal constraints in generative phonological representation became
increasingly apparent in the early 1970s, focus shifted to establishing
universal substantive restrictions based on observed patterns of sound
change. Particular attention was given to the development of distinctive
nasalization, since it appeared to be both cross-linguistically widespread,
and a relatively simple phenomenon, made up of two connected steps: (1)
nasalization; and (2) N-deletion. There was general optimism amongst those
working on phonological universals of sound change that the universal
characteristics of the process of distinctive nasalization could be easily
uncovered through the examination of cross-linguistic data. So-called
universalists of distinctive nasalization (henceforth just 'universalists'),
Chen (1972 and elsewhere), Foley (1975, 1977), Lightner (1970, 1973),
Ruhlen (1973), Schourup (1973) and later Hombert (1986, 1987) considered
in varying detail the effects of inherent properties of both V (height, quality,
presence and absence of stress) and N (place of articulation), as well as the
contextual effects of syllable structure and adjacent segments, on the spread
of distinctive nasalization. Additional motivation for the endeavour lay in
two related areas: (1) defining the universal characteristics, if any, of
language in the context of sound change and of phonology in general; and
for most universalists, (2) determining the phonetic basis assumed to
underlie sound change and phonology.

Whilst the same factors that motivated universalists in the 1970s continue
to provide impetus for this book, there are additional reasons for this present
study of the interrelationship between V and N, and its effect on the spread
of distinctive nasalization. First, reassessment is required of the numerous
conflicting claims which have been made by universalists about the purportedly universal effects of specific factors, such as N place of articulation. Such
conflict is suggestive either of poor methodology or of the absence of any
strictly universal patterning. However, with the exception of small-scale
studies by Hombert (1986, 1987) and possibly Tuttle (1991), there has been
relatively little work on universals of distinctive nasalization since the 1970s.
Additional motivation for a new study lies in continuing advances in
experimental phonetic research, and the explanations these might provide
for patterns of sound change, and ultimately for the nature of phonology.

Finally, the formalisms available to phonologists have altered radically in the last two decades. Autosegmental Phonology now provides for a complex non-linear representation based on hierarchically organized segmental and suprasegmental structures. Within this context of evolving formalism, the implications of formal innovations for the description of sound change, and the implications of sound change for the power of formal representation, remain of primary importance and need to be assessed. Like its generative forebear, autosegmental representation is extremely powerful. In some cases, such as so-called Compensatory Lengthening, its range of formal manipulation seems even greater than that of its generative predecessor. Where formal constraints continue to be weak or absent, substantive restrictions are still required. In other cases, formalistic innovations, such as a developed notion of syllable structure, may allow for better generalizations to be made about the development of distinctive nasalization, as discussed in chapter 8. Innovation in phonological theory is not restricted to the adoption of non-linear representation, but extends also to the Lexical Phonology theory of the organization of grammar, and the place of phonology within it. In Lexical Phonology the component parts of grammar (lexicon, morphology, syntax, phonology) overlap to form a complex grammatical structure. This model of grammar is discussed in chapter 1, and considered to provide valuable insight into the changing nature of sound change over time.

Also in chapter 1, I outline in more detail the factors that motivated the search for universals of distinctive nasalization in the 1970s, and their continuing relevance today. In addition, the notion of language universal is defined, and the expected regularity of patterning across languages is discussed. Also examined are the relationships between phonetics and phonology and suggestions that they overlap to an extent much greater than may once have been thought. Sound change in this present study is assumed to be, at least in the first instance, a phonetically gradual phenomenon, determined by the inherent constraints of the speech mechanism. A listener-oriented model of phonetic sound change is offered, and then related to the complex linguistic structure proposed by the theory of Lexical Phonology. The characteristic features of Autosegmental Phonology are also described, and the diachronic suitability of some formal manipulations is questioned.

Attention in this study is focused, albeit not exclusively, on developments in a small sample of Northern Italian dialects. Distinctive nasalization is a widespread diachronic and synchronic phenomenon in Northern Italy, and any patterning that may be uncovered there could plausibly have important ramifications for universalist claims about distinctive nasalization. In chapter 2, we consider language sampling techniques used in the search for linguistic universals, and conclude that primary reference to a small sample of Northern Italian dialects, with Latin as starting point, is

most suitable in the circumstances. Member dialects are described, and historical background provided.

Whilst the emphasis is on phonological processes as they occur over time, it is also suggested in chapter 1 that conclusions drawn from diachronic observations have important consequences for phonological processes in synchronic derivation. In chapter 3, we consider suggested diachronic and synchronic accounts of the ordering relationship between phonological processes of vowel nasalization and N-deletion (and any possibly intermediate process of N-attrition), as well as the implications of cross-linguistic evidence for both. The accuracy of the traditional universalist assumption that N-deletion is required for vowel nasalization to be distinctive (i.e. VN > Ṽ) is also evaluated, and found to be unmotivated in some cases.

Universalist claims about the development of distinctive nasalization are evaluated in chapters 4 to 7, ordered as follows: vowel length, presence and absence of stress (chapter 4); vowel height (chapter 5); context and syllable structure (chapter 6), N place of articulation (chapter 7). In addition, the influence of foot structure, not referred to previously by universalists, is examined in chapter 4. Once the nature and distribution of sound changes in each case have been established, possible phonetic explanations for any observed patterning are provided. Evidence of interaction between the influence of vowel length and the effect of other factors is reported. Also discussed in chapter 7 are fortitive processes that have the effect of making the development of distinctive nasalization less likely. In chapter 8 the manner of N-deletion is considered in some detail. N-deletion is assumed to involve a gradual reduction over time. Possible intermediate steps on the path to complete loss of any phonetic instantiation are considered and evaluated. The frequently stated hypothesis that motivation for N-deletion lies in syllable structure considerations is also examined. We also consider counter-examples to normal patterns of N-deletion found in Central and Southern Italian, and how they might be reconciled with those reported in Northern Italian and elsewhere.

In chapter 9, we assess the results of the study and the conclusions that can be drawn from them regarding the interrelationship between V and N, and the universal characteristics or otherwise of the development of distinctive nasalization. Consideration is also given to the implications for the formal representation of sound change, and the relationship between phonetics and phonology. Finally, possible avenues for further research are also explored.

1

SOUND CHANGE AND LANGUAGE UNIVERSALS: REPRESENTATIONS AND MODELS OF CHANGE

1.1 Introduction

In this chapter the necessary theoretical groundwork is laid in order to clarify the issues to be investigated in this study. These require preliminary discussion of, amongst other things, the relationship between phonetics and phonology, and between sound change and notions of universality, grammatical structure and formal representation.

1.1.1 *Phonetics, phonology and the non-randomness of sound change*

Whilst phonetics is the study of the physical properties (articulatory, acoustic and perceptual) of sounds used in speech, phonology is the description of the organization and patterning of sounds as they occur in language. The two fields are not independent of each other, but are related by the premise that all languages share the characteristics and limitations of the speech production, perception and processing capabilities common to human speakers. These characteristics and limitations define for any spoken language a universally finite set of phonetically based phonological features and of phonological processes that manipulate such features (Chen 1973b, c; Lindblom 1990). Establishing which are possible phonetic features, and phonological processes, is an important empirical question, and work continues in both areas, e.g. McCarthy (1988; 1989) and Trigo (1990). This study is at least partially an attempt to locate and define possible phonological processes that may occur over time in the context of vowel + nasal consonant (VN).

In a generative grammar, the relationship between phonology and phonetics is not only a defining one, but also derivational: the linguistically important characteristics of speech sounds are captured by the abstract phonological representation which can be given a phonetic realization in physical output (Cohn 1990). However, the precise relation between phonetics and phonology within the grammar is the subject of ongoing investigation. Recent research (e.g. Beddor 1991; Blumstein 1991; Keating 1988, 1991, Lindblom 1992) suggests that (1) the degree of overlap between the two is more extensive than may have been previously thought, and that (2) the degree of phonetic concreteness in phonology is far greater than

normally assumed, even at deeper levels of grammar. This leads to a concomitant decline in presumed levels of phonological abstractness. Whilst the full range of phonological processes – diachronic and synchronic – is still to be delimited, it has often been observed (e.g. Hyman 1975b: 164–72; Escure 1977; Chen 1974a) that phonological processes, particularly sound change over time, exhibit marked cross-linguistic patterning. Such non-randomness suggests that an explanation for sound change lies in the universally shared constraints of the speech mechanism.

Examination of cross-linguistic evidence by Chen (1974a) and Foley (1977) indicates for instance that, whereas the palatalization (and subsequent affrication) of stops before high front vowels, e.g. [gi] > [gʲi] > [ʤi] and [di] > [dʲi] > [ʤi], is a frequently reported phenomenon, the palatalization (and subsequent affrication) of bilabials is relatively unusual. Interaction between stop place and palatalization appears to be universally predictable as at 1 where, on further investigation, velars are most likely and bilabials are least likely to be affected along an implicational scale or parameter:[1]

1 velar dental bilabial
  ——————————→

The finding that bilabials are most resistant to palatalization is not unexpected for physiological reasons: the absence of the lingual articulation found in velars and dentals makes bilabials more resistant to the coarticulatory effects of tongue position in adjacent high front vowels.

The non-random correlation between the spread of palatalization and context is not restricted to stop place but extends, according to Chen and Foley, also to vowel height. Both posit a universal parameter of the type given at 2 where, in the context X, vowel height governs in a universally predictable and implicational fashion the spread of stop palatalization in all languages from left to right:

2 i e ɛ æ
  ——————→

Clear empirical counter-examples to the operation of the parameter at 2 have as yet not been reported.

1.1.2 Language-like vs. logically possible substantive constraints on formal representations

By determining the finite set of phonetically defined phonological features and of phonetically plausible phonological processes, we should be able to distinguish the subset of 'natural' language-like behaviour from the much larger set of logically possible but often 'unnatural' processes that can be posited with the available tools of formal description (Chen 1974a, Archangeli and Pulleyblank 1994). The immense descriptive power of generative formalism is well known, and attempts at constraining it by

incorporating formal means of evaluation into the theory, e.g. markedness, feature counting, and the simplicity metric, have been shown (e.g. Chen 1974a; Lass 1984; Hyman 1975b) to be extremely unsatisfactory. Whilst autosegmental formalism provides for an improved representation, it remains, like its forebear, extremely powerful, and continues, though perhaps to a lesser extent, to permit the representation of phonological processes which never in fact occur. As Ohala (1990b: 259) points out, generative 3a/4a and autosegmental 3b/4b formalisms capture with equal ease the two processes of place assimilation at 3 and 4:

3a [+nasal] $\longrightarrow$ [α PA] / __ $\begin{bmatrix} +\text{stop} \\ \alpha\ \text{PA} \end{bmatrix}$ PA = Point of Articulation

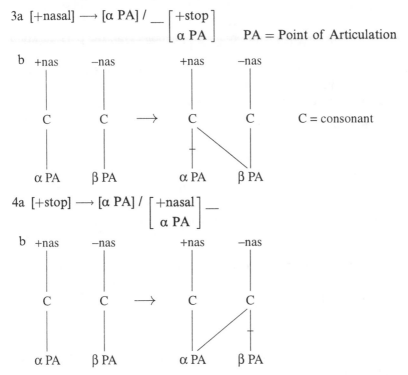

4a [+stop] $\longrightarrow$ [α PA] / $\begin{bmatrix} +\text{nasal} \\ \alpha\ \text{PA} \end{bmatrix}$ __

In contrast to the feature-changing nature of generative notation, in autosegmental analysis assimilation is captured by feature spreading evidenced by the left- or rightward movement of association lines from one segment to another. Notwithstanding the differences in representation, the two formalisms value both types of place assimilation equally. However, whilst the assimilation of N to the place of the following stop, as at 3, is cross-linguistically frequent, its converse, given at 4, is, according to Ohala, 'quite unnatural'.

One solution to the inherent formal difficulties in favouring 'natural', i.e. phonetically plausible, as opposed to logical, but otherwise implausible processes, is to establish substantive constraints. Such constraints may be

determined through examination of phonological processes in and across languages to establish which factors have an effect on phonological processes, and whether such an effect is universal. The goal, as Chen (1973b, c, 1974a) makes clear, is to uncover in language-specific variation non-random universal patterning. Once such patterning has been found, universal scales or parameters of the type already cited at 1 and 2 can then be formulated, according to specific context, to govern phonological processes of sound change across all languages.[2]

As universal parameters come to light, plausible phonetic explanations should then also be sought to account for them. Such scales do not represent, as Foley (1975, 1977) suggests, purely abstract phonological relations devoid of all phonetic content (see Cohen 1971; Cravens 1985; Harris-Northall 1990 for discussion).

The search for substantive constraints has important implications for both diachronic and synchronic phonology. Language reconstruction must be restricted to what is phonetically plausible and empirically verifiable (Comrie 1993).[3] Similarly, the use of substantive universals allows us to assess the relative phonetic 'naturalness', as distinct from the derivational convenience, of synchronic phonological rules (Hyman 1975b: 173–5).

1.1.3 What is a universal?

Outside the realm of distinctive nasalization studies, there is a well-developed literature on the typological notion of 'linguistic universal', mainly as it manifests itself synchronically, e.g. Comrie (1981), Croft (1990), Greenberg et al. (1978), Hawkins (1988), and Maddieson (1984). In synchronic typology three general categories of universal may be distinguished: (1) absolute or strict universal; (2) universal tendency; (3) implicational universal (see Hawkins 1988: 4–5 for details). However, in diachronic phonological typology, cross-linguistic patterning intersects with the generally accepted notion of sound change spreading gradually across a series of related contexts. Hence categories of possible universal are reduced to two: (1) absolute or strict implicational universal; and (2) universal implicational tendency.

Amongst universalists, Chen (1972 and elsewhere) and Foley (1975, 1977) present both the most developed and strictest notion of phonological universals.[4] According to Chen and Foley, phonological universals of sound change related to distinctive nasalization across languages involve strict cross-linguistic adherence, and patterning. Factors which are considered to be directly pertinent to the development of distinctive nasalization, e.g. vowel height and N place of articulation, are assumed, unless otherwise proven, to have a single universal effect over a series of related contexts in all languages where change is reported. Each such factor is given the status of an independent variable operating along its own scalar parameter. As a result,

for each variable, only one pattern forming a strict universal will be expected to appear everywhere, as at 5 where distinctive nasalization is thought to spread in an ordered and implicational fashion from left to right. If a sound change has occurred at any particular point along the parameter at 5, it is implied that all points to the left of it have already undergone a similar change at an earlier stage. Thus, VN_2 may be affected only if VN_1 has already been affected. However, the reverse relationship cannot hold: the fact that VN_1 may be affected in any language does not imply that VN_2 has similarly been affected. In this way, as Hawkins (1988: 4–5) notes, strict ordering along the implicational parameter allows for some variation in observed sound changes across languages, but places restrictions on the type and degree of such variation, so that it always remains predictable.

5   VN_1 VN_2 VN_3 VN_4
    $\longrightarrow$

Unlike Hawkins, however, Chen and Foley do not entertain the possibility of competing non-random patterns of change, i.e. universal implicational tendencies, or perhaps better cross-linguistic implicational tendencies, governing the development of distinctive nasalization. Whereas in some languages VN_1 may always be the first amongst related contexts to be affected by a change along a predictable scale as at 6a, in others it may regularly be the least likely locus for another competing non-random change operating amongst the same set of environments as at 6b.[5]

6a VN_1 VN_2 VN_3 VN_4 vs.   b VN_4 VN_3 VN_2 VN_1
     $\longrightarrow$ $\longrightarrow$

Yet despite the single pattern restriction imposed by Chen and Foley, they sometimes, nevertheless, disagree as to the cross-linguistic effect of any specific factor, e.g. N-place of articulation, and, therefore, the ordering of the related implicational scale. For instance, Chen (1974a) suggests that in any language /Vm/ will have regularly changed to /Ṽ/ before /Vŋ/ > /Ṽ/ is possible. However, according to Foley, the universal order is reversed: in the course of the development of distinctive nasalization in any language /Vŋ/ > /Ṽ/ will always precede /Vm/ > /Ṽ/ (see chapter 7 for further details). Such contradictory views, based on changes reported in the unrelated language samples used by Chen and Foley, suggest that in some cases competing universal tendencies may co-exist in the development of distinctive nasalization. In fact such a pattern of competition is already well known in other circumstances: intervocalic stops may be affected by voicing, fricativization, or glottalization, but not usually a combination of all of these.

As for cross-linguistic adherence to any suggested universal parameter of change, Foley takes the strictest view: no cross-linguistic counter-examples are permitted. Chen, on the other hand, accepts that developments in a very

few languages may be inconsistent with the universal parameter. Provided their incidence is very low, he does not consider counter-examples to immediately invalidate the power of universals, given the otherwise massive cross-linguistic adherence. However, where sufficient cross-linguistic counter-evidence is found, Chen admits that the suggested universal parameter may need to be revised.

I will accept as an initial hypothesis in this study Foley's strict view on absolute adherence to a single parameter of change for each factor considered. Since the possibility of random exceptions, or of non-random areo-genetic patterning is pretheoretically excluded by Foley, such a stance is the most easily falsified. Brief reference above to suggested interaction between nasal place of articulation and the development of distinctive nasalization already suggests that the Foleyan view is inadequate for the characterization of cross-linguistic patterning of sound change. However, it is not immediately obvious that this should always be the case. Evidence will be provided in this study to suggest that the effect of some prosodic factors (e.g. vowel length and stress) may be strictly universal in all languages.

1.1.4 Diachrony and synchrony

The diachronic orientation of this study has been determined by many different factors. In the first instance, since one aim of this study is to reconsider in some detail claims made previously about the cross-linguistically universal character of sound changes in the context VN, then for comparative purposes, the use of a diachronic time-frame is inevitable.

However, the questions of how sound change occurs, and the relationship it may have with linguistic structure at different points in time, are also important issues requiring further investigation. I return to these matters in some detail in section 1.2 below. Additional motivation lies in Greenberg's (1966, 1978, 1979) frequent claim that the study of diachronic change, i.e. the dynamic process of shift from one synchronic state to another over time, often provides insight into synchrony (see also Bybee 1988). For instance, Ferguson's (1966) synchronic observation that the text frequency of nasal vowels is always much less than that of oral vowels in any language may have a plausible diachronic explanation. Greenberg (1966) claims that it is the result of a historical development: the context in which nasal vowels are most frequently reported to develop over time, i.e. in tautosyllabic VN$ sequences, is typically only a limited subset of all possible V + C combinations in any language.

Reference to synchrony in this study is not restricted to the comparison of synchronic states at different points in time. Synchronic data taken from related dialects at approximately the same point in time are used for comparative purposes in the reconstruction of earlier intermediate stages

between Latin and present-day Northern Italian. The methodology involved in such diachronic extrapolation is discussed in some detail in section 2.2. Also, given the phonetic orientation of this study, discussed in more detail below, emphasis is also placed on inferences for sound change that may be drawn from the study of constant synchronic variation in speech, considered to be the source of such change.

The frequent parallel between diachronic and synchronic analysis of phonological data has often been noted, e.g. Posner (1971), Schane (1973a), Klausenburger (1976). For example, the surface alternation of the sort [bõ] vs. [bona] 'good' (m. and f.) found in one form or another in various Romance dialects can be accounted for in synchronic derivation by positing underlying /bon/ and /bon + a/, and consecutive rules of nasalization before syllable-final N, and secondary loss of such N.[6] Such an analysis mirrors the suggested and traditional diachronic explanation for the alternation, i.e. Lat. BONU > [bon] > [bõn] > [bõ] but BONA > [bona].

However, it is not always the case that synchronic derivation recapitulates diachronic change in such a direct fashion, so care should be taken when applying the insights of the former to account for the latter. For instance, the synchronic difference in closely related dialects, e.g. Milanese [būː] and Bergamese [buː] 'good' (m.), can be accounted for diachronically by positing a secondary process of denasalization in Bergamese of a previously nasal vowel, i.e. [būː] > [buː]. However, the greater relative emphasis on formal simplicity in synchronic derivation than on phonetic graduality may result in so-called telescoping and restructuring of the grammar, i.e. omission of an intermediate stage required in diachronic description (cf. Chen 1973b, 1974b). For instance, the surface alternation [bo] vs. [bona] of the type found in some Romance dialects is easily derived from underlying /bon/ and /bon + a/ respectively by a simple rule of word-final /n/-deletion. No rule of vowel nasalization is posited, since there is no evidence of vowel nasalization surfacing in this context. Since N-deletion without vowel nasalization appears to happen, at least in synchronic derivation, it is tempting to infer from such data that N-deletion without vowel nasaliza-tion may also occur diachronically, as has been argued by Foley (1975, 1977), Entenman (1977) and Schourup (1973).

I examine in some detail in chapter 3 synchronic analyses of distinctive nasalization in which a phonological rule of vowel nasalization is not ordered before N-deletion, or any other process affecting N, and consider the diachronic and synchronic implications these may have for an account of distinctive nasalization. Such analyses are found to be inappropriate to diachrony. Evidence is provided to support the hypothesis that loss of N is, with very limited exceptions, typically preceded in time by a phonological process of vowel nasalization. As for synchronic derivation, I accept that N-loss without vowel nasalization is permitted, i.e. UR /VN/ → SR [V]. However, cross-linguistic data demonstrate that in any synchronic analysis

of distinctive nasalization, i.e. UR /VN/ → SR [Ṽ], vowel nasalization should be ordered before N-deletion.

1.1.5 *Diachrony and directionality*

If we adopt the plausible view that greater length of time increases the chance of sound change occurring, the relatively long time frame examined in this study, i.e. approximately 2,000 years from Latin to modern Northern Italian dialects, should allow for an increased frequency and wide range of sound change types. A greater range and number of observed changes should then improve our ability to determine and define any patterning, e.g. in the development of distinctive nasalization, along scales or parameters of the type discussed above, and repeated here at 7:

7 $\underrightarrow{VN_1 \ VN_2 \ VN_3 \ VN_4}$

Our ability to find patterning in changes reported in Northern Italian and then to formulate parameters to describe them as at 7 is of course consistent with the frequently reported repetitive, non-random nature of sound change across languages. The statement at 7 is descriptive in the sense that the changes reported in the examined sample have been codified. Predictive value can also be assigned to the non-random parameter (Chen 1973c): the development of VN > Ṽ in all contexts in a language not previously analyzed can now be broken down into a gradual process that first occurred in VN_1 before spreading progressively to the other listed contexts.

However, parameters of the type at 7 have no teleological value: they do not suggest that ordered changes along the scale are intended or directed unconsciously toward some 'goal', e.g. the elimination of all syllable-final N, as has been proposed by some, e.g. Lightner (1973). In the absence of teleology, the form and nature of universal parameters ultimately have their basis in the articulatory, acoustic and perceptual constraints of speech, and explanations for such parameters should be sought there (Chen 1973c; Ohala 1988 and elsewhere).

Furthermore, we cannot predict in the sense of 'future reference' when sound change or which type of sound change will necessarily occur in a language at any point in time. Universal parameters as at 7 can describe and 'predict' the patterning involved in any particular sound change only when it has occurred (Chen 1973c). Related processes, nasalization and N-deletion, in the context VN compete with conflicting processes of (1) denasalization, i.e. VN > V^CN > VC, and (2) gemination, i.e. VN >VNN, along what may be termed a tridirectional parameter of possible change at 8:

8 $\underleftrightarrow{VC \ V^C N \ VN \ \tilde{V}N \ \tilde{V}}$
$\downarrow$
VNN

Examination of cross-linguistic data suggests that there is some strong, but not universally predictable, directionality along the parameter at 8. Whilst reduction of VN to Ṽ is frequently reported across languages, VN > VNN and VN > VC as regular processes seem comparatively rare. This claim is consistent with the more general observation that reductive processes or 'lenitions', e.g. N-loss, are extremely common in sound change. Their converse, processes which are 'fortitive' to the extent that they make 'lenitions' less likely, are relatively unusual (Pagliuca and Mowrey 1987; Connell 1991). Contextually determined 'fortitions' of N reported in some Southern Italian dialects are discussed briefly in chapter 6. Fortitive processes that block the development and spread of VN > Ṽ are unusual in Northern Italian, and are discussed in some detail in chapter 7.

1.2. SOUND CHANGE, LINGUISTIC STRUCTURE AND LEXICAL PHONOLOGY

The central issue of how sound change occurs in a language has been a matter of great interest to phonologists, amongst whom discussion still continues (cf. Connell 1989, 1991, Labov 1981 and Kiparsky 1988). Wang (1969) formulated a well-known set of idealized sound change scenarios, given at figure 1.1, that he considered to be hypothetically possible in an individual speaker's language. His taxonomy hinged on the competing notions of graduality vs. abruptness of change operating in the phonetics and in the lexicon used by the speaker.

I take the view, one expressed previously by many others, e.g. Dressler (1971), Hooper (1976), Stephen Anderson (1981), Vincent (1978), John Harris (1989), McMahon (1991) and Watson (1991, 1992), that the initial phase of sound change typically involves the modification in a phonetically gradient fashion of low-level phonetic rules.[7] In some languages such phonetically gradual change may sometimes also be lexically gradual, as Connell (1989, 1991) suggests, and as such is a matter requiring further investigation. However, the Neogrammarian Hypothesis of phonetically gradual and lexically abrupt sound change finds wide cross-linguistic confirmation and greater support amongst phonologists (e.g. Labov 1981; Harris 1989; McMahon 1991).[8] I will accept the Neogrammarian Hypothesis as adequate in this study, since it is consistent with the extreme lexical

1 phonetically abrupt and lexically abrupt
2 phonetically abrupt and lexically gradual
    (=Lexical Diffusion)
3 phonetically gradual and lexically abrupt
    (=Neogrammarian Hypothesis)
4 phonetically gradual and lexically gradual

Figure 1.1 Sound Change Scenarios

regularity of distinctive nasalization phenomena found in my Northern Italian sample. In addition, nasalization-related changes evident in Northern Italian appear to share many of the additional characteristics of Neogrammarian-style sound change, reported by Labov (1981: 296), e.g. the absence of morphological conditioning, the presence of phonetic conditioning, and the predictability of effect.

The premise that all sound change is in origin phonetically gradual is not incompatible with sound change as phonetically abrupt, i.e. Lexical Diffusion, if, as Labov (1981) suggests, the two types of sound change can be seen to operate at different levels of the grammar. Whilst Neogrammarian sound change involves alteration of low-level phonetic rules and their entry into the linguistic structure, Lexical Diffusion involves the redistribution of members of phonemically distinct abstract word classes amongst other abstract word classes at a much deeper level of grammar. Confirmation of Labov's hypothesis of relative abstractness is found in recent work by John Harris (1989) and McMahon (1991) on the nature of sound change within the framework of Lexical Phonology (LP). They also claim that the two types of sound change are diachronically related: the originally phonetically gradual and lexically abrupt nature of Neogrammarian-type change, consistent with the view expressed previously that all sound change is phonetic in origin, may be transformed over time into Lexical Diffusion through progressive percolation of the former into the deeper, more abstract regions of linguistic structure. Such a hypothesis is of course also consistent with the views expressed previously by Hyman (1975b; Stephen Anderson 1981) and Vincent (1978) and others working in an earlier generative framework: they had already noted the tendency for phonological processes to become increasingly opaque or phonetically 'denaturalized' over time, as a result of continuing penetration of the grammar, leading to potential morphologization and lexicalization.

The complex structure of grammar envisioned by the theory of Lexical Phonology (cf. Kiparsky 1982, 1985; Goldsmith 1990) is presented in figure 1.2. As Harris and McMahon suggest, different types of sound change can be placed at an appropriate level in the grammar by assessing the nature of phonological rules involved, and the type of interaction, if any, with non-phonological components of the grammar. I will also hypothesize that the distinction between Neogrammarian-type change and Lexical Diffusion operating at different levels of the grammar can be refined further by placing phonetically/lexically abrupt sound change (= Scenario 1 in figure 1.1) at an intermediate level of the grammar. This suggests that Neogrammarian-type (phonetically gradient) change will be transformed first into Scenario 1 (phonetically abrupt) change before a later transformation into Lexical Diffusion at an even deeper level of grammar. I will also suggest, however, that the boundary between phonetically gradual (and lexically abrupt) and phonetically abrupt (and lexically abrupt) sound change is not a clear one.

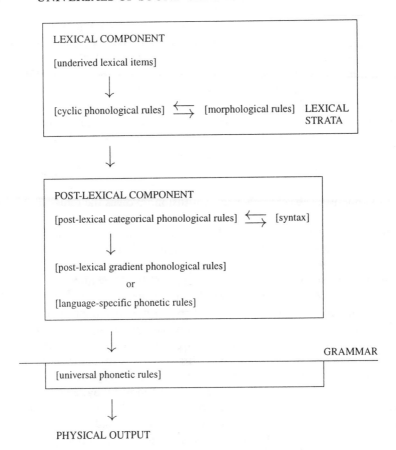

Figure 1.2   A Modified Model of Lexical Phonology

Such indeterminacy presents problems when we try to characterize the phonological nature or otherwise of contextual nasalization, as discussed below in this section, and further in chapter 3.

Although debate continues about the precise nature of Lexical Phonology (cf. Goldsmith 1990; Cohn 1990), all models of Lexical Phonology, including the expanded version I offer in figure 1.2, make a fundamental distinction between the more abstract, deep structure of the lexical component, and the less abstract post-lexical component closer to the surface.

At the deepest level of the grammar, within the lexical component, we find underived and underspecified lexical items. In the course of derivation, these may enter into the lexical strata where they are processed by the interplay between morphological and phonological rules. Phonological rules in the lexical strata have a number of unique characteristics: they apply cyclically, and may make reference to internal word structure. In addition, they permit exceptions.[9] Interaction between the syntactic component and phonology is

not permitted within the lexicon, and no cyclic rule may operate across word-boundaries. Finally, the principle of Structure Preservation (SP) blocks the creation of segments additional to the underlying inventory (but see Harris 1989).

The evolving lexical item then moves into the post-lexical component (or post-lexical phonology) in which the various lexical characteristics of and constraints on phonological operation no longer apply, e.g. cyclicity (and interaction with morphology), and SP. As a result, post-lexical (P-L) rules may create new segments, e.g. UR /VN/ → P-L [Ṽ], and may operate across word boundaries, interacting with the syntactic component, e.g. Spanish intervocalic voiced stop spirantization which occurs whenever phonetic conditions are met. On the other hand, post-lexical rule sensitivity to word-internal syllable structure, as well as to word boundaries, is also permitted (Goldsmith 1990: 239–40). Since full feature specification is not required in the lexicon, redundant feature values are filled in by rule within the post-lexical component (p. 219).

Debate continues as to the categorical vs. gradient nature of rules within the post-lexical component. Some, e.g. Liberman and Pierrehumbert (1984) and Harris (1989), take the radical view that all post-lexical rules are phonologically (and phonetically) gradient, requiring some non-binary specification. However, I will accept as basic the more moderate and more frequently expressed view, e.g. Kiparsky (1985), Keating (1985b, 1988) and Durand (1990: 190), that the post-lexical component allows for both categorical and gradient rules. Whilst there has been relatively little work done to date on the characterization of categorical vs. gradient rules within the post-lexical component, a common view, e.g. Keating (1985b, 1988), Stephen Anderson (1975, 1981), suggests that the latter are language-specific phonetic rules which provide details about redundant, sub-phonemic, allophonic phenomena, and allow for the implementation of binary phonological rules (Durand 1990: 190; Cohn 1990: 1–19). These language-specific rules represent that portion of the phonetic component that differs from what might be expected from any mechanical implementation necessary for speech production (see below for further details). As such, they are considered to be phonologized, and part of the cognitive, non-mechanical linguistic structure, i.e. grammar, since they represent a fact about a particular language, and the competence of its speakers, rather than any mechanical property of speech production and perception (Anderson 1981, Keating 1985b, 1988). This observation is crucial to the definition of what is considered 'phonological' in this study (see below).

The distinction and ordering relationship between categorical and gradient rules are not straightforward, and remain to be clearly defined by phonologists (cf. Cohn 1990; Pierrehumbert 1991; and Durand 1990: 190). In spite of the clearcut division in figure 1.2, it is not always obvious when a rule is categorical or gradient, particularly when the rule in question describes a

strong contextual effect, such as high levels of vowel nasalization before N, or of vowel lengthening before voiced consonants (cf. the contrasting views of Stephen Anderson 1975 and Fromkin 1976). Kiparsky (1985) also reports that some phonetically gradient rules may be perceived as categorical, and are, therefore, easily miscategorized by phonologists.

The traditional generative view (e.g. Chomsky and Halle 1968; Anderson 1975; Keating 1985b) that phonetic rules in the phonology specify language-specific phonetic implementation of binary phonological rules does not in itself allow for an adequate categorization of rule type. Whilst Anderson (1975) accepts that categorical phonological rules are typically ordered first in synchronic derivation, he cites cross-linguistic examples in which the operation of phonologized phonetic rules precedes that of categorical phonological rules in the grammar, as Chomsky and Halle (1968: 65–6) admit. Further complications arise if Cohn (1990), based on phonetic and phonological evidence she presents, is correct in suggesting that vowels adjacent to N may in some languages, e.g. English, be left unspecified for [nasal] in the binary phonological representation, and receive gradient specification in the language-specific phonetic component of the grammar.

The hypothesis that the nature of a sound change may alter over time through progressive percolation into deeper levels of linguistic structure suggests that within the model of LP presented in figure 1.2, a gradient language-specific rule will over time become a categorical phonological rule in the post-lexical component before moving into the lexicon. Therefore, determining the boundary between gradient/phonologized/language-specific phonetic on the one hand and categorical/binary/phonological on the other is relevant to the status within the post-lexical phonology of contextual nasalization. I return to the issue in chapter 3, and consider to what extent independent evaluation of the question may be possible (see also Cohn 1990). But it is always important to bear in mind that I assume throughout, in line with Anderson (1981), Harris (1989) and McMahon (1991), that any rule, gradient or binary, phonologized or categorical, to the extent that it appears in the grammar, is *fully phonological*.[10]

Therefore, in the context of rule indeterminacy, reference to any phonological process of contextual nasalization applies equally to categorical and phonologized assimilation. There is little evidence that secondary changes appearing in the post-lexical component, such as N-deletion, hinge specifically on a distinction between gradient and categorical rules of contextual nasalization. Therefore, reference to a phonologized language-specific rule of contextual nasalization is always sufficient in phonological terms in an account of the development of distinctive nasalization (see also section 3.1).

Phonetic rules that are not language-specific fall within the universal phonetic component outside the grammar, as in figure 1.2, and represent the universal, low-level, mechanical effects of speech production and perception. They are, therefore, not grammatical, and hence not phonological in any

sense – unlike language-specific phonetic rules. All other things being equal, nasal coarticulation on vowels adjacent to nasal consonants is not unexpected, and will be assumed to manifest itself in any language, unless otherwise shown, as one such low-level phenomenon. It is clear, however, that phonetic phenomena that are assumed to apply universally, such as nasal coarticulation, can differ significantly across languages (see Cohn 1988 on differences in contextual vowel nasalization in French and English). The distinction between universal low-level and language-specific phonetic rules is also blurred, and our ability to separate the two is not well developed. I will assume that where a phonetic process is found to be suppressed or increased to a level that diverges considerably from what might be considered the (poorly specified) universal low-level range of variation, then in the first instance we have some indication that phonologization as a language-specific phonetic rule has occurred. I also suggest in section 3.3.2.1, with examples, that since a low-level phonetic rule (e.g. contextual nasalization) can be overridden, it is universal only to the extent that it applies by default.

The process of phonologization of low-level phonetic rules is discussed in more detail in section 1.2.1, and in chapter 3. Whilst the boundary between language-specific and universal phonetic rules remains poorly defined until this point, I provide details in section 3.3.2.2 of how an empirically oriented methodology, first suggested by Hyman (1975b), may allow for a rough categorization of the two types of phonetic rule.

Using the complex linguistic structure of Lexical Phonology at figure 1.2 we can now, in a simple fashion, relate Neogrammarian sound change to the scenario of phonetically and lexically abrupt change (cf. figure 1.1), as well as to Lexical Diffusion. Change in a low-level phonetic rule over time, as a result of language-specific variation, can result in phonologization as a language-specific phonetic rule, and entry into the grammar (see section 1.2.1.1 for further details of the mechanics of phonologization). Further penetration of linguistic structure occurs when phonetically gradual (phonologically gradient) change becomes phonetically abrupt (phonologically categorical), requiring representation as a binary rule. If Kiparsky (1988), Harris (1989) and McMahon (1991) are correct, the sound change will continue to be lexically abrupt since in their view exceptions are not permitted outside the lexicon. Should the sound change percolate deeper into the linguistic structure over time, it will enter the lexical component. Interaction between phonology and morphology may be expected to condition the rise of exceptions, resulting in Lexical Diffusion in the lexical strata. Ultimately, the sound change may become lexicalized and move directly into the underlying representation.

Vowel nasalization and N-deletion processes reported in Northern Italian and many other Romance dialects typically show the characteristics of having been or of being post-lexical phenomena, as Harris (1989) and

McMahon (1991) would predict from the previously noted Neogrammarian characterization. That is, we find that such processes are historically generally exceptionless, and show no evidence of morphological conditioning.[11] In contravention of the Structure Preservation constraint operating in the lexical component, surface nasal vowels are easily derived from underlying VN, e.g. Milanese [sãː] ← UR /saːn/ 'healthy' (m.s.) vs. [san] ← UR /san/ 'healthy' (f.pl.). In addition, nasalization and N-deletion rules are able to operate across word boundaries, showing sensitivity to syntactic structure, e.g. Milanese [būː] 'good' (m.), [pãː e vĩː] 'bread and wine', but [bun amiːg] 'good friend', Catalan [be] 'well', [pa i βi] 'bread and wine', but [ben aɫ] 'quite tall'. However, in some Northern Italian and other Romance dialects, e.g. Imolese, lexicalization of distinctive nasalization has since occurred as the indirect result of unrelated sound changes in other contexts. I discuss in more detail in section 3.5.2 the nature of this phenomenon of lexicalization, and consider briefly its ramifications for the interaction between sound change and the deepest levels of grammar.

In examining patterns of sound change relevant to distinctive nasalization, attention will be focused on developments in the post-lexical component of the grammar, and in particular, at the boundary of grammar/non-grammar where the universal phonetic component and the language-specific phonetic sub-component meet. Having established a grammatical framework for sound change, attention shifts now to the suggested phonetic basis of sound change, and its relationship to Lexical Phonological structure.

1.2.1 The articulo-perceptual basis of sound change

Ohala (1974a and b, 1981, 1986, 1988, 1990a, 1993 and elsewhere) has frequently expressed the view that the emphasis traditionally placed on the role of the speaker in sound change, motivated by the principle of 'Ease of Articulation', is excessive, and would be more profitably directed to that played by the listener. Ohala suggests that sound change is generally perceptual in nature, since it is dependent on the listener's ability to deal with the ambiguous nature of the speech signal. The ambiguity, or 'noise', is the result of articulatory and acoustic constraints inherent to the vocal tract that result in significant and constant variation in phonetic output, over which the speaker has no active control. Well-known examples of such perturbation, Ohala suggests, include differences in pitch in vowels following voiced and voiceless consonants, the acoustic fronting of back vowels adjacent to coronals, the devoicing of geminate voiced stops, and low-level contextual nasalization.

Stability of the sound system depends on the listener's ability to factor out unwanted distortions in the signal by what Ohala terms 'reconstructive rules', as exemplified in figure 1.3 where the speaker intends to utter /an/. According to Ohala (1981), // represents lexical input, and [ ] represents

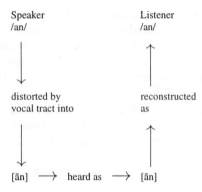

Figure 1.3   Distortion and Reconstruction

surface phonetic output. There is no intermediate phonological component of the sort normally associated with derivation from underlying
representation to surface form.

Low-level contextual nasalization is considered to be an inevitable result
of coarticulatory constraints on production. The listener receives the
distorted signal and is able to eliminate the unwanted distortion by
applying the relevant phonetic 'reconstructive rule', on the proviso that
the environment which causes the particular distortion is also perceived.

It is at this point (and others) that Ohala's view of sound change and my
own diverge significantly. According to Ohala, sound change occurs when
the listener is unable to apply the reconstructive rules, and can no longer
eliminate the low-level distortion, crucially because he or she fails to detect
the presence of the environment that provides the necessary cue, as in
figure 1.4.

In the speaker's output there is the inevitable low-level vowel distortion,
i.e. nasalization, due to slight temporal overlap of velic opening into the

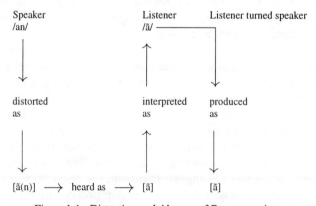

Figure 1.4   Distortion and Absence of Reconstruction

preceding vowel. However, in this case, final /n/ is weakly articulated in some fashion, or is masked by something else, e.g. contextual devoicing of /n/ before a voiceless obstruent. As listeners have '. . . no independent access to the mind of the speaker . . . [they] may be unable to determine what parts of the received signal were intended or what were not . . .' (Hombert et al. 1979: 37). With no perception of the conditioning environment, /n/, the listener in figure 1.4 cannot, therefore, be expected to interpret the signal as the speaker may have intended, and may intentionally reproduce the distortion. In such circumstances, the listener perceives [ã], reinterprets it as /ã/, and begins to produce the original /an/ as if /ã/.

Whilst, according to Ohala, it is ordinarily the case that sound change results from a failure to detect the conditioning environment for whatever reason, he admits that some types of change (but explicitly not distinctive nasalization) develop even when the conditioning environment remains unaffected, e.g. vowel harmony processes. In all cases, however, Ohala suggests that a generalization can be made whereby the mechanical link that previously existed between conditioning environment and conditioned change is lost.

Furthermore, Ohala hypothesizes that once the conditioning environment has been lost, or the mechanical link broken, there may be significant qualitative and quantitative changes in the phonetic characteristics of the original distortion: nasalization of vowels may be significantly increased after N-deletion.

1.2.1.1 A modified articulo-perceptual model of sound change

Whilst Ohala's listener-oriented model of sound change provides valuable insight into the mechanism of sound change, his assumption that there is no intermediate phonological derivation between lexical representation and physical output is incompatible with the complex linguistic structure envisaged by the theory of Lexical Phonology. In contrast to Ohala, I take the view that some articulatory control over contextual phonetic output may be exhibited, and that intermediate phonologization of nasalization, without loss of conditioning environment, is possible.

I have modified the Ohalan model accordingly by incorporating an intermediate phonological component which can then be related to the grammatical structure presupposed by the theory of Lexical Phonology, as seen in figure 1.5.

Evidence of articulatory control is found in major and unpredicted language-specific differences in contextual phonetic phenomena, e.g. the effect of stop voicing on preceding vowel length (Chen 1970), and levels of contextual nasalization (Al-Bamerni 1983; Cohn 1988, 1990; and Clumeck 1975, 1976).[12] Accordingly, I suggest that from the phonetic perspective the first stage of sound change involves a two-step process, exemplified by the proposed development of distinctive nasalization in figure 1.5. As stated

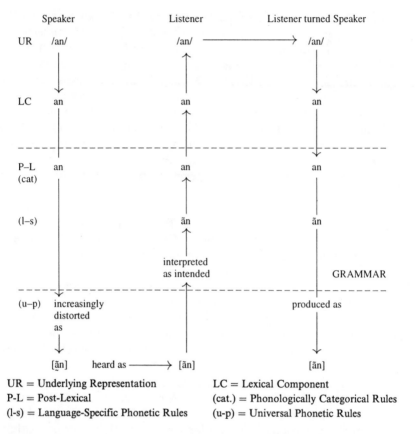

UR = Underlying Representation   LC = Lexical Component
P-L = Post-Lexical   (cat.) = Phonologically Categorical Rules
(l-s) = Language-Specific Phonetic Rules   (u-p) = Universal Phonetic Rules

Figure 1.5 A New Scenario of Sound Change: Distortion, Exaggeration and a Failure to Reconstruct

previously, the level of coarticulation of nasalization in production is at the limit of, or perhaps increased beyond the range of, low-level variation that many phonologists expect to occur. Variation in production is in any case a constant, and may result in gradual, subtle but ultimately cumulative shifts in articulatory and acoustic targets (à la Hockett 1965) in any direction, i.e. towards increased or reduced nasal coarticulation. More specific explanations are also possible: Keating (1985b) considers that decreased performance effort on the part of the speaker, possibly leading to increased coarticulatory effects, may provide the impetus for sound change; Watson (1991, 1992) suggests that within the constant articulatory and acoustic flux of speech the 'increase' is merely one of social variation in performance within the expected range of low-level coarticulation.

Whatever the reason, when the boundary between low-level and language-specific phonetic phenomena is blurred, as has already been suggested, then

the speaker's slightly elevated level of unintended nasalization, marked by two tildes in figure 1.5, may be ambiguous and is potentially reinterpreted by the listener as intended, and he or she will then imitate the change. The listener's reinterpretation or misinterpretation might be viewed as an abductive change (Andersen 1973). Phonologization of contextual nasalization as a language-specific phonetic rule in the first instance is now complete. The gradient quality of contextual nasalization may be further reinterpreted and increased over time by successive generations of listeners until the phenomenon is treated as no longer gradient, but reinterpreted as categorical at a deeper level of the post-lexical component.

An additional factor that can be expected to trigger reinterpretation is a shift in perception over time. Just as there is constant articulatory and acoustic variation in speech, there is constant perceptual variation, evident in significant cross-linguistic differences (Berinstein 1979; Terbeek and Harshman 1971; Watson 1983). Janson (1982) reports sound change in progress in vowel perception across generations in Stockholm Swedish. Shift in perception is likely to increase sensitivity to contextual nasalization (even in the absence of any shift in articulatory levels), and favour its interpretation by listeners as being intended.

There is no reason to suggest, as Ohala (1988, 1990a) does, that the vowel nasalization only becomes phonologically pertinent when the conditioning environment is lost. It is merely sufficient that Ohala's 'mechanical link' between assimilated segment, $\tilde{V}$, and context, N, is lost.

There is independent confirmation of my claim that the phonologization of a contextual effect, in this case vowel nasalization, precedes and is independent of loss of the conditioning environment, N. The phonological phenomenon of prosodic nasalization is frequently reported without reduction and/or loss of N, e.g. Capanahua [hãmãʔõna] 'coming stepping' [bãnawi] 'plant it', Malay [mãjãn] 'stalk' (Piggott 1988a, b). Also, underlyingly contrastive vowel nasalization of the sort /ṼN/ vs. /VN/ (and /Ṽ/), without N-deletion is reported in some languages and discussed in further detail in section 3.5.[13] Finally, Krakow and Beddor (1991) provide experimental evidence showing that listeners are able to distinguish between oral and nasal vowels before N.

The conditioning environment, N, is also subject to contextual distortive effects in production – before and after the phonologization of vowel nasalization (not indicated in figure 1.5). Notwithstanding any contextual distortion, e.g. devoicing before voiceless obstruents, nasal consonants are reported to be quite stable, on the whole, over time (Chen 1972; Connell and Hajek 1991). They are perceptually highly distinct as a class (Ohala 1975) and experiments show nasal consonants to be amongst the most readily identifiable consonants in isolation and adjacent to vowels (Farnetani 1979b). These two factors suggest that most kinds of distortion affecting N, in the absence of strong contextual nasalization, can be easily factored

out by listeners. In some cases, the phonologization of contextual effects affecting N may occur in the absence of phonologized vowel nasalization, e.g. denasalization of N. However, it is likely that the phonologization of nasalization may reduce the ability of the listener to factor out other distortive effects affecting the conditioning environment, N. The listener may then phonologize these accordingly. The smearing effect of nasalization, particularly in the context VN, which lessens the acoustic contrast between V and N (Manuel 1991; Bladon 1986) may ultimately favour a failure to perceive N directly, leading to a corresponding failure on the part of the listener to reproduce N. Although N-deletion (i.e. N > Ø) is a categorical phenomenon easily described by a binary phonological rule, the reduction of N to Ø is assumed to be a gradual process involving intermediate steps, e.g. manner and voicing assimilation. Such steps may be phonologized, and can often be captured in a discrete fashion by autosegmental representation as contextual assimilation phenomena. From the formal phonological point of view, N-deletion involves the loss of the skeletal slot along the timing tier originally associated with N, and any nasalized phonetic instantiation, including intermediate steps associated with it (see section 1.3). As such, N-deletion should be distinguished from (1) transformation of N to oral C (see section 3.4.4), and (2) the gradual vocalization of N to V (see section 8.1.4), in which all trace of nasality originally associated with the nasal consonant is lost, but the skeletal slot is preserved, attached to a full segment at all times.

Changes affecting N and their implications for nasalization and N-loss, are examined in detail in later chapters. I make the claim that, although in some cases phonologization of changes affecting N, e.g. denasalization, may occur in the absence of phonologized vowel nasalization, they do not by implication necessarily trigger a secondary phonological process of contextual nasalization as some have suggested.

The hypothesis that the phonologization of vowel nasalization will normally precede the complete loss of N is an important substantive claim, and has major consequences for the diachronic and synchronic description of distinctive nasalization phenomena. In chapter 3 I consider in some detail analyses of distinctive nasalization, in which the order of vowel nasalization and N-deletion is varied, and show that phonologists such as Piggott (1987, 1988a, b) make empirically unfounded predictions by suggesting that deletion precedes or is simultaneous to the phonologization of vowel nasalization.

1.2.1.2 Sound change, experimental phonetics, teleology, and synchronic variation

By emphasizing the role of the listener in sound change we can avoid the need to invoke teleological explanations for sound change (Ohala 1974b, 1988). Phoneticians and phonologists have often suggested that speakers may alter their pronunciation for reasons of (1) ease of articulation

(Ladefoged 1982), (2) ease of perception (Stephen Anderson 1981), (3) easier language acquisition and (4) phonological system symmetry (Martinet 1955; Hagège and Haudricourt 1978). But as has often been noted, e.g. Bloomfield (1933), Vincent (1978), Ohala (1988), teleological explanations which rely on intent and purpose are easily invoked, providing a ready answer to any question that may be asked. They are, however, difficult to test.

Ohala is particularly critical of the teleological hypothesis offered by Lightner (1970) and Bichakjian (1981), amongst others, whereby vowels become distinctively nasalized after N-deletion, in order to preserve some contrast in lexical identity. As he points out, if such a goal-oriented explanation were valid, there would be no reason for N-deletion to have developed in the first place: if speakers knew in advance that N-deletion would lead to possible confusion, they would not have allowed it. Ironically, vowel nasalization has not prevented copious homophony in French, e.g. [pɛ̃:] *peint/pain/pin* (see also Vincent 1978).

Teleology is in any case often amenable to phonetically oriented causative reinterpretation (Vincent 1978; Dressler 1971). There is no need to speculate that the order of sound change along a possibly universal parameter, given at 5 and repeated here at 9, is the result of a phonological drag chain effect functionally motivated by pattern symmetry and system pressure, i.e. $VN_4 > \tilde{V}N$ because $VN_3 > \tilde{V}N$ because $VN_2 > \tilde{V}N$ because $VN_1 > \tilde{V}N$.

9 VN_1 VN_2 VN_3 VN_4

Instead, according to Ohala (1988: 20–1), parameters like the one at 9 have a plausible causal basis: phonologization of nasalization in $VN_1 > \tilde{V}N$ may sensitize listeners to the presence of nasalization in related contexts along the parameter if the latter are subject to conditions similar to the ones VN_1 was originally subject to.

I accept Ohala's view that emphasis on causal (i.e. non-teleological) explanations for sound change is a reasonable research strategy, having already noted that constant synchronic variation in speech, the result of articulatory, acoustic and perceptual constraints, is considered to provide the source and phonetic basis of sound change. Phoneticians (e.g. Passy 1890; Sievers 1901; Ohala 1974a, 1988; Javkin 1979; Connell 1991) have long been aware of this relation, and consider that explanations for reported sound change can be found in detailed experimental examination of synchronic phonetic variation.

Given the phonetically gradual nature of sound change at onset, reference to experimental phonetic data is useful in accounting for developments reported in this study as well as constraining phonological patterning and representations over time. In line with the emphasis on the sound change as a

concrete phenomenon at least in its initial phase, I will make frequent reference to the results of experimental work, particularly perceptual evidence, and the ramifications these may have for the sound changes I report. By way of contrast, child language data is only rarely cited in this study, e.g. section 6.4. Although Andersen (1973), Stampe (1969) and Donegan and Stampe (1979) emphasize the significant parallels in many instances between child language acquisition data and sound change, the frequently reported discrepancies also limit the usefulness of such evidence (Dressler 1974; Kiparsky 1988; Connell 1991).

1.3 PHONOLOGICAL REPRESENTATIONS

The classic generative view of phonological representation as a unidimensional linear string of segments made up of unordered feature bundles has now been replaced by a complex multilinear representation. Segmental and suprasegmental elements, e.g. articulatory features, stress, length, are no longer placed together in the same unordered feature matrix. Instead, each element is now given its own representation, independent but interconnecting, in the multidimensional hierarchical structure of Autosegmental Phonology.[14]

The central core of autosegmental representation, to which all other structure is ultimately attached by association lines, is the Skeletal Tier, a linear sequence of prosodic timing slots normally represented by a series of Xs. Phonological length is indicated in the representation by the manner in which skeletal slots are connected to feature structure via the intermediate organizing Root Node, as at 10:[15]

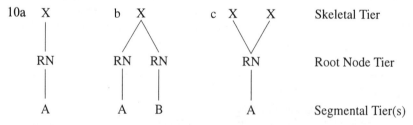

The structure at 10a is typical of simple segments, whilst that of 10b is used to represent short contour segments, such as prenasalized stops. Segments that have a unified feature structure, but are phonologically long, are connected by association line to two timing slots, as at 10c.

In current theory, distinctive features are now hierarchically organized in so-called Feature Geometry. I present at 11 and accept as basic in this dissertation a slightly modified version of feature structure of the types proposed by Sagey (1986) and McCarthy (1988), versions of which are now widely disseminated:

11

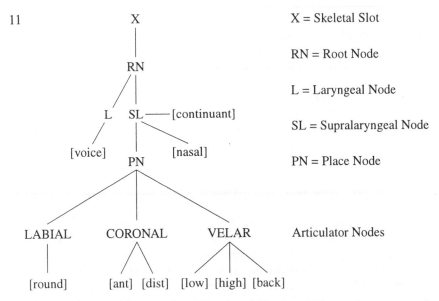

X = Skeletal Slot

RN = Root Node

L = Laryngeal Node

SL = Supralaryngeal Node

PN = Place Node

Articulator Nodes

Suggested modifications involve the following. First, the array of laryngeal features attached by Sagey and McCarthy to the Laryngeal Node has been replaced by a single feature [voice], sufficient for discussion here. In addition, I have simplified the structure slightly by attaching [nasal] directly to the Supralaryngeal Node, rather than to an intermediate Soft Palate Node connected to the Supralaryngeal Node. The presence or absence of the Soft Palate Node is not crucial to any discussion in this thesis. There is furthermore no compelling reason to accept the hypothesis by Piggott (1987, 1988a and b) or Hualde (1989) that [nasal] is attached directly to the Root Node, the supreme subskeletal organizing node.

I follow McCarthy's suggestion that Root Node, in contrast to all the other organizing nodes, has specific featural content, i.e. the major class features [consonantal] and [sonorant]. Standard major class classifications are followed, hence nasal stops have Root Nodes specified [+consonantal, +sonorant].

The association lines which connect the components of the structure are an important and powerful part of multidimensional phonological representation, and are governed by a small number of well-formedness principles. The most important principle relevant for discussion here is the No-Line Crossing Prohibition which forbids the crossing of association lines. As a result, the simple structure in 12a is ill-formed.

From the autosegmental point of view, assimilation processes, such as vowel nasalization, are conceptualized as feature spreading, whereby some association lines are delinked and others spread in a local fashion, as in 12b, but not 12c. By convention, delinked autosegments are automatically deleted.[16]

A well-formed phonological representation requires not only a hierarchically organized segmental structure, but also a hierarchical prosodic or suprasegmental structure placed above and attached to the Skeletal Tier. Skeletal slots with feature content are organized by the syllable as at 13. The so-called Onset-Rhyme model adopted here is of course widely disseminated in the literature, e.g. Lass (1984), and Goldsmith (1990). Described as 'traditional' by Kenstowicz (1994: 253), it is arguably the least controversial of all models of syllable structure. In a context of extensive debate about the syllable, the evidence of phonotactic distribution, predictability of stress patterning, etc., strongly favour accepting the model at 13 over less structured alternatives (see Fudge 1969, 1987; Steriade 1988, Durand 1990 for details).

13 Syllable level

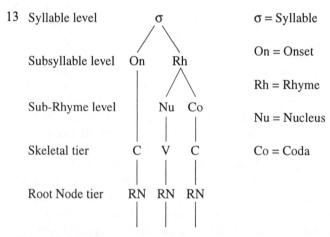

σ = Syllable

On = Onset

Rh = Rhyme

Nu = Nucleus

Co = Coda

The syllable has constituent structure, and is divided between the Onset and the Rhyme. The latter is broken down further into an obligatory Nucleus, and where available, a Coda. All constituents below the syllable may be unary or branching. Syllables are themselves organized into superordinate structure, first the foot and then the highest word-based constituent, the phonological word (see chapter 4 for details).

1.3.1 The diachronic adequacy of autosegmental representation

Notwithstanding the many benefits autosegmental representation has brought to the study and description of phonology, the specifically diachronic adequacy of such a formalism has not been adequately assessed

by phonologists. Certainly, the autosegmental representation of assimilation as a feature-spreading phenomenon is appropriate to the description of phonetic and diachronic phenomena of assimilation, e.g. VN > ṼN. However, I have already noted in section 1.1.2 that substantive limitations still need to be established on the range and type of logically possible assimilations, since the representation allows for assimilatory changes that may never be reported to occur – diachronically or synchronically – in languages.

A more specific problem of adequacy remains. Autosegmental Phonology was developed in the first instance for use in the 'timeless' ambit of a synchronic grammar. Recourse is frequently made in derivation to structures and operations which, whilst formally acceptable, may not have any direct instantiation in speech, e.g. so called Floating Nasal accounts of nasalization discussed in section 3.2.3.[17] Many manipulations of this kind with wide currency in synchronic analysis are now also increasingly and uncritically common in diachronic phonology. Recent attempts at using the same mechanisms to account for sound change phenomena over time include underspecification and Old French lenition (Jakobs and Wetzels 1988), so-called Compensatory Lengthening phenomena (see Hayes 1989, Bickmore 1995 for details and purported diachronic examples), and various manipulations of Feature Geometry.

However, the diachronic adequacy of such operations has to date not been properly evaluated. I suggest that for a posited phonological process to be an empiricially adequate sound change, it must satisfy a small number of basic constraints. First, given the emphasis placed in this study on sound change as a concrete phonetic phenomenon, and on the role of the listener in sound change, an appropriate constraint on formal representation of sound change is that any posited stage should have a phonetic instantiation. This suggests that abstract phonological structures and manipulations are not necessarily suitable for the description of sound change, at least in its first stages. In addition, in any shift from segment A to segment B, sound change should be gradual, minimal and natural in order to be plausible – a point taken up in more detail in chapter 8 (and also Dressler 1971, Picard 1995) and one which also underpins the principle of diachronic extrapolation in reconstruction discussed in section 2.2. I claim that none of these constraints is contro-versial. The first is appropriate in the context described, and the second series of interrelated requirements is generally accepted as fundamental to careful sound change reconstruction. The synchronic alternation between [k] and [s] in English electri[k] and electri[s]ity is, for instance, considered by no-one to be a natural one-step sound change but rather the culmination of a series of gradual and connected changes that allows us to link original velar stop [k] to the final outcome, coronal sibilant [s], i.e. [k] > [kʲ] > [cʲ] > [c] > [tʃ] > [ts] > [s] (cf. Hyman 1975b).

Whilst I do not discuss the issue of diachronic suitability in great detail, I

consider the implications of autosegmental representation, and specific manipulations of feature structure for rule ordering in chapter 3. Evaluation of Feature Geometry continues in chapter 8. Also in chapter 3 there is a brief treatment of one account of distinctive nasalization in which underspecification is invoked with unforeseen and unfortunate consequences. Indeed, emphasis in this study on changes affecting fully-specified segments at or near the surface, as well as lack of any empirical requirement to cite underspecification, specifically mean that at no point is it invoked to account for any diachronic developments reported in my sample. This statement is not inconsistent with the recent hypothesis (e.g. Cohn 1990) of underspecification surviving much closer to the surface than once thought. Although segments may enter the language-specific gradient component only partially specified, they still leave it fully specified before crossing the boundary into the universal component – precisely the initial locus of sound change.

I also refer at various points in this study (e.g. section 4.1.2) to the historical adequacy of so-called Compensatory Lengthening (explained more properly in section 8.1.3), and conclude that abstract operations of this type do not satisfy any of the suggested constraints placed on sound change. Nor in fact is there any empirical necessity to refer to CL to account for changes reported in Northern Italian, as all lengthening phenomena can be independently accounted for. Instead, CL, should be restricted in most circumstances to the representation of secondary synchronic restructuring/ telescoping at more abstract levels of grammar of a previously complex set of gradual changes.

1.3.2 *The feature* [nasal]

All phonological theories posit a single feature [nasal] of some sort to account for the presence or absence of nasality. Whilst Jakobson and Halle (1956) gave their feature [nasal] an acoustically oriented definition, the articulatory definition given to [nasal] by Chomsky and Halle (1968: 316) is current in modern phonological theory:

14 Nasal-Nonnasal
Nasal sounds are produced with a lowered velum which allows the air to escape through the nose; nonnasal sounds are produced with a raised velum so that the air from the lungs can escape only through the mouth.

Although, from the phonetic viewpoint, the degree of velopharyngeal opening, and the consequent nasal output, varies across segments and segment types, it is clear that what is phonologically relevant is a categorical distinction between open and closed velopharyngeal port, i.e. oral vs. nasal. There is little evidence anywhere of a more than binary phonological contrast.[18]

Phonetically, other measures of nasality normally derive from velopharyngeal opening, e.g. duration, nasal airflow, nasal sound pressure levels, acoustic and perceptual effects. Reference will made to each at different points in this study.[19]

Despite Chomsky and Halle's emphasis on an articulatory definition, the phonological feature [nasal] also has some perceptual basis. Experimental evidence shows that there may be velopharyngeal opening through most or all of phonologically oral voiced stops in some languages, e.g. Akan (Huffman 1990), Sindhi (Nihalani 1974, 1991), French (Cohn 1990). Similar evidence of velic opening in oral vowels is also reported, e.g. English (Clumeck 1975, 1976). The effect of such velic opening in these contexts is apparently not perceived or is easily factored out by listeners. Such evidence suggests that Chomsky and Halle's phonetic definition needs to be refined: nasal sounds are produced with sufficient lowering of the velum for them to be perceived as nasal segments.

On the other hand, Ohala (1983) provides acoustic and perceptual evidence demonstrating that velopharyngeal opening is not at all necessary for the perception of nasality in articulatorily oral contexts.[20] Glottal airflow during the production of voiceless fricatives may simulate the acoustic effect of nasalization on adjacent vowels. Listeners may then reinterpret such an effect as involving actual velopharyngeal opening, and nasalize the vowel accordingly, as is reported to occur sporadically in Hindi, e.g. [sã:p] < Sanskrit *sarpa* 'snake'.

It is, nevertheless, the case that contrastive nasalization primarily develops in vowels that were historically adjacent to nasal consonants. Since contextual nasalization of vowels next to nasals is cross-linguistically pervasive, as a result of coarticulated velopharyngeal opening, I will assume, for the purposes of this study, that the articulatory characterization of the feature [nasal] and nasality in general is adequate, bearing in mind that [nasal] also has some, as yet poorly defined, perceptual content.

It must also be pointed out that in the course of this book, following the universalist tradition, I place emphasis on historical developments that occur in only a restricted set of circumstances: unless otherwise made specific, discussion and analysis is generally limited to tautosyllabic VN sequences in stressed syllables, i.e. 'VN$. Also in keeping with earlier studies, I exclude from consideration changes affecting NV sequences, and make limited reference, where specified, to developments affecting heterosyllabic V$NV sequences, and unstressed VN$ syllables.

1.4 CONCLUSION

In the absence of adequate formal constraints on generative and autoseg-mental phonological representation, there is a need to establish substantive constraints based on reported sound changes. Frequently observed non-random patterning has led to the hypothesis that at least some kinds of sound change develop in a universal fashion across languages. In the past, the development of distinctive nasalization, traditionally given as /VN/ > /Ṽ/ was a focal point in the search for such universals. Universalist claims made previously are re-examined in this study.

Any cross-linguistic patterning is assumed to have a phonetic basis, motivated at least partly by the inherent constraints of the speech mechanism. The effects of these constraints can be appropriately observed experimentally in the constant synchronic variation of speech. Sound change as a phonetic phenomenon can be reconciled with the abstract concept of the grammar if we adopt the Lexical Phonology (LP) model of linguistic structure. Accordingly, the phonetic basis and nature of a sound change may over time become obscured as a result of percolation deeper into the grammar. Discussion of the nature of the post-lexical component of the grammar, and the place of sound change, continues in chapter 3. A phonetic model of sound change, in this case a perceptually oriented one, is compatible with the LP model of grammar.

Whilst the hierarchical non-linear representation of Autosegmental Phonology is considered to be a major improvement over classic generative formalism, the diachronic appropriateness of such a synchronically oriented formalism remains to be fully determined.

Finally, although Chomsky and Halle's articulatory characterization of the feature [nasal] is found to be adequate, evidence is provided demonstrating that the feature must also have some perceptual content.

2

THE DATA BASE AND LANGUAGE
SAMPLING: METHODOLOGICAL ISSUES
AND BACKGROUND

2.1 INTRODUCTION

In this chapter general language sampling issues are discussed briefly, so that we can formulate a sample of appropriate quality and time depth necessary for a proper evaluation of sound change universals. A base group of closely related Northern Italian dialects with a shared time frame is established for comparative purposes, although at no time are restrictions placed on the reference to developments elsewhere. After explaining the notion of diachronic extrapolation and the diachronic structure of the sample, I then provide basic information on Latin, the diachronic starting point, and the nine modern members.

2.1.1 *Methodological issues in language sample and data*

The validity of conclusions made in any universalist or typological study of linguistic phenomena will be fundamentally affected by the nature of the data used, and of the source or sources of such data. Given the importance of both language sample and data, methodological issues immediately arise concerning both. These include the number and types of languages involved, the nature and quality of data, the analysis and interpretation of data, and relative time depth. It is somewhat surprising to discover, therefore, that sample and data-related methodological issues have generally evoked little interest amongst universalists examining the development of distinctive nasalization. Discussion of sample and data methodology is absent, or minimal, in Schourup (1973), Foley (1975, 1977), Lightner (1970, 1973), Chen (1973a, b, c, 1974a), Ruhlen (1973), and very limited in Hombert (1986, 1987). Only Chen (1972, 1975) provides some significant detail regarding sources, the type of data used, and of the size and nature of the sample.

2.1.2 *Typological approaches to sampling method*

The Chomskyan or generativist single-language sample and the Greenbergian large-scale cross-linguistic corpus form the two endpoints of the continuum of data bases used in the study of language universals. In the discussion that follows I argue that neither is appropriate for the type of

diachronic study envisioned in this thesis. The single-language sample can be rejected immediately: as universalist claims require cross-linguistic validation at some point, reference to more than one language at the time of formulation is immediately useful. It is not surprising that putative single-language universals, based typically on English, have frequently been disproven once cross-linguistic verification has been attempted; see Comrie (1989: 7–8) for examples.[1]

On the other hand, the criteria used by typologists (e.g. Bell 1978; Perkins 1989; Dryer 1989) in establishing large-scale language samples, such as relative sample size and world-wide distribution, randomness, and the elimination of areo-genetic bias, present their own difficulties, especially for the study of diachronic universals.

Maddieson (1984), typical of the Greenbergian approach, incorporates into his typological study of the world's sound systems a sample of 317 carefully selected languages, each member the sole representative of a language sub-grouping. Although his sample is amongst the largest, the number of languages examined is still a small one relative to the supposed overall number of the world's languages. Explicit attention to relative sample size, as well as to language family and geographical distribution, is intended to reduce areo-genetic influence.

Despite the evolved methodology, the sheer size of large-scale language samples, such as Maddieson's, presents other methodological weaknesses relating to depth and quality of data. Limits are placed on the amount of data incorporated into the typological data base, as well as on the number of possible descriptive sources, to avoid an intolerable burden being placed on the typologist. In some cases, the difficulty in obtaining adequate descriptions of any single member of some less well-known language groupings may lead to their complete exclusion from the sample. Conversely, other languages may be included on the basis of a single available description that may still be lacking in detail, e.g. Maddieson's use of Haudricourt's (1967) very limited account of Lakkia. Furthermore, the huge number of languages in large-scale samples makes more likely the incorporation of erroneous data into the data base, e.g. Maddieson's inclusion of the non-existent extra short nasal vowel /ɨ̃/ in Kashmiri to which his source, Kelkar and Trisal (1964), makes no reference.[2]

Even more problematic, however, than data depth and quality are the very criteria used in establishing large-scale language samples, e.g. large numbers of languages, world-wide distribution, the elimination of areo-genetic bias. Difficult enough to satisfy using synchronic data, they prove insurmountable for diachronic typology. We have relatively little information on the history of the world's languages, and must, therefore, depend on the very restricted set of languages for which we have reasonable historical (preferably attested, but also reconstructed) data.

In the context of difficulties in finding adequate cross-linguistic historical evidence, it is not surprising that relatively small diachronically oriented cross-linguistic samples have been used in universalist studies of distinctive nasalization. Such samples fall into two broad categories: (1) the small scale *ad hoc* sample of the type used, for example, by Lightner (1970, 1973), Foley (1975, 1977); and (2) the small scale genetically oriented sample, as used by Hombert (1986, 1987) and Chen (1972 and elsewhere), in which mother language and a number of daughter languages are compared. Both types of sampling present methodological difficulties, but I shall argue below that both are necessary, and must be combined: the second is useful in creating a 'core' sample, which must remain open to further expansion as well as *ad hoc* accretion for the purposes of empirical verification.

Whilst the construction of *ad hoc* samples appears to have been relatively random, i.e. there appears to be no reasoned process of language choice, strong bias towards Indo-European languages is always evident. Lightner (1970, 1973) considers the development of distinctive nasalization in a sample of eight languages (French, Latin, Old Church Slavonic, Old English, Germanic, Old Norse, Lithuanian and Polish), whilst Foley (1977) restricts discussion to a similarly limited set (French, Portuguese, Old English, German, Polish, Ancient Greek, Sanskrit, Latin, and the Amerindian language Eastern Ojibwa). Of the eleven languages in Ruhlen's (1973) sample, nine are Indo-European, with particular emphasis on French and Portuguese. Schourup (1973) examines developments in thirty-one languages, of which sixteen are Indo-European.

By contrast, Hombert (1986, 1987) and Chen (1972 and elsewhere) selected a set of closely related languages, all sharing a common diachronic starting point. Hombert concentrates on developments in a very small set of Teke (Bantu B.70) languages spoken in central Africa: five languages in 1986 (Ibali, Ndzindziu, Ngungwel, Fumu, Kukua) and only three in 1987 (Ibali, Ndzindziu, Atege). Chen focuses primarily on developments in a set of genetically related Chinese dialects. Although eighteen dialects reportedly make up Chen's (1972, 1973a, b, c, 1974a) sample, he considers developments only in the eleven dialects in which there is evidence of final N-deletion. However, Chen (1975) later expanded his survey to cover 1,364 so-called 'diapoints', 'some in depth, most others quite superficially, an inevitable consequence of the scale and scope aimed at' (p. 23). Chen (1972 and elsewhere) also makes brief reference to other languages, particularly French, to support his findings.

Whilst the emphasis in *ad hoc* studies described above has been on European languages, understandably given the eurocentric bias of Western linguistic research, they also demonstrate a dependency on completely unattested languages with which developments in daughter languages are compared along disparate time frames, e.g. Proto-Slavic with Polish, Proto-Athapascan with Hare (Ruhlen 1973), Proto-Indo-European with

English/Latin (Foley 1977), Proto-Germanic with Gothic (Lightner 1973). There is an obvious danger of circularity in depending on reconstructed starting points that rely at least partly on assumptions about typical sound changes, and then arriving at conclusions about sound change on the basis of such reconstructions. It is true that the methodology is frequently used in all areas of historical linguistics, and that many important findings have been achieved on such a basis, but any diachronic study would be on firmer ground if the historical starting point was one of which we have adequate records, and on which assumptions about sound change and the reconstruction of intermediate forms could be tested.

Whilst the use of an *ad hoc* language sample seems logically to increase the chances of using unattested/reconstructed languages, the same methodological problem is not unknown in genetically oriented samples, as Hombert (1986, 1987) attests with his reliance on Proto-Bantu and Proto-Teke. By comparison, it might seem then that Chen's (1972 and elsewhere) studies of nasalization, based as they are on comparison between an attested language, Middle Chinese, and numerous daughter languages, is methodologically more reliable. However, at no point does Chen discuss the limitations of our knowledge of Middle Chinese. Despite the existence of written records, the traditional logographic representation of Chinese is problematic for our understanding of the phonology of the old language, since it never gives a precise indication of sound. The result is a reconstructed Middle Chinese, laboriously developed by means of modern cross-dialectal comparison, reference to Sino-xenic languages such as Sino-Japanese, and interpretations of Middle Chinese rhyming dictionaries. Even more problematic is the existence of numerous competing and often significantly different reconstructions of Middle Chinese (Norman 1988: 34–42). Given that the use of conflicting reconstructions may lead quite plausibly to different conclusions about the spread of sound change in any language, it is not surprising that Hess (1988) and Chen disagree as to the effect of vowel height on the spread of distinctive nasalization in Chinese dialects (see discussion in chapter 5). The disarray in Sinitic reconstruction is such that Norman, noting the frequent strong criticism of the whole methodology of Middle Chinese reconstruction, suggests the need for a completely new approach. If this is the case, then the reliability of any typological claims based on Chinese diachronic phonology must reasonably be put in doubt.

2.1.3 *A new language sample*

For the purposes of this study, I propose to use a small, genetically oriented core sample, although frequent reference will also be made in a reasonably *ad hoc* fashion, to many other languages for the purposes of empirical confirmation. Eight Northern Italian dialects (Bolognese, Cairese, Imolese, Lughese, Ravennate, Riminese, Milanese, Bergamese) and one Romantsch

dialect (Tavetschan) form this new sample.[3] The common diachronic starting point for the sample is Latin.[4] There are numerous advantages of such a sample over previous samples, although difficulties common to all diachronic studies of this type will inevitably remain. Among the older languages normally cited in universalist nasalization studies, including Middle Chinese, Latin, originally the language of Rome that spread with the expansion of the Roman Empire, is perhaps the best attested with copious written records. Its sound system is also amongst the best understood of all ancient languages, thanks to a relatively penetrable alphabetic writing system, the evidence of Latin grammarians, metre, a long and continuous literary tradition that predates the Christian era, modern cross-dialectal comparison, Latin borrowings into other languages, etc. It is inevitable, however, that areas of uncertainty will persist, e.g. the phonemic status or otherwise of [ŋ] in Latin (cf. Vincent 1988b: 29 and Tekavčić 1972), but these are not considered to affect any discussion in this study.

For diachronic purposes the use of a core sample with a single well-attested diachronic starting point seems preferable to entirely *ad hoc* sampling. The shared time depth for all sample members is useful when comparing developments, and places a constraint on the range of any intermediate reconstruction between endpoints. Furthermore, the need for one or many unattested proto-language starting points is eliminated.

The relatively small scale of the new core sample is not unusual within the context of samples used previously by universalists. Restricting the size of the core sample, at least initially, to nine members allows for a greater bibliographical input for each sample member. To this we can add the inclusion of corroborative fieldwork, more data, detail and discussion for each. At the same time, the Northern Italian sample does not represent a closed data set, but is merely a useful starting point when considering the development of distinctive nasalization. At no point in the thesis do I restrict discussion to the nine sample members: frequent reference is made to other Romance dialects both inside and outside Northern Italy, as well as to many non-Romance languages, including those cited previously by universalists. Other cross-linguistic evidence is used to verify any claims made based on developments in the Northern Italian sample. In this way, I think we can avoid the criticism that may be made of the Greenbergian large-scale language sample, i.e. that it merely represents a closed data set, carefully selected to avoid skewing through areo-genetic bias, which endeavours to find statistical frequency patterns in the corpus.

As for areo-genetic skewing in my own small sample, my initial hypothesis, following Foley, of strict universal patterning in all the world's languages should preclude it as a possibility, since no more than one pattern is hypothetically uncoverable. The validity of such a falsifiable hypothesis is examined in all contexts, and shown in many cases to be disproven.

However, evidence of areo-genetic bias is not in itself fatal to the view expressed in chapter 1 that most sound changes are ultimately phonetically determined. In this context, any areo-genetic patterning will be taken to represent one of many competing non-random patterns, the phonetic basis of which still requires explanation. It should be pointed out too that in any case it may be impossible to eliminate areo-genetic bias no matter how large and carefully selected the language sample: as Janson (1991) points out, areal influence on phonological patterning is evident even in Maddieson's (1984) sample of more than 300 languages.

Whilst areal or genetic factors might be expected *a priori* to lead to an over-representation of a particular phenomenon, and the omission of others, such an outcome is not necessarily the result. In earlier studies (Hajek 1988, 1991a) of the effect of nasality on vowel height, I found an unexpected proliferation of developments in a slightly different Northern Italian sample. Such a result was not expected, given the obvious areal and genetic factors at play, and could not easily be accounted for.

Finally, it should be noted in passing that, in a recent study of nasalization phenomena by Tuttle (1991), most attention is given to developments in varieties of Romance spoken in Northern Italy, with additional frequent reference to changes in other Romance and non-Romance languages. However, there are also major differences in sampling technique and data methodology which suggests that the sample adopted in my own study is more reliable. A far larger number of Northern Italian dialects (at least sixty) cited by Tuttle perforce allows only brief reference for most of them. In contrast, my smaller core sample of nine dialects is described in some detail below, and used consistently throughout the study to test all claims about the development of distinctive nasalization. Tuttle's study also relies on a preponderance of data taken from sources published in the late nineteenth and early twentieth centuries: these are often ambiguous in nature, and in the absence of corroborative fieldwork, their reliability and modern inter-pretation are not guaranteed. As a result, much of the data as well as many of the claims made by Tuttle with regard to the development of distinctive nasalization are, as will be shown, open to reanalysis.

2.2 THE PRINCIPLE OF DIACHRONIC EXTRAPOLATION

Chen (1972, 1973a), uniquely amongst universalists of distinctive nasaliza-tion, makes explicit reference to the methodology underlying the reconstruc-tion of intermediate stages in sound change between Middle Chinese and modern dialectal forms. The so-called principle of 'diachronic extrapolation' or 'latitudinal reconstruction' allows for reconstruction on the basis of comparison of synchronic dialectal reflexes. It rests on 'two empirical assumptions: (i) that it is characteristic of some sound changes to take

place along certain phonological continua; (ii) that closely related linguistic systems share a significant amount of their phonological history' (Chen 1973a: 52).

The use of diachronic extrapolation is best made evident by a simple example: amongst the modern reflexes of Latin CANE 'dog' in Northern Italian we find Bergamese [kaː]. Without the benefit of historical evidence, or of diachronic extrapolation, one could posit the following reconstruction governed solely by the criterion of formal simplicity:

1a   e > Ø / __#   CANE > [kan]
 b   n > Ø / __#   [kan] > [ka]
 c   V > Vː / __#   [ka] > [kaː]

In fact, such a reconstruction appears to be confirmed, at least superficially, by the earliest textual evidence from Old Bergamese where *ca* is the regular reflex of Latin CANE.

Without reference to comparative dialectal data, coupled with the absence of other reflexes of Latin CANE in Bergamese, it is tempting not to posit for Bergamese any intermediate stage of distinctive vowel nasalization.[5] The suggested scenario for Bergamese does not conform with developments elsewhere in Northern Italy, and on the basis of data taken from other Italian dialects, e.g. Italian [kaːne], and the related Lombard dialects, Cremonese [kaːn] ~ [kãːn], and Milanese [kãː], we can extrapolate the following pattern of development as more likely:

2a   'V → 'Vː / __$ CANE > [kaːne]
 b   V → Ø / __#   [kaːne] > [kaːn]
 c   Vː → Ṽː / __n   [kaːn] > [kãːn]
 d   n → Ø / __#   [kãːn] > [kãː]
 e   Ṽ → V   [kãː] > [kaː]

As is evident from the analysis at 2, the guiding principles behind diachronic extrapolation involve: (1) the assumption that change in closely related languages will be expected to be as uniform as possible; (2) graduality leading to the maximization of steps common to all dialects; and (3) delaying of dialect divergence until later stages. In this way, changes in closely related languages can be seen to form part of one interrelated process, rather than many unrelated ones. It has also been suggested, e.g. Greenberg (1978), that diachronic reconstruction may to some extent be constrained by the observed range of synchronic variation. This follows from the Jakobsonian claim that things cannot be reconstructed diachronically if they are not attested anywhere synchronically.[6]

The principle of diachronic extrapolation is commonly applied in historical reconstruction of phonology and sound change, cf. Hall (1976: 1–2), and especially Hock (1986) for details. However, its reliability can be increased or tested by comparative substantive evidence along parts of the

suggested timeframe, such as medieval texts, the prescriptions/descriptions of early grammarians, etc. Chen, in his study of distinctive nasalization phenomena in Chinese dialects, is entirely dependent on diachronic extrapolation, forced upon him by the difficulties in isolating phonological variation over time and space in Chinese logographic representation. By way of contrast, there is a substantial medieval textual evidence for members of my sample.[7] Whilst most frequent reference in this study will be made to modern-day dialectal forms in extrapolating changes from Latin, historical confirmation of the suggested pattern of diachronic development is also possible, and useful in constraining and confirming changes, at least for substantial parts of the time-scale from Latin to the present day.

2.2.1 *Latin and Post-Latin*

Whilst the reconstruction of intermediate steps between Latin and Northern Italian is deemed necessary, given, for example, the divergence between Latin CANE, and Bergamese [kaː] above, I will not assume as absolutely necessary, as proto-Romance reconstructionists have (e.g. Hall 1976, 1978; Leonard 1980), that any shared feature is derived from a particular change occurring at one point in time in a single shared proto-language.

Instead I postulate two major reconstructed stages, Stage 1 and Stage 2, so that changes appear in a coherent and logical manner in historical derivations in the text. However, these stages operate without any underlying assumptions about the existence of uniform proto-languages or about chronological uniformity. Whilst from the synchronic point of view, the same change has occurred in all dialects in question, there is no way of establishing nor any need to assume that the change occurred in all dialects at precisely the same point in time. Only a very restricted set of sound changes will be postulated for each of stages 1 and 2, and these are discussed in detail in the sections that follow.

In most cases, cited Romance reflexes have attested Latin etyma which will normally be provided as the chronological and logical starting point in historical derivations given in the text, e.g. JAM 'already' > Italian ['dʒa]. Very rarely, borrowings into Latin or Romance, and unattested Latin words with a pan-Romance distribution, marked with an asterisk, will also be cited. Reference will normally be made to simple lexical units, generally nouns, and normally part of the basic vocabulary, e.g. 'dog', 'bread', and so on. It is assumed that the basic vocabulary cited in derivations has passed in a continuous and uninterrupted fashion from Latin into modern Romance dialects referred to in the text, and that changes that have occurred have done so in a reasonably uniform manner. Exceptions, of course, may occur, such as Latinisms, Italianisms, and these are recognized by their divergent development from the otherwise normal dialectal outcome. For instance, in Bolognese, instead of the expected *[viːda] for Latin VITA 'life', we find the

historically anomalous form [vetta] with surviving voiceless stop. The modern form seems to represent a Bolognese reinterpretation of a very late borrowing from Italian or Latin.

It is traditional in Romance linguistics to cite Latin forms in small capitals, with or without vowel length markings. I will not ordinarily mark vowel length for typographical reasons. Should length need to be reported, it will be noted for the sake of convenience by the use of the colon (:) , e.g. PA:NIS 'bread' (nom. sg.) but CANIS 'dog' (nom. sg.). Reference to individual Latin segments and sequences of segments may also be made using small capitals, e.g. N represents Latin /n/, NN /nn/, etc. Normal Latin orthography is regular and is assumed to be reasonably transparent. Orthographic c and v are considered by convention to represent [k] and [w] respectively. Cited Latin nominal etyma will normally be given in the accusative, since most Romance nominal forms, at least in the singular, are predictably derivable from the Latin accusative, marked morphologically by final M, e.g. CANEM 'dog' (acc. sg.). However, as accusative -M was lost early and does not survive in any form at all in modern Romance nominal reflexes, final orthographic M is conventionally omitted in derivations, so that where necessary reference will be made to the form CANE and not CANEM in the text. It is only rarely the case that morphological considerations play any role in discussion of the data.

2.2.2 Description of sample members

2.2.2.1 Latin

Latin (Lat.) has a rather simple consonant system, and a slightly more complex vowel system; see the phonemic inventory at 3 (Vincent 1988b: 29):

3   p   b   t   d   k   g k^w g^w
    f   s   h
    m   n
              l
              r

    i: i   u u:
         e: e   o o:
              a: a
    ai,   au,   oi

The vowel system displays contrastive length, e.g. CANIS 'dog' (nom. sg.) v. PA:NIS 'bread' (nom. sg.).

The Latin nasal consonant system is marked by an absence of palatal nasal [ɲ], and velar [ŋ] is allophonic with a highly restricted distribution, i.e. before velar obstruents, e.g. CANCER 'crab', and possibly before /n/ in words like AGNUS 'lamb'. The nasal phonemes /n, m/ have a wide phonotactic

distribution in Latin: they may appear in initial, intervocalic and word-final position, as well as in a variety of clusters, e.g. the accusative forms NASUM 'nose', LANAM 'wool', DENTEM 'tooth', MICAM 'crumb', LIMAM 'file', CAMPUM 'field', and NOMEN 'name'. Like other consonant phonemes, /n/ and /m/ also appear in Latin as contrastively geminate, e.g. FLAMMA 'flame' v. LIMA 'file', ANNU 'year' v. ANU 'anus'.

Stress-placement patterns in Latin, to which there is frequent reference in this study, are traditionally described according to the following tripartite schema: oxytonic (final stress), eg. 'JAM, paroxytonic (penultimate stress), eg. 'LANA, and proparoxytonic (antepenultimate stress), eg. 'ASINU. Final stress is relatively rare in Latin and examples are exclusively monosyllabic.

Radical changes to the phonological system of Latin are apparent from reflexes in the Romance dialects, and are supported by inscriptional evidence, prescriptive texts, and comments by grammarians of the period (Väänänen 1967). Three of the most widespread and apparently earliest changes in the Romance-speaking area are postulated as occurring at Stage 1: (1) transformation of the vowel system; (2) the loss of most word-final nasals; and (3) palatalization. A second series of changes postulated as occurring at Stage 2 is discussed in detail below. Stage 1 changes are postulated to have occurred at some point before Stage 2 changes. In most cases, the latter have a significantly smaller geographic distribution in the Romance area than the former, and are useful in characterizing innovative Northern Italian and Rhaeto-Romantsch (and many other Western Romance dialects) thereby distinguishing them from the more conservative dialects of Central and Southern Italy.

During Stage 1, the structural and distributional characteristics of the original quantity-based Latin vowel system underwent radical alteration (see Vincent 1988b: 28–34 for details). The ten-vowel system of Latin, /a, a:, e, e:, i, i:, o, o:, u, u:/ was apparently reduced to a quality-based seven vowel system of the type given at 4 in most Romance dialects, including Northern Italian, with the exception of Balkano-Romance, Sardinian, and some Southern Italian dialects:

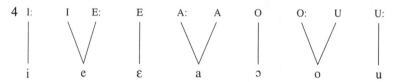

Vowel length is no longer phonemic, and now becomes entirely predictable in distribution: stressed vowels are short in closed syllables, and long in open syllables; unstressed vowels are always short; cf. Vincent (1988b), Saltarelli (1983) and Swiggers (1984).

There was disruption, not detailed here, to this new predictable vowel length distribution in many Northern Italian and Centro-Southern Italian

dialects (Rohlfs 1966: 23–4). Proparoxytonic open syllables were at some point affected by a secondary process of phonetic and phonological vowel shortening, evident in divergent modern vowel reflexes, e.g. LANA 'wool' > [laːna] > Bolognese [lɛːna], but ANIMU 'spirit' > Stage 2 [aːnimu] > *[animu] > [aːnum] parallel to CANNA 'cane' > /kana/ > [kaːna]. The geographical distribution of proparoxytonic shortening is uneven, and the phenomenon shows cross-dialectal variation in implementation.[8] Nevertheless, proparoxytonic shortening before N will be shown in chapter 4 to have important ramifications for the spread of distinctive nasalization. The extensive changes to Latin stressed monosyllables in general, even in the most conservative parts of Romania, suggest a very early dating, and there is some indication (also discussed in chapter 4) that monosyllabic oxytones ending in final N, e.g. NOːN 'no(t)' and JAM 'already' escaped closed syllable shortening as a result.

Whilst orthographic M is an important morphological marker in Latin, phonetic reduction combined with the loss of the Latin declensional system, as well as the simplification of verbal morphology, have eliminated in Romance practically all contexts where Latin /m/ appears in word-final position. Nowhere, in fact, does Latin word-final orthographic M have a reflex /m/ in Romance.[9] In the very few cases where some consonantal reflex has survived into Romance, we find a shift first to /n/, and then to a nasal vowel, e.g. QUEM > Spanish quién [kjen], Portuguese [kẽj] 'who', REM 'thing' (acc.) > French rien [rjɛ̃ː] 'nothing'.[10] Indeed word-final place shift (before eventual loss) is so regular in Romance that final /m/ cannot be reconstructed from modern reflexes. For this reason, Hall (1976: 85) can only reconstruct Proto-Romance CUN for original Latin CUM.

In Northern Italian, Italian, and other Italian dialects, the (non-) appearance of final [n] for Lat. M is stress-conditioned. Final M is completely lost in tonic monosyllables, e.g. JAM 'already' > Bo. [dza], It. [dʒa], and in atonic position in polysyllables, e.g. CANEM 'dog' (acc.) > Bo. [kæŋ], It. [kaːne]. However, in atonic monosyllables, shift to [n] is evident, e.g. CUM 'with' > It. [kon], Bo. [kon]; see sections 4.2.2 and 4.3.2 for further discussion.

Within Latin itself, there is sufficient evidence to suggest that word-final /m/, for which we have comparable cognates in other Indo-European languages, e.g. Lat. equum, Sanskrit aśvam, 'horse', was already prone to weakening and loss. Word-final M is sometimes omitted even in early Latin inscriptions, and Latin grammarians, noting the peculiar behaviour of final M in metre, seem to suggest that word-final M was increasingly elided, leaving a nasal vowel before vowel-initial words.[11] There is some debate today as to whether such a change was already consistent in pre-classical times, perhaps only to be reversed in the written norm of Classical Latin. However, there is evidence to support the notion that Latin word-final M was also consonantal, or had a consonantal allophone at least in some

contexts, in addition to elision and vowel nasalization: (1) in preconsonantal position, the reflex is consonantal which assimilates in place, e.g. inscriptional TAN DURUM for expected TAM DURUM, and the well-known *double entendre* CU[n] NOBIS (Allen 1965: 31); (2) the survival of consonantal reflexes, e.g. CUM > It. *con* 'with', QUEM > Sp. *quién* 'who', SUM > It. *sono* 'am'; (3) the consonantal behaviour of historical M in triggering phonosyntactic doubling in some Southern Italian dialects, e.g. Neapolitan *co ttenə* 'with you' < CUM TI(BI) + *NE, Barese *i' so bbivə* < EGO SUM VIVU 'I am alive' (Rohlfs 1966: 427, n.1). On the basis of the evidence, I will assume that at some stage Latin word-final /Vm#/ had contextually dependent variants [Vm#] and [Ṽ#], but that most evidence of final /m/ was eventually lost very early in Romance through reduction of the sort /Vm#/ > [Ṽm] > [Ṽ] > [V].

Examples of Latin word-final /n/ were relatively rare, and fall primarily into two small sets: (1) particles, e.g. AN (question particle); and (2) the nominative singular masculine (e.g. PECTEN 'comb') or nom./acc. neuter of some nouns. Most of these are neuters which contain the atonic suffix -MEN, e.g. NOMEN 'name' (nom./acc.), FLUMEN 'river', EXAMEN 'swarm'. As the category of neuters declined, these words in -EN came to have Vulgar Latin accusatives based on their oblique/plural stems: *NOMINE(M), *FLUMINE(M), etc. Lexical replacement, particularly of particles, and the pan-Romance preference for the Latin accusative as base form have led to the almost complete elimination of possible etyma with final /n/. Hence Sp. *nombre* < *NOMINE, *enjambre* < *EXAMINE. Modern reflexes of the type e.g. It. *nome*, Fr. *nom* 'name', do not represent, as Rohlfs (1966: 427), Fouché (1961: 652) and Väänänen (1967: 70) suggest, survival of the nominative/accusative form with loss of -N but rather analogical reconstruction based on variation inherent in the forms of the basic but irregular noun SANGUIS (nom. masc.) ~ SANGUEN (nom. neut.) 'blood', SANGUEM (acc. masc.) ~ SANGUINEM (acc. masc.) ~ SANGUEN (acc. neut.). Thus we suppose NOMEN (nom.), *NOMEN (acc.), etc., on the model of SANGUEN, SANGUEM. Exceptionally, only in one small area (Sardinian) do we find unexpected conservation of -N as a result of vowel paragoge, e.g. [frummini], [nomini] (Contini 1987).

As a result of all these processes of elimination of -N, I suggest that the reflexes of only two N-final words with any frequency survive in Northern Italian, and in many other Romance dialects, namely NO:N 'not/no' and IN 'in'. The particular development of these two forms is discussed in some detail in section 4.3.2.

The final Stage 1 change derives from the secondary gliding of post-consonantal front vowels in hiatus, e.g. VINEA > VIN[j]A, SAPIAT > SAP[j]AT. Palatalization follows with far-reaching consequences on the phonologies of Romance dialects, e.g. PUTEU > It. *pozzo* 'well', SAPIAT > It. *sappia*, Fr. *sache* 'knows' (subj.), RABIA > It. *rabbia*, Fr. *rage* 'anger' (Vincent 1988b:

39–40; Rohlfs 1966: 385–6). In parallel fashion, velars C (=/k/) and G were also palatalized before front vowels E, I to /ʧ/ and /ʤ/ respectively throughout most of Romania, e.g. CENTU 'hundred' > It. [ʧɛnto], Sp. [θjento], GENTE 'people' > It. [ʤɛnte], Fr. [ʒɑ̃ː].

The posited Stage 1 changes are illustrated at 5:

5	Latin	/kanem/	/paːnem/	/balneum/
		'dog'	'bread'	'bath'
a. e/i > j / __V				[balnjum]
(b. l > Ø / __n				[banjum])
c. V > Ṽ / –m#		[kanẽm]	[paːnẽm]	[banjũm]
d. m > Ø / __#		[kanẽ]	[paːnũ]	[banjũ]
e. Ṽ > V / __		[kane]	[paːne]	[banju]
f. V > Vː / __$		[kaː$ne]	[paː$ne]	[ban$ju][12]

The phonemic, if not underlying, forms that result after the operation of all the processes listed in 5 are /kane/, /pane/, and /banju/ respectively.

2.2.2.2. The Northern Italian dialects

The Romance dialects found in Northern Italy, an area bordered externally by France, Switzerland, Austria, Yugoslavia, and internally within Italy by Tuscany and the Marches, are normally classified into one of four major dialect groupings. The most important is Gallo-Italian which encompasses the bulk of the Romance dialects spoken in the regions of Northern Italy: Lombard, Ligurian, Veneto, Piedmontese, and Emilian-Romagnol (Pellegrini 1977). In addition, extending in an arc beyond the periphery of Northern Italy, we find Franco-Provençal, Provençal, Rhaeto-Romance (Ladin, Friulan in Northern Italy, and Romantsch in the Swiss Grisons) dialects spoken.

Following Pellegrini (1977), the nine Northern Italian dialects incorporated in the sample have the following very general geolinguistic distribution:

6 Gallo-Italian
    Lombard: Milanese, Bergamese
    Ligurian: Cairese
    Emilian-Romagnol: Bolognese, Imolese, Lughese, Ravennate, Riminese

Rhaeto-Romance
    Romantsch: Tavetschan

Three isoglosses are used to distinguish Rhaeto-Romance, Franco-Provençal and Provençal dialects on the one hand from Gallo-Italian, Italian, and other Centro-Southern Italian dialects on the other: (1) the generalized survival of Latin final -s; (2) the conservation of Latin

obstruent + lateral clusters, FL, BL, PL, CL, GL; and (3) the palatalization of velars in Latin CA and GA clusters, as at 7:

7	Tavetsch	Bolognese	Italian	
NOS	[nuːs]	[no]	[noj]	'we'
CANTAS	[kɔntas]	[kæŋt]	[kanti]	'you sing'(s.)
CANE	[cawn]	[kæŋ]	[kaːne]	'dog'
*GATTU	[ɟat]	[gaːt]	[gatto]	'cat'
FLAMMA	[flɔma]	[fjaːma]	[fjamma]	'flame'
CLAMAT	[klɔma]	[tʃaːma]	[kjaːma]	'calls'

Conversely, a small set of fundamental isoglosses, postulated as Stage 2 changes, allows us to distinguish all the dialects of Northern Italy, as well as many other Western Romance dialects, e.g. French, from the dialects of Central and Southern Italy. The postulated Stage 2 changes are: (1) very early lenition of intervocalic obstruents /p, t, k, b, d, g, s, f/; (2) reduction of Latin geminates to simple consonants; (3) the loss of final atonic vowels, except /a/; and (4) fusion of NJ to [ɲ]. Limited data drawn from two dialects, Bolognese, and Tavetschan, typical of all sample members, as well as equivalent material from Italian, are provided for simple comparative purposes in 8:[13]

8a	Italian	Bolognese	Tavetschan	
ROTA	[rwɔːta]	[roːda]	[roːdə]	'wheel'
ORTICA	[ortiːka]	[urtiːga]		'nettle'
ASINU	[aːzino]	[ɛːzen]	[aːzən]	'donkey'
CAUDA	[koːda]	[ko]	[kuːə]	'tail'
b				
*GATTA	[gatta]	[gaːta]	[ɟatə]	'cat' (f.)
VACCA	[vakka]	[vaːka]	[vakə]	'cow'
c				
*GATTU	[gatto]	[gaːt]	[ɟat]	'cat'
MURU	[muːro]	[muːr]	[miːr]	'wall'
LACTE	[latte]	[laːt]	[lac]	'milk'
but				
BARBA	[barba]	[bɛːrba]	[barbə]	'beard'
LUNA	[luːna]	[loŋna]	[ʎiːnə]	'moon'
d				
*BANJAT	[baɲɲa]	[baːɲa]	[bɔɲa]	'bathes'

In contrast to Northern Italian [ɲ] < NJ, the regular Centro-Southern Italian outcome is geminate [ɲː], as at 8d. In many Sardinian and Corsican dialects, NJ was never simplified, and hardening of the glide occurred, e.g. VINEA 'vineyard' > Stage 1 /vinja/ > Fr. [viɲ], It. [viɲːa], Occ., Sp., Cat., Pt. [viɲa], but Sard. [bindʒa], Cors. [binɟa] (Contini 1987: 140–2, Rohlfs 1966: 399, n. 1).

Degemination and final vowel loss have a fundamental effect on word structure in Northern Italian. The former interacts with the earlier Stage 1 innovation of predictable distribution of vowel length, i.e. long vowels in open syllables, and short vowels in closed syllables, to create a new phonemic contrast in vowel length, at least in Latin paroxytones: previously predictably short vowels before geminates at Stage 1 remain short even after degemination at Stage 2, as evident at 9a and b.[14] The distinction is important, since it will be demonstrated at various points in this study that vowel length plays a crucial role in the development of vowel nasalization and N-deletion in Northern Italian. For the sake of convenience, I will distinguish the Stage 2 reflexes of Latin N and NN as $/n_1/$ and $/n_2/$ respectively when referred to in isolation.

The deletion of most final vowels, coupled with the rise of palatal $/\text{ɲ}/$, allows for an entirely new three-way place contrast in word-final nasals unknown to Latin, as at 9c:

9a		PANE	PANNU	*BANJU	LANA	CANNA
		'bread'	'cloth'	'bath'	'wool'	'cane'
	Stage 1	/pane/	/pannu/	/banju/	/lana/	/kanna/
	[ ]	[paːne]	[pannu]	[banju]	[laːna]	[kanna]
	Stage 2					
	degem.	[paːne]	[panu]	[banju]	[laːna]	[kana]
	NJ > ɲ			[baɲu]		
	FVL	[paːn]	[pan]	[baɲ]	[laːna]	[kana]
	/ /	/paːn/	/pan/	/baɲ/	/laːna/	/kana/
b		CLAMAT	>	/klaːma/	'calls'	
		FLAMMA	>	/flama/	'flame'	
c		PANE	>	/paːn/	(and PANNU > /pan/)	
		*BANJU	>	/baɲ/		
		(AE)RAMEN	>	/raːm/	'copper'	

/ / = underlying representation[15]   degem. = degemination
[ ] = surface representation   FVL = final vowel loss

Secondary developments in individual dialects, such as diphthongization of long vowels, glide hardening, secondary lengthening/shortening, may obscure the simple vowel length opposition in many Northern Italian dialects today. Some of these changes affecting vowel length are referred to and discussed in the brief descriptions of sample dialects below, and throughout the text where relevant (cf. also Saunders 1975, 1978). However, the existence of an earlier vowel length contrast can still be inferred from the divergent development of Stage 2 long and short vowels even in dialects where Stage 2 vowel length distinctions are lost or obscured. For example, the Bolognese examples in 10 indicate that fronting of Stage 2 /aː/ must have preceded the later lengthening of Stage 2 /a/:

10	Stage 1	Stage 2	Bolognese	
CARU	[kaːru]	[kaːr]	[kɛːr]	'dear'
CARRU	[karru]	[kar]	[kaːr]	'cart'
PASTA	[pasta]	[pasta]	[paːsta]	'pasta'

In addition to allowing for a new contrast in final nasals, final vowel deletion has a fundamental effect on general patterns of word-structure in Northern Italian: Latin oxytones remain as such, e.g. JAM 'already' > It. *già*, Bo. [dza], but paroxytones and proparoxytones terminating in U, I, O, E become oxytones and paroxytones respectively, e.g. 'CANE 'dog' > Bo. [kæŋ], but It. *cane*, 'PECTINE 'comb' > Bo. ['peːten], but It. *pettine*.

2.2.3 *Choosing the sample*

Different factors governed the choice of dialects to be included in the sample. Of primary importance was the availability of reliable data, synchronic and diachronic, the quality of primary sources, supported by adequate secondary sources, e.g. additional descriptions, dictionaries, and linguistic atlas material. Recordings were available of most dialects, and I undertook additional fieldwork to check the accuracy of primary sources. Although the sample has in itself an inherent genetic and areal bias, as discussed previously, the sample is further skewed by the preponderance of dialects from Emilia-Romagna. The decision to include such a large number of dialects from one area was initially determined solely by the high quality of data provided by Schürr (1917 and elsewhere). The decision to select Imolese, Lughese, Ravennate and Riminese from amongst the many Romagnol dialects described by Schürr was at the outset random, but has demonstrated itself to be quite felicitous. These four Romagnol dialects and Bolognese present different degrees of innovation with regard to the development of vowel nasalization and N-deletion. Relative degree of innovativeness appears to correspond with the distribution of the dialects on or near the famous Roman *Via Emilia* which extends throughout Emilia-Romagna, i.e., as one moves westwards along the *Via Emilia* from the easternmost and most conservative, Riminese, developments become progressively more innovative in Ravennate, and even more so in Imolese and Lughese, until they reach their most radical in the westernmost dialect, Bolognese. Despite the restricted geographical distribution of the five dialects even within Emilia-Romagna, it was felt important to include them so that any small-scale attested differences in development could be incorporated into the sample, and used in the reconstruction of sound changes discussed in this study.

2.2.3.1 Lombard: Milanese and Bergamese

Two Lombard dialects, Milanese (Mi.) and Bergamese (Bg.), have been included in the sample. They are representative of Western and Eastern

Lombard respectively, the two major dialect zones within Lombardy, and the core of the Lombard speaking area. Milan and Bergamo are represented by *AIS* (*Atlante italo-svizzero*) points 261 and 246.

The primary source used here for details of Milanese phonology is Salvioni (1884, 1975), supported by Pavia (1928), Sanga (1988a, b), Beretta (1980), Nicoli (1983), Massariello Merzagora (1988). Additional, primarily lexical, sources include Arrighi (1896) and Angiolini (1897). Beretta and Luzzi (1982), amongst others, provide details of medieval records in Milanese, the earliest of which date from the thirteenth century. Unusually for Northern Italian, there is also an early description of the phonological system of Milanese, entitled *Prissian da Milan della parnonzia Milanesa*, and first published in 1606 (Lepschy 1965).

All sources agree that contrastive vowel length is highly characteristic of Milanese, at least in word-final position, e.g. [kan'ta] 'to sing' v. [kan'tɑː] 'sung' (m. sg.). However, as in many other Northern Italian dialects, secondary vowel shortening is regular before /m/, e.g. *LAMA 'blade' > Stage 2 /laːma/ > Mi. [lama]. More unusually, however, the expected long vowels are reported by Salvioni (1884), Pavia (1928), Sanga (1988a) and Nicoli (1983) to be regularly reduced by many speakers before /n₁/, e.g. Stage 1 /saːna/ > Mi. [sana] 'healthy' (f. sg.), and St. 1 /saːne/ > [san] (f. pl.).[16]

Distinctive nasalization, first explicitly reported in the *Prissian* of 1606, remains a regular feature of Milanese, e.g. CANE > Stage 2 /kaːn/ > Mi. [kɑ̃ː], VINU 'wine' > Stage 2 /viːn/ > [vĩː], CENTU 'hundred' > Mi. [tʃɛ̃ːt].

For Bergamese, the primary sources are Sanga (1987a), and Sanga and Bernini (1987). Tiraboschi (1873, 1879), and Sanga (1987b) provide additional material on both the dialect of Bergamo city and the rustic Bergamese of the surrounding valleys. Lorck (1893), Tomasoni (1984) and Ciociola (1979, 1986), amongst others, provide details of Old Bergamese, which is reasonably well attested, and for which we have texts dating back to the thirteenth century.

Contrastive vowel length, remnants of which survived in the late nineteenth century, e.g. *caar* < CARU 'dear' (m.sg.) v. *car* < CARRU 'cart', is now lost, and stressed vowels may be optionally lengthened, e.g. Stage 2 /an/ 'year' > [a(ː)n] (Sanga 1987b).

Highly characteristic of Bergamese and other Eastern Lombard dialects are the historical deletion of secondary word-final /n/ (< Lat. N, but not < NN) and of nasals before voiceless obstruents, and the complete denasalization of expected nasal vowels in these contexts e.g. CANE > Bg. [kaː], CAMPU 'field' > [kaːp], TANTU 'so' > [taːt], PONTE 'bridge' > [puːt], but *GAMBA 'leg' > [gamba], PLUMBU 'lead' > [pjomp], ANNU 'year' > [a(ː)n]. These once regularly long vowels are also subject to optional reduction, e.g. [kaː] ~ [ka], [kaːp] ~ [kap], etc. Doublets may arise, as the influence of Italian has led in some cases to the reintroduction of nasalization and nasal consonants before voiceless obstruents, e.g. [tã:(ⁿ)t] ~ [taːt] 'so', mainly in

the urban variety of Bergamese. The phenomenon of complete denasalization, quite regular in Eastern Lombard, is not generalized anywhere else in Northern Italy.

2.2.3.2 Ligurian: Cairese

Cairese (Ca.), the dialect of Cairo Montenotte situated in the Ligurian province of Savona, close to the Piedmontese border, is the sole representative of dialects spoken in Liguria. Parry (1984) provides a detailed description of the dialect, including a glossary. In addition, Forner (1988, 1989) and van den Bergh (1979) provide general overviews of Ligurian, with details of sub-groupings in the region. There is no AIS survey of Cairo Montenotte, which is located between AIS pts. 184 (Calizzano) and 177 (Sassello). Whilst we find in Cairese the Ligurian characteristics of (af)frication of Lat. FL, BL and PL clusters, e.g. FLAMMA > [ʃama] 'flame', Gmc. *BLANK > [dʒaŋk] 'white', PLANTA > [tʃaŋta] 'plant', and rhotacism of intervocalic /l/, e.g. ALA > [eːra] 'wing', the dialect belongs to a mixed Ligurian-Piedmontese zone that straddles the Ligurian-Piedmontese border to the north of Savona and Genoa. Parry (1984) and Forner (1988, 1989) both note the preponderance of Piedmontese features in the dialects such as Cairese, spoken in the western half of the mixed zone. Parry (1984: 378) reports that, of a set of fifteen sound change variables, the Ligurian result is evident in only five cases, whilst the Piedmontese outcome is adopted in six. The remainder represent unexpectedly strong Lombard influence, normally considered to be more typical of the Monferrato area north of Cairo Montenotte.

Distinctive nasalization is no longer a regular synchronic feature of Cairese. Stage 2 syllable-final /n/ (< Lat. N), e.g. /tant/, /kaːn/, appears today as velarized, e.g. [taŋt], [kaŋ]. However, patterns of synchronic alternation suggest that distinctive nasalization was once the norm, and that velarization is the relatively recent result of a process of nasalized glide hardening, e.g. LANA > Stage 2 /laːna/ > *[lãjna] ~ [lãw̃na] > [lajna] ~ [laŋna] (and [laːna]), LUNA > Stage 2 /luːna/ > *[lỹw̃na] > (1) [lywna] and (2) > [lỹŋna] > [lyŋna], alongside CANE > Stage 2 /kaːn/ > *[kãj] ~ [kãw̃] > [kãŋ] > [kaŋ]. Whilst vowels may still be nasalized before [ŋ] in casual speech, denasalization occurs in careful citation speech. Glide velarization is also systematic in another sample dialect, Bolognese, and the mechanics of the process are discussed in chapter 8. In very rapid speech, contextual vowel nasalization can be strong, and subsequent optional [ŋ]-deletion permitted, as is common everywhere in Northern Italy (Galassi and Trumper 1975, Mioni and Trumper 1977).

The Stage 2 vowel length contrast before nasals survives, sometimes obscured, e.g. Stage 2 /laːna/ > [lajna] ~ [laŋna] (and [laːna]), but Stage 2 /kana/ > [kɐna].[17]

2.2.3.3. Emilian-Romagnol

The traditional isogloss used by Pellegrini (1977), amongst others, to characterize Emilian-Romagnol dialects is the fronting of Lat. A in open syllables, e.g. Med. Lat. BLADA 'fodder' > Bolognese, Piacentino [bjɛːva], Imolese, Ravennate [bjeᵊva], Riminese [bjɛːda], but Milanese [bjaːda] ~ [bjaːva], Bergamese [bjaˑa], Italian *biada* .

Also characteristic, but not unique to Emilia-Romagna, is the lengthening of all vowels before liquid + consonant clusters. The phenomenon must have occurred early in Emilia-Romagna, since the development of these secondary long vowels coincides, unlike elsewhere, e.g. Milanese, with that of long vowels in Latin open syllables, e.g. SALE 'salt' > Bo. [sɛːl], Im. [seᵊl], ALA 'wing' > Bo. [ɛːla], ALTU 'high' > Bo. [ɛːlt], BARBA 'beard' > Bo. [bɛːrba], Im. [beᵊrba], CURTU 'short' > Bo., Im. [kuːrt], cf. *MATTU 'crazy' > Stage 2 /mat/ > Bo., Im. [maːt]. Historically more recent, given the vowel quality, is the consistent lengthening of Stage 1 low vowels /a, ɛ, ɔ/ before oral consonants in historically closed syllables, e.g. CABALLU 'horse' > Stage 2 /kaval/ > Bo., Im., Lg., Ri., Ra. [kavaːl], PASTA > Bo. [paːsta]. Stage 1 /e, o, i, u/ remain short, e.g. FUSTE > Bo., Im. [fost] 'stem'.

The sub-categorization of dialects within Emilia-Romagna has never been fully determined, and discussion in the literature is vague; see Foresti (1988). The major sub-division corresponds largely to the internal geographical boundary, i.e. between Emilia and Emilian dialects on the one hand and Romagna and Romagnol on the other. The general view is that dialects spoken in the Romagnol provinces of Forlì and Ravenna (Lughese, Riminese and Ravennate in our sample) are Romagnol. To this group must be added Imolese which is spoken in the traditionally Emilian province of Bologna very close to the Bolognese-Romagnol border and represents the westernmost limit of Romagnol; see Bottiglioni (1919), Schürr (1917 and elsewhere) and data below. The other dialects of Emilia (Piacenza, Parma, Reggio nell'Emilia, Modena, Ferrara, and Bologna) are classified as Emilian. Centralizing diphthongs frequently found in Romagnol are absent in Bolognese, and other Emilian dialects, e.g. BLADA > Emilian (Bo., Piac.) [bjɛːda], but Romagnol (Im., Ra.) [bjeᵊva]. In addition, the presence of word-final velar nasals, common in dialects of the Emilian plain, is also generalized in Bolognese, but rarely found in Romagna, e.g. CANE > Stage 2 /kaːn/ > Bo. [kæŋ], Piac. [kaŋ], but Romagnol (Im., Lg.) [kẽː], cf. also *AIS* V 985 PANE. However, whilst there is general agreement that Bolognese is fundamentally Emilian, Romagnol features are also evident, e.g. use of Romagnol lexical items, such as clitic pronominal [i] rather than typically Emilian [g] 'to him, to it, there'. Also, the front rounded vowels [y] and [ø] (< U: and U/O: respectively), present in large parts of Emilia, are completely absent in Romagnol and Bolognese, e.g. DU:RU 'hard' > [dyːr] in Piacentino and Appenine Emilian, but [duːr] in Bolognese, and Romagnol.

2.2.3.4 Romagnol: Imolese, Lughese, Ravennate, Riminese

The various works on Romagnol by Schürr (1917 and elsewhere) represent the primary sources for the four Romagnol dialects included in the sample. Secondary sources include Bottiglioni (1919), Pelliciardi (1977), Baldassari (1979), Bellosi and Quondamatteo (1979) and Delmonte (1983). Schürr (1918, 1974: 63–95) also discusses in detail medieval and late medieval Romagnol texts. Imolese (Im.) and Ravennate (Ra.) are represented by points 467 and 459 respectively in the *AIS*. Lugo (Lg.) is closest to Fusignano (point 458), whilst Rimini (Ri.) is located some distance away from the closest points, 479 (Cesenatico) and 499 (Saludecio).

Schürr's descriptions of Romagnol dialects are, in general, highly detailed and accurate.[18] The results of my own fieldwork largely reflected Schürr's findings for Imolese, Lughese and Ravennate. In the case of Riminese, Schürr did not consider contextual nasalization to be a regular phenomenon, although it was sometimes noted on long vowels before word-final $/n_1/$, e.g. [pɛːn] ~ [pɛ̃ːn] 'bread'. Contextual nasalization of all long vowels before N is now regular in the Riminese of today, e.g. [padroʷn] (Schürr 1917 and elsewhere) > [padrõw̃ⁿ] 'boss' (Hajek 1991a, confirmed by Delmonte 1983). I will continue, however, to make primary reference to the dialect described by Schürr, whilst noting more recent changes.

Distinctive nasalization is reported by Schürr to be a stable synchronic feature of Imolese, Lughese, and Ravennate, e.g. CANE 'dog' > Im., Lg. [kɛ̃ː], Ra. [kɑ̃ː].

2.2.3.5 Bolognese

There are numerous synchronic descriptions of Bolognese (Bo.), e.g. Gaudenzi (1889), Trauzzi (1901), Mainoldi (1950), and my primary source, Coco (1970).[19] Additional sources on modern Bolognese include Ferrari (1835), Mainoldi (1967), Coco (1971), Rizzi (1984), Vincenzi (1978), Minghè (1950) and Saunders (1979). Bolognese is also represented by *AIS* point 456. The dialect of the medieval and early modern period is amply attested, and studied, e.g. Toja (1954), Foresti (1983), Accorsi (1980) and Balducci (1980). There are, in addition to all the material on the dialect of Bologna *città*, numerous studies of rural Bolognese dialects, e.g. S. Giovanni in Persiceto (Froehlich 1967), Alpine Bolognese (Bruzzi Tantucci 1962 and Malagoli 1930). Poggi (1934), Contavalli (1963) and Badini (1972) discuss the dialect boundary between Bologna and Romagnol-speaking Imola.

Distinctive nasalization is no longer a stable synchronic phenomenon in Bolognese. Although well attested in nineteenth-century descriptions of Bolognese, e.g. Ferrari (1835) and Gaudenzi (1889), Coco (1970) found it to be an archaic feature today. Although I found nasalized diphthongs to appear with some frequency in rapid speech, the process of 'denasalization' as velarization in Bolognese shows clear parallels with developments in

Cairese: hardening of nasalized glides occurs with [Ṽŋ] in casual speech, and [Vŋ] with vowel denasalization now appears regularly in citation forms, e.g. CANE 'dog' > [kæ̃ĵ] ~ [kæ̃ũ̯] > [kæ̃ŋ] > [kæŋ], LUNA 'moon' > [lõw̃na] > [lõŋna] > [loŋna].

A particular characteristic of Bolognese, uniquely in my Northern Italian sample, is a marked process of secondary gemination, after primary and secondary short tonic vowels, e.g. It. 'duca > ['dokka] 'duke', 'PIPERE 'pepper' > ['pavver], and 'LIMA 'file' > Stage 2 /liːma/ > *[lima] > ['lemma].

2.2.3.6 Rhaeto-Romance: Tavetschan

The only Rhaeto-Romance dialect to be included in the sample is Tavetschan (Ta.), spoken in the westernmost extremity of the Swiss Grisons, just across the Northern Italian border. The primary source is Caduff (1952), supported by Loriot (1952) and Plangg (1985).[20] Haiman (1988) as well as Gartner (1910) and Ascoli (1873) discuss in detail the characteristics of Rhaeto-Romance, its major subdivisions into Romantsch, Ladin and Friulan, as well as the further subdivisions of Romantsch. Tavetschan belongs to the Sursilvan sub-branch of Romantsch, although it demonstrates some affinities with distant Engadine Romantsch dialects (Hall 1953). The first late medieval attestations of Sursilvan are discussed by Ascoli (1882).

Tavetschan is relatively isolated from the other dialects in the sample. Geographically, it sits close to the Lombard of the Swiss Ticino, and there is very limited evidence of Ticinese influence. However, there is no reason to believe that any other dialect in the sample has had any direct contact with or influence on Tavetschan. In addition, unlike the Gallo-Italian dialects in the sample, all Romantsch dialects, including Tavetschan, have been strongly influenced by Swiss German (Haiman 1988).

Relative to the rest of the sample, Tavetschan is conservative: nasalization, language-specific or distinctive, is not reported, and there is no evidence to suggest that it has ever occurred in Tavetschan. In addition, the vowel length distinction survives, at least before $/n_1/$ and $/n_2/$, although slightly obscured by vowel quality changes, e.g. CANE > Stage 2 /kaːn/ > [cawn], but ANNU > Stage 2 /an/ > [ɔn].

2.3 CONCLUSION

Different types of language samples, including those used in previous studies of distinctive nasalization, were considered in some detail in sections 2.1.1 to 2.1.3. All were found to present some difficulties. The Chomskyan single-language and Greenbergian large-scale samples were found to be particularly inappropriate for the purposes of a comparative diachronic study. In the circumstances, I suggested that a small initial sample of closely related (in this case Northern Italian) dialects or languages with a common time frame

and well-attested starting point (Latin) was the most suitable approach for the purposes of comparison and intermediate reconstruction. The possibility of areo-genetic bias was not considered to be a problem, and if found, still needed to be accounted for. The nine-member base sample is not a closed set and may be expanded at any point. Reference to other languages, related or otherwise, is made during the course of this study for the purposes of cross-linguistic verification for any patterning observed in the Northern Italian sample.

In section 2.2.1 I provided a brief description of Latin phonology, and outlined the major changes to the Latin sound system. Their implications for distinguishing Northern Italian from other Romance dialects, as well as the reconstruction of intermediate stages between Latin and Northern Italian today, were discussed. From section 2.2.2.2 to 2.2.3.6 some of the character-izing features of the nine members of the sample were described. In at least four dialects (Milanese, Imolese, Ravennate, Lughese) distinctive nasaliza-tion is reported to be a regular synchronic feature. In one dialect (Bergamese) complete denasalization of distinctively nasalized vowels has occurred, whilst in two other dialects (Bolognese and Cairese) historically nasalized vowels are found to have been affected by a process of nasalized glide hardening.

3

DISTINCTIVE VOWEL NASALIZATION
AND RULE ORDERING

3.1 INTRODUCTION

Whilst the process of distinctive nasalization, normally given as /VN/ > /Ṽ/, is considered to spread gradually across contexts over time, in this chapter its two basic components, phonological rules of vowel nasalization and of N-deletion (or any other process of N reduction), are abstracted from factor-specific conditioning, and the diachronic and synchronic relationship between them is examined in detail.

Various formal models of distinctive nasalization have been proposed in the past, but have to date not been properly evaluated. Predictions made by these models are tested in specific circumstances. Cross-linguistic examples are provided demonstrating that the phonological process of vowel nasalization, regardless of whether it involves a phonologized language-specific phonetic or phonologically categorical rule, is independent of N-deletion, or any other operation on N. It is also shown that languages are able to contrast phonologically oral and nasal vowels before N in the absence of any reduction of N. This contrast is fully lexicalized, i.e. it must be assigned to the underlying representation in any synchronic analysis. A diachronic account of how such a contrast before N may arise is also provided and consideration is given to the implications of such lexicalization for the relationship between sound change and Lexical Phonology. Finally, so-called local nasalization, typical of Northern Italian and French, and so-called prosodic or long-distance nasalization are shown to be related, rather than independent, phenomena. Prosodic nasalization, without N-deletion, also provides further evidence that contextual nasalization may be phonologized in the absence of N-deletion or any other process affecting N.

3.1.1 Synchronic approaches to distinctive nasalization

There are fundamentally two approaches to the underlying status of surface contrastive nasal vowels (e.g. Fr. [bɔ̃] *bon* vs. [bo] *beau*) in generative and post-generative traditions:

1   the view that nasal vowels, at least in French, are underlying and appear in the lexicon as such, taken by Bibeau (1975), Wetzels (1987), Tranel (1981), Landry (1985), and Johnson (1987);[1]

2   the more traditional generative approach that all vowels that appear as contrastively nasal at the surface are derivable from underlying /VN/ sequences, e.g. Fr. [bɔ̃] ← UR /bɔn/; cf. Durand (1977, 1990), Plénat (1985, 1987), Harms (1968), Schane (1968), Morin (1977), and Patterson (1978).

The reasons for the generative preference for underlying /VN/ sequences are well-known, e.g. frequent pattern congruity between nasal vowels and VC$ syllables, a reduction in the number of underlying phonemes, coupled with a shift in emphasis from the lexicon to derivation by rule (Ruhlen 1973: 18–21; Schane 1968: 46–8, n. 37).

Methods used by phonologists in deriving surface [Ṽ] from underlying /VN/ differ somewhat, and one can make a distinction between two very general categories of derivation, according to their treatment of rule ordering. Where the approach is to order a phonological rule of vowel nasalization before N-deletion or independently of any other rule of N-attrition/reduction, this may be called the Vowel Nasalization (V-NAS) model. All other cases where the rules affecting V and N are ordered simultaneously, or where N-deletion or any other operation affecting N is ordered before vowel nasalization, are representative of what I shall call for the sake of convenience the N-deletion (N-DEL) model. The question of ordering has important implications not only for synchronic analysis, but also, as we shall see, for any diachronic account of distinctive nasalization.

3.1.2 The diachronic approach to distinctive nasalization

From the diachronic point of view, two major issues arise when considering the development of distinctive nasalization in Northern Italian:

1   the relationship over time between an earlier surface [VN] in Latin and a later surface contrastive /Ṽ/ in Romance;
2   the manner in which the component parts of distinctive nasalization penetrate the phonological structure of a language. This second issue leads to a further question of whether penetration over time can be so deep that nasal vowels become fully lexicalized in the underlying representation.

The frequent parallels between synchronic and diachronic description, the former from the underlying to the surface, and the latter from one point in time to another, are, as reported previously, well known. In these circumstances, synchronic binary and V-NAS models are easily transposed to diachronic analysis and often have been in the past. Moreover, in some analyses detailed in the sections that follow, the time frame is particularly ambiguous, and little explicit distinction appears to be made between the synchronic and the diachronic. Given the frequently observed synchronic

recapitulation of diachronic processes, there is nothing inconsistent in evaluating the effectiveness of an analysis previously used only for synchronic derivation or alternatively only for diachronic description from both synchronic and diachronic perspectives.

In assessing the diachronic adequacy of any phonological account of the development of distinctive nasalization, we must consider, in line with our model of sound change–grammar interaction, not only rule ordering, but also the integration, or otherwise, of three different processes: (1) low-level phonetic contextual nasalization of vowels before N operating outside the grammar; (2) a phonological rule of vowel nasalization somewhere in the grammar; and (3) N-deletion or any other phonological process of N-attrition.

3.2 THE N-DEL MODEL

There are numerous variants of the N-DEL model, and these fall into four general sub-categories: (1) Coalescence; (2) Floating Nasal; (3) N-Attenuation; and (4) Ohalan Phonetic. An essential characteristic of all variants is the failure to order a phonological rule of vowel nasalization before any phonological process directly affecting N, e.g. deletion. With the prime exception of the Ohalan Phonetic model, few variants of the N-DEL model refer to phonetic processes of vowel nasalization. In so doing, they avoid the issue of low-level contextual nasalization, and its possible integration into an account of distinctive nasalization. Some, e.g. Piggott (1987: 227, n. 3), are explicit that phonological nasalization is completely unrelated to any phonetic contextual nasalization that one might find in vowels adjacent to nasals at the surface.

3.2.1 *Coalescence*

According to the Coalescence analysis of distinctive nasalization, phonological rules of vowel nasalization and N-deletion are assumed to apply simultaneously as part of a single process as can be seen from the generative and autosegmental versions at 1a (Entenman 1971) and 1b (Hayes 1986b) respectively:

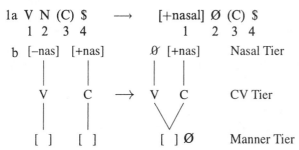

1a V N (C) $ ⟶   [+nasal] Ø (C) $
   1 2 3 4   1   2 3 4

Entenman (1977), Selkirk (1972), Narang and Becker (1971) and Schane (1973a: 68) on the one hand, and Hayes (1986b) and Levin (1988: 259) on the other, adopt the generative and autosegmental versions of the coalescence rule respectively. None of these sources provides explicit discussion of any relationship between phonetic and phonological nasalization. However, Entenman (1977: 7) suggests that a diachronic account combining simultaneous N-deletion and phonologization of vowel nasalization is preferable to an analysis involving two ordered rules of vowel nasalization and N-deletion on two grounds: (1) the former is simpler in terms of feature counting; and (2) rule ordering is eliminated. He claims that no independent phonological confirmation has been found to date that rule ordering plays any role in the development of distinctive nasalization-related phenomena. Such a claim is easily disproved by the examples cited in sections 3.5 to 3.5.3 of the phonologization of contextual nasalization in the absence of N-deletion.

3.2.2 Other versions of the N-DEL model

In contrast to the coalescence account, the other versions of the N-DEL model assume that any operation on N must be ordered *before* any phonological process of vowel nasalization can occur. In cases of N-deletion, such ordering is in contrast to the traditional generative analysis of distinctive nasalization (e.g. Hyman 1975b: 130–1) where a constraint in favour of logical relationship operates to control the ordering of vowel nasalization and N-deletion as at 2a. N-deletion must follow vowel nasalization, since the latter cannot be logically ordered after the former and still be related, as seen at 2b:

2a Logically Related   b Logically Unrelated

   i. $V \longrightarrow \tilde{V} \, / \, \_\_N$ i. $N \longrightarrow \emptyset \, / \, V\_\_$

   ii. $N \longrightarrow \emptyset \, / \, \tilde{V}\_\_$ ii. $V \longrightarrow \tilde{V}$

However, in more recent times phonologists have have been tempted to use the power of autosegmental formalism to break this ordering relationship. The logical ordering constraint need not apply in a non-linear representation if means can be found to eliminate all of N except [+nasal], so that phonological vowel nasalization may be ordered as a post-deletion phenomenon. If this is possible, we must conclude, at least in this context, that autosegmental representation is more powerful, and less constrained than the linear generative model that preceded it. Given the already excessive power of generative formalism, and the problems associated with it, any increase must be viewed in a negative light. Greater representational power merely increases the range of possible phonological processes, and hence the number and type of predictions about hypothetical sound changes that are unlikely to occur in fact.

3.2.3 *The Floating Nasal*

Perhaps the best example of using a less constrained formalism to describe nasalization and N-deletion processes is the Floating Nasal analysis, versions of which have been advocated by Piggott (1987, 1988a, b), D'Andrade and Kihm (1988), Halle and Vergnaud (1981) and Bouchard (1983). The bare bones of Piggott's account, and typical of other Floating Nasal analyses, is that all segmental information of an underlying nasal is deleted, with the exception of the feature [+nasal], at some point before full feature specification in the representation. Newly floating [+nasal] then reattaches itself by convention to the rightmost available anchor point of the word, up to this point unspecified for nasality, i.e. in this case the preceding vowel. A phonologically nasal vowel results, as in the treatment of Fr. *bon* at 3:

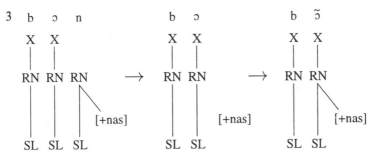

X = Skeletal Tier   RN = Root Node   SL = Supralaryngeal Node

Piggott's floating nasal analysis is problematic on many counts. The most obvious difficulty is how to motivate and justify deletion of the Root Node, and all supralaryngeal features attached to it, whilst still permitting the seemingly *ad hoc* survival of [+nasal] also previously attached to the Root Node. In the more restrictive model of Feature Geometry adopted in this study, [nasal] would simply disappear with all other features dependent on a higher organizing node, the Root Node in Piggott's analysis or the Supralaryngeal Node in my model. This follows from the previously mentioned constraint (see section 1.3) requiring immediate elimination of any feature structure or individual features not attached to the superordinate skeletal slot. It should be noted that even Piggott's initial representation of /bɔn/ breaches this constraint: although the absence of a skeletal slot to which the Root Node of /n/ would ordinarily be linked relates to liaison phenomena of no direct consequence here, what is in effect a floating Root Node would also be automatically lost. The skeleton is a sequence of timing elements that provide temporality and hence the possibility of phonetic instantiation to feature structures below it. The absence of any constraint requiring deletion of unattached features dramatically increases the power of

autosegmental formalism: abstract phonologists such as Piggott are now easily tempted to manipulate the representation and derivation in such a way as to control very closely the loss of undesirable feature structure, whilst trying to preserve targeted features.

Equally undesirable is Piggott's failure to consider the empirical consequences of his floating nasal analysis: it makes completely erroneous predictions about the effect of N-deletion elsewhere in French. The regular alternation *hiver* – *hiverner* 'winter' – 'to winter' suggests the following underlying forms /iveʁn/ – /iveʁn+er/.[2] Given the segmental structure of word-final /n/ posited by Piggott, the floating [+nasal], after deletion of the Supralaryngeal Node, would anchor to the nearest available point, i.e. /ʁ/. The result is obvious, but completely unattested: *[iveːʁ̃]. That the final rhotic would be predicted to surface as nasalized follows from the Underspecification approach adopted by Piggott and the interaction of underspecification with phonological processes such as relinking of the Floating Nasal. It appears possible in his account for all segments, except for underlyingly contrastive oral-nasal pairs /m–b/ and /n–d/, to be underspecified for nasality through most of the derivation. Predictable specification, normally as [−nasal], is assumed to occur late in the derivation after phonological rules that attach/spread [+nasal] have applied. /ʁ/ clearly has no underlying specification for [nasal], since it does not contrast with a nasal uvular rhotic in French. It is, therefore, available for relinking of [+nasal].

Similarly, in a word like French *chanter* 'sing', presumably represented underlyingly as /ʃante/, Piggott would incorrectly predict the surface result *[ʃatẽ]. Since no segment in the word, except /n/, requires underlying specification for nasality, the newly floating [+nasal] must attach itself by convention to the rightmost available node, i.e. final /e/. The intervening segment /t/ does not block the rightward movement of [+nasal], since it is a voiceless obstruent and, therefore predictably non-nasal. In Piggott's analysis, it need not be redundantly specified as [−nasal] until the last moment, i.e. only after relinking of [+nasal] has occurred.

The major empirical drawbacks of the Floating Nasal analysis highlight the potential dangers of using Underspecification in the description (synchronic or diachronic) of nasalization-related phenomena. The rise of Underspecification Theory as a formal tool to be used in tandem with autosegmental representation clearly allows for the elimination of constraints that full feature specification (redundant and non-redundant) places on any representation. An analysis with total specification of features before nasalization and N-deletion processes occur simply would not permit floating [+nasal] to attach – with such disastrous consequences – to final /e/ in *chanter* or to /ʁ/ in *hiver*. The presence of [−nasal] attached to the intervening /t/ in the former and to /ʁ/ in the latter would, according to basic autosegmental principles, have blocked the rightward movement of [+nasal] to the end of the word.

If underspecification can have such unforeseen consequences in the description of phonological processes, we must ask ourselves whether in fact we need to avail ourselves of this analytical tool in the description of sound change. The answer is both yes and no, according to the relative abstractness of the sound change in question. In synchronic description underspecification and full specification are not incompatible, they merely operate at different points in the derivation: the former occurs at deeper, less concrete levels of the grammar until eliminated by feature specification as late as possible in the derivation (Durand 1990). This distinction can be correlated to different types of sound change at different levels of the grammar: underspecification is consistent therefore with sound change that has already percolated deep into the grammar, i.e. Lexical Diffusion. It appears less compatible, however, with the first manifestation of sound change as a regular, Neogrammarian-style surface phenomenon that occurs at the outer edge of the grammar, i.e. at the boundary between the post-lexical component in the grammar and the universal phonetics component just outside. Phonological feature specification has already occurred by this point in any derivation: underspecification is simply no longer present and must be viewed as irrelevant to the phonologization of sound change. Since it is precisely this initial phase of interaction between sound change and the grammar that is the focus of interest in this study, reference to under-specification (and its potential dangers or misapplication) in the description of sound changes reported here is unnecessary. It is important to note too that recent suggestions (e.g. Cohn 1990, 1993; Pulleyblank 1995) that feature underspecification survives much closer to the surface than is usually thought, i.e. into the language-specific component, are still consistent with the view of sound change adopted here. This new model of underspeci-fication focuses on the relationship between feature specification and the shift from categorical to language-specific post-lexical rules. Even under this model, full specification (phonetic or phonological) has occurred by the time the boundary between language-specific and universal phonetics is reached.

3.2.4 N-attenuation

In an effort to avoid problems associated with the Floating Nasal, Hualde (1989), D'Introno et al. (1989), and Trigo (1988) derive distinctive nasaliza-tion in such a way that [+nasal] remains attached at all times to the suprahierarchical structure. In the view of these authors, the first step in any process of distinctive nasalization is the phonological reduction or attenuation in some fashion of N, e.g. elimination of underlying place features, or of the entire supralaryngeal structure. In Hualde's model of Feature Geometry at 4 (1989: 191), all manner and place features are attached to the Supralaryngeal Node. Vowel nasalization occurs after

delinking of the Supralaryngeal Node: [+nasal] survives attached to the Root, but must spread to the adjacent vowel in order to surface phonetically.

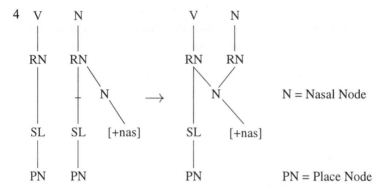

Hualde's account seems in any case incomplete: he makes no mention of how the surviving skeletal slot and Root Node are to be interpreted phonetically. The only directly subordinate structure remaining is [+nasal], and in the absence of other features of class, manner and place, phonetic instantiation of the skeletal slot appears impossible.

Trigo (1990) presents a slightly modified version of the Ohalan diachronic account of distinctive nasalization referred to immediately below: phonologization of low-level contextual nasalization may occur over time previous to complete N-deletion as a result of some phonetically conditioned phonological process of attenuation or attrition of N, e.g. contextual devoicing of N. Evidence will be provided in later sections of this chapter demonstrating that models reliant on some sort of N-attenuation to trigger the diachronic or synchronic phonologization of contextual nasalization make empirically incorrect predictions about such phonologization.

3.2.5 Ohalan Phonetic

Ohala's (1981: 186, 1988: 15–16) diachronic account of distinctive nasalization, based on his listener-oriented phonetic model has been adopted, at least partly, by Kawasaki (1986), Hombert (1986: 360) and Chen (1973a, b, 1974a, 1975).[3] Already detailed in chapter 1, the account is outlined again here. Nasalization is ordered before N-deletion as a (low-level) phonetic process outside the grammar. While N is still perceived to be present, vowel nasalization is simply factored out by the listener. Once N-deletion has occurred, nasalized vowels are lexicalized as phonologically distinctive. Since no intermediate structure of the sort normally associated with phonology between the lexicon and physical output is assumed, there is need to refer to an intermediate phonological stage, [ṼN], and the grammatical process is reduced over time to two steps, as at 5:

5 /VN/ > /Ṽ/

I have already suggested in chapter 1 that the Ohalan model of distinctive nasalization is oversimplified and is empirically contradicted by the phenomenon of prosodic nasalization reported in many languages, e.g. Malay [mēɲãw̃ãl] 'to guard', Capanahua [hãmãʔõna] 'coming stepping'. I return to the issue of prosodic nasalization in more detail in section 3.5.3.

Ohala (1988) also hypothesizes that once N-deletion has occurred, and the listener begins to treat vowel nasalization as distinctive, the level of nasalization on such vowels may undergo a phonetic increase or 'exaggeration'. However, such a claim does not find universal confirmation. Whilst Al-Bamerni (1983) found the amplitude and duration of velic opening in distinctively nasalized vowels in French to be substantially greater than that of contextually nasalized vowels, Clumeck (1975: 144) and Ruhlen (1973: 5) report no apparent phonetic differences in kind between contextual and distinctive nasalization in a number of other languages, e.g. Breton, Bengali, and the Fynish dialect of Danish. Manjari Ohala (1975, 1983) provides experimental nasographic evidence demonstrating no appreciable differences in the nature and duration of the velic opening gesture between contextually and distinctively nasalized vowels in Hindi. In at least one language, Bengali, contextual nasalization before N is reported to be markedly greater than the degree of nasality evident in phonemic nasal vowels in the same language (Ferguson and Chowdhury 1965: 37).

3.3 THE V-NAS MODEL

As stated previously, the most traditional and widely disseminated account of distinctive nasalization is what I shall call the Vowel Nasalization (V-NAS) model, whereby a phonological rule of vowel nasalization is ordered before any operation on N, most typically N-deletion, as at 6:

6a V ⟶ Ṽ / __N

b N ⟶ Ø / Ṽ__

The process described in 6 is favoured by traditional generative formalism, and whilst some variation in formulation occurs, e.g. the environment for N-deletion, it is the one most generally favoured by diachronic universalists, such as Lightner (1970, 1973), Schourup (1973) and Ferguson (1975), describing sound change, as well as by synchronists deriving surface [Ṽ] from underlying /VN/ sequences, e.g. Durand (1977, 1990), Morin (1977), Plénat (1985, 1987), Patterson (1978), and Schane (1968).

3.3.1 *A new V-NAS model*

In line with the Lexical Phonology and phonetic models of sound change detailed previously in chapter 1, some refinement of the V-NAS model is, however, in order. The traditional V-NAS model is under-articulated to the extent that no explicit reference is made to any difference between low-level universal and phonologized/phonological rules of nasalization seen to be crucial in the description of the sound changes involved in the development of distinctive nasalization. A new V-NAS model is proposed which allows for more explicit phonetic and phonological content, and for a more coherent categorization of different processes of vowel nasalization and N-deletion over time. Additional motivation will be shown to lie in the sorts of predictions the new model makes, with the assistance of a small number of operational constraints, about the diachronic and synchronic relationship between N-deletion and vowel nasalization. It makes, however, no explicit claims concerning the lexicalization of nasal vowels.

The new V-NAS model has the following form:

7a Low-level contextual nasalization
 b Language-specific contextual nasalization
 c N-deletion.

Each step is governed by rule (gradual or categorical as the case may be):

8a V $\longrightarrow$ Ṽ / __N
 b V $\longrightarrow$ Ṽ / __N
 c N $\longrightarrow$ Ø / Ṽ__

The first and second rules at 8a and b are normally formalized in a similar fashion by phonologists and phoneticians, but are presumed to operate in different components of the model of Lexical Phonology. The low-level rule of nasalization operates in the universal phonetics component, outside the grammar. The second rule of vowel nasalization is phonologized, and appears in the post-lexical phonological component of the grammar. Explicit reference in the new V-NAS model to changes affecting N is restricted to deletion, which must be ordered after the phonologization of vowel nasalization. I suggest that phonologized vowel nasalization is not dependent on any pre-deletion process of N-attrition or attenuation.

The first restriction on the operation of the model is the Linear Ordering Constraint: a vowel may proceed over time from a to c, but must pass through stage b of the model to do so, as at 9:

9a [VN] or [V̯N]
  ↓
 b [ṼN]
  ↓
 c [Ṽ]

To avoid confusion it is perhaps better here to use a different symbolization for low-level nasalization, as in 9a: it may be indicated by the absence of a tilde, or where necessary, by the use of subscript [˷] instead of [˜]. Such vowels bearing only slight contextual nasalization may even be called 'oral' for the sake of clarity.

The direct passage over time from [VN] to [Ṽ], without an intermediate stage [ṼN], as predicted by at least some versions of the N-DEL model, is not allowed by V-NAS models. This particular constraint on diachronic ordering in phonological analyses is supported, in the first instance, by a large body of cross-linguistic evidence demonstrating synchronic variability between heavily nasalized vowels before N and post-deletion nasal vowels, i.e. [ṼN] and [Ṽ], as in Australian English, Bengali and many other languages (see also Kawasaki 1986: 83).

N-deletion at Stage a is strongly disfavoured as a diachronic process by the model, and phonetic reasons for this constraint have already been provided in chapter 1, eg. relative ease of perception of N, and absence of nasalized smearing between V and N. It was also observed that N-deletion, a categorical phenomenon easily captured by a binary phonological rule, should be seen as the last step in a previously phonetically gradual process of N-reduction. The synchronic derivation of surface [V] from underlying /VN/ by simple N-deletion, e.g. Catalan [bɔ] ← UR /bɔn/ 'good' (m.), is of course telescoping of a previously more complex diachronic process involving nasalization, subsequent N-deletion, and then denasalization.

Different stages of the new V-NAS model may present themselves variously across languages at the same point in time. There is evidence of Stages b and c of the model operating in at least some varieties of Portuguese as at 10:

10 Stage b   [pẽna]   < POENA   'pain'
            [kẽ\ᵐpu] < CAMPU   'field'
    Stage c   [lẽ]   < LANA   'wool'

Vowel nasalization is clearly distinctive in word-final position, and strong language-specific nasalization is permitted before all synchronic nasals as a regular phenomenon; see Lipski (1975). In French, all three categories can be found to occur synchronically, as at 11:

11 Stage a   [bɔn ami]   *bonne amie/bon ami*   'good friend' (f./m.)
    Stage b   [mɔ̃n ami]   *mon ami*   'my friend' (m.)
    Stage c   [bɔ̃], [mɔ̃]   *bon/mon*   'good' (m.), 'my' (m.)

3.3.1.1 The hyperarticulated V-NAS model: a digression

Tuttle (1991: 50) suggests that the 'trajectory of voiced nasal weakening' and hence of distinctive nasalization is the following: [VN] > [Ṽ̃N] > [Ṽ̃ᵑN] > [Ṽŋ] > [Ṽŋ] > [Ṽ]. This hyperarticulated account is based on a faulty

interpretation of Northern Italian data, including the appearance of velar nasals in Bolognese, e.g. /loŋna/ from LUNA. It can, however, be rejected out of hand as being excessively structured and supported neither by developments in Northern Italian or elsewhere. The appearance of a velar nasal is not a universal component of any part of the distinctive nasalization process, and does not by itself trigger deletion of an adjacent N. All available evidence – synchronic and diachronic (including orthographic and explicit descriptive material) clearly shows that the appearance of velar nasals in Bolognese, as in other Northern Italian dialects, is chronologically subsequent to N-deletion (see Hajek 1991c and chapter 8 for details). Similarly, in varieties of English where allophonic N-deletion is common (e.g. Australian [kãːnt] ~ [kãːⁿt] ~ [kãːt], there has never been any suggestion of the spontaneous appearance of any kind of velar nasal after nasalized vowels nor of velarization of N.

3.3.2 The nature of the new V-NAS model

3.3.2.1 Low-level regressive coarticulatory nasalization

Low-level regressive coarticulatory nasalization is generally not considered to be an unexpected feature of vowels in VN sequences. It is a phonetic property of adjacency, where in the sequence VN, some anticipatory velic opening on V occurs through a failed synchronization with the oral closure of N (Ohala 1971). It is not correct, however, to suggest that such coarticulation is a necessarily universal feature of V in VN sequences across languages, since it can be overridden in one of two ways: (1) there may be a language-specific increase in levels of contextual nasalization, as predicted by all so-called V-NAS models, and exemplified at 9 above; or (2) in some languages, denasalization, partial or complete, of N in VN sequences entirely excludes the possibility of any nasal coarticulation on the vowel (Kawasaki 1986: 85–7; Hyman 1975a: 255–7). In Cornish and Manx, word-final nasals are affected by optional partial denasalization, e.g. Cornish *pen* > [peᵈn] 'head' (Brown 1984: 19), Manx *feeyn* > [fiːn] ~ [fiːᵈn] 'wine' (Jackson 1955: 113–14). Hyman suggests that in some languages, denasalization of N is a phonologically conditioned process which keeps distinct an oral-nasal vowel opposition before nasal consonants, as is evident in the synchronic derivation of Land Dayak data at 12 (1975a: 256):

12	'game'	'cloth'	
UR	/pimain/	/kain/	
a	[pimãĩn]		$V \longrightarrow \tilde{V} / N \_\_$
b		[kaiᵈn]	$N \longrightarrow {}^{C}N / [-nas] \_\_$
			V

In his view, the partial denasalization rule blocks the presence of regressive nasal coarticulation, and eliminates the possibility of any confusion between

regressive and progressive nasalization before word-final nasals. However, this teleological explanation for denasalization is now known to have no cross-linguistic basis: Kawasaki (1986: 85) notes that similar denasalization of N occurs in languages, e.g. Asmat, Cham, Cantonese and Korean, in which there is no phonological process of vowel nasalization.

Where denasalization occurs, a post-lexical rule of (partial) denasalization of N may operate. The absence of any phonetic adjacency between V and the nasal component of N eliminates the possibility of low-level phonetic overlap of velic opening in N onto V.

This evidence confirms my earlier suggestion that limited nasal coarticulation of V in VN occurs universally only by default. It is not possible to predict without error across languages the presence or extent of contextual nasal coarticulation in VN sequences, since in some cases regressive coarticulation may be blocked, and in others it may be phonologized, and increased beyond the expected low levels of coarticulation.

3.3.2.2 Low-level vs. language-specific contextual nasalization

The boundary between low-level phonetic and phonologized language-specific rules is of course blurred, and it may not always be clear whether a particular contextual phenomenon is due to one or the other. In most descriptions of languages, the assessment of the degree of contextual nasalization has largely been based on individual impressionistic evaluation. Many observers would agree that nasalization, of whatever type, is impressionistically greater in Brazilian Portuguese than in French and Spanish. Contextual nasalization is generally considered to be significantly greater in English than in French, an impression confirmed experimentally. Similarly, such nasalization is often judged to be markedly greater in Australian and American English than in British English.

However, judgements based on impressionistic evaluation by the individual phonologist, although extremely important, are idiosyncratic, difficult to compare, and provide us with no clear mechanism to distinguish between non-phonological universal and phonological language-specific levels of nasalization. Hyman (1975b: 172–3) provides details of how experimental evidence might be used to evaluate relative levels of contextual phenomena, and to allow for a rough empirical distinction to be made between low-level and language-specific phenomena.[4]

For instance, he considers the language-specific divergence in the well-known effect of obstruent voicing on vowel lengthening. On the basis of statistical comparison of articulatory measurements, he concludes that in a sample of six languages, vowel lengthening is so exaggerated in one, i.e. English, as to be phonologized. We may add at this point that within the context of a listener-oriented model of sound change adopted in this study, assessment should not rely on articulatory evidence alone. Perceptual

confirmation should also be sought for any initial hypothesis based on articulatory data.[5]

The first step, following the methodology set out by Hyman (1975b), is to gather sufficient experimental production data on contextual nasalization, e.g. duration and amplitude of velic opening and nasal airflow. Significant exaggeration of the degree of contextual nasalization in one language relative to other languages in the sample will be considered to be a partial indication of a language-specific rule applying in the former.[6] Available cross-linguistic data, e.g. velopharyngeal opening (Clumeck 1976) and nasal airflow (Cohn 1988), demonstrate that the level of contextual nasalization is significantly greater in English than in French. Such a discrepancy leads to the initial hypothesis that contextual nasalization is a phonological phenomenon of some sort in English, but not in French. Reenen (1982a) is adamant that contextual nasalization in American English is a categorical phenomenon: the articulatory pattern is markedly different from that for contextual nasalization found in European French, but conforms instead to the pattern found for distinctively nasalized vowels, /Ṽ/, reported for other languages. Perceptual data discussed below also provides support for this conclusion.

The next step involves perceptual verification of articulatory data. Krakow and Beddor (1991) found listeners to be sensitive to contextual nasalization differences and to be able to consistently distinguish between [V] and [Ṽ] in the context N__N. Such perceptual sensitivity leads to the following tentative hypothesis (cf. also Reenen 1982a). Where contextual nasalization is great, then the splicing out of N in VN sequences in experimental conditions might be expected to result in: (1) the perception of distinctively nasal vowels; or (2) the ability of listeners to factor back in the missing nasal. Conversely, where there is only limited coarticulatory nasalization, splicing out of N should be expected to result in: (1) the perception of functionally oral vowels, or at least in only marginal identification of these vowels as nasalized; and (2) the failure to identify the following segment as nasal.

Reenen (1982a) suggests that the results of perceptual experiments in which nasal consonants in (C)VN\$ syllables were attenuated or spliced out confirm the hypothesis.[7] Kawasaki (1986), and Ali et al. (1971) using American English nonsense and normal speech tokens respectively, tested the perception by American subjects of contextual nasalization: listeners perceived English vowel tokens, after N-deletion, to be nasalized in a significant fashion. Kawasaki (1986) also found American listeners were able to use vowel nasalization to identify the following consonant as nasal. Lahiri and Jongman (1990) uncovered a similar effect for British English speakers. Conversely, Clumeck (1971) found that American listeners could not reliably judge whether such vowels in French tokens were followed by a nasal consonant or not.

Whilst more experimental research is required, the cited evidence provides some confirmation of the impressionistically based hypothesis that contextual nasalization may have different phonological status across languages. On the basis of both articulatory and perceptual evidence, contextual nasalization in French and English must now be categorized differently according to the new V-NAS model: contextual nasalization is a low-level phenomenon in French, and some sort of phonological phenomenon in English.

3.3.2.3 Language-specific vs. categorical rules in the post-lexical phonology

Blurring between rule types is not restricted to the distinction between low-level rules outside the phonology and language-specific rules within the phonology: the boundary is yet to be clearly determined between phonologically gradient (i.e. language-specific phonetic) rules and phonologically categorical (i.e. binary phonological) rules of contextual assimilation in the post-lexical component of grammar (cf. Durand 1990: 190, Cohn 1990). In some cases, assessment may be made after the fact. For instance, it is tempting to conclude that vowel nasalization in [Ṽ] derived from underlying /VN/ is the result of a categorical assimilation rule applied before a categorical rule of N-deletion. But Stephen Anderson (1975) provides examples in which the assumed ordering relationship of categorical/binary rules before gradient rules is reversed in derivation. If this is the case, then we cannot immediately assume that surface contrastive vowel nasalization is the result of a synchronic categorical rule.[8]

In the tradition of Hyman (1975b), Cohn (1990: 15–16) suggests that gradient and categorical phonological rules have phonetically different manifestations that can be determined by experimental analysis. If the nasal assimilation rule in VN > ṼN is categorical, then the whole vowel might be expected to be phonetically nasal in a plateau-like fashion from start to finish. Conversely, articulatory measurements would be expected to show that a gradient rule affects only part of the vowel in a cline-like or varying fashion. There is insufficient cross-linguistic evidence available at present to assess properly the validity of Cohn's claim. Experimental results for French, for instance, are inconsistent: some (e.g. Cohn 1990) have found distinctive nasal vowels in French, e.g. [fɛ̃ː] *faim* 'hunger', to be nasalized in the categorical fashion described by Cohn, whilst others (e.g. Linthorst 1973, Watson 1991) suggest such vowels are only partly nasalized in a cline-like fashion. I conclude that whilst Cohn's suggested methodology may allow for a very general categorization of gradient and categorical rules to be made, the overlap between the two remains appreciable and indeterminate.

3.4 COMPARING MODELS

3.4.1 *The new V-NAS model and N-deletion*

Although in all variants of the V-NAS model N-deletion is ordered after the application of some phonological rule of vowel nasalization, the relationship between the rules can be variably intrinsic or extrinsic according to one's formalization. Formalization of the two rules as intrinsically ordered results in the operation of a clear restriction which I shall call the N-Deletion Constraint. In other formulations, where ordering is extrinsic, the constraint is no longer apparent in the rules, but remains implicit in the ordering, as in the typical accounts at 13a and b (cf. Entenman 1977: 70):

13a i $V \longrightarrow \tilde{V} \ / \ \_N$

　　ii $N \longrightarrow \emptyset \ / \ \tilde{V}\_$

　b i $V \longrightarrow \tilde{V} \ / \ \_N$

　　ii $N \longrightarrow \emptyset \ / \ \_\$$

The reasons for a phonologist's choice of one version of ordering over the other vary (e.g. pattern congruity, phonetic plausibility) and the same phonologist may not be consistent. Schane (1972: 204) prefers intrinsic ordering because '[according to rule 13a(i)] a nasal consonant causes a preceding vowel to become nasalized. Only then can the nasal consonant be deleted – that is, it seems that what is natural is that the nasal consonant is deletable only if it has left a vestige of itself in the preceding vowel'. But soon after, Schane (1973b: 821, n. 3) expresses a preference for 13b because 'although there is an intimate relation between vowel nasalization and nasal consonant deletion, these are separate processes. Vowel nasalization can take place independently of nasal consonant deletion – e.g. *ũn̠ ami* – and nasal consonant deletion can occur independently of vowel nasalization – e.g. *dorm̠ + ons*, *dor(m̠) + s*.' The formulation of the new V-NAS model restricts reference to VN sequences only, and makes no predictions as to the development of CN sequences. Whilst it may be convenient in a synchronic analysis of a particular language, e.g. French, to group all types of N-deletion under one rule, there is no reason to believe that changes affecting N in VN and CN sequences are in fact historically related or similar.

From the diachronic perspective, the intrinsically ordered new V-NAS model clearly disfavours N-deletion after vowels bearing only low-level coarticulatory nasalization, and I will argue that this constraint makes important claims about when N-deletion may or may not occur over time. N-deletion will not normally be expected to occur unless phonologization of contextual vowel nasalization has already preceded it. Such a claim follows naturally from the claim already made that in the absence of strong contextual vowel nasalization, N is easily perceived, and is, therefore, not ordinarily prone to deletion on the part of the listener. However, if

N-deletion were possible at the first stage of the model, the operation of the Linear Ordering Constraint referred to previously predicts that deletion will result only in an oral vowel [V], and never in a phonologically nasalized vowel, i.e. [VN] > *[Ṽ]. Synchronic derivation is less restrictive to the extent that vowel nasalization is of course not a prerequisite for N-deletion. However, without a rule of vowel nasalization in the grammar preceding N-deletion, the same prediction holds in synchronic derivation: the resulting surface vowel will be oral. Hence the already cited [bɔ] ← UR /bɔn/ 'good' (m.) alongside [bɔnə] ← /bɔna/ (f.) in Catalan. This diachronic and synchronic prediction, which finds support in the experimental perceptual evidence discussed above, is in clear contrast with that made by versions of the N-DEL model according to which phonologization of vowel nasalization (Piggott 1987, 1988a, b), or lexicalization (Ohala 1981, 1988) is subsequent to N-deletion, i.e. UR /VN/ → SR [Ṽ] and Time$_1$ UR /VN/ > Time$_2$ UR /Ṽ/.

The N-Deletion and Linear Ordering Constraints have an important role in any analysis of the historical development of vowel nasalization and N-deletion in languages. It follows that, even where there is no clear-cut orthographic evidence of nasalization, e.g. the use of a tilde, and only synchronic evidence of N-deletion accompanied by apparent vowel denasalization, it is appropriate to assume that, historically, N-deletion occurred following phonologization of contextual nasalization.[9] Therefore, given Old English *fi:f*, and Gothic *fimf*, the traditional and, I believe, correct assumption amongst many universalists is to posit for Old English intermediate stages of vowel nasalization and N-deletion in line with the new V-NAS model. Some, such as Entenman (1977) and Foley (1977) have interpreted the absence of any explicit marking of vowel nasalization as indicative of straightforward N-deletion without intermediate vowel nasalization. The weakness of their case is easily demonstrated: it is not immediately obvious from modern French orthography that any vowels are distinctively nasalized, e.g. *pain*. With the same limited data we have for Old English, we could not easily assume that *pain* represented [pɛ̃ː] rather than [pajn] in modern French.

Examination of cross-linguistic data shows that N-deletion (of sorts) after vowels bearing only low-level coarticulatory nasalization normally occurs diachronically in only one very restricted circumstance that I have ascertained up to this point, i.e. during simplification of nasal geminates, e.g. VNNV > VNV. The nature of this phenomenon, and of other processes of N-attenuation without deletion, as well as the implications all of these processes may have for models of distinctive nasalization are discussed in the sections that follow.

3.4.2 *Degemination*

The comparative applicability of V-NAS and N-DEL models can be tested in those circumstances where they make different predictions about the effect

on vowel nasalization of any process affecting N. One example of divergence in predicted outcomes arises in the degemination of long nasals, NN. The Northern Italian sample proves itself very useful here, since simplification of Latin geminates, including NN, is posited as a Stage 2 development in Northern Italian, e.g. CANNA 'cane' > Stage 2 /kana/.

Most versions of the N-DEL model would not predict the triggering of phonological vowel nasalization as a result of degemination of long nasals. Given that a nasal consonant survives (albeit reduced now to a single skeletal slot in formal representation) [+nasal] remains attached at all times to a consonantal segment. It is never floating and therefore not available for reassignment to an adjacent vowel. Similarly, according to Ohala's model, the mere presence of some kind of nasal consonant allows listeners to factor out contextual vowel nasalization. However, it seems clear that in a model such as Trigo's (1988), where any kind of attenuation of N is a sufficient trigger for the phonologization of nasalization, degemination of NN must be treated as a temporal reduction, and therefore attenuation. Hence /VN$NV/ > [Ṽ$NV], and /VNN$/ > [ṼN$] are expected.

In contrast, the various manifestations of the V-NAS model predict that distinctive vowel nasalization would only result from degemination of NN if a phonological rule of nasalization had been ordered previously.

Evidence from the Northern Italian sample clearly supports the predictions made by the V-NAS model about the effect of NN-degemination on the status of vowel nasalization. There is no rule of vowel nasalization, and degemination results in the deletion of one skeletal slot assigned to the geminate, as at 14:

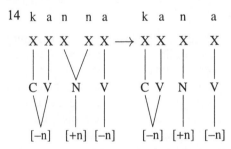

14 k a n   n a   k a n   a

Nowhere in Northern Italy do we find as a result of degemination the form */kãna/, and there is certainly no evidence of any underlying or surface contrast that might be expected, i.e. */kãna/ vs. /lana/ or [kãna] vs. [laːna]:

15	CANNA 'cane'	LANA 'wool'	PINNA 'feather'	VENA 'vein'
Ca.	[kana]	[laŋna] (< [lãṹna])	[pena]	[vɛjna]
Lg.	[kaːna]	[lɛ̃ːna]	[pena]	[vẽjna]
Bo.	[kaːna]	[lɛːna]	[panna] (< [pena])	[veŋna]

	ANNU 'year'	PANE 'bread'
Ca.	[an]	[paŋ] (< [pãᵘ̃])
Ta.	[ɔn]	[pawn]
Lg.	[aːn]	[pɛ̃ː]
Bo.	[aːn]	[pæŋ]

Vowel lengthening in the modern reflexes of Stage 2 short /a/ found in some dialects, e.g. Bo. [kaːna], is a much later secondary phenomenon unrelated to degemination. In particularly innovative Romance dialects, e.g. Imolese, and French, Lat. /VNN/ and /VN/ may have fallen together synchronically in structural terms in most respects, e.g. Fr. /pɛ̃ː/ < PANE, /ɑ̃ː/ < ANNU. However, from the diachronic point of view, differences in vowel quality in these French reflexes are indicative of two (chrono)logically separate cycles of distinctive nasalization, governed by vowel length differences, as at 16:

16		PANE	ANNU
	Stage 2	/paːn/	/an/
Cycle 1	Vː ⟶ Ṽː / __N	[pãĩ̯n]	[an]
	N ⟶ Ø / Ṽː__	[pãĩ̯]	[an]
	V ⟶ Vː / __N	[pãĩ̯]	[aːn]
Cycle 2	Vː ⟶ Ṽː / __N	[pãĩ̯]	[ãːn]
	N ⟶ Ø / Ṽː__	[pãĩ̯]	[ãː]
	Mod. French	[pɛ̃ː]	[ɑ̃ː]

3.4.3 Nasal dissimilation

Nasal dissimilation, in which expected nasality is lost but consonantality unaffected, is not infrequent in Northern Italian, e.g. *lome* < *nome* 'name', *domà* < *nomà* 'only' < NON MAGIS, *alema* < ANIMA 'soul' (Rohlfs 1966: 461) and other Romance dialects, e.g. Old French *arme* < ANIMA, Andalucian *cormigo* < *conmigo* 'with me' (Posner 1961). It is, however, sporadic, and not a regular Neogrammarian sound change envisioned by the study. In addition, as the examples show, nasal dissimilation is triggered by the proximity of another nasal consonant, not by vowel nasalization. Conversely, modern reflexes show that nasal dissimilation does not trigger vowel nasalization. It is therefore, unrelated to any process of vowel nasalization, and does not fall within the scope of any V-NAS model. According to some versions of the N-DEL model (Ohalan Phonetic and Trigo's N-attenuation account) N-dissimilation must be predicted to trigger phonological vowel nasalization: with the loss of consonantal nasality listeners can no longer factor out contextual effects and must assume low-level contextual vowel nasality to be intended and phonological. However, expected *[kõɾmigo] and *[ãɾma] are never reported.

3.4.4 *Total cluster assimilation*

Total NC > Cː assimilation most typically occurs in N + voiceless obstruent clusters. A well-known example frequently cited in universalist studies of nasalization is Old Norse, as at 17:

17 Old Norse *drekka* cf. OE *drincan*   'drink'
            kappi   *cempa*   'fight'

There is some dispute amongst universalists as to nature of the process. Lightner (1973: 18–19) suggests intermediate stages of contextual and distinctive nasalization, i.e. *drinka > *drẽnka > *drẽkka* > *drekka*. This account is correctly rejected by Schourup (1973), given the lack of evidence (internal or cross-linguistic) for the posited intermediate stages. Evidence from other languages indicates that total NC > Cː assimilation generally involves two ordered steps: (1) assimilatory devoicing of N before a voiceless obstruent; (2) subsequent complete denasalization triggered by the reduced perceptual saliency of nasality on newly devoiced N̥.

In Logudorese Sardinian, Latin [nf, ns] clusters are completely assimilated to [ff] and [ss] respectively, e.g. INFERNU > [ifferru] 'hell', and PENSARE > [pessare] 'to think'. Total assimilation of this sort affects no other NC clusters, either voiced or voiceless, e.g. CANTARE > [kantaːri] 'to sing', UMBRA > [umbra] 'shadow', INVENTARE > [imbentaːri] 'to invent'. In Contini's (1987) highly detailed cross-dialectal study of Sardinian, there is no evidence at all of nasalization of vowels before assimilated clusters in any Logudorese dialect, including the small group of peripheral dialects where one finds synchronic alternation between survival of [Vns, Vnf], and simplification to [Vss, Vff]. Comparison of the synchronic data drawn from this group of dialects does not lead to the conclusion that there may have been at any point in time an intermediate nasalizing stage, e.g. [Ṽff]. Furthermore, there is no reported evidence in any Logudorese dialect of vowel nasalization before any other cluster.

Similar processes of cluster assimilation, without evidence of vowel nasalization, are found in other languages, as at 18 (Hayes 1986a: 480):

18 Toba Batak   /baoa an peddek/ > [baoa ap peddek]
                  'that man is eating'
                  /lean lali/ > [leal lali]
                  'give a hen-harrier'

Some variants of the N-DEL model, such as Trigo's (1988, 1990) N-attenuation model, and the Ohalan Phonetic model, would predict once again that phonological vowel nasalization will result from total NC > Cː assimilation. Since elimination of the [+nasal] element in N is a clear attenuation of the contextual cue of nasality, then low-level contextual vowel nasalization would logically be expected to be phonologized as a consequence.[10]

Total assimilation presents no problem for any version of the V-NAS model: there is no deletion of N, so there is no obligation to posit an intermediate stage of vowel nasalization. It is worth noting that I have been unable to find any cross-linguistic evidence that structures as at 19, where Ṽ is a short nasal vowel, and CC is an oral geminate, are permitted anywhere:

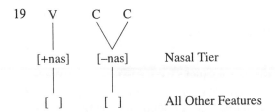

This apparent cross-linguistic constraint suggests that nasalization and total assimilation of NC to Cː are in most languages unrelated processes. Should cross-linguistic counter-examples to such a claim be found, i.e. [VNC] > [VN̥C] > [ṼN̥C] > [ṼCː], the evidence relating to the influence of vowel length on nasalization processes, discussed in chapter 4, indicates that such a structure would be highly marked, unstable and likely to be quickly eliminated.

3.4.4.1 Partial and complete denasalization

Some binary models of distinctive nasalization that rely on N-attenuation as the first step seem logically to predict that partial or complete denasalization of N in the absence of contextual devoicing should also result in phonological vowel nasalization. With the partial or total loss of the immediate contextual source of nasalization, both the Ohalan model and Trigo's (1990) model would hypothesize that that listeners could no longer predictably factor out contextual vowel nasalization, resulting in its phonologization, e.g. Time$_1$ [Vn] > Time$_2$ [Ṽ^{d}n], or [Ṽd]. Such a prediction, however, is not supported by cross-linguistic evidence, and is rejected as incorrect and unproven by Hyman (1975a: 259). As discussed previously, denasalization of N leads to total denasalization of the preceding vowel, e.g. Apinayé /ũm/ [ũm] 'dirty (water)', but /om/ [om] ~ [obm] 'mixture', Manx *feeyn* [fiːn] ~ [fiː^{d}n], Land Dayak /kain/ > [kai^{d}n] (see Kawasaki 1986 for other examples).

Once again, the V-NAS model has no difficulty in dealing with denasalization. Given that N is (partially) denasalized, but not deleted, there is no need to posit a preceding rule of vowel nasalization. In fact, denasalization of N will be expected to block any phonetic or phonological process of contextual vowel nasalization.

3.5 Distinctive Nasalization without Attenuation, Attrition or Deletion

All studies of the process of distinctive nasalization regardless of choice of time frame, or of model of nasalization, have operated on the premise that distinctive vowel nasalization, whether contrastive solely at the surface or underlyingly, develops typically as a result of N-deletion, i.e. /VN/ > surface contrastive and/or underlying /Ṽ/ vs. /V/. The association between vowel nasalization and N-deletion is hardly surprising given the large body of diachronic and synchronic cross-linguistic evidence that supports it, e.g. Lat. BENE 'well' > Pt. [bẽj] *bem*, Fr. [bjɛ̃ː] *bien*. However, whilst the development of distinctive vowel nasalization is most frequently associated with N-deletion across languages, there is evidence to show that a surface or underlying contrast between nasal and oral vowels may occur in the synchronic grammar in the absence of N-deletion, or any other operation on N in VN sequences.[11]

In the course of my investigations for this study, I have uncovered numerous examples of languages which present a surface, if not underlying, contrast between phonologically oral and nasal vowels before nasal consonants: /VN/ vs. /ṼN/. In some cases, the contrast is a surface phenomenon, derived by rule. In others, contrast is not predictable by rule, and should, in any synchronic account, be seen as underlying. A number of examples of an oral vs. nasal distinction are found in the Romance-speaking area, and more particularly in Northern Italy, including dialects in my sample.

Many Romagnol dialects, described by Schürr (1919), present at least a surface contrast between [VːN] and [ṼːN], as at, for example, 20:

20 Cesenate

[læ̃ːna] < LANA 'wool'	but	[kaːna] < CANNA 'cane'
[læ̃ːma] < *LAMA 'blade'		[maːma] < MAMMA 'mummy'
		[pena] < PINNA 'feather'
Sant'Arcangelo		
[lẽːna]		[kaːna]
[lẽːma]		[maːma]
		[pɛna]
Lughese		
[lẽːna]		[kaːna]
[tʃẽːma] < CLAMAT 'calls'		[maːma]

In these dialects, the nasalization contrast before N is derived diachronically from the historical distinction between Stage 2 /VːN/ and /VN/ (see below for more details). If vowel quality and vowel length differences are taken to be underlying, as other evidence not cited here suggests, then in a synchronic account the nasalized vowels given at 20 may be derived by rule.

In other Romagnol dialects in Schürr's sample, e.g. Imolese, Ravennate,

the spread of vowel nasalization is more extensive, with a concomitant reduction in possible contrasts, as at 21:

21 Imolese
[lẽːna] < LANA   [kẽːna] < CANNA
[lẽːma] < *LAMA   [mẽːma] < MAMMA
[sẽːna] < CENA 'dinner'   [pena] < PINNA
but [bɔ̃ːna] < BONA 'good'   vs.   [nɔːna] < NONNA 'grandmother'

Nevertheless, as near-minimal pairs such as [bɔ̃ːna] vs. [nɔːna] make clear, where the vowel contrast rests solely on the presence or absence of nasalization, then the nasalization contrast should be analyzed as fully lexicalized in the underlying representation.

In Bolognese, surface contrast between non-identical oral and nasal nuclei in the more archaic form of the dialect, and in rapid speech today, is also possible, e.g. [paːna] < *PANNA 'cream', but [vãĩna] ~ [vãũna] (and [vaŋna]) < VENA 'vein'. In any case, the existence of apparently unetymological syllable-final [ŋ], found regularly in Bolognese and Cairese of the sort LUNA > Bo. [loŋna], Ca. [lyŋna] ~ [lywna], is indicative of a vowel nasalization rule without N-deletion having once operated regularly in these dialects. In both cases, secondary nasalized diphthongs have undergone subsequent glide hardening, e.g. LUNA > Bo. [lõw̃na] > [lõŋna], [loŋna], Ca. [lỹw̃na] > [lỹŋna] > [lyŋna] (see chapter 8 for more details).

In the Gallo-Italian dialects of Lunigiana, described by Rossi (1976), non-nasalized forms such as [aːnu] < ANNU 'year' and [maːna] < MANNA 'manna' contrast in different dialects with nasalized forms like [sãːna], [sãŋna], [sãw̃na] < SANA 'healthy' (f.).[12] Notwithstanding the variation in [sãːna], [sãŋna], [sãw̃na] all forms are entirely derivable, according to Rossi (596–7), from underlying /ã/.

More tentative, and requiring further confirmation, is the evidence of contrast given by Saunders (1979) in the Emilian dialect of Nonantola, e.g. [veːna] < VENA 'vein', vs. [galẽːna] < GALLINA 'hen'.

Contrastive nasalization without deletion is found elsewhere in the Romance-speaking area, particularly in the Franco-Provençal dialects of France and Switzerland. The *Tableaux phonétiques des patois suisses romands* (*TP*) give consistent examples of near-minimal pairs throughout much of Suisse Romande, e.g. [lãːna] (and [laŋna]) 'wool' (< LANA) vs. [tsaːno] 'oak' (< *CASSANU) in many of the Franco-Provençal dialects of the Valais, Fribourg, and Vaud. Similarly, we find [lãːn] vs. [ʧaːn] in numerous Neuchâtellois Franco-Provençal and Jura French dialects to the north.[13]

Confirmation of contrast before N in Suisse Romande (West Switzerland), with the same pattern of general geographical distribution, is found in the *Atlas Linguistique de la France* (*ALF*), e.g. widespread, especially in Valaisan, [lãːna] vs. [aːno] (< ASINU 'donkey'), [kabaːna] (< CAPANNA 'hut'), [zaːna] (< GALBINA 'yellow'); see *ALF* maps 41 ÂNE, 190 CABANE,

716 JAUNE, 744 LAINE.[14] The same *ALF* maps also show similar contrasts of the type [lãːn(a)] vs. [kabaːn(a)], [aːn(o)] in many Franco-Provençal dialects of France, e.g. pts 913, 915, 924, 926, 935 in the Ain *département*.

Dialect-specific descriptive materials also confirm the existence of surface, and probably underlying, /VN/ vs. /ṼN/ contrasts throughout much of the Franco-Provençal area. In Switzerland, Nendaz Valaisan contrasts /ãna/ 'wool' vs. /pana/ (< *PANNA 'cream'), /kana/ (< CANNA), /ano/ (< ASINU) (Schüle 1963). Similarly, we find [aːne] (< ASINU) vs. [grãːna] < GRANA 'grain' in Vionnaz Valaisan (Gilliéron 1880), and /lãna/ vs. /tsana/ (< CANNA) in Ollon Vaudois (Hasselrot 1937). Duraffour (1932), Ahlborn (1946), Duc (1988), Dupraz (1975) and Hering (1936) provide similar evidence of contrast in Franco-Provençal dialects spoken in different French *départements*.

Elsewhere, some Portuguese dialects use contrastive nasalization to distinguish between the first person plural of the preterite and present tenses, e.g. *am*[ẽ]*mos* 'we love' (< AMAMUS), and *am*[a]*mos* (< *AMAMMUS) 'we loved' (Dunn 1930: 37; Entenman 1977: 102).

Surface contrast between oral and nasalized vowels before /N/ without N-deletion is also possible in French liaison, e.g. [bɔnami] *bon ami*/*bonne amie* 'good friend' (m./f.) vs. *ton ami* [tɔ̃nami] 'your friend' (m. sg.).

Underlying contrast between /ṼN/ and /VN/ is not infrequent in the French Creoles of the Caribbean, e.g. (1) Martinique Creole [sõnet] *sonnette* 'bell' vs. [tunẽ] *tourner* 'to turn' (Chen 1973b: 243); (2) Haitian Creole /vjãn/ *viande* 'meat' vs. /leogan/ *Léogane* (name), /ʃãm/ [ʃãːm] *chambre* 'room' vs. /ʃam/ [ʃaːm] *charme* 'charm', /pan/ *panne* 'breakdown' vs. /pãn/ *pendre* 'hang' (Hall 1950; Szabo 1973; Tinelli 1974; Valdman 1970, 1977). Valdman (1974) reports similar contrasts to exist in Dominican, Guyanese and St. Lucian Creole.

Finally, examples of underlying contrastive nasalization without N-deletion are also found outside of Romania, e.g.: (1) Apinayé /ũm/ [ũm] 'dirty (water)' vs. /om/ [om] ~ [obm] 'mixture' (Kawasaki 1986: 85); (2) Viennese German [βĩːn] *Wien* 'Vienna' vs. [βiːn] *Wieden* 'How so', [rẽːna] *Renner* 'winner' vs. [reːn] *reden* 'to talk', [ʃtũːm] *stumm* 'dumb' vs. [ʃtuːm] *Stube* 'room' (Koekoek 1955); and (3) Argol Breton /tom/ *tomm* 'hot' vs. /plõm/ *plom* 'steady' (Bothorel 1982: 226–7).

3.5.1 *Diachronic and synchronic aspects of* VN *vs.* V$N

The diachronic explanation for a phonological contrast between oral and nasal vowels before synchronic N appears to be fairly transparent in most of the cases cited above. Most typically, at least in Romance, a synchronic contrast between VN and ṼN has its historical basis in the earlier underlying VN vs. VNN contrast in Latin, e.g. Lat. LANA VS. CANNA. As a result of degemination and vowel lengthening phenomena, underlying contrast

shifted to the preceding vowel, e.g. Stage 2 /laːna/ vs. /kana/.[15] For reasons discussed in chapter 4, and supported by cross-linguistic evidence, there is preferential nasalization of long vowels, i.e. /laːna/ > [lãːna], but /kana/ > [kana]. Subsequent to nasalization, secondary vowel lengthening may then affect short vowels before /n/. Where vowel quality and length coincide perfectly, nasalization becomes the only contrastive feature, e.g. [lãːna] vs. [kaːna], and must be marked as such in the underlying representation.

Another frequent source of contrast between oral and nasalized vowels before N, noted in Franco-Provençal, French Creole and Viennese German, is loss of a pre-nasal consonant, e.g. Franco-Provençal [lãːna] < LANA 'wool' vs. [aːno] < *[aznu] < ASINU 'donkey', [zaːna] < *[dʒalna] 'yellow', Haitian [ʃãːm] < Fr. chambre 'room', but [ʃaːm] < Fr. charme 'charm'. The pre-nasal consonant clearly had a blocking effect at the time of the diachronic application of nasalization rules. However, when C-deletion occurred, the vowel nasalization rule was evidently no longer productive, and oral-nasal vowel contrast resulted. Since the blocking consonant no longer surfaces synchronically, there is no reason to posit its existence at any level of the representation, and here too the oral-nasal vowel contrast must appear underlyingly.

A slightly less frequent source of the /VN/ vs. /ṼN/ contrast is nasalization of obstruents adjacent to nasal vowels, e.g. Haitian Creole /pan/ < Fr. [pan] panne vs. /pãn/ < Fr. [pãːd(ʀ)] pendre, /vjãn/ < Fr. [vjãːd] viande. The oral-nasal contrast in Breton appears to be the result of two intersecting processes: degemination and obstruent nasalization, e.g. /tom/ < /tomm/ but /plõm/ < OFr. /plõb/ 'lead'.

The diachronic explanation appears more complex for surface contrast between /VN/ and /ṼN/ in French liaison, e.g. [bɔn ami] 'good friend' vs. [tɔ̃n ami] 'your friend'. Vowels before surface N are ordinarily not nasal in French, e.g. [bɔn] bonne, and the presence of nasal vowels before /n/ in liaison appears to be restricted to a very small set of words, e.g. bien 'well', rien 'nothing', on 'one', en 'in', mon 'my', ton 'your', son 'his/her', un 'one', aucun 'not one', commun 'common' (Encrevé 1988). Historical and synchronic evidence indicates that today's oral-nasal contrast is merely the final stage in a long process of sound change transformation through the grammar, i.e. from post-lexical (regular/Neogrammarian) to lexical (Lexical Diffusion/restricted/exceptionful/morphologically conditioned) until ultimately underlying. Notwithstanding apparent full lexicalization, interaction with lexical/cyclic and post-lexical components is still residually evident today. Syntactic conditioning of vowel nasalization and N-deletion in liaison is clearly post-lexical, e.g. [bɔ̃ e bo] bon et beau 'good and nice' but [bɔn ami] bon ami 'good friend' (m. sg.). Morphological conditioning, typical of the lexical component, is also apparent, cf. [okœ̃#] 'not one' (m. sg.) vs. [okyn#] (f. sg.), and [okœ̃n ami] aucun ami 'no friend' (m. sg.) vs. [okyn ami] aucune amie 'no friend' (f. sg.). Sources, e.g. Pope (1952), Entenman (1977), agree that

during an earlier phase vowel nasalization was generalized before all nasals, e.g. [bõn] ~ [bõ] 'good' (m. sg.) alongside [bõnə] (f. sg.). Partial denasalization in the Late Medieval period – before historically intervocalic nasals only – often coincided with gender marking of the feminine in French. Hence the rise of morphological conditioning and the absence of contextual nasalization today in feminine [okyn ami], previously [okỹn ãmiə]. By the nineteenth and twentieth centuries the set of lexical items involved in N-liaison with vowel nasalization has become greatly reduced, and the influence of analogy, an additional characteristic of Lexical Diffusion, seems increasingly evident – *ton/son* on the basis of *mon* 'my', and *aucun/ commun* on *un*.

Regardless of the historical derivation of the contrast in French, it is evident that in this language and others cited as examples of /VN/ vs. /ṼN/, there is no rule of N-deletion operating that allows us to predict the appearance of phonological vowel nasalization. In some languages, such as certain Romagnol dialects noted at example 20 above, oral and nasal vowels before N present qualitative and quantitative differences, and the presence of vowel nasalization before N is synchronically derivable by rule. In others, however, the presence of vowel nasalization cannot be derived, and must, therefore, be lexical. Developments in Northern Italian dialects show that lexicalization, however, is not the result of any process directly affecting [ṼN] where V > Ṽ / __N, but is the 'accidental' result of historical processes affecting the rest of the lexicon, as at 22:

22   LANA

CANNA

		'wool'	'cane'
Stage 2	UR	/laːna/	/kana/
	SR	[laːna]	[kana]
Time₁	UR	/laːna/	/kana/
V: ⟶ Ṽː / __N		[lãːna]	[kana]
Time₂	UR	/laːna/	/kana/
V ⟶ V: / __N		[lãːna]	[kaːna]
relexicalization		/lãna/	/kana/
Time₃	UR	/lãna/	/kana/
V ⟶ V: / __N		[lãːna]	[kaːna]

If we compare synchronic grammars at different points in time, the rule of nasalization at Time₁ is predictable and easily derived. However, secondary lengthening at Time₂ of previously short vowels means that the output of the nasalization rule is no longer predictable, and must be encoded in the underlying representation. It is worth pointing out that the vowel lengthen-ing rule which triggered lexicalization of nasalization is not itself restricted or

eliminated as a result. In fact, by Time$_3$ its scope is increased: it now applies to nasal vowels as well.

The process of lexicalization is not dependent on N-deletion, nor is it rule-governed or an easily predictable one, e.g. the loss of the Lat. /VN/ vs. /VNN/ contrast in Romagnol and Franco-Provençal, loss of a blocking consonant in /VCN/ in Haitian Creole and in Franco-Provençal. Therefore, no explicit reference to lexicalization should be made in any model of distinctive nasalization.

3.5.2 *The implications for sound change and Lexical Phonology*

The process of lexicalization of vowel nasality reported here has interesting implications for the suggested relationship between sound change and the structure of grammar. According to John Harris (1989) and McMahon (1991), sound change is progressively transformed in nature as it percolates over time into the deeper structure of grammar. Initially phonetically gradual, but lexically abrupt (Neogrammarian-type) sound change operating in the post-lexical phonology may over the course of time enter the Lexical Phonology, and become phonetically abrupt and lexically gradual (Lexical Diffusion). In so doing, the rules accounting for such change display all the characteristics of lexical rules, e.g. cyclicity, morphological conditioning, and exceptions. Ultimately, however, the output of the change may percolate deeper into the grammar, and become fully lexicalized in the underlying representation (see figure 1.2). The cross-linguistic evidence suggests that this fine-grained view of grammar percolation is not obligatory. Of all the languages examined, only the French data seem to fit this account. The changes reported in Northern Italian, and elsewhere, suggest that a sound change may still be operating in the post-lexical component before its output is fully lexicalized. The nasalization phenomena reported (with the exception of French) show no diachronic or synchronic evidence of ever operating in the lexical component: as already noted in chapter 1, there is no evidence of exceptions, cyclic application and morphological interaction affecting developments in Northern Italian. In these circumstances we need to modify slightly the original hypothesis regarding the diachronic relationship between sound change and the grammar. Whilst Lexical Diffusion and operation in the lexical component is often an intermediate step between the entry of a sound change into the post-lexical component of grammar and ultimate lexicalization, it is not a universal requirement for lexicalization to occur. It can instead be a collateral result of other sound changes that cause new underlying contrasts to arise.

3.5.3 *Local vs. prosodic nasalization*

Proponents of the N-DEL model are forced to distinguish between two types of (synchronic and presumably diachronic) nasalization processes: (1) local;

and (2) prosodic (long-distance). The former is apparently characterized by N-deletion and local nasalization of an immediately adjacent vowel, e.g. Fr. *océan* [oseɑ̃ː] ← UR /osean/, but *océ*[an]*ique*. The latter is typified by (left- and/or rightward) long-distance spreading of nasalization, and by retention of N, as demonstrated by the examples at 23 (Piggott 1988b):

23 right-spreading:

Malay	[mãjãn]	'stalk'
	[mãʔãp]	'pardon'
	[mẽw̃ãh]	'be luxurious'
Warao	[inãw̃ãhã]	'summer'
	[mõhõkohi]	'shadow'

left-spreading:

| Capanahua | [hãmawi] | 'step on it' |
| | [hãmãʔõna] | 'coming stepping' |

It is clear that in such circumstances, the N-DEL model is, as Trigo (1990) and Piggott (1987, 1988a and b) explicitly state, incapable of accounting for prosodic nasalization where N is not affected in any way. The suggestion that local and prosodic nasalization processes are two unrelated phenomena, requiring different explanations, is a convenient one for proponents of the N-DEL model. However, for the V-NAS model there is no need to posit any such dichotomy. The distinction between prosodic and local nasalization is also an unlikely and unnecessary one, since it is evident that long-distance spreading of nasalization and N-deletion can both occur in the same language. This happens, as Piggott (1987, 1988a and b) admits, in Capanahua where N is optionally deleted in word-final position and before glides:

24 Capanahua	[põjã(n)]	'arm'
	[bãw̃ĩ(n)]	'catfish'
UR /wiran + ai/ ⟶	[wirãnai]	'I pushed it'
/wiran + wi/ ⟶	[wirãw̃ĩ]	'push it over'

Whilst it is true that the emphasis in this study is largely on examples of so-called 'local' nasalization in Northern Italian and elsewhere, there is no reason to suggest that local and prosodic nasalization cannot be governed by the same model. It seems redundant to suggest, as Piggott (1988b: 147) does, that there are two separate phenomena of local and prosodic nasalization operating in Capanahua and other languages, governed by completely different principles and parameters.

The new V-NAS model is precisely a model that can deal with non-spreading and spreading nasalization: in both cases vowel nasalization is ordered before N-deletion. The absence or presence of N-deletion is indicative simply of different stages of the new V-NAS model, i.e. Stage b

or c. The type of nasalization spreading, local or prosodic, can be accounted for, for instance, by the operation of simple universal parameters of the type Piggott himself favours:

25a Nasalization Spreading Parameter
    Vowel nasalization spreads in a long-distance fashion: Yes/No
    Yes: Capanahua, Malay, Warao
    No: French, Northern Italian
  b Direction of Spreading
    Leftward: Capanahua
    Rightward: Malay, Warao

In some languages, long-distance spreading is blocked, and we find local nasalization, as in French [oseã:] ← UR /osean/ 'ocean'. In others where long-distance spreading is reported, spreading may be leftward or rightward.

3.6 CONCLUSIONS

Claims that the diachronic phonologization or synchronic phonological rule of vowel nasalization is determined by attenuation or deletion processes affecting N are shown not to be supported by diachronic and synchronic empirical evidence. Phonological rules of contextual nasalization, independent of N-deletion or any kind of N-attenuation, are seen to operate over time and in derivation. A strict ordering relationship between nasalization and N-deletion over time allows us to conclude that whenever we have synchronic evidence of N-deletion, without clear diachronic or synchronic attestation of nasalization, we can assume nevertheless that deletion was once preceded at some point in time by some phonological process of contextual nasalization. Similarly, in synchronic derivation of surface [Ṽ] from underlying /VN/, a rule of vowel nasalization should be ordered in the grammar before N-deletion.

With reference to diachronic change and its relationship to the grammar, it has been shown that the independence of the nasalization process allows for lexicalization of nasalized vowels without deletion. It was also found that the output of a lexically abrupt post-lexical rule may pass directly into the underlying representation without, at an intermediate point in time, showing evidence of having been transformed into a Lexical Diffusion phenomenon operating in the lexical strata.

4

UNIVERSAL FEATURES OF VOWEL NASALIZATION AND N-DELETION: THE EFFECT OF VOWEL LENGTH, STRESS AND THE FOOT

4.1 INTRODUCTION

For the first time in this study, factor-specific effects on the gradual spread of vowel nasalization and N-deletion are examined in detail. In this chapter our attention is turned to the influence of a series of prosodic factors (vowel length, stress differences, and the stress foot) on developments in Northern Italian and elsewhere. All of these are found to have a discernible and significant effect – to an extent not previously reported by or known to universalists. On the basis of the cross-linguistic evidence it is possible to formulate a set of parameters of sound change. These are found to be interrelated, the result of a shared phonetic basis of which details are provided and discussed.

Also described is the distribution, behaviour and development of so-called phonemic short nasal vowels in a small number of languages reported to have them. Such vowels are found to be highly marked and in the end to fall outside the scope of this study. Finally, in discussion of foot-level conditioning of sound change, specific attention is also given to the development of oxytonic vowel length in Italy, found to be cross-linguistically somewhat atypical.

4.1.1 *The graduality of distinctive nasalization*

Universalist studies of distinctive nasalization by Chen (1972 and elsewhere), Lightner (1970, 1973), Ruhlen (1973), Schourup (1973), Foley (1975, 1977) and Hombert (1986, 1987) make clear that whilst rules of the type given at 1 below, and discussed in detail in chapter 3, can be valued for their convenient descriptive power, they are diachronically inadequate. Excessively telescoped in nature, they fail to make any reference to the componential nature over time of nasalization and N-deletion phenomena.

1a $V \longrightarrow \tilde{V} / \_\_N$

  b $N \longrightarrow \emptyset / \tilde{V}\_\_$

For universalists, the process of distinctive nasalization spreads gradually

over time along defined universal parameters, according to context and type, as described in section 1.1.3.[1] However, whilst all seem to agree that universal parameters exist, conclusions differ as to their formulation. Contradictory claims made about parameters of vowel nasalization and N-deletion square poorly with the purportedly universal nature of such parameters, and suggest one of two things: (1) no universal parameters exist; or (2) some conclusions are erroneous. It is in these circumstances that I wish to assess the relative merit of suggested parameters by comparing developments in my Northern Italian sample. Experimental evidence, and possible phonetic explanations, as well as additional comparative linguistic material, will be offered where possible in support or otherwise of different claims.

4.1.2 *Vowel length, nasalization and N-deletion*

The issue of vowel length and its relationship with vowel nasalization and N-deletion has generated relatively little interest amongst universalists studying distinctive nasalization. Apparently most typical is the view that the development of nasalization and N-deletion is in no way dependent on vowel length, but that rather the reverse applies: nasal vowels are frequently affected by an immediate process of Compensatory Lengthening (CL) triggered by deletion of all segmental content of N as at 2. Such is the general view amongst universalists, e.g. Ruhlen (1973: 12), and Chen (1974a: 916). Foley (1977: 64–65) is generally accepting, although he notes that pre-deletion vowel lengthening is more typical before N + Fricative clusters. Only Lightner (1970, 1973) is unsympathetic to the notion of CL – of any type and in any context.[2] A CL model of vowel lengthening triggered by N-deletion is also adopted by many other phonologists, e.g. Lass (1980: 74, ex. 3), Goldsmith (1990: 74), Hayes (1986b).

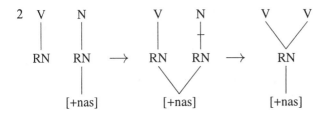

The diachronic adequacy of the formal representation of Compensatory Lengthening (CL) of the type given in 2 is discussed in restricted fashion in this chapter, but is evaluated in some detail in chapter 8.

Hombert (1986, 1987) is unique amongst universalists in suggesting that vowel-length differences affect the development of distinctive nasalization.

According to Hombert, vowel nasalization and N-deletion develop preferentially in the environment of long vowels, before spreading to short vowels. Whilst the concept of CL has received a significant amount of attention in recent work on phonological theory, e.g. Hayes (1989), I will attempt to demonstrate that the available evidence cited in this chapter supports Hombert's suggestion of a predictable vowel-length effect.[3] In some languages, including Northern Italian dialects, there is evidence that vowels must always be phonologically long *before* they can be phonologically nasalized, as described in sections 4.1.3 to 4.1.4. In such cases, the need to postulate post-deletion CL as a historical phenomenon to account for the phonological length of nasal vowels is eliminated.

Hombert draws support for his vowel-length parameter from developments in a small sample of Teke (Bantu B.70) languages spoken in Central Africa; see the set of structural correspondences abstracted by Hombert (1987: 274) through comparison of cognate word-tokens, and given at 3:

3 Atege	Ibali	Ndzindziu
$C_1 im V_2$	$C_1 im V_2$	$C_1^j\tilde{\mathrm{o}}$
$C_1 em V_2$	$C_1 em V_2$	$C_1^j\tilde{\mathrm{o}}$
$C_1 am V_2$	$C_1 am V_2$	$C_1\tilde{\mathrm{o}}$
$C_1 om V_2$	$C_1 om V_2$	$C_1\tilde{\mathrm{o}}$
$C_1 um V_2$	$C_1 um V_2$	$C_1 o\tilde{\mathrm{o}}$, $C_1\tilde{\mathrm{o}}$
$C_1 iim V_2$	$C_1 iim V_2$	$C_1 i\tilde{\mathrm{o}}$
$C_1 iem V_2$	$C_1 i\tilde{\mathrm{o}}$	$C_1 i\tilde{\mathrm{o}}$
$C_1 aam V_2$	$C_1 \tilde{a}\tilde{a}$	$C_1 a\tilde{\mathrm{o}}$
$C_1 uom V_2$	$C_1 u\tilde{\mathrm{o}}$	$C_1 u\tilde{\mathrm{o}}$
$C_1 uum V_2$	$C_1 uum V_2$	$C_1 u\tilde{\mathrm{o}}$, $C_1 u\tilde{\mathrm{o}}$

In conservative Atege, intervocalic /m/ and contrastive vowel length before it are preserved. By comparison, in Ibali, vowel nasalization and N-deletion have begun to appear in the context of some phonologically long vowels only, whilst short vowels remain untouched. More radical changes in Ndzindziu affect both long and short vowels. From such data, Hombert concludes that vowel nasalization and N-deletion preferentially affect long vowels before N.

Despite Hombert's observation, a restricted sample of three closely related languages with an unattested proto-language is unlikely to be adequate for the formulation of a universally applicable parameter of sound change, at least without supporting evidence from other language areas. Such confirmation of a vowel-length parameter is found in my Northern Italian sample and elsewhere.

The underlying vowel-length contrast that resulted as a by-product of Stage 2 degemination in Northern Italian and other Romance dialects, and given at 4, conveniently allows one to evaluate the cross-linguistic validity of Hombert's vowel-length hypothesis.

4	CANE	ANNU
	'dog'	'year'
Stage 1	[kaːne]	[annu]
Stage 2	/kaːn/	/an/
Tavetsch	[cawn]	[ɔn]
Milan	[kɑ̃ː]	[an]
Cairo	[kaŋ] (< [kã ̃ᵘ])	[an]
Bergamo	[ka(ː)]	[a(ː)n]
Bologna	[kæŋ] (< [kæ̃ ̃ᵘ])	[aːn]
Rimini 1917	[kɛːn] ~ [kɛ̃ːn]	[aːn]
Rimini 1991	[kɛ̃ːn]	[ãːn]
Lugo	[kɛ̃ː]	[aːn]
Imola	[kɛ̃ː]	[ɛ̃ːn]
Ravenna	[kʌː]	[ʌːn]

In Romagnol (Rimini, Lugo, Imola and Ravenna) and Bolognese, expected short Stage 2 /a/ (like /ɛ ɔ/) demonstrates a marked tendency towards secondary lengthening in all contexts, as seen at 4. Such a development obscures slightly the length contrast postulated at Stage 2 which still survives more obviously elsewhere in the modern vowel system; cf. the present-day reflexes of Stage 2 /eː/ vs. /e/ in VENA and PINNA at 5:

5	LANA	CANNA	VENA	PINNA
Stage 2	/laːna/	/kana/	/veːna/	/pena/
Imola	[lɛ̃ːna]	[kɛ̃ːna]	[vɛ̃ːna]	[pena]
Ravenna	[lʌːna]	[kʌːna]	[vẽːna]	[pena]
Rimini 1917	[leːna]	[kaːna]	[vəʲna]	[pɛna]
Rimini 1991	[lɛ̃ːna]	[kãːna]	[və̃ʲna]	[pɛna]
Bologna	[leːna]	[kaːna]	[vaŋna]	[panna]

It is clear from both a diachronic and synchronic point of view that nasalization and N-deletion apply in a preferential manner in the context /VːN/ in all listed dialects. As the data sets demonstrate, vowels that appear today as short are not reported to be nasalized. Conversely, synchronically nasalized vowels, regardless of historic length, are always long, e.g. Im. [kɛ̃ːna] < Stage 2 /kana/ and [lɛ̃ːna] < Stage 2 /laːna/. A similar relationship between vowel length and N-deletion is also found in the data: whilst deletion of final /n#/ after historical long /aː/, once nasalized, is quite frequent, there are no examples in the sample of final [n]-deletion in modern reflexes of Stage 2 /an/, even in those dialects where secondary lengthening has occurred, e.g. Im. [kɛ̃ː] < Stage 2 /kaːn/, but [ɛ̃ːn] < *[aːn] < Stage 2 /an/. Interaction between vowel length and the spread of vowel nasalization is confirmed by developments in Riminese over the last seventy years: whereas as in 1917 Schürr found contextual nasalization to be an optional or sporadic characteristic of long vowels, by 1992 all long vowels

before N are obligatorily nasalized. Short vowels, however, remain unnasalized.

In comparison with Hombert's Teke data, the correlation between vowel length and vowel nasalization and N-deletion is even more striking: nowhere in the Northern Italian sample are vowel nasalization and N-deletion reported to occur in the context of synchronic short vowels before N. From the diachronic point of view, vowel nasalization only affects historically short vowels once they have been lengthened. N-deletion, even after vowel lengthening, is still unknown. In some places, secondary vowel lengthening has not as yet been followed by a secondary wave of nasalization, e.g. Bo. and Lg. [aːn]

A similar pattern of preferential nasalization of phonologically long vowels, coupled with subsequent N-deletion is found in numerous German dialects. Schirmunski (1962: 385–6) notes that whilst final /n/ after tonic long vowels is eliminated in a large part of the German-speaking area, N-deletion after historically short tonic vowels is restricted to a much smaller sub-area within the first. In any case, all distinctively nasalized tonic vowels are predictably long, regardless of historical derivation.

Thinnes (1981), amongst others, also confirms the effect of tonic vowel length before N on the historical pattern of N-deletion and nasalization in the context of long vowels in German dialects. He also provides more specific evidence of nasalization and N-deletion in the Rhine Franconian dialect of Wackernheim demonstrating that underlying short vowels are not nasalized, and that N-deletion does not occur after them, i.e. /VN/ > *[ṼN] or *[Ṽ]. There are very sporadic examples of secondary shortening of long nasal vowels, but in general, all nasal vowels are long, and N-deletion occurs only in the context /VːN/. The same diachronic and synchronic correlation between long vowels and nasalization and N-deletion is reported to occur in Banat German by Barba (1982: 82), e.g. MHG bîn (i.e. /biːn/) > [põ̃] 'bee' but bin (/bin/) > [pin] 'am', as well as in other German dialects, e.g. Corell (1936: 14), Schwartz (1939), Friebertshäuser (1961) and Martin (1957: 101).

Elsewhere, Karttunen (1976) notes that distinctive nasalization affects only VːN$ and not VN$ in Veracruz Nahuatl. In Ceylon Gypsy Telugu, and some Irish Gaelic dialects, contextual nasalization is markedly stronger on long vowels than on short vowels before N (Karunatilake 1974 and Breatnach 1947: 61). A similar pattern is found in Charleroi French by de Reuse (1987: 103–4), e.g. [fam] 'woman' vs. [mɛ̃ːm] 'same'.[4] In Sardinian and Corsican dialects where contextual nasalization of tonic vowels before intervocalic /n/ is reported to be strong in some circumstances, only long vowels appear to be affected, e.g. [pãːne] 'bread' but [kanne] and in some Corsican dialects even [kane] 'canes' (pl.) (Contini 1987; Dalbera-Stefanaggi 1989). In the Gallo-Romance dialect of Damprichard spoken near the

Franco-Swiss border only long vowels are nasalized before N, all short vowels are oral: [pjẽːn] < PLANA 'flat', [fĩːn] < FINA 'fine', but [avwɔn] < AVENA 'oats' and [bwɔn] < BONA 'good' (Grammont 1892–8). Finally, Bloch (1934: 45–6) reports that spontaneous nasalization in Indo-Aryan languages is most likely when the vowel affected is long.

4.1.3 The Vowel Length Parameter

The apparent correlation between the length of pre-nasal vowels and the development of nasalization and N-deletion in my Northern Italian sample, as well as the evidence drawn from Teke, German and elsewhere, support Hombert's suggestion of a Vowel Length Parameter (VLP). The historical development of distinctive nasalization patterns predictably, possibly in a universal fashion along the parameter given at 6, whereby vowel nasalization and N-deletion, as separate and successive processes, occur preferentially in the context of phonologically long vowels before spreading to short vowels:

6 Vowel Length Parameter (VLP)

$$\underrightarrow{\text{VːN VN}}$$

It may be too strong to claim, on the basis of developments in Northern Italian and German dialects alone, that short nasal vowels can never develop in the context VN, since Ndzindziu, cited above at 3, appears to have a restricted number of short nasal vowels.[5] However, the evidence may be interpreted as indicating that the VLP operates with relative degrees of restrictiveness over time in different languages. In Teke the parameter appears to be fully operational, and earlier /VN/ can become today's contrastive /Ṽ/, once /VːN/ has become /Ṽː/, as seen at 7a where the suggested patterns of development are given along a time axis:

7a VːN > ṼːN > Ṽː

$$\underrightarrow{\text{VN} > \text{ṼN} > \text{Ṽ}} \quad \text{(Teke)}$$

T₁   T₂   T₃   T₄   T₅

b VːN > ṼːN > Ṽː

$$\underrightarrow{\text{VN} > \text{VːN} > \text{ṼːN} > \text{Ṽː}} \quad \text{(N.It. and Gmn)}$$

T₁   T₂   T₃   T₄

In Northern Italian and German dialects, operation of the parameter is severely restricted, at least in the context of tonic vowels before N#. Short tonic vowels must be lengthened before phonologization of nasalization is recorded, as seen at 7b. In these circumstances the VLP may be reduced to

one item, as at 8, which suggests that nasalization and N-deletion will occur only when the vowel before N is phonologically long:

8 Restricted VLP

$$\underset{\longrightarrow}{V:N}$$

Although at this point I restrict my observation about a correlation between phonological vowel length and the development of distinctive nasalization to tonic vowels before N#, it will become apparent in the course of this study that the same correlation appears to extend to tonic VN in other contexts in Northern Italian.

Most of the languages that I cite in support of the VLP show evidence of a diachronic or synchronic underlying contrast between /V:N/ and /VN/. However, developments in Sardinian and Corsican indicate that the operation of the VLP is not dependent on an underlying vowel length contrast. In these Romance dialects the length of stressed vowels is phonologically conditioned by syllable structure, i.e. ['V:$CV#] but ['VC$CV#]. Vowel length distribution interacts with vowel nasalization (and subsequent N-deletion): only long vowels are nasalized, e.g. LANA > [lãːna] (and >[lãː]) 'wool', but CANNA > [kanna] 'cane' (and in some Corsican dialects [kana]) in all of them.[6] However, the Restricted VLP does not operate in all parts of Centro-Southern Italy. Exceptionally in Tuscan elevated levels of contextual nasalization are now pervasive: as a result, all vowels – long or short – adjacent to N, are nasalized, eg. [lãːnã], [kãnnã] and [gãmba] 'leg' (Giannelli and Savoia 1978). But even here stressed long vowel nasalization is favoured to the extent that optional deletion affects only short N and not long N:, i.e. [lãː(n)ã] but always [kãnnã]. Also, in section 6.4 evidence is provided of a correlation between a non-contrastive secondary vowel lengthening before NC clusters and the spread of distinctive nasalization in Northern Italian. More surprising, however, are the results of perceptual tests, discussed below, which indicate that even small differences in vowel duration affect listeners' perception of vowel nasalization.

4.1.4 *Phonetic evidence for the Vowel Length Parameter*

The results of experimental research on the effect, if any, of vowel duration on perceived vowel nasality are consistent in suggesting that the perception of vowel nasalization is favoured by increasing vowel duration.

In a series of three experiments, Whalen and Beddor (1989) synthesized by means of an articulatory synthesizer three vowels, /a i u/, with five durations (50, 100, 150, 200 and 250 ms.) and with six degrees of velar port opening for /a/ and four for /i, u/, ranging from 'oral' to heavily nasalized. Twelve speakers of American English were then presented with tokens in randomized order and asked to rate each token from 1 ('least nasalized') to 5

('most nasalized'). The former rating corresponded to the stimulus with zero velic coupling, and the latter with the greatest velic coupling of 36 mm². As expected, the average nasality rating increased with an increase in velar port opening for all vowels, as shown in figure 4.1. However, more significant is the finding that the nasality rating also increased with an increase in vowel duration for all vowels. These and other experiments established that the link between perceived nasality and duration was not dependent on vowel height, fundamental frequency, or amplitude.

Whalen and Beddor (472) can provide no phonetic explanation for the correlation between perceived nasality and duration, other than to suggest a poorly defined summation effect. In another experiment using stimuli based on recordings of Western Abenaki, Whalen and Beddor (475–7) found no evidence that oral vowels might be perceived as inherently more nasal as their length was increased. However, they did find that the perceived nasality of similar stimuli based on vowels in nasal contexts did correlate to some small but significant degree with duration.

Delattre and Monnot (1981) using synthesized tokens manipulated for length and interpretable as French *l'aide* vs. *l'Inde*, tested the effect of vowel length on the perception of vowel nasalization by French and American English speakers. In this experiment tokens were nasalized throughout.

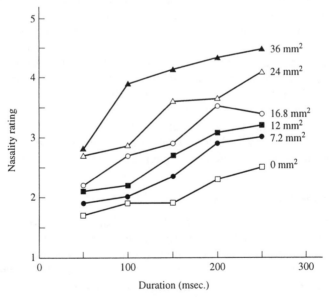

Whalen and Beddor (1989) suggest that the midpoint value '3' represents a conceivable boundary between oral and nasal vowel.

Figure 4.1   Averaged Responses of Twelve Subjects to [a] Synthesized with Six Degrees of Nasalization at Five Durations. Source: Whalen and Beddor (1989: 462)

However, the acoustic cue for nasality was affected by lowering the intensity of the first formant, so that it fell between that normally found for a nasal and an oral vowel respectively. There was a clear correlation between length and nasality for both groups. From one endpoint to the other, the rate of perception of the vowel as nasal increased from 0% at 100 ms. to 90% at 260 ms. for English-speakers, and from 5% at 100 ms. to 100% by 260 ms. for French-speakers. The cross-over (50% oral-50% nasal) point was 180 ms. and 200 ms. for English-speakers and Francophones respectively.

Similar experimental results have been reported by others, eg. Casablanca (1987) for Puerto Rican Spanish, and Lahiri and Marslen-Wilson (1991) for Bengali and English. The latter found a similar correlation between increased vowel length and the correct identification by British English listeners of spliced out syllable-final N. Also, the perception of oral, as opposed to nasal vowels, by Bengali listeners correlated inversely with decreasing vowel length.

Cagliari (1977), in a sound-segmentation experiment, found that duration affected the perception of vowel nasality in Brazilian Portuguese. In a context where the vowel is expected to be articulatorily nasalized throughout, e.g. /NVGN$/, vowels which were perceived as nasal when the entire duration of the vocalic segment was heard were no longer perceived as such if the same segment was temporally reduced.

Finally, Lintz and Sherman (1961), using unedited normal speech, found that in phonologically oral contexts, contextually determined vowel duration differences correlated directly with the perception of nasality by American listeners on six of seven vowels tested, i.e. [i, ɛ, ʌ, ɑ, ʊ, u], but not [æ] which was inexplicably perceived as strongly nasal in all contexts.

That duration affects the perception of vowel nasality in the manner suggested by Cagliari (1977), Delattre and Monnot (1981) and Whalen and Beddor (1989) has long been reported, e.g. Petrovici (1930: 74, n. 1), Rousselot (1924: 539) and Straka (1955: 257). Given the experimental evidence cited above, we have a phonetic basis for the claim that phonologically long vowels provide the preferential environment for the phonologization of contextual vowel nasalization and subsequent N-deletion in V(ː)N$ syllables. That a monotonic relationship between vowel duration and the perceptibility of nasalization exists is clear: as the former is increased, so is the latter. There is no phonetic evidence at all for Tuttle's (1991: 37) claim that some maximum duration-perception threshold exists beyond which vowels become too long to be nasalized. He is forced to suggest this in order to deal with otherwise inexplicable discrepancies in his account of developments in Northern Italian. If LANA appears today as /lɛːna/ in Bolognese alongside /loŋna/ < LUNA, it is simply, contra Tuttle, that when hardening of nasalized glides occurred in this dialect the tonic vowel in /lɛːna/ was monophthongal and had no glide to harden unlike [lõw̃na] > [lõŋna] (see chapter 8 for further details).

We can also hypothesize from a perceptual perspective why phonologically

short vowels before geminate nasals are not reported to be nasal in languages such as Sardinian and Corsican, e.g. Sard. [kanna] < CANNA 'cane' but [lãː] < LANA 'wool'. Any contextual nasalization of the pre-geminate vowel is presumably not easily perceived since the shortness of the vowel seems to adversely affect the perception of vowel nasality. Even after degemination, when N-reduction might be expected to result in the phonologization of any contextual vowel nasalization as some N-DEL models of distinctive nasalization might predict, retained vowel shortness continues to affect the perception of any coarticulated nasality (see section 3.4.2); hence [kana] and not *[kãna] in degeminating varieties of Corsican. The experimental evidence leads us to suggest that cases of languages with regular vowel nasalization before geminate nasals will be less frequent. In addition, we can predict that in these languages all long vowels before nasal consonants will also always be nasalized – precisely the situation in Tuscan today where contextual nasalization is pervasive before all nasals, eg. [kãnna] alongside [gãmba] 'leg', [pãːne] 'bread', and [lãːna] (see Giannelli and Savoia 1978 for details).

4.1.5 Short nasal vowels, their origins and behaviour

Whilst all the cross-linguistic evidence referred to in this chapter indicates that phonologically short nasal vowels are strongly disfavoured, some languages are nevertheless reported to have them, sometimes in surface, if not underlying, contrast with long nasal vowels, e.g. Norman French /mã/ vs. /mãː/ 'hand/s' (Lepelley 1974: 50).

Maddieson (1984) makes explicit reference to seven languages (Chipewyan, Hindi-Urdu, Irish, Lakkia, Navaho, Tolowa, !Xũ) in which short nasal vowels contrast, at least on the surface, with their long counterparts. In order to determine further the relationship between distinctive nasalization and vowel length, I examined characteristics of short nasal vowels in at least some of these languages. A clear areo-genetic distribution is evident. Three of the languages (Navaho, Chipewyan and Tolowa) are Athapascan. In addition to Hindi-Urdu, evidence from related Sindhi (Yegorova 1977: 23) and Panjabi (Tolstoya 1981: 41) shows that the short-long nasal vowel distinction is found in many Indo-European languages of India and Pakistan.

In at least three languages (Irish, Lakkia, Hindi), the phonemic status of short nasal vowels is somewhat precarious, since they may never appear in true isolation. In Irish, short nasal vowels seem in most cases to be contextually nasalized by adjacent approximants and continuants, with which they form long nasalized contours, e.g. 9:

9a [kr̃ũk]   < cnoc 'hill'
 b [sãw̃ru] < OIr. sa[ṽ]radh 'summer'
 c [tõs̃]   < *[tõw̃s] < OIr. to[ṽ]as 'act of measuring'

A similar pattern of distribution seems evident in Lakkia where all short vowels, e.g. *wăk* 'soft', are preceded by a glide apparently derived from an earlier N. If so, it is likely the remnant glide is also nasalized. Unfortunately, Haudricourt (1967) provides insufficient detail for proper evaluation.

At the level of phonological representation, the result in Irish, Lakkia and presumably elsewhere, is a binary branching structure not unlike that of long nasal vowels:

Regardless of their status as surface contrastive phonemes, short nasal vowels are in any case subject to a strong cross-linguistic tendency towards elimination. They may be subject to: (1) regular lengthening, e.g. Cois Fhairrge Irish, [kr̃ãːg] < *[kr̃ãg] < *cnag* 'rap' (de Bhaldraithe 1945); (2) regular denasalization, e.g. Tourmakeady Irish [kɾap] < *cnap* 'lump', but [kũːg] < *cumhang* 'narrow' (De Búrca 1958), Hindi [hə̃si] > [həsi] 'laughter' (Manjari Ohala 1975: 318–19); or alternatively, (3) the epenthesis of a nasal consonant before obstruents, e.g. Hindi [hə̃si] > [hənsi] 'laughter' (318–19).

Towards the end of chapter 1 I was explicit in stating that this study focuses on developments affecting tonic VN$ sequences. Consequently, unless otherwise specified, any conclusions reached about the spread of distinctive nasalization are normally to be restricted to such sequences. Examination of historical evidence for three languages indicates that the development of short nasal vowels in Hindi, Irish and Lakkia, falls outside the scope of this study, and is, therefore, not relevant to the operation or otherwise of the VLP. In Lakkia, and Irish, they are the result of weakening of the prevocalic N in (C)NV sequences, e.g. Irish [kr̃ãũk] < *cnoc* 'hill'. Short nasal vowels may also arise from the reduction of nasalized diphthongs most typically when adjacent to voiceless fricatives, e.g. Irish [tõs] < *[tõw̃s] < Old Irish *to*[ṽ]*as*. 'act of measuring'. That short nasal vowels in Irish are frequently found adjacent to sibilants /s ʃ/ and voiceless glottal /h/ (e.g. [kõhəru] *comhartha* 'sign') is not unexpected: voiceless airflow through the open glottis during the production of these voiceless fricatives simulates the acoustic effect of nasal coupling and may indeed be accompanied by substantial nasal airflow (Ali 1984, Manjari Ohala 1975). This would in turn enhance the perception of nasality on the adjacent short nasal vowel. Given the distributional characteristics of such vowels in Irish, it is likely too that velic opening during articulation of the fricatives themselves is substantial if listeners have reinterpreted accidental nasality on these segments as intended.

In Hindi, short nasal vowels are typically the result of: (1) an abbreviation of earlier long vowels, a process evident in lexical derivation e.g. [sĩʧaj]

'irrigation' ← [siːʧ] 'to irrigate'; and (2) spontaneous nasalization when adjacent to voiceless fricatives, e.g. Hindi [ãsu] < Skt. *ashru* 'tear' (Manjari Ohala 1975: 321; Srivastav 1989: 426).

Finally, it should also be pointed out that the notion 'short nasal vowel' could well be an analytical artefact of a contrast between two segment types, one apparently shorter in duration than the other. It is indeed quite possible that so-called short nasal vowels are not phonetically short at all. In the absence of any experimental data, it cannot be determined whether short nasal vowels share the duration characteristics of other apparently short vowels in the same language. It is possible that the purportedly short and long nasal vowels are really phonetically long and extralong respectively. The latter hypothesis is plausible, if the following historical derivation is correct for previously cited Norman French:

11		MANU	MANU + S
Stage 2		/maːn/	/maːn + s/
N ⟶ ø /__$		mãː	mãːs
s ⟶ h /__$			mãːh
h ⟶ V /__$			mãːː

4.2 STRESS AND DISTINCTIVE NASALIZATION

Northern Italian dialects provide an interesting case study of the interaction between stress, or lack thereof, and the historical development of distinctive nasalization. To date, universalists such as Foley (1975, 1977) and Schourup (1973), have restricted their analyses to only the simplest distinction between stressed and unstressed syllables. I take the opportunity to examine the more subtle distinction in atonic syllables, to determine whether pretonic and post-tonic positions have differing effects on nasalization processes.

4.2.1 *The effect of stressed vs. unstressed position*

There are conflicting views among universalists about the relationship between stress and the development of the components of distinctive nasalization. Foley (1975: 201, 1977: 60–1), based on purported developments in Sanskrit and Ancient Greek, formulated a strict universal according to which N-deletion occurs first (without nasalization in these languages) in unstressed/atonic syllables, before spreading to stressed/tonic syllables, as in 12a.

12a Foley   ^VN 'VN
           ―――――→

  b Schourup   'VN ^VN   ^ = unstressed/atonic
              ―――――→   ' = stressed/tonic

In contrast to Foley, Schourup (1973: 192) provides slightly more extensive data to support his finding that distinctive nasalization develops and survives preferentially in stressed syllables; see 12b. Schourup found no counter-examples to such an observation.

Developments in my Northern Italian sample lend weight to Schourup's view that the presence of stress on the vowel immediately before N favours the development of distinctive nasalization:

13	'CANE	'ASINU
	'dog'	'donkey'
Stage 2	/'kaːn/	/'azin/
Tavetschan	['cawn]	['aːzən]
Riminese	['kɛːn] ~ [kẽːn]	['ɛːznə]
Bolognese	['kæŋ]	['ɛːzen]
	(< [kæ̃ᵚ])	
Imolese	['kẽ̝ː]	['eᵊzən]
Lughese	['kẽː]	['eᵊzən]
Ravennate	['kʎː]	['eᵊzən]
Milanese	['kɑ̃ː]	['aːzen]
Bergamese	['ka]	['aːzen]
Cairese	['kaŋ]	['ɐːzu][7]
	(< [kã̃ᵚ])	

In six dialects with historical or synchronic distinctive nasalization (Bolognese, Imolese, Lughese, Ravennate, Bergamese and Milanese), word-final /n#/, always preserved after atonic vowels, is regularly deleted after tonic vowels.[8] There is, furthermore, no evidence of significant contextual vowel nasalization in atonic /Vn#/ syllables in the same dialects. Loss of word-final atonic /n/ is restricted to Cairese in the sample, and is typical of Piedmont and Northern Liguria, eg. Piedmontese *frasu* < 'FRAXINU 'ash', *Stéu* < 'STEPHANU. The final oral vowel [u] is the result of secondary denasalization some time after final atonic N-deletion occurred (see below).

Additional confirmation of Schourup's Tonic ≫ Atonic parameter is found elsewhere. In Tuscan and Standard Italian final /n/ of Latin NO:N was lost in stressed phrase-final position, but preserved when phrasal unstressed, e.g. ['nɔ## ɛ 'mːiːo] 'No! It's mine' but [non ɛ 'mːiːo] 'It's not mine'. In German dialects, where deletion of word-final /n/ in stressed syllables is geographically quite widespread, deletion of word-final /n/ in unstressed syllables (e.g. Gmn '*Magen* 'stomach') seems to be limited to a smaller portion of the same region (Schirmunski 1962: 385–8). In some dialects, especially Swabian, earlier unstressed final [ən#] still appears as a nasal vowel [ə̃#]. In most others, secondary unstressed [ə̃#] has denasalized, even where tonic nasal vowels survive. Finally, markedly greater contextual nasalization of tonic 'VN$ syllables, relative to atonic ^VN$, is frequently

reported in Irish dialects, e.g. Holmer (1962: 63), de Búrca (1958: 58) and Breatnach (1947: 61).

4.2.2 Pretonic vs. post-tonic position

There is only limited evidence in my sample of a differential effect of pretonic and post-tonic syllable position on the development of distinctive nasalization. The evidence at 14 shows that in most sample dialects, i.e. Bergamese, Tavetschan, Bolognese, Imolese (and the remaining Romagnol dialects), there is no trace of phonologized contextual nasalization and N-deletion in atonic syllables, whether pretonic or post-tonic.

14	Pretonic		Post-tonic	
Bg.	*furmentù*	< FRUMEN'TONE 'corn'	*asen*	< 'ASINU 'donkey'
Im.	[kanta'ra]	< CANTARE + HABET 'he will sing'	[eᵊzən]	
Ta.	[kum'praː]	< COMPARARE 'to buy'	[aːzən]	
Bo.	[mun'taːɲa]	< MON'TANEA 'mountain'	[ɛːzen]	
Mi.	[mũn'taɲa]/ [mũ'taɲa]	< MON'TANEA 'mountain'	[aːzen]	
Ca.	[kaŋ'tɛ]	< CAN'TARE 'to sing'	[ɐːzu]	

However, whilst such an observation is correct for post-tonic syllables in Milanese, N-deletion, and to a lesser degree vowel nasalization, are optional in pretonic syllables in the same dialect. In Cairese the presence of syllable-final [ŋ] in pretonic (C)VN$ syllables is evidence of an earlier stage of pretonic nasalization and N-deletion, i.e. CAN'TARE > *[kãũ̃'tɛ] > [kaŋ'tɛ].[9] Final atonic [u] in Cairese [ɐːzu] for atonic [VN] found in other dialects is the result of a secondary denasalization of an intermediate distinctively nasal vowel, i.e. 'VCVN# > 'VCṼN# > 'VCṼ# > 'VCV#. Such denasalization of post-tonic /Vn#/ syllables in Cairese is indicative of the converse relationship nasalization/N-deletion and denasalization have with stress, also reported by Tuttle (1991). Unstressed syllables, the last to be affected by vowel nasalization and N-deletion, are, however, the first to be denasalized. The basis for such a claim lies in the evidence given previously in this chapter. First, whilst long vowels before N are preferentially nasalized, short nasal vowels, Ṽ, are relatively uncommon and prone to elimination. Second, as vowel duration is reduced, so is perceptibility of nasalization. Unlike stressed vowels, atonic vowels are usually short in Italian dialects, and hence an unstable locus for nasalization.[10] The same pattern of preferential atonic denasalization is noted elsewhere, e.g. Med. French (*effant* < IN'FANTE 'child',

covent < CON'VENTU), Breton and Old Icelandic (Schourup 1973: 192). In Standard Portuguese both stressed and unstressed nasal vowels appear, eg. [pẽw̃] < PANE 'bread', and *'hom*[ẽj] < 'HOMINE 'man'. However, in more colloquial varieties, especially those spoken in Brazil, optional denasalization occurs, but only of atonic nasal vowels, eg. *'hom*[ẽj] > *'hom*[ə] (Carvalho 1989; Votre 1981).

It is possible to extrapolate from the Milanese data at 14 in which there is pretonic nasalization and optional N-deletion (e.g. [mũntaɲa] ~ [mũtaɲa]), but no change to final unstressed VN (eg. [aːzen]) that pretonic and post-tonic VN were not affected by nasalization and denasalization processes at the same time in Cairese. By taking into account the distinction between pretonic and post-tonic, as well as developmental differences between tonic and atonic position in Northern Italian, we can very tentatively formulate an extended nasalization/stress parameter as follows:

15 Extended Stress Parameter (ESP)

$$\overrightarrow{\text{'VN }^{+}\text{VN }^{-}\text{VN}}$$

'V = stressed vowel
$^{+}$V = pretonic vowel
$^{-}$V = post-tonic vowel

According to the ESP, nasalization and N-deletion develop successively in a predictable manner, occurring first in tonic 'VN syllables, before spreading to pretonic unstressed $^{+}$VN syllables, and finally to post-tonic $^{-}$VN syllables. Conversely, vowel denasalization will be expected to spread gradually in the reverse direction from right to left along the same parameter.

With the aid of the ESP, we can now provide a detailed account seen at 16 of changes in Cairese:

16	CANE	INFERNU	ASINU	
Time	'dog'	'hell'	'donkey'	
1	/'kaːn/	/in'fern/	/'aːzin/	Stage 2
2	['kãːn]	[in'fern]	['aːzin]	tonic VNAS
3		[ĩn'fern]		pretonic VNAS
4			['aːzõn]	post-tonic VNAS
5	['kãː]			tonic N-DEL
6		[ĩ'fern]		pretonic N-DEL
7			['aːzã][11]	post-tonic N-DEL
8	['kãw̃]	[ĩw̃'fern]	['aːzãw]	gliding[12]
9			['aːzəw]	post-tonic DENAS
10	['kãŋ]	[ĩŋ'fern]		velarization
11		[iŋ'fern]		pretonic DENAS
12	['kaŋ]			tonic DENAS
13			['ɐːzu]	monophthongization

Once vowel nasalization (Time 2–4) and subsequent N-deletion (Time 5–7) had spread gradually to the different stress-governed contexts in Cairese, nasalized vowels were denasalized first in post-tonic /Vn#/ syllables. Tonic and pretonic vowels in Cairese continued to be nasalized, and were later affected by a process of velarization, whence the modern reflexes ['kaŋ] and [iŋ'fɛrn].

Whilst the spread of nasalization and N-deletion along the length of the extended parameter is evident in only one dialect in my sample, i.e. Cairese, the spread of distinctive nasalization along the length of the ESP is evident in many other Romance dialects outside Northern Italy, e.g. Portuguese, Galician, Gascon and French, as exemplified at 17:

17a Braz. Pt.[ẽ'kõtrãw̃]   < *IN'CONTRANT 'they meet' (Major 1985)
  b French [ʃãːt]   < 'CANTAT
    [ʃãːte]   < CAN'TARE
    [ʃãːt]   < [ʃãːtə] < *[ʃãːtə̃] < *[ʃãːtə̃t] < 'CANTANT[13]

In an attempt to verify the validity of the extended stress parameter outside the Northern Italian sample, developments in four Romance dialects known to delete intervocalic /n/, i.e. Portuguese, Galician, Gascon and Sardinian, were examined.[14] Words containing the sequence /-Vna-/, but with differing stress patterns relative to /Vn/, were collected and compared, as exemplified at 18. Sequences in question are underlined.

18 tonic[15]	'LANA	'wool'	'CENA	'dinner'
pretonic	SEMI'NARE	'to sow'	CE'NARE	'to dine'
post-tonic	'FEMINA	'woman'	'SABANA	'sheet'

In Portuguese, Galician and Gascon, there is evidence of the process of distinctive nasalization (i.e. vowel nasalization and N-deletion) once extending to all positions along the ESP. However, secondary denasalization is now extensive everywhere, and is almost complete in Gascon, cf. 19. In all three languages, distinctive nasalization survives best in tonic position, and tonic denasalization occurs largely in hiatus, e.g. Pt. *lã* < LANA 'wool', but *boa* < *bõa* < BONA 'good'(f.). Some confirmation of the need to distinguish between pretonic and post-tonic position along any stress parameter is found in Portuguese and Galician where denasalization appears to be significantly more frequent in the latter than in the former; see 19 (primary source: Fagan 1972):

19a tonic:
  Pt.   *lã* 'wool'   but *boa* < BONA 'good' (f.)
  Gal.   *la[ŋ], la*
  Gasc.   *la, lã, la[ŋ]*

b pretonic:
Pt.   *semear* 'to sow'   but *tendes* < TE'NETIS[16] 'have' (2 pl.)
Gal.   *semear*   but *canle* < CA'NALE[17] 'channel'
Gasc. *semiá*
       grè < GRA'NARIU 'granary'
c post-tonic:
Pt.   *fêmea* 'woman', *savaa* 'sheet'
Gal.   *femia, sava*
Gasc. *hemi, hémio*
       pàdio < 'PATINA 'shallow pan'

Much stronger support for the extended stress parameter is found in Sardinian: as expected, vowel nasalization and N-deletion are regular in tonic position, but substantially less widespread in pretonic position, and even less so post-tonically (Fagan 1972; Contini 1987: 454–8). Denasalization sometimes occurs post-tonically, and much less frequently in pretonic position, as at 20:

20a tonic:
Sard. ['lãː] 'wool', ['kẽːã] 'dinner'
b pretonic:
Sard. [ke'nai] 'dine'
but also [frõ'nesta] ~ [frõ'esta] < FE'NESTRA 'window'
c post-tonic:
Sard. ['femmĩna] ~ ['femmĩa] ~ ['femmja] 'woman'

The present-day absence of most Latin word-final nasals in synchronically non-nasalizing Romance dialects, such as Italian, also appears to be compatible with the Extended Stress Parameter. Examination of nasal reflexes in word-final position shows differences to be stress-conditioned:

21a -M# tonic: JAM#   > '*già*   'already'
     but atonic: CUM   > *con*   'with'
                  'CANEM   > *cane*   'dog'
b -N# tonic: NOːN#   > '*no*   'no'
   but atonic: NOːN   > *non* '*canta* 'doesn't sing'
                  IN   > *in*   'in'

Although examples of surviving tonic monosyllables are rare, the loss of the final nasal in monosyllables, as is evident in 21, is regular only in tonic syllables. In final atonic syllables, M survives as fully consonantal [n] in monosyllables. However, the complete loss of any sort of reflex for atonic final M# in Latin polysyllables suggests that secondary denasalization of final atonic Ṽ occurs preferentially in polysyllables.

In light of the Romance and non-Romance evidence in support of Schourup's Tonic ≫ Atonic parameter, and the extended stress parameter,

we are also able to now reassess the data referred to by Foley (1975, 1977) in support of his own version of the stress parameter. Foley's suggestion that N-deletion affected only unstressed syllables in Sanskrit and Ancient Greek is based solely on his interpretation of a limited set of orthographical data, examples of which are provided at 22 (1977: 60–1):

22a Sanskrit
    hathá (2 pl.) < *hanthá*, but *hánmi* (1 sg.)   'strike'
    baddhá (part.)   but *bandh*   'bind'
  b Ancient Greek
    épathon < *épenthon* 'I suffered' but *pénthos* 'lament'

However, if we accept the proposition, even if only tentatively, that the stress parameter found to govern developments in Romance can be said to apply in all languages unless proven otherwise, there is reason to suggest that distinctive nasalization occurred in both stressed and unstressed syllables in Sanskrit and Ancient Greek. At a later stage, unstressed nasalized vowels were denasalized. The appearance of orthographic nasal stops in stressed syllables, evident in Romanized forms, may be interpreted in one of three manners: (1) conservation of original nasal stops, per Foley (1975, 1977); (2) evidence of a later process of secondary N-epenthesis in nasalized syllables as has been suggested for Hindi (Manjari Ohala and Ohala 1991) and Portuguese (Ruhlen 1973); (3) a purely orthographic convention to represent nasal vowels, i.e. $VN = [\tilde{V}ː]$, as in French, e.g. *chante* [ʃɑ̃ːt] '(he) sings', *champ* [ʃɑ̃ː] 'field'.

There is support for the hypothesis that orthographic nasal stops, at least in Sanskrit, are used conventionally to represent something other than nasal stops. The traditional view is that they represent, at least at the phonetic level, distinctive vowel nasalization or a nasalized vocoid fragment, known as *anusvara* (Srivastava 1972, Trigo 1988). If this is the correct interpretation, then Foley's Sanskrit data is easily squared with the extended stress parameter, i.e. conservation of tonic nasalization, but atonic denasalization, e.g. ['hã̃ːmi] *hánmi*, but *hathá* < *[hã'tʰa]* < *hanthá*.

Closer examination of developments in Ancient Greek finds Foley to have been led astray by his superficial use of data. That stress is not a conditioning factor in the development of related *épathon* and *pénthos* given at (22b) can be seen when comparing related forms: *pásko:* 'I suffer' (< *pṇthsko:), alongside *pépontha* 'I have suffered'. In the former, a nasal consonant is apparently lost in a stressed syllable in apparent contrast to *pénthos*, but retained in an unstressed syllable in the other, again in contrast to *épathon*. More importantly, however, it should be pointed out that the original nasal contexts in the related forms *épathon* and *pénthos* are not in fact directly comparable. They have quite differently reconstructed nasals: in the former *a* is derived from an earlier Proto-Indo-European (PIE) syllabic nasal *ṇ, and in the latter the original PIE *en remains. And in each case the reflex is entirely

regular in Ancient Greek: syllabic nasals *n̩ and *m̩ appear as *a* in all syllables, stressed and unstressed. On the other hand, PIE sequences of V + N generally survive unaffected across all contents – regardless of stress patterning (Buck 1933). Lejeune (1947) reports loss of pre-consonantal N in some dialects of Ancient Greek, but the evidence he cites provides further evidence against Foley: Lejeune's examples appear to reflect loss in stressed syllables. In any case he suggests that N-loss is not a marker of distinctive nasalization, but of denasalization and secondary degemination, ie. NC > CC > C.

4.2.3 *Explaining the Tonic ≫ Atonic stress parameter*

The Vowel Length Parameter that was found to govern the development of distinctive nasalization in tonic/stressed syllables has a phonetic parallel in stress-related patterning. Schourup's Tonic ≫ Atonic parameter found to regulate the development of distinctive nasalization in Northern Italian and elsewhere, appears to have its basis in stress-conditioned durational differences. That is, vowel nasalization (and later N-deletion) appears to develop preferentially in the context of phonetically longer tonic vowel 'V + N, before spreading to phonetically shorter atonic vowel ^V + N. This observation is in line with experimental evidence already discussed in this chapter in which the perception by listeners of contextual nasalization appears to be favoured by increasing phonetic vowel length. An increased ability on the part of the listener to perceive such nasalization would then, in accordance with the articulo-perceptual model of sound change, favour its reinterpretation by the listener as intended, and therefore, phonological. A direct

Table 4.1   Mean Tonic vs. Atonic Length in Milliseconds

	'V	^V	Ratio	Subj. No.
Arg. Sp.	86.6	57	1.52	4
Italian	207	103	2.0	3
	'σ	^σ	Ratio	Subj. No.
English	300	140	2.14	1
Swedish	290	125	2.32	1
French	220	130	1.69	1
Braz. Pt. (1)[18]	219	125	1.7	1
Braz. Pt. (2)[19]	243	136	1.79	3

Sources: Argentinian Spanish (Borzone and Signorini 1983: 120), Italian (Vogel 1982: 39), English, French, and Swedish (Fant et al. 1991a, b); Brazilian Portuguese (Major 1981: 346). Figures for Brazilian Portuguese are rounded to the nearest millisecond.

correlation between relative accentual prominence and phonetic vowel (and syllable) length is well known. Durational measurements from different languages are consistent in showing unstressed vowels (and syllables) to be phonetically much shorter than their stressed counterparts, as in table 4.1.

Whilst, in the case of Borzone and Signorini's study of Argentinian Spanish, only non-prepausal vowel duration was examined, a similar tonic/atonic correlation is reported for Castilian Spanish (Carrió i Font and Ríos Mestre 1991) and Catalan (Recasens 1991) across all contexts.

Isochronic type, i.e. stress-timing vs. syllable-timing, appears not to affect the general correlation between reduced duration and atonic vowels and syllables. The substantial divergence in tonic vs. atonic vowel and syllable length is apparent in both so-called stress-timed languages (e.g. English, Swedish) and syllable-timed languages (e.g. Italian, French, Spanish, Catalan). Compression of unstressed vowel duration is of course to be expected in so-called stress-timed languages: since stress is thought to occur at regular intervals, an increase in the number of intertonic syllables should lead to greater atonic reduction. However, the same result is not expected in syllable-timed languages in which syllables – regardless of stress-type – are thought to appear at regular intervals without a compressive effect on atonic duration.[20]

Table 4.2   Mean Pretonic, Tonic and Post-Tonic Syllable Length for the Nonsense Token [la'lala] in Milliseconds (ms.) in Brazilian Portuguese

Subj. No.	Durations (ms.)			Std Dev. (ms.)			Token No.
	$^+\sigma_1$	$'\sigma_2$	$^-\sigma_3$	$^+\sigma_1$	$'\sigma_2$	$^-\sigma_3$	
S1	148	240	99	17	25	18	30
S2	168	235	125	22	30	19	17
S3	164	255	111	20	26	17	38
S1–3	160	243	112				85

Durational Ratios	$'\sigma_2/^+\sigma_1$	$'\sigma_2/^-\sigma_3$	$^+\sigma_1/^-\sigma_3$
S1	1.62	2.42	1.50
S2	1.40	1.88	1.34
S3	1.55	2.30	1.48
S1–3	1.52	2.18	1.43

Levels of significance: mean durations between all syllables (for each speaker) are significant to > 0.01. Source: Major 1985: 261.

Similar experimental evidence also exists in support of the refinement of the original Tonic ≫ Atonic parameter into the Extended Stress Parameter (ESP). Measurements taken by Major (1985), and further supported by Major (1981), of syllable length in Brazilian Portuguese indicate a marked correlation between tonic/pretonic/post-tonic stress-type and syllable (and vowel) duration, at least in that language. As the figures in table 4.2 show, for all speakers tonic syllable duration was substantially greater than for all other syllable types and the duration of pretonic syllables was much longer than that of post-tonic syllables. Since the duration of the same syllable-initial consonant, /l/, was found to be fairly constant across contexts, vowel and syllable duration run in tandem.

If phonetic differences in relative vowel length do have an effect on the perception, and, therefore, on the phonologization of vowel nasalization (and consequently therefore on later N-deletion), then the ESP is consistent with relative vowel and syllable duration according to stress position, as at 23a and b:

23a Relative Duration   Tonic Pretonic Post-Tonic
                                ⎯⎯⎯⎯⎯⎯⎯⎯⎯⎯⎯⎯⎯⎯⎯⎯⎯⎯⎯⎯⟶

  b ESP   Tonic Pretonic Post-Tonic
                                ⎯⎯⎯⎯⎯⎯⎯⎯⎯⎯⎯⎯⎯⎯⎯⎯⎯⎯⎯⎯⟶

  c Relative Prominence   Tonic Pretonic Post-Tonic
                                ⎯⎯⎯⎯⎯⎯⎯⎯⎯⎯⎯⎯⎯⎯⎯⎯⎯⎯⎯⎯⟶

The parameters at 23a and b also appear to reflect the relative degree of prominence of tonic, pretonic and post-tonic position, at least in Brazilian Portuguese, as noted at 23c. Major (1985) found native speaker intuitions resulted in predictable assignment of primary prominence to the tonic, secondary prominence to the pretonic, and absence of any prominence to the post-tonic syllable. In addition to predictable differences in duration and relative prominence, Major found post-tonic syllables had the lowest syllable weight, and were most prone to vowel reduction processes. Finally, the tendency in Brazilian Portuguese towards preferential denasalization of final post-tonic nasal vowels has already been reported, e.g. [oméj̃] > [omᵊ] 'man'.

Should the relationship in duration and prominence between the two atonic positions (pretonic and post-tonic) be found to be reversed in some languages, then we might expect that, if the atonic spread of distinctive nasalization is sensitive to duration, it would be favoured in post-tonic, rather than pretonic, contexts in these languages. Where the atonic timing relationship is shown to be reversed, an additional and competing ESP with a different relative ordering of pretonic and post-tonic positions may need to be posited to account for developments in such languages. Although I have found no convincing evidence to date that the timing relationship between pretonic and post-tonic vowels and syllables is reversed in some languages, further investigation is clearly required.[21] It is possible that the suggested

phonetic basis of the ESP reflects the type of syllable organization expected in languages with so-called left-headed feet, such as Latin, most of its daughters, as well as English and Swedish. In other languages where stress position tends to the right end of the word (so-called right-headed), patterns of syllable organization and compression (and hence the spread of distinctive nasalization) could plausibly be different. We might expect in these languages greater temporal compression of pretonic than of post-tonic syllables. Were this hypothesis to be confirmed, our ability to account for stress-conditioning universally is not diminished. Our expectation is that each ESP variant would apply only to languages with a particular foothead-edness and related pattern of syllable compression.[22]

4.3 Distinctive Nasalization and the Stress Foot

The limited universalist interest in the 1970s in suprasegmental or prosodic conditioning of the development of distinctive nasalization reflects the essentially (sub-)segmental orientation of phonological theory of the time. As a result, universalists restricted themselves largely to what was then the still relatively controversial notion of the syllable boundary ($), and to a rather general discussion of stress-related conditioning. Since that time, phonological theory has come to incorporate as integral a highly developed suprasegmental structure, including stress-conditioned organization of syllables into feet.

Very conveniently for our purposes, we are able to determine foot-level conditioning of sound change in Romance: words in Latin (and Romance for that matter) are traditionally divided into three categories according to syllable-stress placement counting from the rightmost word-boundary:

24a	word-final	$'\sigma\#$	$'$JAM	'already'
	(oxytone)		$'$NO:N	'no'
b	penultimate	$'\sigma\ \sigma\#$	$'$LANA	'wool'
	(paroxytone)		$'$VINU	'wine'
c	antepenultimate	$'\sigma\ \sigma\ \sigma\#$	$'$ASINU	'donkey'
	(proparoxytone)		$'$ANIMA	'soul'

Stress position determines the length of the accentual domain known as the *foot* (Durand 1990; Goldsmith 1990 for details). In current phonological representation, syllables (σ) are of course not the highest prosodic constituent, but are themselves organized by the foot (Σ), and the highest word-based constituent, the phonological word (w). Only one stressed or strong syllable appears in each foot, and is automatically placed in a parametric fashion at the left or right boundary of the foot. In Latin and generally in Romance (with the exception of French) all feet are left-headed, i.e. the stressed syllable appears to the left, as at 25. The foot may in addition be

bounded or unbounded, i.e. always contain the same fixed number or contain any number of syllables respectively. Since only one stressed, i.e. strong, syllable is permitted per foot, length of the foot is determined by the number of unstressed weak syllables. Whilst the foot is technically unbounded in Latin and Romance, in practice the number of permissible post-tonic weak syllables before the word-boundary varies from zero to two. As a result, feet may be mono-, bi-, or maximally trisyllabic:

25a oxytone   b paroxytone   c proparoxytone

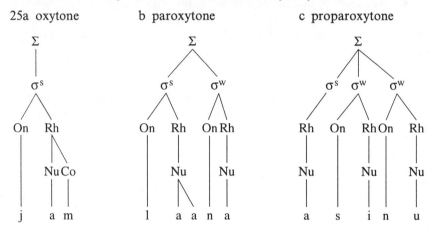

σ = syllable   Σ = foot

^{s} = strong (i.e. stressed) ^{w} = weak (i.e. unstressed)

Pretonic syllables located to the left of the Latin stressed syllable are not incorporated into the left-headed stress-foot, e.g. IMPOR'TANTE. According to Nespor and Vogel (1986: 89), atonic syllables outside the stress foot form their own foot without a strong element, as at (26):

26

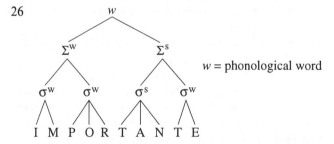

w = phonological word

Nespor and Vogel's suggestion that pretonic syllables can form their own, albeit weak, foot, appears to fall in line both with: (1) claims made by Major (1985) that they bear some stress, in contrast to the completely stress-free nature of post-tonic syllables; and (2) the Extended Stress Parameter which places the pretonic between the tonic and post-tonic in behaviour.

4.3.1 *Oxytones, paroxytones and proparoxytones*

I noted in section 2.2.2.1 that the predictable distribution of vowel length found in paroxytones, that resulted from changes to the Latin vowel system, was disrupted – at least before nasals – by phonologized proparoxytonic open syllable shortening in many dialects of Northern and Southern Italy: the modern reflexes of proparoxytonic vowels in open syllables are typically the same as those of short vowels in closed syllables, e.g. Bo. [leːna] < 'LANA 'wool', but [aːnma] < 'ANIMA 'soul', [aːnum] < 'ANIMU 'spirit' like [aːn] < 'ANNU 'year', [tajla] < 'TELA 'cloth', but [pavver] < 'PIPERE 'pepper', [tatta] < *'TITTA 'teat'.[23]

The distribution of stress feet found in Latin underwent some alteration as a result of the Stage 2 sound changes posited for Northern Italian. Stage 2 final vowel loss led to the restructuring of paroxytonic and proparoxytonic words not ending in /a/, as oxytonic and paroxytonic respectively; see 27:

27 'σ σ σ#	'σ σ#	'σ#	
UMIDA			'humid' (f. s.)
UMIDU >	/umid/		'humid' (m. s.)
ANIMU >	/anim/		'soul'
	CANE >	/kaːn/	'dog'
	ANNU >	/an/	'year'
	TANTU >	/tant/	'so' (m. s.)
	TANTA		'so' (f. s.)
	LANA		'wool'
		NOːN	'no'
		JAM	'already'

As a result of restructuring, earlier foot-governed differences in vowel length are now contrastive, e.g. LANA 'wool' > Stage 2 /'laːna/ but ANIMU 'spirit' > Stage 2 /'anim/. Such vowel length differences are seen below in section 4.3.3 to influence the spread of distinctive nasalization processes in Northern Italian in line with the VLP.

In more innovative Northern Italian dialects, such as Bolognese and Romagnol, surviving proparoxytones and secondary paroxytones were normally further reduced by additional post-tonic vowel deletion, e.g. 'UMIDA 'humid' (f.) > Bo. [omːda], 'MANICU 'sleeve' > Bo. [maːndg], 'STOMACHU 'stomach' > Im. [stonk], Bo. [stamːg]. Elsewhere in Northern Italy, historical proparoxytones in final /a/ generally survive as such, e.g. UMIDA > Mi., Ca. /'ymida/, Bg. *ömeda* (Rohlfs 1966: 172).

4.3.2 *Oxytonic distinctive nasalization*

There were few N-final oxytones in Latin, of which an even smaller number passed into Northern Italian, e.g. NOːN, and JAM.[24] It is evident, however,

that oxytonic final N in these forms was lost very early, i.e. Stage 1, since nowhere in the Romance-speaking area does the original nasal ordinarily survive intact, as at 28:[25]

28	JAM	NO:N[26]
Ta.	[ɟjeː]	—
Bg.	[za]	[nɔ]
Mi.	[dʒa]	[nɔ]
Bo.	[dza]	[na]
Ra.	[za]	[nɔ]
It.	[dʒa]	[nɔ]
Sp.	[ja]	[no]
Fr.	dé[ʒa]	[nɔ̃ː]
Pt.	[ʒa]	[nẽw̃]
Gasc.	[ʒa]	[nu]

Of course, the New V-NAS model (NVM) predicts that oxytonic N-deletion was preceded by an intermediate stage of phonologized vowel nasalization, i.e. NO:N > Stage 2 /non/ > *[nõn] > [nõ]. However, if the Vowel Length Parameter (VLP) has always operated in Northern Italian in the same restrictive fashion as it appears to now, then one must also assume that oxytonic vowels were first phonologically lengthened before any nasalization-related process developed, i.e. NO:N > Stage 2 /non/ > *[noːn] > [nõːn] > [nõː].[27] There is some evidence of this suggested oxytonic lengthening persisting in many areas, including western varieties of Romance such as Portuguese, e.g. NO:N > Pt. [nẽw̃] and Fr. [nɔ̃ː]. The lengthening before final N appears to be part, at least for French, of a process affecting all closed monosyllables, including items with an original Latin short vowel, such as TRES > O. Fr. [trejs] *treis,* and MEL > Fr. *miel* (Fouché 1958). Lengthening also survives in large parts of Northern and Southern Italy, eg. Ticinese Lombard [nɔː] ~ [nuː] (AIS IV 841), and JAM > Ta. [ɟjeː], Altamurese [dʒeʲ] (Loporcaro 1988: 46). In Engadine Romantsch, a close relative of Tavetschan and also spoken close to the Italian-Swiss border, we find conditioned lengthening before final nasals, e.g. stressed ['suːn] < SUM, but normally unstressed [kun] < CUM (Schneider 1968: 195). As noted below in section 4.3.6, generalized oxytonic lengthening before final consonants (nasal and oral), as in French, appears to be widespread in Romantsch, including Tavetschan.

Denasalization of oxytonic/stressed monosyllabic nasal vowels followed in most places, and in many parts of Italy and most of the sample, oxytonic oral vowels in open syllables were subjected to a typologically unusual shortening process, e.g. *[nõː] > *[noː] > *[nɔ] > Bo. [na].[28] The Tavetschan reflex [ɟjeː] of JAM is the only example in the sample of a surviving lengthened vowel, but this survival is not unexpected, given that the language in question is the phonologically most conservative member.

A glance at the typical sample data at 29 may give the impression that secondary oxytones and surviving paroxytones do not differ, at least superficially, with regard to the development of distinctive nasalization.

29 Bg.   *ca* [kaː]   < *[kãː]   < Stage 2 /kaːn/ < CANE 'dog'
            tat [taːt]   < *[tãːt]   /tant/ < TANTU 'so'
            tata [taːta] < *[tãːta]   /tanta/ < TANTA 'so'

In some circumstances, however, factors known to affect the development of distinctive nasalization are favoured in oxytonic position, e.g. historical vowel length differences, tautosyllabicity, and non-cluster position, as the wider range of Bergamese data at 30 demonstrate:

30 Bg.   *bu*   [buː]   < Stage 2 /bɔːn$/   < BONU   'good' (m.)
    but   *buna* [buːna] <   /bɔː$na/   < BONA   'good' (f.)
            an   [aːn]   <   /an/   < ANNU   'year'
            grand [grant] <   /grand/   < GRANDE 'big'

In the closely related, but more conservative, Lombard dialect of Salò, evidence of distinctive nasalization (and subsequent denasalization, i.e. ṼːN > Ṽː > Vː) in original Latin paroxytones is restricted to only second-ary oxytonic /Vːn#/, e.g. Salodiano *ca* 'dog', *bu* 'good' (m. s), but *tant* 'so' (m.), *tanta* 'so' (f.), *buna* 'good' (f.), *an* 'year', *grant* 'big' (Razzi 1984).

4.3.3. *Proparoxytonic (antepenultimate) vs. paroxytonic (penultimate) position*

There is evidence within the sample that the development of distinctive nasalization is disfavoured in proparoxytones. In Bergamese, evidence of earlier distinctive nasalization and later denasalization, found in the oxytonic and paroxytonic reflexes of Latin paroxytones, does not extend to the new paroxytonic and surviving proparoxytonic reflexes of Latin proparoxytones:

31 Bg.   [teːp] < *[tẽːp] < /temp/   < TEMPU   'time'
         [kaːp] < *[kãːp] < /kamp/   < CAMPU   'field'
         [taːta] < *[tãːta] < /tanta/   < TANTA   'so' (f.)
    but   ['tɛmpra]   < /'tempera/ < 'TEMPERAT   'tempers'
         ['lampeda]   < /'lampada/ < 'LAMPADA   'lamp'
         ['sɛntola]   < /'ʧentula/ < 'CINCTU+ULA   'belt'

In Bolognese, evidence of nasalization and subsequent hardening of nasalized glides before intervocalic /n/ is restricted to historical paroxytones. In surviving proparoxytones, tonic vowels before intervocalic /n₁/ are pre-dictably short, blocking the spread of nasalization. Secondary gemination after tonic short vowels, normal in Bolognese, then follows:

32 Bo.　['loŋna]　< ['lõw̃na]　< 'LUNA 'moon'
　　　　　['veŋna]　< ['vẽjna]　< 'VENA 'vein'
　　　　　['veŋ]　　< ['vẽj]　　< 'VINU 'wine'
　but　　['onneka] < */'unika/ < 'UNICA 'unique' (f.)
　　　　　['onnek]　< */'unik/　< 'UNICU 'unique' (m.)[29]

Absence of so-called 'intervocalic' nasalization in historical proparoxytones
is reported elsewhere in Northern Italy, e.g. in Piacentino where the short
proparoxytonic tonic vowel, in line with the operation of the VLP in
Northern Italian, has blocked the spread of vowel nasalization even in
secondary paroxytones, as seen at 33 (Gorra 1890).

33　Piacentino
　　s[aː]　　　< St. 2 /'saːn/　< 'SANU 'healthy' (m.)
　　s[aː]na　　<　　　/'saːna/　< 'SANA 'healthy' (f.)
　　g[aː]mba <　　< /'gamba/ < *GAMBA 'leg'
but ánaz　　　<　　　/'anitʃ/　< 'ANISU 'aniseed'
　　mánag　　<　　　/'manig/ < 'MANICU 'handle'
　　mánga　　<　　　/'maniga/ < 'MANICA 'sleeve'

As the reflexes of *GAMBA and MANICA demonstrate, a distinction between
original and secondary paroxytones in Piacentino is still evident in the
presence of strong contextual nasalization of lengthened vowels before
clusters in the former but not in the latter where vowels remain short. A
similar pattern is reported for Val Graveglia Ligurian, where the appearance
of secondary [ŋ] as a marker of an earlier stage of vowel nasalization is found
only in paroxytones with expected long vowels, e.g. /'laŋa/ < ['laŋna] <
['lãũ̃na] < ['lãːna] < 'LANA 'wool', in contrast to /'manega/ 'sleeve' <
/'maniga/ < 'MANICA 'handle' (Plomteux 1975). Unusually, in the neighbouring Ligurian dialect of Genoa proparoxytonic /a/ was apparently never
shortened, or at least relengthened very early on. As a result, alongside
expected /'laŋa/ < ['lãŋna] < *['lãːna] < 'LANA, we find evidence of proparoxytonic nasalization: /'aŋnima/ < *['ãːnima] < 'ANIMA 'soul' (Parodi 1902:
352).

4.3.4　A possible Foot Parameter

On the basis of developments in the sample dialects, and in other Northern
Italian dialects referred to above, it appears possible to formulate in a tentative
fashion a foot-governed parameter of distinctive nasalization, as at 34:

34　A Foot Parameter

　　'σ#　'σ σ#　'σ σ σ#
　　─────────────────→

According to 34, nasalization will be phonologized first on oxytone vowels

before N, subsequently on penultimate stressed vowels and then last on antepenultimate stressed vowels. The spread of N-deletion will follow nasalization in a similar fashion: it occurs first after oxytonic nasalized vowels, subsequently after paroxytonic nasalized vowels, and only last after proparoxytonic nasalized vowels.

Confirmation that operation of the Foot Parameter is not restricted to Northern Italian is found in other Romance dialects. Even in the most conservative varieties, N-deletion and denasalization in stressed monosyllables occurred long ago, eg. Std It. and Corsican [nɔ] < NON, [dʒa] < JAM. In Corsican a current process of vowel nasalization and optional intervocalic /n/-deletion is found only in paroxytones and does not as yet extend to proparoxytones, e.g. [lãː(n)a] < LANA 'wool' but ['annema] ~ ['anema] < ANIMA 'soul'.

Similarly, in Sardinian, regular intervocalic /n/-deletion in paroxytones, is much less frequent in proparoxytones, e.g. 'MANU > ['mãw̃] 'hand', but DO'MINICA > [du'miniɣa] 'Sunday' (Contini 1987: 455). In the more innovative Romance dialects, Portuguese, Galician and Gascon, both paroxytones and proparoxytones are equally affected by historical nasalization and N-deletion; see 35 (Fagan 1972):

35 'LUNA   > *[lũːna]   > [lũːã] > Pt.   *lua*   'moon'
                                         Gal   *lua*
                                         Gasc   *luwe, lũo, luo*
   'GENERU   > *[dʒẽer]   >   OGasc.   *gier*   'son-in-law'
   CA'NONICU > *[kãõigo] >   OPt./OGal. *cooigo* 'canon'

4.3.5 *An explanation for the Foot Parameter*

Like both the Tonic ≫ Atonic Parameter and the more evolved Extended Stress Parameter, the nature of the Foot Parameter can be related to predictable differences in phonetic vowel length, and the effect such differences are thought to have on perception of contextual vowel nasalization. Durational measurements, given in table 4.3, exemplify the correlation between foot-type and tonic vowel length reported to exist in many languages.

Oxytonic vowels are found in table 4.3 to be phonetically much longer than similar paroxytonic and proparoxytonic vowels. This pattern of oxytonic shortening, confirmed by available experimental evidence, is widely reported across languages, including German, Swedish, Dutch, Hungarian, Spanish, Lappish, and Polish (Fischer-Jørgensen 1982, Toledo 1989, Richter 1987). The correlation extends beyond tonic vowel length to tonic syllable length. Phonological evidence of oxytonic lengthening in modern French is also reported (Morin 1986). It is not unexpected, therefore, that vowel nasalization and N-deletion should develop preferentially in

Table 4.3 Foot-Related Tonic Vowel Length Measurements in Milliseconds and Relative Ratios in Two Languages

a	Oxy.	Par.	Prop.	Subj. No.
Tamil[30]	243.6	185.2	152.2	4
English	204.0	105.0	97.0	6

b	Oxy./Par.	Oxy./Prop.	Par./Prop.	Subj. No.
Tamil	1.32	1.60	1.27	4
English	1.94	2.10	1.08	6

Sources: Tamil (Balasubramanian 1981: 157); English (Fowler 1981: 42).

the context of oxytones, in accordance with the VLP, and with experimental findings of sensitivity in the perception of nasality to phonetic vowel length differences. Similarly, that paroxytones were found to be a more favourable locus for the development of nasalization, and successive N-deletion, than proparoxytones may be determined by the relative phonetic length of the former.

The same cumulative compressive effect of post-tonic syllables is not restricted to the phonetic length of tonic vowels, but extends to the whole tonic syllable. As such, tonic syllable compression has been amply reported to occur in a statistically significant fashion across languages, e.g. Brazilian Portuguese (Major 1981: 347), Argentinian Spanish (Toledo 1989), Catalan (Recasens 1991), Swedish, Dutch (Vayra 1989: 74–5) and English (Hoequist 1983).

The formulation of the Foot Parameter at 34 appears to be adequate for both stress- and syllable-timed languages. Hypothetically, only stress-timed languages should be characterized by a post-tonic compressive effect in an effort to regularize inter-stress intervals. In syllable-timed languages, syllables are expected to be regularly spaced. However, such a hypothesis is disconfirmed by reports of statistically significant tonic compression even in these languages, e.g. Spanish (Toledo 1989), and Catalan (Recasens 1991).

Toledo (1989: 212) also provides figures showing foot-governed compression to be absent in mora-timed languages, such as Japanese.[31] If this is the case, then there may be no need to posit some sort of Foot Parameter to account for the development of distinctive nasalization in these languages. However, further investigation is required.

Finally, the effect of left- vs. right-headed feet on tonic compression also needs to be investigated. All the languages referred to above (English, Tamil, Brazilian Portuguese, Argentinian Spanish, Catalan, Swedish, Dutch), with

the exception of mora-timed Japanese, may be characterized as left-headed. Whilst anticipatory tonic compression is regular, pretonic syllables show little compressive effect on stressed syllables (Vayra 1989; Lindblom and Rapp 1973; Fowler 1981). In languages with right-headed feet, the compressive effect may be reversed in direction, i.e. pretonic rather than post-tonic syllables may be expected to have the greatest compressive effect on tonic vowels and syllables. If this is the case, and historical developments are found to correlate with this phonetic hypothesis, an additional Foot Parameter may also need to be formulated for right-headed languages. We might expect distinctive nasalization to develop preferentially in proparoxytones and oxytonic monosyllables, rather than plurisyllabic oxytones and paroxytones. Unfortunately, the matter must be left to future investigation, as I have no experimental evidence at present with which to test the hypothesis.

The possible influence of foot structure on the perception of contextual nasalization has not to date been specifically addressed in experimental research. Therefore, the hypothesis made here, that an observed historical correlation between foot length and the development of distinctive nasalization derives from a suggested correlation between relative vowel duration and the perception of contextual nasalization (see section 4.1.4), remains somewhat tentative. The claim is of course consistent with available experimental evidence, but requires further investigation.

4.3.6 Oxytonic vowels in Italy: long or short?

The cross-linguistic evidence that oxytonic vowels are markedly longer phonetically than paroxy- and proparoxytonic vowels, as well as the claim made previously in section 4.3.2 that pre-nasal oxytonic vowels may have been lengthened in Romance, is in apparent conflict with the frequent observation that primary oxytonic vowels are short – both phonetically and phonologically – in parts of Northern and Centro-Southern Italy, e.g. PLUS > It. ['pju], Bo. ['pjo] 'more', alongside LACUS > It. [laːgo], Bo. [lɛːg] 'lake' (Rohlfs 1966: 24–5; Vincent 1988c). However, the experimental evidence for Standard Italian given in table 4.4 is not conclusive. Vogel (1982: 39) found oxytonic vowels to be relatively short. Conversely, Toledo (1989: 212), based on Vayra et al. (1984: 543), found expected foot-related differences, whilst Vayra (1989) reports major inter-speaker variation.

The contradictory findings reflect the instability of oxytonic vowel length in Standard Italian. Lengthening of oxytonic short vowels is optional and is particularly common in Northern, but also some Central and Southern, varieties of Italian (Trumper et al. 1991; Camilli 1965; Nespor and Vogel 1979).[32] The apparent source of short oxytonic vowels in Italian and Northern Italian dialects is pre-pausal glottalization of open syllables reported to occur in some varieties of spoken Italian, as well as Northern

Table 4.4   Tonic Vowel Length in Open Syllables in Milliseconds and Relative Ratios in Italian

	Oxy.	Par.	Prop.	Subj. No.
Toledo[34]	274	236	196	1
Vogel	113	207	—	3
Vayra 1	183	268	219	1
Vayra 2	159	234	180	1
Vayra 3	244	264	180	1

	Oxy./Par.	Oxy./Prop.	Par./Prop.	Subj. No.
Toledo	1.16	1.40	1.20	1
Vogel	0.55	—	—	3
Vayra 1	0.68	0.84	1.49	1
Vayra 2	0.68	0.88	1.47	1
Vayra 3	0.92	1.36	1.47	1

Sources: Toledo (1989), Vogel (1982), Vayra et al. (1984).

Italian, and known to reduce vowel length in languages, e.g. [da$^{(?)}$] '(he) gives' (Trumper et al. 1991; Vayra 1989, 1991).[33]

In any case, oxytonic shortening appears to be a relatively recent phenomenon restricted to open syllables. We see at 36a and b that the results for historical oxytones, and unexpected secondary open-syllable oxytones, in Italian and Northern Italian converge. Expected long oral vowels normally appear as short when in open final position.

36a It.   [la]   < [IL]LAC 'there'
           [ʧit'ta] < /ʧit'taːde/   < CIVI'TATE 'city'
           expected: *[ʧit'taːde]
           [kan'tɔ] < [kan'tao]   < CAN'TAVIT '(he) sang'

  b Bo.   [la]   < [IL]LAC 'there'
           [a'za]   < Stage 2 /aʧeːd/ < ACETU 'vinegar'
           expected: *[a'zajd]
           cf.   ['sajd] < Stage 2 /seːd/   < SITE 'thirst'

  c Ta.   [ple]   < Stage 2 /plus/ < PLUS   'more'
           [te]   < /tuː/   < TU 'you (s.)'
      but [noːs]   < /nos/   < NOS 'us'
           [trajs]   < /tres/   < TRES 'three'
      and [ɟjeː]   < JAM 'already'

Where consonant-final oxytones survive, as in Tavetsch at 36c, and Romantsch in general, Stage 2 short tonic vowels have undergone regular lengthening (Rupp 1963 and Schneider 1968). I have suggested previously in section 4.3.2 that a similar phenomenon may have occurred in Northern Italian, and elsewhere, in nasal-final oxytones, so that NO:N > Stage 2 /non/ > *[noːn], if not simply always preserved /noːn/ from NO:N.

4.3.7 *Proparoxytonic vowel length*

Experimental evidence demonstrating the relative shortness of proparoxytonic vowels in Italian (table 4.4) and elsewhere (table 4.3) finds confirmation in the characteristic treatment of such vowels throughout much of Italy as phonologically short in terms of permissible syllable and word structure (see section 4.3.1, Vincent 1988c; Repetti 1989; Coco 1970; Loporcaro 1988). In all sample members, with the partial exception of Tavetschan, the development of proparoxytonic vowels in open syllables generally coincides with that of short tonic vowels in paroxytonic (and proparoxytonic) closed syllables, cf. section 4.3.1, as the Bolognese examples, repeated at 37, make clear:

37 Bo.   ['dabbel] < Stage 2 ['debil]   < 'DE:BILE 'weak'
   cf.   ['tatta] < ['teta]   < *'TITTA 'teat'
           ['vaskuv] < [e'beskov]   < E'PISCOPU 'bishop'
   but   ['tajla] < ['teːla]   < 'TE:LA   'cloth'

In Standard Italian and Tuscan, proparoxytonic and paroxytonic vowels in open syllables are described as predictably phonologically long. However, as Vincent (1988c) notes, divergent historical development is indicative of phonetic vowel compression in proparoxytones, confirmed by durational measurements given above at table 4.4. Expected open syllable diphthongization of long vowels is normally blocked in proparoxytones, e.g. PEDE > Stage 1 ['peːde] > ['pjɛde] 'foot', but 'PECORA > Stage 1 and It. ['pɛːkora] instead of expected *['pjɛkora] 'sheep'. Indeed the figures suggest that they are in fact phonetically (and arguably phonologically) short. This claim is entirely consistent with my own fieldwork observations that antepenultimate vowels in Tuscan, and Standard Italian are preceptually quite often very short, i.e. ['pɛkora] or at the most only half-lengthened, i.e. ['pɛˑkora], rather than fully lengthened ['pɛːkora] as traditionally described in the absence of experimental data.[35] This proparoxytonic vowel length reduction sometimes interacts with a regular phonotactic constraint against short tonic vowels in non-final open syllables, thereby triggering sporadic secondary gemination of the post-tonic consonant, e.g. ['fabbrica] < 'FABRICA 'factory', ['pillola] < PILULA 'pill' (Repetti 1989: 23–5). Elsewhere, in some parts of Central and Southern Italy, but also in the North, such secondary gemination is more advanced, although not usually regular. However,

complete generalization to other historical proparoxytones is not unknown, e.g. Senigalliese ['stuppidǝ] < 'STUPIDU 'stupid', ['unnikǝ] < 'UNICU 'unique' (m.) and Bolognese semi-learned ['ommida] < 'UMIDA 'humid' (f.).[36]

The phonological effect of phonetic vowel compression in proparoxytones is not unique to Italian dialects, and is well-known in English as Trisyllabic Shortening, e.g. *divine* [dɪvajn] vs. *divinity* [dɪvɪnɪtɪ], *serene* vs. *serenity* (Durand 1990: 114–15; Goldsmith 1990: 246).

4.4 CONCLUSIONS

In this chapter, factor-specific effects on the development of distinctive nasalization were examined in detail for the first time. Initial results are promising, and seem to indicate that prosodic phenomena, such as vowel length, presence and absence of stress, and stress-foot length, may have a universally predictable effect over time. No credible counter-examples have been found to date to disprove the universal applicability of the Vowel Length Parameter (VLP), the Foot Parameter, Schourup's Tonic ≫ Atonic stress parameter, and the more evolved Extended Stress Parameter (ESP). Formulations remain tentative, nevertheless, and require further cross-linguistic verification. In particular, it was suggested that differences in timing type (stress, syllable and mora), as well in foot structure (left-headed and right-headed) may affect the development of distinctive nasalization. Suggested parameters may have to be modified or additional parameters formulated accordingly, should different effects be reported.

The particularly strict manner of operation of the VLP in Northern Italian, and elsewhere, that is, distinctive nasalization in the context of tonic vowels develops only when the vowel is phonologically long, is unexpected, but is shown in the following chapters to have important ramifications in other contexts not discussed in this chapter. Given the operation of the 'restricted' VLP in Northern Italian, there has been no need to this point to refer to any process of Compensatory Lengthening to account for the length of word-final nasal vowels, e.g. Mi. [kɑ̃ː] < /kaːn/ < CANE 'dog'. More unexpected is the finding that vowel duration effects may also account for the formulation of the Foot Parameter, Schourup's Tonic ≫ Atonic parameter, and the ESP.

5

VOWEL HEIGHT, VOWEL QUALITY AND THE DEVELOPMENT OF DISTINCTIVE NASALIZATION

5.1 INTRODUCTION

5.1.1 *Universalists and vowel height*

Whilst details differ, universalists Schourup (1973: 192), Lightner (1973), Chen (1972 and elsewhere), Ruhlen (1973), Foley (1975, 1977) and Hombert (1986, 1987) are in general agreement that vowel height has the same ordered effect on the phonologization of vowel nasalization and/or N-deletion. That is, the development of some or all parts of the distinctive nasalization process occurs preferentially in the context of low vowels before spreading gradually to mid and then finally to high vowels in pre-nasal position, as in 1a.[1] Opinion is divided, however, as to whether the Vowel Height Parameter (VHP) also interacts with a Front vs. Back Parameter as in 1b:

1a Vowel Height Parameter (VHP)

low mid high

b a o u   a e o i u
  e i
(Foley)   (Ruhlen)

There is further disagreement as to which part or parts of the process of distinctive nasalization are affected by the VHP. Lightner and Ruhlen indicate that vowel height is relevant only to the spread of phonologized vowel nasalization before N. Conversely, Schourup and Chen appear to allow vowel height to affect distinctive nasalization as a unitary process, i.e. N-deletion triggering concomitant phonologization of vowel nasalization, e.g. $T_1VN > T_2\tilde{V}$. Foley, on the other hand, emphasizes the effect of the VHP on N-deletion. My own approach, in keeping with the methodology adopted in other chapters of this study, is to distinguish between vowel nasalization and N-deletion, and to examine the effect, if any, of vowel height on each as a separate processes. Nevertheless, I will concentrate on the effect of vowel height on nasalization, to which most available phonetic evidence refers. The question of possible interaction between front v. back

vowel quality and the development of distinctive nasalization is treated separately in section 5.4.

5.1.2 Evidence in support of the VHP: Old French

With the exception of Hombert, all universalists make reference, sole or partial, to purported historical developments in French in support of the suggested vowel height parameter. Typical is Chen's schematized account given in figure 5.1 of the purported spread (marked by +) in Old French of distinctive nasalization in the context VN.

The evidence used by universalists to support the suggested VHP has been drawn primarily from Pope (1952) and Straka (1955) who, like many others, considered it possible to decipher the development of nasalization in Old French by looking at the behaviour of Old French VC and VN in medieval assonating poetry. Briefly, in assonating rhyme, only stressed vowel nuclei are paired, e.g. *vint/pris* – in contrast to so-called perfect rhyme combining both nuclei and codas, e.g. *virginitét/honestét*. Theoretically, assonance is useful in that it allows for the quality of vowels to be compared independently of context, e.g. *a*N/*a*C, and is, therefore, valuable in showing whether the same vowel has changed in different, i.e. oral and nasal, contexts.

Whilst Pope and Straka differ slightly in chronological detail, they are in general agreement that by the end of the end of the tenth century *a*C and *a*N no longer assonated together in Old French. By the eleventh century, the pairs *ai*N/*ai*C and *e*N/*e*C no longer assonated together as they once did. Higher vowel pairs, however, did not diverge till much later, i.e. *o*N/*o*C in the twelfth, and *i*N/*i*C and *u*N/*u*C in the thirteenth centuries respectively.[2] Pope and Straka, like others, conclude that the failure of VN and VC to assonate, affecting low vowels first before extending over time to affect higher vowels, is the result of the blocking effect of contextual nasalization, i.e. *ã*N ≠ *a*C.

Although Pope and Straka's account of gradual vowel-height related nasalization in Old French is a convenient one, the apparently uniform picture of developments in Old French, referred to by universalists, masks a

a	e	ay	ey	o	oy	i	u	
+								End 10th/11th C
+	+	+						First half of 11th C
+	+	+	+					Mid 11th C
+	+	+	+	+				Mid 12th C
+	+	+	+	+	+			End 12th/13th C
+	+	+	+	+	+	+		Mid 13th C
+	+	+	+	+	+	+	+	14th C

Source: Chen 1973b: 187.

Figure 5.1   Chronology of Distinctive Nasalization in Old French

number of serious difficulties. First, Chen and Foley inadvertently cite Pope (1952) and Straka (1955) to support their respective claims regarding vowel-height governed N-deletion. Pope, like Straka and others, expresses the traditional view that vowel height affected only the spread of vowel nasalization in Old French. Loss of N is generally assumed by French historical linguists to have been a much later secondary phenomenon which occurred simultaneously after all vowels by the early Middle French period.

Significantly, no mention is made by universalists of the clear split in opinion amongst French historical linguists: the gradualist vowel height hypothesis of nasalization is rejected by many who espouse an alternative hypothesis of simultaneous phonologization of contextual vowel nasaliza-tion regardless of height, e.g. Rochet (1976), Matte (1984), Reenen (1982b, 1985, 1987), and also Entenman (1977).[3]

Such anti-gradualists take the view that the failure of related vowels in the contexts VN and VC to assonate is not indicative of any differential process of vowel nasalization, but of contextually governed vowel quality changes. Matte (1984) reanalyses the textual data, and comes to the conclusion that the quality of a before N and C was [ɛ̃] and [æ] respectively: despite the presence of vowel nasalization, the early absence of assonance between aN and aC simply reflects the important vowel quality difference. The possibility of higher vowels, such as iN and iC assonating together, even when aN and aC did not, is not indicative of a difference in the spread of vowel nasalization, but reflects the fact that the quality of i before N and C remained stable for a relatively long period. Even members of the gradualist camp accept that the purported chronology of changing patterns of assonance and therefore nasalization runs parallel to, and is associated with that of vowel quality changes in Old French. Hence Delattre's (1970) statement that 'on doit supposer que la rime entre voyelle orale et voyelle nasalisée correspondante n'a cessé d'être possible que lorsque la voyelle nasalisée a subi un certain degré de modification de timbre' (p. 224). But as Entenman (1977: 117–19) points out, while nasality may have an effect on vowel quality, nasality, *per se*, need have no effect on assonance: in both medieval and modern Portuguese poetry, oral and nasal vowels, of similar quality, appear to assonate in all contexts.

More tellingly, the vowel height schema appears to have no factual basis. There is absolutely no textual evidence which allows for the positing of nasalization of low aN before that of mid eN. Both are equally and fully separated from aC and eC respectively from the earliest texts going back to the ninth century. As a result, some linguists, e.g. Straka (1955) and Fouché (1958), are forced to presume that a was necessarily nasalized before e was for physiological reasons, i.e. as a result of universally greater velic opening on the former (see below). Moreover, detailed statistical analyses of the distribution of assonance in Old French by Reenen (1985, 1987) do not confirm the vowel height hypothesis of nasalization in Old French. Reenen

(1987) found assonance to be morphologically conditioned, i.e. there was a conscious grouping of so-called 'masculine' VN–VN pairs, but regular 'feminine' VN–VC assonance where V was orthographically the same vowel in height and quality. Such a dichotomy is not predicted by the vowel height hypothesis, and is not easily accounted for. In addition, the gradualist hypothesis makes the prediction that the frequency of nasalized vowels will increase over time, as nasalization spreads along the height parameter. In terms of assonance, such a claim will manifest itself by an increase in the proportion of VN assonating only with VN in later texts, as more vowels before N are progressively affected by nasalization. However, Reenen (1987) found the inverse to be correct: VN is most frequently paired with VN, i.e. does not assonate with VC, in the earliest texts examined, *La Vie de St. Alexis* (c. 1050) and *Chanson de Roland* (early twelfth century). The frequency of VN–VN assonance declines with the later dating of a text, and is absent in the most recent text examined, *Aucassin et Nicolette* (thirteenth century).

Given the problems with the Old French data, and with their interpretation, there appears to be no compelling reason to accept the hypothesis that the spread of nasalization from low to high vowels is discernible from changing patterns of assonance in Old French (Hajek 1993a).

5.1.3 *Evidence in support of the VHP in other languages*

Whilst conflicting interpretation strongly undermines the reliability of the Old French data as confirmation of the VHP, examples of other languages to support the VHP have also been offered.[4]

Hombert (1986, 1987) claims that reconstructed Proto-Bantu open /*a, *e, *o/ before N are more likely than close /*i, *u/ to be affected by distinctive nasalization in a small set of Teke languages. No finer distinction between low and mid vowels can be made from the data.

In addition to changes in Old French, Chen (1972 and elsewhere) claims to find extensive synchronic and diachronic evidence in support of the VHP in Chinese dialects. In a simple synchronic lexicostatistical count of oral and nasal vowels in a sample of eleven dialects (20,829 lexical items checked), Chen (1975) reports that for $\tilde{V}_1 \sim V_1 N$ pairs, where V_1 has the same quality, but differs with regard to distinctive nasalization, e.g. /ĩ/ vs. /in/, an inverse relationship holds between vowel height and the relative frequency of nasal vowels: the percentages for high, mid and low nasal vowels, when compared with their oral counterparts, were 10%, 12% and 24% respectively. Chen's initial hypothesis is that this distribution is accounted for by: (1) preferential nasalization of low vowels over time; (2) a tendency for nasal vowels to lower, and (3) the preferential denasalization of high nasal vowels. In order to evaluate the impact of each of these factors, Chen goes on to examine patterns of nasalization – synchronic and diachronic – in over 1,200 Chinese dialects. He finds (2) and (3) not to hold as stated, but the empirical basis for

(1) appears to be extremely strong. N-deletion where it is reported occurs in substantially more dialects after Middle Chinese /a/, the number of dialects dropping as vowel height increases. Representative figures for original /an, aŋ, əm, əŋ, uŋ/ are 414, 243, 193, 134 and 24 dialects respectively with N-deletion.

It is very difficult for non-Sinitic linguists to evaluate properly synchronic and diachronic developments in Chinese. As a result only the following observations are made here. First, his lexicostatistical figures are not internally consistent: a break-down of figures shows major variability in nasal vowel frequency, e.g. high /ĩ/ 46%, but /ĩ/ 11%, low /æ̃/ 94%, but /ã/ 19%. The relative frequency of /ĩ/, when compared to that of /ã/, is simply not predicted. Moreover, the biasing effect of interdialectal borrowing, known to be extensive in the Sinitic area, in favour of low vowel nasalization has not been accounted for by Chen. Although unquantified, such skewing is confirmed by Entenman's (1977: 67) observation that in Xiamen, one of Chen's sample dialects, the modern native reflex of Middle Chinese [miŋ] is [mẽ] with lowering, alongside the borrowed reflex [bin]. Borrowing of forms with a high oral vowel before N, if frequent and widespread enough, has the potential to dramatically affect the proportion of $\tilde{V}$ to VN for that vowel height, by reducing the relative frequency of high nasal vowels.

With regard to both the synchronic and diachronic data, Chen's findings appear to be further seriously affected by his failure to consider the impact of secondary hardening of nasalized off-glides, e.g. [VN] > [$\tilde{V}$] > [$\tilde{V}\tilde{G}$] > [$\tilde{V}$ŋ]. Precisely this sequence of diphthongization and subsequent glide hardening is common in Northern Italian, especially in the context of non-low vowels, e.g. LUNA > [lõw̃na] > [lõŋna] 'moon' but LANA > [lã:na] > [lɛ̃:na] > [lɛ̃:na] ~ [lɛ:na] 'wool' in Bolognese (see discussion below and chapter 8). Chen's (1975) presentation of data regarding developments affecting vowels before final coronal /n/ in 129 Hebei dialects (table 16, p. 52) is, in our view, entirely consistent with this observation: full velar nasals appear only after the reflexes of historically non-low vowels, e.g. /en/, /in/, /uen/ > /eŋ/, /iŋ/, /oŋ/ respectively (but /an/ > /ã, aⁿ, a, ɛ/). Chen treats the former as simple N-place shift: /en/ > /eŋ/, etc. However, not all dialects have developed non-low /eŋ, iŋ, oŋ/. A second group has secondarily developed denasalized off-glided /ei, iei, uei/ and a third has nasalized /ẽ, iẽ, uẽ/. These data can be interpreted in the following manner: the third group with nasal monophthongs is the most conservative. Elsewhere these vowels were diphthongized. Full denasalization in the second group blocked glide-hardening, whilst in the first group nasalized off-glides were consonantized. If our scenario is correct, then developments in 129 Hebei dialects cannot be cited in favour of preferential low vowel nasalization, and the quantitative case in favour of low vowel nasalization is substantially reduced. It is likely that developments in many more dialects are amenable to reinterpretation on the basis of preferential glide hardening to [ŋ] after high vowels.

The purported diachronic patterning is also affected by the nature of the

Middle Chinese reconstruction used: Hess (1988), using a different reconstruction when considering the development of nasal vowels in Wu Chinese
dialects, found, unlike Chen, that low /a/ and low mid /ɛ, ɔ/ before N could
not be distinguished.

Like the Old French data, the Chinese data Chen refers to in support of
the VHP is problematic. The apparent biasing effect of interdialectal
borrowing and of glide-hardening combine to seriously undermine the
reliability of Chen's massive sample. As a result, any conclusions based on
the sample data should be not accepted before proper re-evaluation of all
such data has occurred.

5.1.4 *Developments in Northern Italian*

Examination of the sample data indicates that, in most cases, there is very
little synchronic evidence of diachronic interaction between the VHP and the
spread of nasalization and N-deletion. Where the two phenomena have
developed most frequently, i.e. Stage 2 /Vːn#/, they appear in the context of
all vowels, regardless of height, e.g. Mi. [paː] < Stage 2 /paːn/ 'bread',
[viː] < /viːn/ 'wine', [karbuː] < /karboːn/ 'coal'.

Whilst the synchronic consistency of nasalization and N-deletion across
vowel height may be interpreted as indicating simultaneous application of
each process in the context of all vowels before N, consistent synchronic
patterning may also be the telescoped outcome of previously gradual
processes, as seen in the possible scenario at 2. In the absence of clear
historical evidence, it is impossible to resolve the matter.

2 /aːn/	ãːn		ãː		ãː
/eːn/		ẽːn	ẽː		ẽː
/iːn/	ĩːn			ĩː	ĩː
	1	2	3	4	5 6

$\xrightarrow{}$ Time

Limited evidence in favour of preferential low vowel nasalization may be
found in other contexts where nasalization is reported to occur only rarely in
the sample, e.g. Stage 2 /Vn(V)/ and /VNStop[+v]/.[5] Nasalization of Stage
2 /a/ is reported by Schürr (1919) to occur in these contexts in Imolese,
Ravennate and many other Romagnol dialects, but only after secondary
lengthening; see 3a. The same restricted conditions of nasalization are
reported to occur before /ɲ/; see 3b:

3a Im.	[gẽːmba]	< *GAMBA but /ɛ/ [membar]	> MEMBRU	'member'
	[kẽːna]	< CANNA /e/ [pena]	> PINNA	'feather'
b	[bẽːɲ]	< *BANJU but /ɛ/ [veɲ]	> VENIO	'I come'
c Im	[kẽːna]	< CANNA but [nɔːna]	< *NONNA	'grandmother'
		[nɔːn]	< NONNU	'grandfather'
		[dɔːna]	< *DONNA < DOMINA	'lady'

Whilst secondary lengthening is normally restricted to Stage 2 /a/, Stage 2 / ɔ/ before /n/ (< Lat. /nn/) also lengthens in many Romagnol dialects (including those in the sample). Nasalization, however, is not reported anywhere; see 3c where typically Romagnol results reported for Imolese are given. It is not certain that the difference in nasalization patterns reported at 3c provides support, however limited, for the VHP. Secondary lengthening of Stage 2 /ɔ/ appears to be very recent, as yet not reported in many other Romagnol dialects, e.g. Forlivese [nɔna] < *NONNA 'grandmother', but [kʌːna] < CANNA 'cane'. The apparent vowel-height related pattern of nasalization may simply be an indication of a recent change in the productivity of nasalization: nasalization, governed by the Vowel Length Parameter (VLP), and productive when Stage 2 /a/ was lengthened, may have ceased to be productive by the time /ɛ/ was lengthened. If this is the case, then operation of the VLP, independent of the VHP, would be sufficient to account for restricted low vowel nasalization where reported in Romagnol.[6]

Tuttle (1991) claims to have uncovered clear interaction between vowel height and nasalization phenomena in his *ad hoc* survey of Northern Italian and other Romance dialects, allowing him to formulate a scale of so-called nasalization receptivity in the following order: a ≫ o ≫ e ≫ u ≫ i. Although this follows the low ≫ mid ≫ high suggested by universalists, interaction with vowel quality is quite different to Ruhlen's specific ordering a ≫ e ≫ o ≫ i ≫ u, already listed at 1b. As well as referring to Old French (unreliable – see 5.1.2.), he cites developments in a handful of other Romance varieties, all of which are open to reinterpretation. In Bonneval Savoyard spoken in Eastern France, Tuttle claims only earlier [aN] and [oN] are subject to (distinctive) nasalization in reputed contrast to [eN], [iN] and [uN], and hence orders [a] and [o] before other vowels on his scale. However, some examples of [ẽ] are also found in the source (Gilliéron 1880), and absence of nasalization in [eN], [iN] and [uN] appears in fact to be conditioned by vowel length: unlike [a] and [o], all other vowels have undergone secondary shortening before N, e.g. MOLINU > St. 2 */moliːn/ > [meˈlɛn] 'mill'.[7] This process, in accordance with the Vowel Length Parameter, has either blocked the spread of nasalization if early enough, or eliminated it through preferential denasalization of short vowels (see chapter 4). Interaction with vowel height in this Romance variety should be viewed as, at best, only indirect.

Tuttle's other examples in support of low vowel nasalization generally relate to the appearance of velar nasals after some but not all vowels in some areas of Northern Italy, e.g. Piveronese *lãɲa* < St. 2 */laːna/ < LANA 'wool' but *buna* < */bɔːna/ < BONA 'good' and *lüna* < */luːna/ < LUNA 'moon'. However, this reputed patterning in favour of low vowel nasalization has a more plausible alternative explanation: [ɲ] is in all such cases the result of a secondary consonantization of an earlier off-glided diphthong. In Piveronese, apparently only low /aː/ was diphthongized. Higher vowels

were subject to shortening, thereby blocking nasalization (according to the Restricted VLP) and diphthongization. Even Tuttle has to report that in some parts of Northern Italy, conditions appear to be reversed: in Bolognese (and elsewhere, as noted by Tuttle himself) an epenthetic [ŋ] appears after all stressed vowels other than Latin /a/ before intervocalic /nɪ/, e.g. /loŋna/ < LUNA, /boŋna/ < BONA but /lɛːna/ < LANA. Although he notes the intimate relationship between long vowels and nasalization, he can only suggest – without corroborative evidence of any kind – that low vowel /aː/ in Bolognese was simply too long to be nasalized. Such an assertion is not supported at all by the available experimental evidence, e.g. Whalen and Beddor (1989), in which a monotonic relationship between vowel duration and perceived nasalization is reported (see section 4.1.4 for details). As vowel duration rises, so do levels of perceived nasalization. No maximum limit on interaction between the two factors is found. The apparently aberrant absence of [ŋ] after Stage 2 low /aː/ in Bolognese (and elsewhere) has a straightforward explanation: it is the only vowel not to have been diphthongized before intervocalic /n/, as confirmed by traditional orthographic convention dating back to the eighteenth century, e.g. *bouna, louna* but *lana ~ läna* (Hajek 1991c and d, and also chapter 8 below on glide hardening)

The difficulties of relying on *ad hoc* data samples can be seen when one compares Tuttle's conclusions with those of Montreuil (1991). Montreuil undertook a simple nasal vowel/oral vowel count before NC clusters in a sample of Northern Italian dialects included in the main Italian linguistic atlas, *Atlante italo-svizzero (AIS)*. Unlike Tuttle, he found the order of preferential nasalization to be reversed: higher vowels are much more likely to be affected than low vowels. The reliability of such a conclusion is on closer examination dubious: (1) on his own figures [u] appears to be as equally resistant to nasalization as low [a]; (2) interaction with factors able to influence the development of nasalization, such as vowel length and voicing in NC clusters, is not controlled for; and (3) the transcriptions themselves are of a somewhat unknown reliability with regard to the qualitative marking of nasalization and vowel duration.

The conclusions drawn by Tuttle (1991) and Montreuil (1991) are conflicting, open to straightforward reanalysis, and are best left to one side.

5.1.5 *Cross-linguistic counter-examples to the VHP*

Counter-examples to the VHP can be found. In Chamorro a phonological rule of vowel nasalization applies obligatorily to high vowels when adjacent to /m/, only optionally to mid vowels and never to low vowels (Witucki 1974). In Akan only high vowels /i ɪ ʊ u/ are subject to regressive nasalization, e.g. [dũmʔ], [dĩŋ] but [dam], [dɛŋ] (Schachter and Fromkin 1968). In Gunu (Robinson 1984) and Voute (Guarisma 1978) only high vowels /i u/ are nasalized in the context N__N. In Valaisan Franco-Provençal

a regular phonological process of progressive nasalization affects only reflexes of earlier /iː, uː/, e.g. NIDU > [niː] > [nẽ̄ĩ] 'nest' but NOVU > [noː] > [nou] 'new' (Bjerrome 1959). Spontaneous nasalization of word-final stressed vowels in Picard is restricted to historical high vowels, e.g. SPICU > /epi/ > [ɛ'pẽ̄ⁱ] 'ear', but /kilo/ > [tʃi'lu] 'kilo' (Flutre 1955).

With regard to N-deletion, Cedergren and Sankoff (1975), in a study of the sociolinguistic spread of distinctive nasalization in Panamanian Spanish, report that loss of syllable-final N in the context ṼN$ is strongly favoured when the vowel in question is high. Mid and low vowels are reported to have an inhibiting effect on N-deletion.

Chen (1975) reports two genuine counter-examples of preferential high vowel distinctive nasalization in his sample of more than 1,200 dialects. However, reanalysis of some of the very limited data provided by Chen for a handful of other dialects allows us to add at least three more: Mengzi, Kaiyuan and Huaning.[8]

Even if one accepts Chen's (1973b: 189) suggestion that sporadic counter-examples do not invalidate claims about the development of distinctive nasalization, such as the VHP, they can only be excluded as trivial when they are countered by cross-linguistically consistent evidence in support of a substantive claim. Examination of language data cited by universalists in support of the VHP, e.g. Old French, indicates that neither criterion is fully satisfied. In these circumstances, counter-examples to the VHP seem to demonstrate that contradictory tendencies can manifest themselves across languages, and need to be accounted for. That different cross-linguistic patterns may be reported to exist is not surprising in a context where inconsistencies in the available phonetic evidence discussed below allow for different predictions about the effect of vowel height to be made.

We have at present very little reliable cross-linguistic evidence in support of any vowel-height related effect on the spread of distinctive nasalization – the influence of other factors such as vowel length tends often to obscure direct independent interaction between vowel height and nasalization phenomena. This is not to suggest, however, that reliable cross-linguistic evidence of a consistent, but not necessarily universal, vowel-height effect may not be uncovered in the future.

5.2 PHONETIC EXPLANATIONS FOR A POSSIBLE VOWEL-HEIGHT EFFECT ON THE DEVELOPMENT OF DISTINCTIVE NASALIZATION

5.2.1 *Vowel height and articulatory correlates of vowel nasalization*

Universalists have emphasized the importance of a purportedly universal inverse correlation between velopharyngeal, or velic, opening and relative vowel height as an explanation for the VHP. However, other articulatorily

dependent measures of relative vowel nasality interact differently with vowel height. As a result, different claims about the possible effect of vowel height on the development of distinctive nasalization may be made, if development is thought to correlate with one particular articulatory measure. Problems also arise when, on closer examination, it becomes evident that the interaction between a suggested parameter (e.g. velic opening) and vowel height is not consistent enough to support the purportedly universal vowel-height related parameter of distinctive nasalization, given at 1.

5.2.2 The velic opening hypothesis

Universalists, e.g. Ruhlen (1973: 11), Hombert (1987: 274) and Chen and Wang (1975: 276–8), who offer a phonetic explanation for the suggested VHP, claim that the parameter has an articulatory basis in vowel-height governed differences in velopharyngeal or velic opening (VPO).[9] Chen and Wang note that low vowels in oral contexts may be produced with an open velum in some languages. This is confirmed experimentally (see Clumeck 1976: 344, and Ohala 1975 for details). Furthermore, experimental results, based on fibroscopic and X-ray studies of languages such as English, Hindi and Chinese, are reported to show that the relative degree of velic opening in a vowel in nasal contexts is inversely related to increased vowel height (see Chen and Wang 1975; Bell-Berti 1993). Low vowels are produced with an amount of velic opening far greater than that reported for high vowels in the same nasal context.

Despite the approval afforded by universalists to the velic opening account of the VHP, it is not clear that such a hypothesis is supported by cross-linguistic evidence of sound change or by the results of phonetic (articulatory, acoustic and perceptual) research. First, if we accept, at least initially, that a strictly articulatory account of the VHP is acceptable, one could argue that the velic opening hypothesis, which is gradient in nature, runs counter to Chomsky and Halle's (1968) simple articulatory definition of the phonological feature [nasal] as relating to the presence vs. absence of velopharyngeal opening (see section 1.3.2). If theirs is the correct characterization of [nasal], mere presence, rather than degree, of velopharyngeal opening on any individual vowel could arguably be sufficient for the phonologization of vowel nasalization.

Notwithstanding Chomsky and Halle's simple definition, there is no reason to believe that for all vowels there is one unitary level of sufficient velic opening necessary for the phonologization of nasalization, a level which low vowels for articulatory reasons are most likely to exceed. It is implicit in the universalists' argumentation, supported by their cited experimental evidence, that levels of velic opening are intrinsically different according to vowel height. Therefore, the level of velic opening in high vowels, even when

maximum, may never approach that found in low vowels. In these circumstances, individual velic opening targets for phonologization must be established for each vowel.[10] Otherwise, nasalization of high vowels might never be possible. As a result, intrinsic differences in velic opening between vowels of different vowel heights should not be considered to be automatic causes of a differential process of nasalization (contextual and/or distinctive), as universalists wish to suggest.

Second, as Clumeck (1976) and Al-Bamerni (1983) point out, it is not clear at all that the degree of velic opening is in fact the critical articulatorily dependent marker of vowel nasalization. It has been suggested that other correlates, such as: (1) relative duration of vowel nasalization and (2) nasal airflow levels, may be better measures with potentially more important roles in the development of distinctive nasalization. Given the perceptually oriented model of sound change adopted in this study, we need in the first instance to assess how acoustic measures of nasality, such as vowel-height related variation in nasal sound-pressure levels, and the acoustic effect of nasal coupling on individual vowel spectra, correlate with articulatory measures of nasality. We need then to establish how listeners respond to acoustic cues of vowel nasality (cf. section 5.3 for details).

Third, examination of cross-linguistic experimental evidence does not support the hypothesis of a strict inverse correlation, as suggested by universalists and others, between the amount of velic opening and vowel height. Al-Bamerni (1983: 254, table 8), in a nasographic study of VPO in VN sequences in seven languages, found a statistically significant difference in velic opening between high and low vowels on the one hand, and low and mid vowels on the other, in only five languages (English, French, Kurdish, Arabic and Norwegian). In two of these languages (French and English), there was no statistically significant difference between mid and high vowel velic opening, and individual speaker variation was high. More striking is the finding that in two languages, Gujarati and Hindi, differences in vowel height had no statistically significant effect on velic opening. Unexpectedly, in both languages, the highest levels of velic opening occurred in mid and high back vowels (p. 249, figure 20). Similarly, Clumeck (1976) in another nasographic study of nasal coarticulation before N in six languages (American English, French, Amoy Chinese, Brazilian Portuguese, Swedish and Hindi) found that only five speakers out of thirteen examined showed statistically significant differences between low and high vowels with regard to the amount of velic opening. Even fewer speakers showed the predicted differences between high and mid (2/5) and mid and low (3/5) vowels respectively.

The major cross-linguistic and inter-speaker variation reported by Al-Bamerni (1983) and Clumeck (1976) indicates that velic opening does not correlate as predicted with vowel height. As a result, the hypothesis of a strict universally held inverse correlation between vowel height and velic opening

must be rejected as empirically unsupported, although a tendency towards such a correlation may be apparent in some languages. Furthermore, the suggested correlation between velic opening and vowel height in oral contexts may also be put in doubt: velic opening is not restricted to low vowels as some universalists suggest, but may extend to high vowels, as reported in Ontario French and English (Bream 1968), in North African French (Condax et al. 1976), and variably (2 out of 10 speakers) in American English (Moll 1962).

In any case, velic opening in oral low vowels, normally uncovered only as a result of experimental work, would appear to be irrelevant to the phonologization of contextual nasalization. The extreme sporadicity of spontaneous nasalization of oral vowels in the world's languages suggests that low levels of velic opening, particularly in low vowels, are not perceived or are easily factored out by listeners.

If the development of distinctive nasalization is dependent on relative velic opening, as universalists suggest, then the effect of vowel height on patterns of development will be language-specific in line with the findings of cross-linguistic variation in vowel height-related velic opening. Therefore, for instance, in a language which exhibited the same patterns of velic opening as reported in Gujarati and Hindi by Al-Bamerni, we might expect the phonologization of vowel nasalization and subsequent N-deletion to occur preferentially in the context of mid and high back vowels before spreading to front and low vowels.

5.2.3 *Relative duration of vowel nasalization*

Clumeck (1976) has suggested that timing of velic lowering may be the crucial factor in the perception of vowel nasalization. Al-Bamerni's (1983) cross-linguistic experimental results do not demonstrate a necessary correlation between the relative duration of nasalization and velic opening. In these circumstances, they may be viewed as independent parameters.[11] If an inverse correlation exists between the duration of nasalization (as a proportion of total vowel length) and vowel height, as Clumeck suggests, i.e. relative duration decreases with increased vowel height, then we may have, as an alternative to the velic opening hypothesis, a plausible articulatory basis for the purportedly universal VHP.[12]

However, Clumeck's own experimental results demonstrate that the correlation between vowel height and relative nasalization duration is cross-linguistically variable. Statistically significant cross-category differences in relative nasalization duration between low and high vowels are reported in five languages examined (French, Amoy Chinese, American English, Swedish and Hindi). Significant cross-category differences in line with the VHP, i.e. low ≫ mid ≫ high, were reported in French only. In Swedish (/V:/ only) and American English, there were no significant differences in relative nasalization duration between low and mid vowels.

More surprising results were found for Brazilian Portuguese, in which CVNV and CVNCV were tested. Overall, it was found that relative nasalization duration was greatest in low and high vowels as one group, to the exclusion of mid vowels. In CVNCV, duration was greatest in high vowels, and least in mid vowels. Differences across the three categories (high, mid and low) were found to be significant. No significant cross-category differences were found, however, in CVNV. A similar absence of correlation was reported in Swedish short vowels.

Al-Bamerni (1983) found greater cross-linguistic consistency than Clumeck: significant cross-category differences between low and high vowels in favour of the former were found in all seven languages tested. Cross-linguistic consistency in correlation between vowel height and duration decreased between low and mid vowels, and between mid and high vowels. And in at least one language, Hindi, no such correlation was found. Inter-speaker variation within the same language (French and English) was also marked.

Whilst an overall correlation appears to exist between relative nasalization duration and low vs. high vowels in general agreement with the VHP, important cross-linguistic differences uncovered by Al-Bamerni and Clumeck do not support a correlation with the finer articulation of the VHP as low $\gg$ mid $\gg$ high. If relative duration of nasalization is to be taken as the primary articulatory (and perceptual) cue for the phonologization of contextual vowel nasalization, then it could be argued that in some contexts and in some languages, e.g. Portuguese, phonologization may affect all vowels at the same time, or high vowels before mid vowels.

5.2.4 Nasal airflow and nasal sound pressure levels

Al-Bamerni (1983) suggests that nasal airflow patterns provide an alternative articulatory parameter along which the phonologization of contextual vowel nasalization may be determined. Indeed, Warren et al. (1993: 133–4, and fig. 12) provide evidence that increased airflow volume correlates with increased perceived nasality. Lubker and Moll (1965), McDonald and Baker (1951) and Al-Bamerni (1983: 231–2) report a direct association between nasal airflow levels and vowel height: in the context VN nasal airflow is substantially greater in high vowels than in low vowels. Greater constriction in the oral cavity, as a result of increased tongue height, results in increased impedance to oral airflow. As a consequence, more air will be directed to the nasal cavity in the production of high vowels. The location of tongue constriction is also reported to be crucial: Al-Bamerni found that where Kurdish [iː] and [uː] shared a similar degree of velic opening, the more posterior constriction in [uː] resulted in greater nasal airflow in this vowel than in [iː].

Nasal sound-pressure level, an articulatorily dependent acoustic measure, is considered by some to be the primary correlate of vowel nasalization, and, therefore, most relevant to the development of distinctive nasalization. Clarke and Mackiewicz-Krassowska (1977) and Rochet and Rochet (1991), who do in fact consider nasal sound-pressure differences to mark relative vowel nasality, measured levels before N in Australian English and Canadian English and French, and found the greatest levels in high and front vowels, in particular /i/. Relative tongue height, with concomitant effects on relative oral constriction also appears responsible for these results. In this case, however, the highest levels are achieved with an anterior oral constriction. Clarke and Mackiewicz-Krassowska are explicit in suggesting a strong correlation between the greatest nasal sound-pressure levels in high vowels and earlier perceptual studies of cleft palate speech in which high vowels were rated as most nasal.

If nasal airflow is considered to be the primary articulatory marker of relative vowel nasalization then, according to the same argumentation used by universalists, there is no basis for the suggested VHP: high vowels are more nasal than low vowels because of greater nasal airflow. A similar conclusion is reached if nasal sound-pressure levels are taken to be the primary correlate of vowel nasalization (Farnetani 1979b: 43). The two possible correlates of vowel nasalization are not, of course, entirely compatible: nasal airflow results indicate that high back vowels are articulatorily the most nasalized, but the evidence of nasal sound pressure variation favours the nasalization of high front vowels.

If nasal airflow and nasal sound pressure are taken to be the primary correlates not only of phonetic but also of phonologized vowel nasalization, the same logic used by universalists to suggest the velic opening hypothesis in support of the VHP allows us to suggest a counter-hypothesis: the development over time of (phonologized) vowel nasalization before N is favoured in high vowels, and is least likely in low vowels. However, the same criticisms made of the velic opening hypothesis apply, such as the need to distinguish between intrinsic and extrinsic levels of coarticulation.

The assessment of relative vowel nasality is thus found to this point to be a difficult matter. Unexpected cross-linguistic variation in velic opening makes clear that the velic opening hypothesis does not hold universally, and cannot, therefore, be used to support the VHP as a strictly universal phenomenon. Alternative parameters of nasalization discussed above, when placed alongside VPO, result in conflicting claims about the effect of vowel height on relative nasalization: low vowels are the most nasal in terms of relative velic opening and vowel nasalization duration, but high vowels are the most nasal in terms of nasal airflow and nasal sound-pressure levels.

5.3 VOWEL HEIGHT AND THE PERCEPTION OF NASALIZATION

If sound change is primarily a perceptually motivated phenomenon as suggested in sections 1.2.1 to 1.2.1.1, we need to establish to what degree and in what fashion the perceptual assessment of nasalization is affected by vowel height. If we can determine what perceptual weight is given to different articulatory parameters of nasalization, then we may be able to make some predictions based on these about the effect of vowel height on the development of nasalization and N-deletion. Unfortunately, experimental results indicate that there is no strict correlation between articulatory and perceptual measures of nasalization, and no single prediction can be made about the effect of vowel height on the perception of vowel nasalization. The absence of a consistent correlation between the perception of nasalization and suggested acoustic or articulatory parameters of nasalization suggests that listeners, within and across languages, use different perceptual cues, giving weight to different articulatory parameters, to assess relative nasality.[13] From the perspective of sound change, the possibility of different perceptual parameters available to the listener would allow for different diachronic patterns of interaction between vowel height and nasalization to occur, as the cross-linguistic evidence previously discussed in sections 5.1.2 to 5.1.5 seems to indicate.

5.3.1 Evidence for a high ≫ low parameter

Operating on the assumption that a general correlation exists between increased vowel height and decreased velic opening, Al-Bamerni (1983) hypothesizes that, if listening tests show low vowels to be perceptually more nasal than high vowels, then we have evidence that perceived nasalization is related to the amount of velic opening. If high vowels are found to be perceptually more nasal, then perceived nasalization correlates with relative nasal airflow. However, the integration of articulatory, acoustic and perceptual parameters of nasalization is not as straightforward as Al-Bamerni suggests.

The acoustic effect of velic opening does not correlate with the purported VHP in the simple manner universalists claim. Ohala (1975: 299), Lubker (1968) and Maeda (1982, 1989), amongst others, suggest that high vowels are acoustically the least able to tolerate velic opening: small levels of velic opening are reported to have a substantial effect on high vowel spectra. In comparison, at the same levels of velic opening, little spectral change is reported in low vowels.[14] A far greater amount of velic opening is required to achieve the same degree of acoustic distortion as is reported in high vowels with only limited velic opening. As Ohala notes, at low levels of velic opening, nasalization is likely to be perceptually more salient in high vowels. Phonologization of high vowel nasalization will be favoured if the

ability of listeners to factor out acoustic distortion decreases as the amount of distortion increases even at low levels of velic opening. Conversely, in the same situation listeners may plausibly continue to treat contextually nasalized low vowels as phonologically oral, since the lesser acoustic distortion will be more easily eliminated. As a consequence, velic opening in low vowels will need to be markedly increased before nasalization is perceived and then phonologized. This is consistent with the observation made earlier in section 5.2.2 that small amounts of velic opening sometimes reported in oral low vowels appear to have little acoustic effect, and are easily factored out by speakers.

That some sort of relationship exists between levels of velic opening and perceived nasalization is not in dispute, and has been reported by House and Stevens (1956), Maeda (1982, 1989, 1993), Abramson et al. (1981) and Benguerel and Lafargue (1981): for each individual vowel, perception of nasalization normally increases along with velic opening. However, in line with the hypothesis of relative acoustic distortion, the rate of increased responsiveness varies according to vowel height: the perception of low vowel nasalization, in contrast to that of high vowels, is reported to rise only slowly with increased velic opening.

Perceptual evidence, based on manipulation of both synthetic and natural speech, in support of preferential nasalization of high vowels is not lacking. House and Stevens (1956) report that in listening tests using synthetic tokens low vowels require almost three times as much velic opening as high vowels before they are identified as nasalized by American listeners. The results of perceptual experiments conducted by Stevens et al. (1987) using synthesized imitations of natural Gujarati tokens also indicate that at the lowest levels of modification of the acoustic spectrum perceived nasality of [u, i] responded most rapidly. Abramson et al. (1981) tested the effect of vowel height and relative velic opening on oral/nasal consonant perception in the syllable type /nV#, dV#/ using synthetic speech. Of the three vowels tested, /i, ʌ, a/, it was found that the lower the vowel the greater the amount of velopharyngeal opening necessary for the perception of prevocalic /n/.

Maeda (1982, 1989, 1993) reached similar conclusions about the interaction between vowel height and velic opening, based on perceptual evaluation of synthesized vowel nasalization. With no nasal coupling, [a] was perceived as marginally more nasal than [i, u]. However, once nasal coupling began, perception of nasalization of [u], and especially of [i], increased dramatically. Conversely, perceived nasalization of [a] *decreased* at very low levels of velic opening, before recovering slowly until achieving a level only marginally greater than that of [i] at peak magnitude of velic opening. At most levels of opening, [i, u] were consistently perceived as more nasalized than low vowel [a]; see figure 5.2. Abramson et al. (1981: 330) note that many earlier investigators found the linguistically useful range of nasal coupling in natural speech to lie between zero cm^2 and little more than one

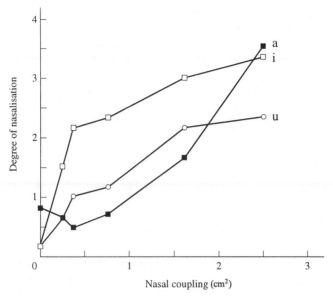

The scale of perceived nasality along the vertical axis ranges from '0' (not nasalized) to '4' (heavily nasalized).
Source: Maeda (1989: 26).

Figure 5.2   Averaged Responses of Eight Subjects to [a, i, u] Synthesized with Six Degrees of Velic Opening (0.0, 0.2, 0.4, 0.8, 1.6, 2.5 cm²)

cm². If such an observation is correct, then the results of experiments using synthesized speech suggest that, within the normal range of velic opening, [i] and [u] are perceptually more nasal across most points, as seen in figure 5.2.

Benguerel and Lafargue (1981) manipulated natural stimuli to find that French nasal mid vowels /ɛ̃, ɔ̃/ were perceived as more nasal than /ã/ at smaller levels of velopharyngeal opening.

The results of these experiments are consistent with cross-linguistic reports that high vowels are perceptually most nasalized before N in Bengali (Ferguson and Chowdury 1965), Chamorro (Witucki 1974) and Portuguese (Parkinson 1979), and that high /ũ/ is most nasal and low /ã/ is least so in Molinos Mixtec (Hunter and Pike 1969).

5.3.2 Perceptual evidence for a low ≫ high parameter

In contradiction to the experimental results that we have just discussed, there is a smaller body of experimental work that indicates that low vowels before N are perceptually the most nasal.[15]

Ali et al. (1971) in an experiment with American English subjects using edited tokens reported that perception of deleted final N was significantly greater after low /a/ than after /u, eɪ , ɛ/.

Lintz and Sherman (1961) tested the perception of vowel nasality in the non-nasal contexts CVC# and CV# in unmanipulated American English speech. Low vowels /æ, a/ were rated by listeners to be substantially more nasal than other vowels tested, for which the severity of nasality declined in the following order: /ɛ/ ≫ /i/ ≫ /ʌ/ ≫ /ʊ/ ≫ /u/. However, Massengill and Bryson (1967) found no significant differences in the nasality ratings of /i, u, æ, a/ produced by American English speakers without velopharyngeal opening.

Bream (1968) tested the perception of vowel nasalization before N in Canadian and Standard French, as well as in Canadian English. Overall results indicate the following parameter of decreasing nasality in (Ontario and Standard) French: /a, ɛ/ ≫ /i/ ≫ /ɔ/. For Canadian English the ordering was in all contexts: /ʌ/ ≫ /ɛ/ ≫ /ɪ/ ≫ /i/.

5.3.3 Evidence against a Vowel Height Parameter

Clumeck (1971) tested the ability of American listeners to perceive contextual nasalization in French when syllable-final N in VN$ was deleted, and found that vowel-height differences had little effect on vowel-nasalization perception. Reenen (1982a) suggests that Clumeck's findings support the hypothesis that the perception of vowel nasalization is not affected by vowel height. However, the available evidence is scanty and not sufficient, at this stage, to provide an adequate phonetic basis for such a hypothesis.

5.4 Nasalization, N-deletion and Front vs. Back Vowels

Agreement amongst universalists as to the purported effect of vowel height on the development of the different components of distinctive nasalization does not extend to the possibly universal effect of front or back vowel quality.[16] Opinion is split three ways. Foley (1975, 1977), Hombert (1987) and Lightner (1973) make no specific claim, implying an absence of interaction between vowel quality and the VHP (see 1b above). Schourup (1973: 192) suggests that nasalization is phonologized more readily on back vowels than on their front counterparts. Unfortunately, he mentions only examples of perseverative nasalization, i.e. NV, which are irrelevant for the purposes of this study. Conversely, other universalists believe that in the context VN, front vowels are preferentially affected by the development of nasalization (Ruhlen 1973) and N-deletion (Chen 1972 and elsewhere).

There is at present very little reliable cross-linguistic evidence of sound change that allows claims to be made about the differential effect of front or back quality on the development of distinctive nasalization. This is not to suggest that further cross-linguistic investigation in the future may not uncover clear evidence of patterning.

Much the same examples cited in support of the VHP are used to support the front ≫ back parameter, i.e. diachronic patterns of Old French

assonance, and the synchronic distribution of nasal vowels in modern Chinese dialects.[17] For the same reasons given previously in sections 5.1.2 and 5.1.3, the Old French and Chinese evidence can be rejected as unproven and unreliable respectively. There is no compelling reason to believe that a gradual spread of nasalization in Old French is discernible from changes in Old French assonance. Nor is there any reason to believe that diachronic patterns of distinctive nasalization correlate in a direct and straightforward fashion with the synchronic frequency of nasal vowels in Chinese. Relatively low rate of appearance of back $\tilde{V}$ may simply reflect tendencies to: (1) fronting; or (2) [ŋ]-'epenthesis', if complete velar closure is plausibly favoured after back vowels. In addition, the figures Chen typically provides of the frequency of $\tilde{V}_1$, relative to V_1N, for front (18%) and back vowels (7%), continue to mask major inter-vowel variation not predicted by him. For example, whilst the average frequency of surface contrastive $\tilde{V}$ (relative to identical oral V) for all low vowels is 24%, the reported frequencies for individual low vowels are 98% for rounded back /ɒ̃/ (2% /ɒ/) but 0% for its unrounded counterpart /ɑ̃/, 19% for central /ã/, and 94% for front /æ̃/.

Other evidence is generally not conclusive. The results of a survey by Cedergren and Sankoff (1975) of the sociolinguistic spread of distinctive nasalization in Panamanian Spanish show little difference in the frequency of N-deletion after front and back vowels.

As for my sample of Northern Italian dialects, there is no evidence that differences in front and back vowel quality have affected the development of vowel nasalization and N-deletion, e.g. Mi. [vĩː] < VINU 'wine' and [vỹː] < UNU 'one'. The only indication of a vowel quality effect I have found is in two Romagnol dialects not in the sample, Faentino and Forlivese, as described by Schürr (1919). Deletion of Stage 2 word-final /m/ appears to be regular after nasalized back vowels, and rare or non-existent after non-back vowels:

4   Faentino/Forlivese

| /o/ [nõː] | < Stage 2 /noːm/ | < NOME 'name' |
| /u/ [lũː] | < | /luːm/ | < LUME 'light' |

but /a/ [fʌ̃ː(m)]	<	/faːm/	< FAME 'hunger'
/e/ [prem]	<	/preːm/	< PREMIT 'he presses'
/i/ [prem]	<	/priːm/	< PRIMU 'first'

The Romagnol evidence remains scanty, however, and the apparently preferential loss of labial /m/ after back vowels may be conditioned by other factors, such as labial dissimilation.

5.4.1 *Experimental evidence for a front vs. back distinction*

The experimental phonetic evidence is contradictory, as it was for vowel height. Hence, no universal generalizations can be made about a universal

effect of front vs. back vowel quality on the development of nasalization and N-deletion.

Al-Bamerni's (1983) measurements of velic opening in six languages do not demonstrate any universal correlation between levels of velic opening and the front vs. back distinction. Instead, marked cross-linguistic variation is reported. In similar fashion, Moll (1962) found that the front vs. back distinction had no significant difference on levels of velic opening in American English.

Also, while levels of nasal sound pressure were found by Clarke and Mackiewicz-Krassowska (1977) and Rochet and Rochet (1991) to be greatest for front vowels, Al-Bamerni (1983) reports nasal airflow to be markedly higher in back vowels, because of posterior tongue constriction.

The results of many perceptual experiments are more consistent and indicate a preferential nasalization of front vowels, e.g. Maeda (1982, 1989), House and Stevens (1956), Bream (1968), and Lintz and Sherman (1961).

5.5 CONCLUSIONS

Whilst there is no evidence that the development of one or all component parts of distinctive nasalization in the context VN is completely random, the strict universalist hypothesis of a low $\gg$ mid $\gg$ high vowel-height parameter is not found to be empirically supported. Examination of cross-linguistic evidence regularly cited in favour of the VHP shows that much of the data is unproven, e.g. Old French, or plausibly biased and requiring complete re-evaluation, e.g. Chinese. Counter-examples in which VN > ṼN > Ṽ is favoured in the context of high vowels are also reported. Although currently few in number, their presence suggests that the effect of vowel height, if any, on the development of distinctive nasalization is cross-linguistically governed by competing non-random tendencies, i.e. low $\gg$ high, but also high $\gg$ low. The general paucity of reliable cross-linguistic examples in support of either tendency, despite the fact that many languages contrast oral and nasal vowels today, also allows for the hypothesis that the spread of nasalization (and later N-deletion) may in some languages have affected all vowels simultaneously, regardless of height. Further investigation of historical developments across languages may, however, allow for more consistent cross-linguistic patterning to be uncovered, in which one non-random tendency may appear to be substantially more frequent than others.

The universalist hypothesis that low vowels are inherently more nasal than mid and high vowels because of a purportedly universal inverse correlation between the degree of velic opening and vowel height is also not confirmed. Unexpected cross-linguistic and cross-speaker variation in levels of velic opening was reported in section 5.2.2. Other articulatory measures of vowel

nasality, e.g. relative duration of velic opening, nasal airflow and nasal sound-pressure levels, were also found to be inconsistent with the universalist hypothesis.

More striking are the conflicting results of perceptual experiments: in some cases high vowels are reported to be most nasal, in others low vowels are favoured, whilst in others still an absence of any vowel-height effect is reported. This inconsistency suggests that the many acoustic and articulatory cues of nasalization available to listeners may not be integrated in the same manner across languages or at different points in time.[18] As a result, the effect of vowel height on the perception and the subsequent phonologization of contextual nasalization will vary. In these circumstances, no single universal effect of vowel height on the development of nasalization and N-deletion is likely, a claim which finds confirmation in the different cross-linguistic patterns reported above.

One factor, only mentioned in passing in this chapter but requiring further attention, that may greatly influence interaction between vowel height and distinctive nasalization processes, is vowel length and the VLP. Differences in vowel length, conditioned by vowel height, appear to have affected the spread of nasalization, e.g. preferential nasalization of Stage 2 /a/ after secondary lengthening in Romagnol, e.g. ANNU > Stage 2 /an/ > Lg. [aːn] > Im. [ɛ̃ːn]. Hombert (1987) suggests that low-level phonetic differences may be sufficient to account for any vowel-height patterning of distinctive nasalization. Certainly, Lintz and Sherman (1961) found the perception of nasality on the same vowel to correlate directly with phonetically conditioned increases in vowel duration. However, whilst it is generally considered that vowel duration decreases predictably with increased vowel height, the cross-linguistic figures of vowel length before N provided by Al-Bamerni (1983) and Rochet and Rochet (1991) indicate that such patterning is not universal. If vowel length does influence the spread of nasalization according to vowel height, their results suggest only a cross-linguistic tendency, rather than a strict universal, towards low vowel nasalization. In languages where non-low vowels are reported to be phonetically longer, the preferential phonologization of nasalization on these vowels might then be expected.

Finally, it was observed in section 5.4 that there is at present very little reliable evidence that differences in front and back vowel quality affect the development of distinctive nasalization. The cross-linguistic evidence – diachronic (French) and synchronic (Chinese) – cited by universalists remains of questionable value. The little evidence in Northern Italian that N-deletion may be favoured after nasalized back vowels also appears easily discounted. Whilst further investigation of the development of distinctive nasalization is clearly required, conflicting experimental results suggests that evidence of alternative front ≫ back and back ≫ front parameters of distinctive nasalization may be expected.

6

CONTEXTUAL ORDERING OF DISTINCTIVE NASALIZATION

6.1 INTRODUCTION

Universalist claims about the effect of contextual factors, e.g. syllable structure and the nature of the post-nasal segment, on the spread of distinctive nasalization are examined before I turn to developments in my Northern Italian sample and elsewhere. Although contextual parameters posited for Northern Italian are found not to hold universally, some ordering relationships along the two parameters appear to apply more generally – for which possible phonetic explanations need to be found.

6.1.1 *Universalist claims about contextual effects*

Opinions differ somewhat amongst universalists as to the effect of context on the development of nasalization and N-deletion processes. Whilst Ruhlen (1973: 13) makes no suggestion that contextual or language-specific nasalization is determined by any factor other than the height of the vowel preceding N, he does claim that N-deletion develops in an ordered manner according to the position of N and the nature of the following segment if any. In Ruhlen's view, N is deleted preferentially before consonants word-medially. Deletion of word-final N follows, first before consonants and then before vowels. Lastly, intervocalic N may be lost, as in my schematized representation at 1a:

1a Ruhlen   NC N#C N#V NV $\longrightarrow$

b   NFric NStop NStop
                           [−v]   [+v] $\longrightarrow$

Although Ruhlen, a specialist in French linguistics, makes no explicit reference, his account seems to have been formulated largely with French in mind, as seen in the following examples: [tɑ̃ː#] *temps* 'time' ≫ [bɔ̃ː# tɑ̃ː#] *bon temps* 'good time' ≫ [bɔn#ami] *bon ami* 'good friend', but [lɛn] *laine* < LANA 'wool', [ane] *année* 'year'.

As far as the nature of the post-nasal consonant has any effect on N-deletion, Ruhlen notes that N-deletion is restricted to pre-fricative position in Portuguese and Polish. The voicing contrast in post-nasal stops also appears to be an important factor: N is deleted only before voiceless stops in

American English, e.g. [kæːt] *can't*, but [kæːnd] *canned*. A parameter can be formulated to account for such cross-linguistic evidence; see 1b. Ruhlen, however, is uncertain as to how universal such a parameter might be, in the light of Malécot's (1960) claim that nasal consonants are lost before stops but not before fricatives in American English, e.g. *[dɛ̃ːs] *dense*, but [kæːt] *can't*.[1]

Foley (1975, 1977) posits two universal patterns of ordered N-deletion according to context that I have schematized in parametric fashion at 2:

2a Foley $\underrightarrow{\text{VN\$ V\$NV}}$

 b $\underrightarrow{\text{VNFric VNStop VNV}}$[2]

Foley agrees with other universalists, e.g. Ruhlen, that nasals in syllable-final position, like all consonants, are inherently weaker than strong syllable-initial intervocalic nasals and are, therefore, preferentially deleted, e.g. Fr. [fɛ̃ː\$] *faim* 'hunger', but [a\$mi] *ami* 'friend' (m.). As for nasal clusters, preferential N-deletion before fricatives is the result of the interaction of two different phenomena: (1) the relative weakness of syllable-final position, and (2) the quantitative fortition of the preceding vowels as a result of preferential lengthening before N+Fricative clusters. Such fortition results in an additional weakening of the post-vocalic nasal consonant, thereby favouring its deletion (even in the absence of vowel nasalization). The process, *per* Foley (1975: 202), is recorded in Old English:

3 Germanic	gans	hund	
	gaːns	hund	vowel lengthening
	gaːnˉs	hund	weakening of element after strong element
	gaːs	hund	N-deletion
OE	goːs	hund	
	'goose'	'dog'	

Unlike Ruhlen, Foley makes no reference to any difference in preferential N-deletion between word-final and preconsonantal position. As a result, it becomes impossible to categorize the two positions individually along the second parameter at 2b.

Like Ruhlen and Foley, Schourup (1973) also found syllable position to be important: nasalization before intervocalic nasals was found to occur only if nasalization phenomena were already evident in tautosyllabic VN\$ sequences. Schourup was also aware of finer distinctions: tautosyllabic distinctive nasalization developed sooner word-finally than in pre-consonantal position.[3] In preconsonantal position, distinctive nasalization developed preferentially before continuants. Schourup's findings, more explicit than those of Foley, can be summarized in one parameter as follows:

4 Schourup VN# VNC[+cont] VNC[−cont] VNV
                                                    ⟶

Comparison of the suggested contextual parameters at 1, 2 and 4, demonstrates only partial agreement amongst universalists as to the effect of context on vowel nasalization and/or N-deletion. First, Ruhlen and Foley restrict their observations on context to N-deletion, since they consider other factors, primarily vowel height, to account largely for vowel nasalization. Schourup, on the other hand, extends his observations to distinctive nasalization, i.e. vowel nasalization and N-deletion. Whilst all concur that the position of N within the syllable has a predictable effect on any change, agreement extends little further. Schourup considers word-final position to be the most favourable position for change, whilst Ruhlen considers it to be only second most favourable. Foley makes no special claim about it at all. Finally, only Ruhlen refers to the effect of a post-nasal voicing contrast on preferential N-deletion, whilst Schourup alone distinguishes between continuant and non-continuant nasal clusters.

6.1.2 *Contextual effects in Northern Italian and other Romance dialects*

The conflicting claims about the contextual ordering of nasalization can easily be tested by developments in my Northern Italian sample. In fact, the historical phonotactic structure of Northern Italian dialects allows me to examine in an integrated fashion a number of context types that universalists have not properly treated or touched upon, e.g. the voicing contrast in post-nasal stops. Further, unlike Foley, Ruhlen and Schourup, I consider the effect of context on the development of both phonologized contextual nasalization and N-deletion as separate processes.

When considering developments in the Northern Italian sample, explicit reference to nasals in non-cluster position will normally be restricted to Latin /n/ (Stage 2 /n₁/), since it is this nasal which most frequently undergoes change throughout the sample. More limited reference is also made to Latin /nn/ (>Stage 2 /n₂/). There is, however, no reason to believe that the spread of vowel nasalization and N-deletion reported in the context of dental nasals will not develop in the same fashion, once they occur, at other places of articulation in Northern Italian, or elsewhere. Of course, only changes in the context of tonic vowels are considered unless stated otherwise.

Initially, reference to Latin Nasal+Continuant clusters is restricted to NS since this is the only such cluster to appear within native morphemes, e.g. PE:NSAT 'he thinks', but 'IN+FAME 'infamous'. N+Continuant clusters of the type N+L, N+R, N+J, N+W have a complex and special history in Latin and in Romance, which is considered separately and in detail in section 6.2. I will argue, *contra* Schourup, that it is impossible to categorize

in a uniform manner the effect of different post-nasal continuants on the development of vowel nasalization and N-deletion.

The elimination of Latin /n/ before /s/ (and before /f/) appears to have been under way, although not entirely complete, within Latin; see Väänänen (1967: 66–7) for examples.[4] As a result, examples of /ns/ (and also /nf/) clusters found in Romance dialects today are often considered to have been reintroduced under learned and semi-learned pressure, often resulting in doublets, e.g. PE:NSAT > It., Mi. *pensa*, Fr. *pense*, 'thinks', but It., Mi. *pesa*, Fr. *pèse*, 'weighs'; cf. Allen (1965: 28–30), Rohlfs (1966: 381), Sanga (1979: 236; fn. 96) and Väänänen (1967). The reduction of NS can be tied to a first cycle of vowel nasalization and N-deletion apparently already in progress in Latin, and complete very early in Romance, e.g. oxytonic JAM 'already' > *[d͡ʒãː], NO:N > *[nõː], and also final atonic PANEM 'bread' > *[paːnẽ]; see sections 2.2.2.1 and 4.3.2. The results of this cycle are found in all Romance dialects, including Northern Italian, e.g. JAM > It., Mi. *già*, Sp. *ya*, Fr. *déjà*, Bo. [dza], Ta. [ɟjeː], but also PANEM > Fr. *pain*, Sp. *pan*, It. *pane*, Bo. [pæŋ]. In most cases denasalization followed the first cycle, as made evident by the examples, and 'NO:N > Bo. [na], but Fr. [nɔ̃ː].

In these circumstances, I distinguish between two sets of N+Fric clusters: (1) the original Latin set of NS (and NF), affected by the first cycle of distinctive nasalization, e.g. PE:NSAT > *[pẽːsat] > It., Mi. *pesa* 'weighs'; and (2) a second set of NS (and NF) clusters reintroduced in Romance, or preserved when they otherwise would have been lost, as a result of learned influence, e.g. PE:NSAT > It., Mi. *pensa* 'thinks'.

I have tabulated the development of vowel nasalization and N-deletion in each sample dialect according to specific context in tables 6.1 and 6.2 respectively. Original Latin 'VNFric sequences and N-final oxytones, although few in number, are listed above the distinguishing line in each table as part of the first cycle of distinctive nasalization. As is evident both from the tables, and from the discussion above, nasalization and N-deletion in these two contexts occurred early everywhere. Below the line in each table, I list specific contexts that passed into Romance relatively untouched, or that arose secondarily as a result of changes posited at Stages 1 and 2. Examples of the former include voiceless clusters, e.g. TANTA 'so' (f.) > Stage 2 /tanta/; see table 6.1e, and of the latter, degemination, e.g. CANNA 'cane' > Stage 2 /kana/, ANNU 'year' > Stage 2 /an/ at h, and secondary oxytones at c, e.g. CANE 'dog' > Stage 2 /kaːn/. With regard to Bolognese and Cairese, formerly quite clear patterns of distinctive nasalization (although now reversed by secondary hardening of nasalized glides) are easily inferred by the presence of velar nasals in specific contexts. Similarly, the absence of N in the denasalizing dialect of Bergamese allows for earlier patterns of nasalization and N-loss to be established. As for Riminese, Schürr (1919) did not consider vowel nasalization to be regular in this dialect, although his recordings (and transcriptions) show that nasalization was to some degree optional on long

Table 6.1   Nasalization Patterns before N in Northern Italian

	Ta.	Ri.	Bg.	Lg.	Bo.	Ca.	Mi.	Im.	Ra.
a V(:)N#(1)	+	+	+	+	+	+	+	+	+
b V:NFric(1)	+	+	+	+	+	+	+	+	+
c V:n#(2)	−	±	+	+	+	+	+	+	+
d VNFric(2)	−	−	+	+	+	+	+	+	+
e VNStop [−v]	−	−	+	+	+	+	+	+	+
f VNStop [+v]	−	−	−	−	+	+	+	±	±
g V:nV	−	−	−	+	+	+	−	+	+
h Vn(V)	−	−	−	−	−	−	−	±	±

Key: + regular, − not reported, ± restricted distribution or optional.
a V(:)N#(1)   original Latin N-final oxytones, e.g. NON, JAM
b V:NFric(1) original Latin NS, NF clusters (1st cycle)
c V:n#(2)   Stage 2 /n/-final oxytones, e.g. /ka:n/ < CANE
d VNFric(2)   (semi-)learned NS, NF in Romance, e.g. PE:NSAT
e VNStop   e.g. Stage 2 /tant(a)/ < TANTU-A
   [−v]
f VNStop   e.g. Stage 2 /grand/ < GRANDE
   [+v]
g V:nV   e.g. Stage 2 /la:na/ < LANA
h Vn(V)   e.g. Stage 2 /kana/ < CANNA, /an/ < ANNU

vowels before word-final /n₁/, e.g. [pɛːn] ~ [pɛ̃ːn] 'bread'. Today however, nasalization of long vowels is regular, e.g. [pɛ̃ːn] < Stage 2 /paːn/ < PANE, [dẽĵⁿt] < DENTE 'tooth', [gãːmba] < *GAMBA, [lẽːna] < LANA, [lẽːma] < *LAMA 'blade', but [pɛna] < PINNA 'feather', [vɛnd] < VENDIT 'sells', [fum] < FUMU 'smoke'. N-deletion is not really known, although N may be so reduced after nasalized vowels today that it is often difficult to hear. Conditions for Riminese reported in the tables are those described for the early part of this century.

Examination of table 6.1 indicates that vowel nasalization has developed most frequently before word-final /n#/, and voiceless NFric and NStop clusters. N-deletion is entirely regular only before Stage 2 /n#/, since in Milanese, pre-consonantal N-deletion remains optional, e.g. [tãː(ⁿ)t] < TANTU.

We can infer from developments in other Romance dialects inside (e.g. Salodiano, closely related to Bergamese) and outside Northern Italy (e.g. Anconetano, Catalan) that distinctive nasalization develops preferentially before Latin /n/ in secondary final position (i.e. Stage 2 /V:n#/). At 5 we see that in these dialects evidence of a past process of distinctive nasalization does not extend to VNC or any other context.

Table 6.2   N-deletion Patterns in Northern Italian

	Ta.	Ri.	Bg.	Lg.	Ca.	Bo.	Mi.	Im.	Ra.
a V(ː)N#(1)	+	+	+	+	+	+	+	+	+
b Vː NFric(1)	+	+	+	+	+	+	+	+	+
c Vː n#(2)	−	−	+	+	+	+	+	+	+
d VNFric(2)	−	−	+	+	+	+	±	+	+
e VNStop [−v]	−	−	+	+	+	+	±	+	+
f VNStop [+v]	−	−	−	−	+	+	±	−	−
g Vː nV	−	−	−	−	−	−	−	−	−
h Vn(V)	−	−	−	−	−	−	−	−	−

See table 6.1 for key.

5a Salodiano
  ca < *[kãː] < Stage 2 /kaːn/[5] < CANE 'dog'
  pa < *[pãː] <   /paːn/ < PANE 'bread'
  but $pónt$ < Stage 2 /pɔnt/ < PONTE 'bridge'
  $mènt$ <   /mɛnt/ < MENTE 'mind'
  $lónch$ <   /lɔng/ < LONGUS 'long'
  an <   /an/ < ANNU 'year'

                                    (Razzi 1984: 125)

  b Anconetano (The Marches)
  [saˈvoː]   < *[saˈvõː] < Stage 2 /savoːn/ < SAPONE 'soap'
  [viː]   < *[vĩː]   <   /viːn/ < VINU 'wine'
  but [gamba]   < *GAMBA 'leg'
  [sant]   < SANCTU 'holy'
  [grande]   < GRANDE 'large'
  [an°]   < ANNU 'year'

                                    (*AIS* pt.539)

  c Catalan
  ma [ma]   < *[mãː] < MANU but $mans$ [mans] 'hand(s)'
  vi [bi]   < *[bĩː] < VINU $vins$ [bins] 'wine(s)'
  be [be]   < BENE but [ben rik] $ben ric$ 'quite rich'
                         [ben al] $ben alt$ 'quite high'
  bo [bɔ]   < BONU but [bɔn diə] $bon dia$ 'good day'
  $camp$ [kam] < CAMPU 'field'
  $vent$ [ben] < VENTU 'wind'
  any [aɲ]   < ANNU 'year'

                                    (Badía Margarit 1951: 225)[6]

Despite their special status, (semi-)learned /Vns, Vnf/ sequences behave in a manner that is entirely compatible with the general conditions of nasalization and N-deletion recorded in individual Northern Italian dialects. For example, N-deletion in Milanese is optional before obstruents, whether fricatives or stops. Similarly, in Bolognese and Cairese, VNFric, like other clusters, is affected by historical distinctive nasalization and secondary velarization, e.g. Bo. [pæŋsa] < [pæ̃ɥ̃sa] < [pæ̃ȷ̃sa] < PE:NSAT 'thinks', [praŋta] < [prɔ̃w̃ta] < PRO:MPTA 'ready' (f.).

Voicing differences in post-nasal consonants clearly affect the development of distinctive nasalization, as seen in tables 6.1e and f and 6.2e and f, and as also reported for Northern Italian by Tuttle (1991). Evidence of vowel nasalization and N-deletion before voiceless stops is found in seven dialects, including Bergamese, Lughese, Imolese and Ravennate. However, before voiced stops, the same phenomena are absent in Bergamese and Lughese, as is evident in the examples at 6a. In Imolese and Ravennate, N-deletion is similarly absent, and vowel nasalization extends only to Stage 2 /a/, after secondary vowel lengthening, as at 6b:

6a	Bg.	*cap*	< *[kã:p]	< CAMPU	'field'
	but	*gamba*		< *GAMBA	'leg'
	Lg.	[kwẽ:t]		< QUANTU	'how much'
	but	[dma:nda]		< DEMANDAT	'(he) entrusts'
b	Im.	[pjẽ:ta]		< PLANTA	'plant'
		[grẽ:nda]		< GRANDE	'big' (f.)
	but	[leŋgwa]		< LINGUA	'tongue'

A phonological process of nasalization, as a diachronic or synchronic phenomenon, of long vowels before Latin intervocalic /n/ is regular in five dialects in the sample, although deletion of intervocalic /n/ is unknown, e.g. LANA 'wool' > Stage 2 /la:na/ > Im. [lẽ:na], Ca. [laŋna]; see table 6.1g. Perhaps somewhat unexpectedly, nasalization of long vowels before intervocalic /n/ is more regular in the sample than before voiced clusters.[7] Such a pattern finds confirmation in other Northern Italian dialects, e.g. Genoese (Parodi 1902: 351–2), Parmigiano (Piagnoli 1904), Piacentino (Gorra 1890), where synchronic or historical evidence of nasalization before voiced N+Stop clusters is always accompanied by nasalization before intervocalic /n$_1$/, e.g. Piac. [lã:na] and [gã:mba]. Nasalization of Stage 2 short vowels before /n$_2$/ (< Lat. /nn/) is rare, and associated with secondary vowel lengthening: only Stage 2 /a/ in Imolese and Ravennate is affected, as seen at 7a and b with corroborating evidence from Piacentino. Secondary /n$_2$/ (< Lat. /nn/), whether final or intervocalic, is never lost in the sample:

7a Im.   [kẽːna] < Stage 2 /kana/ < CANNA   'cane'
           [ẽːn]   <   /an/   < ANNU   'year'
      but [pena] <   /pena/ < PINNA   'feather'
    Ra.   [ʌ̃ːn]   < Stage 2 /an/   < ANNU   'year'
      but [nɔːn] <   /nɔn/ < *NONNU 'grandfather'
cf. Lg.   [kaːna]
           [aːn]
      but [kẽː]   < CANE   'dog'

b Piac.   lãna   [lãːna] < LANA   'wool'
      but ann   [an]   < ANNU   'year'
          canna [kana] < CANNA 'cane'

                                                (Gorra 1890)

The distributional characteristics of vowel nasalization and N-deletion in Northern Italian make it possible to formulate two contextual parameters that account for the spread of each phenomenon respectively in an ordered and predictable manner, as at 8a and b:

8a Nasalization Contextual Parameter

Vːn# VNFric VNStop VːnV VNStop Vn#
     [−v]   [+v] VnV
                         Vnn(V)
    ─────────────────────────────────→

b N-deletion Contextual Parameter

Vːn# VNFric VNStop VNStop VːnV VnV Vnn(V)
     [−v]   [+v]   Vn#
    ─────────────────────────────────→

Accordingly, vowel nasalization and N-deletion spread in an implicational fashion along their respective parameters from left to right. In both cases, I suggest that change is more likely to affect VNFric than VNStop on the basis of the preferential simplification of N+Fricative clusters already under way in Latin. Confirmation of such a distinction is provided by Tuttle (1991): he reports that whilst VNStop is conserved as such in Val d'Antrona Novarese, nasalization is regular and N-deletion optional before secondary fricatives, e.g. [camp] 'field' < CAMPU, [ɟamba] 'leg' < *GAMBA, but [rãːⁿʃ] ~ [rãːʃ] 'rancid' < RANCIDU, [sũːⁿʒa] ~ [sũːʒa] 'suet' < AXUNGIA. Additional non-Romance evidence in support of this claim is easily uncovered, and is reported below in section 6.4.1.1.

Although Stage 2 /VːnV/ (< VNV) and /VnV/ (< VNNV and related /Vn#/) appear equally resistant to N-deletion in the sample, developments elsewhere in Northern Italy show that in the former N can be lost, e.g. rustic Parmigiano lõa < lõna [lõːna] < LUNA 'moon', but pena [pɛna] < PINNA 'feather' (Piagnoli 1904: 26). A similar pattern is reported in many other Romance

dialects (Portuguese, Gascon, degeminating varieties of Corsican), e.g. Pt. *lã* < LANA, but *cana* < CANNA. I have also incorporated geminate contexts, Vnn(V), into the parameters. As found previously for Vn# and VnV, vowel nasalization is predictably blocked by the phonologically short vowel before geminates in [Vnn(V)], e.g. Bo. [panna] < Stage 2 /pena/ < PINNA 'feather'. Furthermore, as discussed below, vowel nasalization is unusual before geminates in otherwise nasalizing Centro-Southern Italian dialects, e.g. Sard., Cors. [kanna] < CANNA. but [lãːna] < LANA. Exceptionally, only in Tuscan are vowels nasalized when adjacent to geminate nasals, e.g. [kãnnã], [pẽnnã], just as they are next to any nasal in all contexts, e.g. [tãnto], [lãːnã] (Giannelli and Savoia 1978). Everywhere in Romance, complete loss of simple N remains more likely than the relatively rare loss of N:, and simplification of geminates is via degemination to a short nasal, i.e., [Vnn(v)] > [Vn(V)].

VNStop sequences should properly refer also to N+Affricate clusters, in which the stop element survives, since they appear to pattern together, equally affected by a post-nasal voicing contrast, as at 9. Tuttle (1991) suggests that a similar voicing contrast effect on nasalization and N-deletion is apparent in the context of Romance N+Fric clusters, /nf/ and /nv/, e.g. INFERNU 'hell' vs. *INVERNU 'winter'. I have seen no clear evidence in Romance of this, although such a result would be expected. Fujimura (1977: 119) notes that nasal consonants are significantly reduced or even deleted before voiceless stops and fricatives, when compared to nasals before their voiced counterparts (see also section 6.4.1.4 below). For the moment, however, N+Fricative clusters are not differentiated along the parameters.

9 Im.   [vẽːʧ]   < *[vinʧ]   < VINCULU 'band'
   but [ondᶻa] < *[undʤa] < UNGULA 'fingernail'
Bg.   [u(ː)ʧa]< *[unʧa]   < UNCTA   'greasy'
   but [ondʤa] < *[ondʤa] < UNGULA 'fingernail'

The contextual deletion parameter at 8b supports the contention by Ruhlen (1973) and Foley (1975, 1977) that N-deletion is more likely in syllable-final, i.e. Coda position, than in syllable-initial (intervocalic) position. Nowhere in the sample is intervocalic or word-initial /n/ lost, e.g. Im. [kẽ:] < Stage 2 /kaːn/ < CANE, but [lẽːna] < LANA, [nom] < *NOME. However, the role of syllable position is less clear-cut in the operation of the nasalization contextual parameter: nasalization before syllable-initial intervocalic /n/ is more likely than before syllable-final N in N+voiced stop clusters. This apparent aberration can be accounted for and an explanation for it is given in section 6.4.

The parameters also appear to operate across word boundaries, so that # may be inserted after /n/ or N along the length of the parameters, as suggested by the French data previously given in the text and the Catalan data at 5c.

Table 6.3   Nasalization Patterns before Stage 2 /n/ and NC

a	No nasalization	Tavetsch
b	V:n#	Riminese (Salodiano, Catalan, Lengadocian Occitan, Anconetano)
c	VNFric	(Val d'Antrona Novarese)
d	VNStop [−v]	Bergamese
e	V:nV	Lughese
f	VNStop [+v]	Bolognese, Cairese, Milanese[8]
g	Vn# VnV	Imolese, Ravennate[9]

In an effort to make the relative position of individual dialects along the contextual parameters clearer, the patterns of nasalization found in the sample of nine dialects and listed in table 6.1 have been tabulated in table 6.3. Only Stage 2 contexts are included. The first cycle of nasalization and N-deletion already underway in Latin is not referred to as all dialects are affected equally. In a similar fashion, relative position along the N-deletion contextual parameter is listed in table 6.4. Both tables are set out in a strictly implicational manner from top to bottom, i.e. g ≥ a–g, unless otherwise stated. Also included in parentheses are other Northern Italian and Romance varieties also mentioned or exemplified with regard to contextual effects on the development of distinctive nasalization.

Whilst the two contextual parameters are not strictly comparable, it is evident that, in accordance with the NTM whereby vowel nasalization always precedes N-deletion over time, the extent of nasalization according to context in Northern Italian is greater than that of N-deletion, as can be seen in table 6.5.

Table 6.4   Patterns of /n/-deletion

a	No /n/-deletion	Tavetsch, Riminese
b	V:n#	(Salodiano, Catalan, Lengadocian, Anconetano)
c	VNFric	(Val d'Antrona Novarese)
d	VNStop [−v]	Bergamese, Imolese, Lughese, Ravennate
e	VNStop [+v]	Cairese, Bolognese, Milanese [10]
f	V:nV	no examples
g	VnV Vn#	no examples

Table 6.5   Comparative Spread of Nasalization and N-deletion

	Nasalization	N-deletion
Tavetsch	a	a
Riminese	b	a
Bergamese	d	d
Lughese	e	d
Milanese	f	e
Bolognese	f	e
Cairese	f	e
Imolese	g	d
Ravennate	g	d

6.2. [+ Continuant] and Contextual Parameters

In some non-Romance languages, the spread of distinctive nasalization appears preferentially before all continuants, in accordance with Schourup's (1973) claim, as in Brussels Flemish at 10 (De Vriendt and Goyvaerts 1989: 54):

10 Brussels Flemish
   [nəm#boːʀ]   *een boer*   'a farmer'
   [ən#tuŋ]   *een tong*   'a tongue'
   [ɔ̃#vʀaː]   *een vrouw*   'a woman'
   [tɛ̃ː#juːʀ]   *tien jaar*   'ten years'

However, the changes reported in Northern Italian dialects, as in many other Romance dialects, show little or no evidence of vowel nasalization and N-deletion developing preferentially before continuants. Instead, more typically we find changes that render the development of distinctive nasalization less likely through (1) total assimilation of N to C; or (2) 'fortitive' processes that alter or eliminate the post-nasal continuant, or result in the gemination of N, with the effect of rendering more difficult the spread of distinctive nasalization (see section 7.2).

With regard to historical developments in my Northern Italian sample, morpheme-internal /nl, nr, nj, nw, nf/ as native clusters were unknown to Latin. Examples of such clusters in native words could theoretically appear only across morphemes as a result of prefixation, e.g. IN+RIGARE, CON+IUGARE, IN+FLUENTIA.[11] However, N before L/R regularly underwent full liquid assimilation, rather than deletion, e.g. IN+RIGARE > IRRIGARE > Mi. *irigâ*, It. *irrigare* 'to irrigate', IN+LEGALE > ILLEGALE > Mi. *ilegâl*, It. *illegale* 'illegal'.

In many Northern Italian dialects, as in other Western Romance dialects, a new set of secondary *N'R, *N'L, *M'L, *M'R after tonic vowels developed when intertonic vowels were deleted, e.g. CAMERA 'room' > *CAM'RA, TENERA 'tender' > *TEN'RA (Rohlfs 1966: 355, 382). Secondary N+Liquid clusters were eliminated in one of two ways, apparently chronologically unrelated: (1) a very early process of total assimilation, evidence of which is also found sporadically in Central and Southern Italy; and (2) homorganic stop epenthesis; see Rohlfs (1966: 355) and 11a and b:

11a SPINULA 'pin'   > *SPIN'LA   > Bo. ['spella]
                                    Bg. ['spila]
                                    cf. Tusc. *spilla*

  b TEN'RA 'tender' > *[tɛndra] > Bo. ['tæŋdra]
                                    Bg. ['tɛndra] ~ ['trɛnda]
                                    cf. OFr. *tendre* > Fr. [tãːdʀ]
                                    but Tusc. *tenera*

Across morpheme boundaries in Northern Italian, as in many other Romance dialects, Latin /w/ in post-nasal position generally hardened to [v], e.g. Lat. /in+wiːtaːre/ > It. *invitare*, Mi. *invidà* 'invite'. In Southern Italy, Lat. /n+w/ strengthened further to [mb], before passing to [mː] in some areas:

12 INVITARE > S. Calabrian *imbitare* 'invite'
             Sicilian   *mmitare*   (Rohlfs 1966: 360)
             Altamurese [mmətɛʲ]   (Loporcaro 1988: 147)

Secondary *[nw] also developed within morphemes, as a result of secondary prevocalic gliding, e.g. TENUIS > *[tenwis] 'thin'. The subsequent development of *[nw] in Romance is extremely complex. Regularly simplified to [n] in Northern Italian, e.g. JANUARIU > Ta. [ɟə'nɛː], Bo. [dznɛːr], Mi. *genar* 'January', one finds a multiplicity of results for *[nw] across Romance and within the same Romance dialect:[12]

13a gemination and delabialization: [nw] > [nnw] > [nn]
    TENUIT   > Sard. *tenni(t)*, It. *tenne*, 'he held'
    MANUARIA > It. *mannaia* 'axe'

  b simple delabialization: [nw] > [n][13]
    MANUARIA > Bo. *manèra* 'axe', Sp. *manera*, Pt. *maneira*, Fr. *manière*,
                'manner'
    JANUARIU > OProv. *janier* 'January'

  c velar assimilation and epenthesis: [nw] > [ŋw] > [ŋg(w)]
    *MINUARE > Sp. *menguar*, Pt. *minguar*, 'decrease'
    TENUI   > OProv. *tinc,* OCat. *tenc(h)*, 'I held'

  d bilabial assimilation and hardening: [nw] > [mβ] > [mb]
    MANUALE > OProv. *mambal* 'manual'

e labiodentalization: [Vnw] > [Vɱv] (> [Ṽv] > [Vv])
JANUARIU > Fr. *janvier*, OProv. *gevier, girvier*, 'January'
TENUE   > OFr. *tenve* 'fine'

In (semi-)learned forms, Latin pretonic [u] survived as a vowel, e.g. MANUALE > It. *manovale* 'manual', in which case intervocalic /n/ was deleted in Portuguese and Galician, e.g. Pt. *moual*, Gal. *manle*.

There is no evidence of N-deletion before [w] itself in Romance; /n/ survived everywhere, in some areas undergoing fortition through gemination, e.g. TENUIT > Tusc. *tenne* '(he) held'. Post-nasal [w] itself is eliminated, or fully consonantized as [v] or [b]. Only then is labiodentalized [ɱ] lost as in Old Provençal and French, e.g. CONVENTU > *couvent* 'convent'.

The derived cluster N+J was preserved as such in Latin: neither N-deletion nor alternatively total assimilation are reported, e.g. CON+IUGE 'spouse'. In Italian dialects, this post-nasal but morpheme-initial /j/ is normally hardened to /ʤ/ (> [dz, z, ʒ]) in most Italian dialects, as if in word-initial position; see 14:

14 CON+IUNGERE > It. [konʤunʤere] ~ [konjunʤere]
              Bo. [kondzondzer] 'to conjoin'
   cf. IOCU   > It. [ʤɔːko]
              Bo. [dzuːk] 'game'

Similarly, the development in Romance of secondary morpheme-medial NJ, e.g. VINEA 'vineyard' > *VINJA, does not conform to any predictions about preferential N-loss and nasalization in the context [Vnj]. In Northern Italian, as elsewhere in Romance, NJ became [ɲ], e.g. *BANJU 'bath' > Bo. [baːɲ]. In Central and Southern Italian, N, like other consonants, was lengthened before J, whence modern [ɲː], e.g. Tusc. [viɲːa] 'vineyard' < *VINNJA < *VINJA (Rohlfs 1966: 399). In many Sardinian and Corsican dialects, N is preserved as [n], but J has been variously strengthened; see 15:

15 *VINJA 'vineyard' >
   Sard. [binʤa], [bindza], [binʒa], [bintsa], [binʒa], [binɟa]
                           (Contini 1987, map 38)
   Cors. [vinɟa]   (Rohlfs 1966: 399, n.1)

The development of N+Continuant clusters in Romance and Latin does not support Schourup's claim that distinctive nasalization develops in a uniform fashion before all continuants. The evidence suggests that [+cont] does not characterize in Romance at least a natural class for the purposes of sound change. Nor is the hypothesis confirmed that distinctive nasalization develops preferentially in the context of N+Continuant clusters, relative to any other type of nasal cluster. Whilst distinctive nasalization has developed in Latin /V(ː)ns/, changes reported in Northern Italian and other Romance

dialects show that the development of other N+Continuant clusters does not necessarily fall within the framework of distinctive nasalization processes. According to the nature of the continuant, and the Romance dialect, N+Continuant clusters may be variously affected, for instance, by N-gemination, loss or obstruentization of the continuant, stop epenthesis, and total assimilation. One element of change unforeseen by universalists, such as Schourup (1973) and Foley (1975, 1977), is that N may be prone to fortition, just as it may be prone to weakening and deletion. The gemination of N before [w, j] found in Central and Southern Italy is not predicted by Schourup (1973), and renders reduction of N to Ø even less likely. Furthermore, if we accept at least as an initial premise Schourup's claim that all N+Continuant clusters present the most favoured context for the development of distinctive nasalization, the reported obstruentization of post-nasal continuants in some cases also has the effect of rendering the development of distinctive nasalization less likely by pushing clusters further to the right along his own contextual parameter given previously at 4.

6.3   ARE CONTEXTUAL PARAMETERS UNIVERSAL?

The uniform pattern of implementation of nasalization and N-deletion processes in Northern Italian along the respective contextual parameters given at 8 above would seem to augur well for the more general, possibly universal, applicability of such parameters elsewhere.

One expected strong point of the N-deletion contextual parameter at 8d is the reference it makes to the relative weakness of syllable-final or Coda-position N(C)\$, in contrast to its syllable-initial or Onset-position counterpart \$N. Universalists agree that N-deletion develops preferentially in syllable-final rather than syllable-initial (intervocalic) position, a finding apparently confirmed by developments in Northern Italian, e.g. Bg. [taːt] < TAN\$TU, but [laːna] < LA\$NA. However, important counter-examples demonstrate that in some Romance dialects the expected strength relationship between (supposedly weak) tautosyllabic VN\$ and (strong) heterosyllabic V\$NV positions appears to be unexpectedly reversed.[14] In Sardinian and many Corsican dialects vowel nasalization is recorded only before historic intervocalic /n/ which is then deleted, e.g. Sard. [mãw̃] < [mãːnu] < MANU 'hand', but [tanta] < TANTA 'so' (f.), [limba] < LINGUA 'tongue' (Contini 1987). Dalbera-Stefanaggi (1989) provides evidence of different stages of development in a number of Corsican dialects, as at 16:

16	Vero	Loreto	Galeria[15]	
-ONE	[-ɔːni]	[-õːne]	[-ɔ̃ː]	
PANE	[paːni]	[pãːne]	[pãːe]	'bread'

In Tuscan changes have been more extensive. Giannelli and Savoia (1978: 47–50) report the weakening of historical /n/ and /m/ to corresponding nasalized approximants [ɪ̃] and [β̃] respectively, between vowels, after continuants /l, r, z/, and even in phrase-initial position. In word-medial and phonosyntactic intervocalic position, these nasalized approximants may be deleted, as exemplified at 17:

17 Tuscan

a /domani/   > [ðõ'β̃ãɪ̃]   > [ðõ'ãɪ̃]   'tomorrow'
b /la#notte/ > [l̃ã'ɪ̃ɔ̃tːe] > [l̃ã 'ɔ̃tːe] 'the night'
c /naskondilo/ > [ɪ̃ãskõndilo] 'hide it!'
d /lo#smonta/ > [lo 'zβ̃õnta] 'dismantles it'
e /kalmo/   > ['kalβ̃o]   'calm'

The preferential development of distinctive nasalization in the context V\$NV, in contrast to the apparent stability of VN\$ in Sardinian, Corsican and Tuscan, is extremely surprising given the claim by Ruhlen (1973), Schourup (1973), Foley (1975, 1977) and myself that the opposite should always be the case. I have suggested elsewhere (Hajek 1993b) that the divergent patterns of development noted in Northern vs. Centro-Southern Italian dialects, such as Sardinian and Corsican, may depend at least partially on important structural differences that separate the two groups, e.g. the conservation in Centro-Southern Italian of final vowels, and of historical gemination.[16] Some weight must also be given the extremely advanced process of intervocalic lenition of obstruents and sonorants within and across words noted in these dialects.[17]

A further difference may lie in differences in the relative weight given to prosodic vs. melodic factors in the development of distinctive nasalization processes. That is, in Northern Italian and elsewhere, syllable structure above the skeleton, i.e. onset vs. coda position of N, may be the most significant factor, rendering other factors less important. Conversely, in Centro-Southern Italian, the melodic configuration of features below the skeleton may override the operation of expected syllable-structure constraints. It is well known that geminates and partial geminates, such as homorganic NC clusters, frequently exhibit so-called 'inalterability' behaviour (Hayes 1986b and Schein and Steriade 1986). As such, they resist the operation of rules that affect non-geminate segments, e.g. Sard. [kanna] < CANNA 'cane', [limba] < LINGUA 'tongue', but [lãː] < LANA 'wool'.

Alternatively, operation of the Vowel-Length Parameter (VLP) may account for developments in Centro-Southern Italian: in these dialects, vowel nasalization and N-deletion most characteristically affect VːN, leaving VN untouched, regardless of any hypothetical syllable-structure constraints, e.g. LANA 'wool' > [laːna] > Sard. [lãː], but TANTU 'so' (m.) > [tantu]. Such an account of developments in Centro-Southern Italian is not incompatible with the operation of contextual parameters in Northern

Italian, which also appear to be governed, at least partially, by vowel length; see 8 above, but especially discussion below in section 6.5.[18]

6.3.1 Non-Romance counter-examples to the revised context parameter

The non-universality of contextual parameters, whether posited by myself or others, is further demonstrated by developments in non-Romance languages. There is ample evidence, diachronic and synchronic, in Germanic dialects, of preferential deletion of preconsonantal N, presumably preceded by vowel nasalization, in contrast to the preservation of word-final /n#/ even after long vowels. Preconsonantal deletion is especially common before voiceless fricatives, as at 18:

18a English
    [kæ:t] 'can't'   but [mæ:n] 'man'   (Hooper 1976)

  b Old English
    us (cf. Gothic uns)   but man(n)   (Foley 1977)

  c Low German
    us 'us'   but mon 'man'   (Schirmunski 1962)[19]

  d Afrikaans
    [afrəkã:s] 'Afrikaans'   but [duəsəin] 'dozen'   (Taylor and Uys 1988)

  e Brussels Flemish
    [mẽ:s] 'person'   but [te:n] 'ten' (De Vriendt and Goyvaerts 1989)

6.3.2 Conclusions about universal contextual parameters

The body of evidence within and without Romance demonstrates the non-universality of posited contextual parameters. The deletion of inter-vocalic /n/ in Tuscan, Sardinian and Corsican, whilst tautosyllabic /n/ remains unaffected, is completely unexpected within the theories proposed by universalists. Factors such as the conservation of final vowels and geminate consonants, and the scope of intervocalic lenition, may be responsible for the particular pattern of N-deletion and distinctive nasalization noted in these dialects. This overrides the expected application of the contextual parameters I proposed on the basis of developments in Northern Italian. However, it also appears that apparently divergent developments in Northern and Centro-Southern are not as incompatible as they might seem, if an explanation for patterns lies, not ultimately in the nature of context, but in the operation of the Vowel-Length Parameter, as is suggested briefly above, and further discussed below.

Despite the existence of apparent counter-examples such as those found in Centro-Southern Italy, it remains possible that parts of the revised contextual parameter have universal validity. For instance, I have found

no counter-evidence to the claim that the development of distinctive nasalization is predictably affected by the voicing contrast in post-nasal consonants, e.g.: (1) Lg. [tẽːta] 'so' (f.) < TANTA, but [gaːmba] 'leg' < *GAMBA; and (2) Hindi [dãːta] < Skt. *danta* 'tooth', but [tʃãːnda] < Skt *candra* 'moon'.

6.4 EXPLANATIONS FOR THE CONTEXTUAL PARAMETERS: A ROLE FOR THE VOWEL-LENGTH PARAMETER?

Despite the non-universal applicability of the contextual parameters posited by universalists and myself, it remains true that: (1) developments in Northern Italian seem to have occurred in a non-random fashion; (2) counter-examples have not been found to certain ordering patterns along the parameters, given at 8a and b and repeated at 19, for which plausible phonetic explanations are available. In these circumstances, it remains necessary to account for such patterning.:

19a Nasalization Contextual Parameter

Vːn# VNFric VNStop VːnV VNStop Vn#
    [−v]   [+v] VnV
                            Vnn(V)

———————————————————————————————▶

  b N-deletion Contextual Parameter

Vːn# VNFric VNStop VNStop VːnV VnV Vnn(V)
    [−v]   [+v]   Vn#

———————————————————————————————▶

Even a cursory glance at 19 shows that the VLP plays some role in the operation of the contextual parameters. For instance, reference to word-final position, supposedly very weak because syllable-final, is in itself insufficient to account for developments in Northern Italian, since final /n/ appears at both ends of the parameters as both the most likely and one of the least likely contexts for nasalization and N-deletion, e.g. Mi. [pãː] < Stage 2 /paːn/ 'bread', but [an] < Stage 2 /an/ 'year'.[20]

Word-final N-deletion after tonic short vowels is unknown in the sample, and the limited evidence of vowel nasalization in some Romagnol dialects is preceded by secondary vowel lengthening, e.g. Stage 2 /an/ > Lg. [aːn] > Im. [ẽːn].

Some additional confirmation that word-final position alone is not the only factor in the development of distinctive nasalization in the context of word-final N is found in child-language acquisition data for Spanish (Hernández-Chaves et al. 1975) and English (Hooper 1977): whilst nasals before voiceless stops are lost, word-final nasals are not deleted,

e.g. English [grɪk] *drink*, [fak] *spank*, but [fun] *spoon*, [wan] *one*, [ram] *lamb*.[21]

There is evidence to suggest that the effect of the VLP is not restricted to word-final position, and, in fact, may be pervasive along both contextual parameters. The development of nasalization and N-deletion in the context of intervocalic N also coincides with the expected operation of the VLP, i.e. VːNV ≫ VNV. More surprisingly, even the distribution of different types of NC clusters along the parameters appears to be governed by a parameter of preferential vowel lengthening, as at 20:

20   Preferential Vowel-Lengthening Parameter

$$\underset{\underset{[+\text{v}]}{\longrightarrow}}{\overset{\text{VNFric   VNStop   VNStop}}{\underline{\hspace{1cm}[-\text{v}]\hspace{1cm}}}}$$

Foley (1975, 1977) was the first to suggest that preferential effacement of N in nasal+fricative clusters is the result of a similarly preferential phonological process of vowel lengthening in that context, e.g. Old English *goːs* < **gaːns* < **gans* 'goose', but *hund* < *hund* 'hound'. The early elimination of nasal+fricative clusters that first began in Latin may also be tied to a preceding stage of regular vowel lengthening not found before other NC clusters, e.g. MEːNSA 'table' but MENTE 'mind', DEːNS (nom.) – DENTEM (acc.) 'tooth', CEːNSOR 'censor' but CENTU 'hundred'.[22] Similarly, in Val d'Antrona Novarese, regular nasalization and optional N-deletion before fricatives were preceded by vowel lengthening, e.g. [rãː[(n)]ʃ] 'rancid' < RANCIDU, [sũː[(n)]ʃa] 'suet' < AXUNGIA, but [camp] 'camp' < CAMPU, [ɟamba] 'leg' < *GAMBA.

The effect of the stop voicing contrast on secondary vowel lengthening before nasal clusters in Northern Italian dialects is widespread. Preferential vowel lengthening before N+Stop[−voice] clusters, in contrast to the preservation of short vowels before N+Stop[+voice] clusters, also confirmed by Tuttle (1991), is reported throughout Northern Italy, including much of Emilia-Romagna:

21a Frignano
   [teːnt] < TANTU 'so'   but [grand]   < GRANDE   'large'
   [teːmp] < TEMPU 'time'   but [setamber] < SEPTEMBRE
                                                           (Uguzzoni 1975)

  b Collagna
   [teːŋp] < TEMPU 'time'   but [rəŋd]   < RENDIT   'renders'
   [poːŋt] < PONTE 'bridge' but [kloŋb]   < COLOMBA   'pigeon'
                                                           (Malagoli 1943)

  c Rimini
   [teːnt] < TANTU 'so'   but [gaːmba]   < *GAMBA   'leg'
   [dɛjnt] < DENTE 'tooth'   but [veŋ[k]]   < *VENGO   'I come'
   [mo[w]nt] < MONTE 'mount' but [laŋga]   < LONGA   'long' (f.)
                                                           (Schürr 1919)

Similar facts are reported in other more distant Emilian dialects such as Valestra (Malagoli 1934), and Novellara (Malagoli 1910). The AIS also shows secondary lengthening in Northern Italy to be far more extensive before N+Stop[−voice] than before N+Stop[+voice] clusters; cf. VII 1416 CAMPO and I 10 GRANDE, I 159 GAMBA. In numerous Romagnol dialects, as exemplified by Riminese at 21c, vowel lengthening has now extended in a very restricted fashion to the low vowel /a/ before N+Stop[+voice] clusters. Elsewhere in more innovative Northern Italian dialects, vowel lengthening has subsequently spread to affect vowels before all N+Stop clusters; see 22. Even here relative chronological ordering can often be established: in the dialect of Rovigno, lengthening and secondary diphthongization before voiceless clusters is assumed to have occurred before subsequent lengthening before related voiced clusters.

22a Rovigno

  [vɛjnto] < VENTU 'wind' [sɛjmpro] < SEMPER 'always'
  [veːndi] < VENDERE 'sell' [moːndo] < MUNDU 'world'
  (Tekavčić 1985)
 b Lizzano
  [kãːŋta] < CANTAT 'sings' [ʧẽːŋto] < CENTU 'hundred'
  [gãːŋba] < *GAMBA 'leg' [vẽːŋde] < VENDERE 'sell'
  (Malagoli 1930)

The interaction between secondary lengthening before clusters and the rise of nasalization is evident when comparing developments in closely related Imolese and Lughese, e.g. DEMANDAT > Lg. [dmaːnda] > Im. [dmẽːnda] 'asks', but MERENDA 'lunch' > Lg. and Im. [brenda].

If, as I suggest on the basis of developments in Northern Italian, pre-cluster vowel lengthening regularly precedes the development of distinctive nasalization in the context VNC, then once more we have no reason, at least for Northern Italian dialects, to posit any post-deletion Compensatory Lengthening (CL) (see section 4.1.2) to account for the length of nasal vowels Ṽː derived from an earlier VNC.

The secondary lengthening of vowels before N+C, or any other type of cluster for that matter, contra Hayes (1989: 261, n. 2), is not an unusual phenomenon across languages. Indeed, in Northern Italy secondary lengthening is not restricted to vowels before nasal clusters. Lengthening before oral clusters is quite regular in many dialects, e.g. Bo. [ɛːlt], Mi. [aːlt] < ALTU 'high', Bo. [kuːrt] < CURTU 'short', Bo. [paːsta] < PASTA 'pasta'. Elsewhere lengthening before N+C is, for example, regular in: (1) English, e.g. prof[aʊ]nd < Fr. profond (cf. Eng. profundity), pint [paɪnt] < Fr. pinte, find [faɪnd] < OE finden, (2) Apinayé (Burgess and Ham 1968), e.g. /tɔm + piʧ/ → [tɔːmpiʧ] 'just a freckle', /meɲ + za/ → [mɛːɲza] 'this honey'; (3) Malay (Trigo 1990: 21, n.18) /bəntuk/ → [bəːntoʔ] 'form', / gurindam/ → [guriːndam] (a type of poetry), /baɲci/ → [baːɲci] 'census';

and finally (4) Herbert (1977, 1986: 134–8) also reports frequent lengthening before prenasalized stops and N+C clusters in many African languages.

6.4.1 *Phonetic explanations for the contextual parameters*

Whilst the double effect of syllable structure and secondary vowel lengthening accounts to a large degree for the ordering of the contextual parameters at 19, at the phonetic level they may also interact with context-specific factors that favour the development of distinctive nasalization. Some of these phonetic factors are considered in the sections that follow.

6.4.1.1 Nasal+fricative clusters

The finding that vowel nasalization and reduction and deletion of N in nasal clusters occur preferentially before fricatives rather than before stops is a frequent one in languages around the world, e.g. Italian, Spanish, Romanian (Petrovici 1930), Japanese (Hattori et al. 1958), Polish (Rubach 1977, Gussman 1980: 85), Icelandic (Einarsson 1949), Luganda (de Chene 1985: 254), Afrikaans (Taylor and Uys 1988) and Dutch (Trommelen 1984: 176). One needs, however, to bear in mind that reduction of N (and, indeed, nasalization) before fricatives is not a universal process. In many Romance dialects, N+Fric clusters, /ns/, /nf/ and /nv/ ($<$ [n] + [w], *[nw]) may be variously affected by stop epenthesis, fricative voicing, fricative hardening and total assimilation, whereby the nasal segment becomes fully occluded, and in some dialects even geminated, i.e. /ns/ $>$ [nz] $>$ [ndz], /nf/ $>$ [nv] or [mp] ($>$[mb]), /nv/ $>$ [mb] ($>$ [mm]), e.g. Altamurese [pəndzɛʲ] $<$ PENSARE 'to think', [tamb] 'bad odour' $<$ It. *tanfo*, [mbɛjm] $<$ INFAME 'infamous', [mːətɛʲ] $<$ INVITARE 'invite' (Loporcaro 1988, and Rohlfs 1966).

Furthermore, it should be noted that the length of distinctively nasalized vowels before fricatives can also be accounted for by vowel lengthening independent of any reduction and loss of prefricative N, e.g. Mi. [pẽːⁿsa] 'thinks' $<$ PEːNSAT, Val d'Antrona [rãːⁿʃ] 'rancid' $<$ RANCIDU, [sũːⁿʒa] 'suet' $<$ AXUNGIA. Whilst prefricative N may have undergone intermediate reduction, such reduction seems to have led ultimately in my Northern Italian sample to complete loss of N as slot deletion, i.e. N $>$ F̃ $>$ G̃ $>$ Ø, rather than complete vocalization, i.e. N $>$ F̃ $>$ G̃ $>$ Ṽ.

In many other languages, a gradual conditioned reduction in occlusion has led to the weakening of nasals before spirants and other continuants, in progressive steps from nasal stop to nasal vowel; see de Chene and Anderson (1979: 529). In such circumstances, deocclusion may be completely independent of the VLP, and vowel lengthening before such clusters may not be a necessary precondition for the development of distinctive nasalization, but rather the result of gradual vocalization.[23]

First, nasal stops undergo manner assimilation, as at 23:

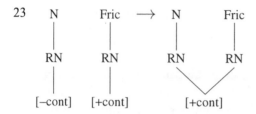

The nasalized fricatives that result are frequently reported in the literature, e.g. Japanese (Hattori et al. 1958), Romanian (Petrovici 1930), English (Ali 1982, 1984) and Icelandic [dažsa] *dansa* 'dance' (Einarsson 1949: 19).

After manner assimilation, further weakening of nasalized fricatives to nasalized glides is recorded in some languages, as at 24:

24 Polish
[koj͂ ski] *konski* 'equine' (Rubach 1977, Gussman 1980: 85)

Visperterminen German
[bãix] *Bank* 'bank'
[dẽixu] *denken* 'think' (Stephen Anderson 1981: 516–17)

Complete vocalization of secondary nasalized glides may follow, as noted in Luganda, Afrikaans, Dutch and Low German, and given at 25:

25 Luganda
[ẽːva] < /en + va/ 'relish'
[ẽːsiri] < /en + siri/ 'mosquito' (de Chene 1985: 254)

Dutch
[tõː# ɣeːl] *ton geel* '. . . butt yellow . . .' (Trommelen 1984: 176)

The preferential elimination of nasalized fricatives, when compared with nasal stops, is presumably a result of the articulatory instability of the former. With reference to nasalized fricatives, Mayerthaler (1982: 225) notes that the passage of air through the nasal cavity affects the level of the airflow through the oral cavity, thereby reducing the amount of turbulence/friction normally associated with (oral) fricatives. Reduced turbulence combines with the masking effect of voicing to affect the perceptual saliency of such segments: they may be missed by listeners or reanalysed as nasalized approximants. At the phonological level, this inherent phonetic 'weakness' translates into the notable cross-linguistic infrequency of phonemic nasalized fricatives, supported also by their tendency towards deletion, and their late acquisition by children. Maddieson (1984) finds no phonemic nasalized fricatives in his sample of 317 languages, although rare cases of nasalized approximants arise: two examples of /j̃/, one of /w̃/, and one example of the nasalized voiced velar approximant /ɰ̃/. By comparison, plain bilabial /m/ is found in 299 languages. Cohn (1987), in a sample of 165 languages, finds only three languages with some sort of phonemic nasalized fricatives of the

type such as /ṽ/, and six languages with phonemic nasalized glides of the type /w̃, j̃, h̃, ɥ̃/.

6.4.1.2 Devoicing and N-deletion

N-loss before voiceless stops and other obstruents may be favoured by a phonetic process of contextual devoicing. Devoicing of N without a concomitant increase in nasal airflow, and therefore, nasal turbulence, has a major effect on perceptual saliency, which may lead to complete N-deletion (Ohala 1975). However, N-deletion does not appear to be the inevitable result of contextual devoicing. Elsewhere in sections 3.4.3 and 8.1.6, I have noted that devoicing of N leads in many languages, e.g. Sardinian, Toba Batak, Old Norse, to complete assimilation to the following voiceless obstruent, e.g. Sard. [pessare] < PENSARE 'to think'. Preferential N-deletion before voiceless stops, and other obstruents, may be more frequently accounted for by the phonetic effect of obstruent voicelessness on the duration of N, as discussed below in the following section.

6.4.1.3 The voicing contrast in N+Stop clusters

The effect of the voicing contrast in post-nasal stops in determining the length of pre-stop nasals has been extensively studied in English e.g. Raphael et al. (1975), Hooper (1977), Lehiste (1972), Fujimura and Lovins (1978, 1982), Malécot (1960) and Chen (1970) and also in Swedish (Lovins 1978). The duration of nasal consonants is found to be significantly reduced before voiceless stops within and across syllable syllables (Lovins 1978). For instance, Zue and Sia (1982), in comparative studies of tautosyllabic /Vnt$/ and /Vnd$/ in English, found a highly significant 130% greater mean length of /n/ before /d/ than before /t/: mean nasal murmur duration for /n/ in /nt/ clusters was only 43 ms., compared to a mean duration of approximately 100 ms. before /d/. Raphael et al. (1975: 395) found that individual excesses in length of N before voiced stops ranged from 26.7% to 425% (!).

The difference in N-duration is so marked that Zue and Sia and Raphael et al. suggest that N-duration is the most significant factor in the perception of stop voicing, and is, in fact, adjusted specifically for that purpose. Fujimura and Lovins (1978, 1982) argue that the extreme reduction in duration of nasals before tense (i.e. voiceless) stops is largely the result of conflict between the muscle contraction necessary for the articulation of a tense (i.e. voiceless) stop, and the muscle relaxation necessary for velum lowering. This element of articulatory incompatibility, with tenseness predominating, results in the reduced occlusion of N.

Malécot (1960) and Fujimura (1977: 115) report that the durational reduction of N before a voiceless consonant may be so extreme that complete loss of the nasal consonant is frequent. Such a finding is confirmed, as Parker (1977) points out, by the difficulty Raphael et al. often had in isolating nasal murmurs before voiceless stops. Since the only evidence of nasal resonance

remains entirely on the vowel, Malécot also suggests that vowel nasalization may be used by listeners as the major perceptual cue for stop voicelessness. He also found vowel nasalization to function as a cue for the perception of absent nasal consonants before voiceless stops in American English: listeners reconstituted the missing N on the basis of cues provided in the preceding vowel. In one experiment Malécot tested the perceptual effect of deleting N in *amble*, and found the word was perceived as *ample* in 76% of cases.

In addition to the voicing contrast effect, there is experimental evidence indicating an interaction between vowel length and the phonetic reduction of N before stops. Fujimura and Lovins (1982) and Lovins (1978) both report N to be phonetically longer after short V in CVNC than after long V: in CV:NC in absolute terms, regardless of whether the post-nasal C is voiced or voiceless (Lovins 1978: 242, table 1). Such vowel-length related reduction of N is of course compatible with the operation of the VLP which predicts preferential reduction and elimination of N after long vowels.

Finally, further confirmation of preferential deletion of N before voiceless, rather than voiced, stops is provided by child language acquisition data referred to previously. Hooper (1977: 154) and Neilson Smith (1973) give numerous examples in English, e.g. [bap] *bump*, [mɛn] *mend* and [buːn] *spoon*. Hooper (1977) is led to the conclusion that small children treat VNC sequences (where C = voiceless stop) as if phonemically /ṼC/. N is absent, since vowels are phonemically nasalized. According to Hooper, nasalization does not surface at this early stage, since it is not accurately mastered till much later. Similar results were obtained by Vogel (1975: 207) and Hernández-Chaves et al. (1975: 239–40) working on the acquisition by children of nasals in Chicano Spanish: N was never deleted before under-lying voiced stops in the sequence /VNC#/, which surfaced with diminishing frequency from left to right as $[VNC] > [V^NC] > [ṼN(ː)] > [Ṽ^N]$. In contrast, N-deletion is frequent before voiceless stops, and the insertion of preconsonantal N was only mastered slowly with increasing age in the following order: $[VC] > [ṼC] > [Ṽ^NC] > [VNC]$.

6.5 Conclusion

Examination of contextual effects on the spread of distinctive nasalization in Northern Italian allows for complex contextual parameters to be posited, which are compatible with claims made by both Foley (1975, 1977) and Schourup (1973). However, two different contextual parameters are required because of slight ordering differences between Stage 2 /V:nV/, and VNStop[+voice]. The effects of syllable structure, and, to a lesser degree, of interaction with the VLP, are immediately obvious in the formulation of both contextual parameters. Further investigation shows that the ordering among NC clusters may coincide with vowel lengthening

phenomena that favour the spread of distinctive nasalization. Whilst overall the two parameters are not found to hold universally (counter-examples are reported in Centro-Southern Italian, and Germanic languages), some ordering relationships along the parameters have as yet not been contradicted, and phonetic explanations have been provided which may account for them. Finally, it was also seen in discussion of the development of N+Continuant clusters that vowel nasalization and N-deletion are not inevitable over time. In some cases, fortitive changes to both N and the post-nasal continuant make the spread of distinctive nasalization less likely.

7

HISTORICAL DEVELOPMENT OF NASAL CONSONANTS AND THE EFFECT OF N PLACE ON DISTINCTIVE NASALIZATION

7.1 INTRODUCTION

In the first part of this chapter we examine universalist claims regarding the effect of the place of articulation of N on the development of distinctive nasalization. It comes as little surprise to find such claims to be conflicting. The evidence cited by universalists is inconsistent, and no universal effect of N-place can be established. Our attention then turns to developments in Northern Italy in an attempt to uncover any regular patterning. We also consider the possible phonetic basis of developments in Northern Italian, as well as possible discrepancies noted elsewhere in the Romance-speaking world. Finally, N-place can also be shown to interact with so-called fortition processes that block the spread of nasalization and N-deletion by interacting with the Vowel Length Parameter. The phonetic basis of fortition is also discussed and evaluated.

7.1.1 *Place of articulation, nasalization and N-deletion*

Foley (1975, 1977) and Lightner (1973), differing only in the fine detail, both suggest that N-deletion (and the distinctive nasalization that normally results) spreads progressively in an ordered fashion from 'weakest' [ŋ], [ɲ] to 'strongest' [m], along what would be, in Foley's terms, a parameter of relative strength, as at 1a and 1b respectively:

1a Foley   ŋ n m⟶

  b Lightner   ŋ ɲ n m⟶

The substantive basis for the formulations at 1 seems extremely weak. Foley, for instance, extrapolates a universal correlation between preferential N-loss and relative backness from a rather cursory set of examples drawn from two languages. That velar [ŋ] is more prone to loss than [n] is inferred from patterns of N-deletion before voiceless fricatives in German: *dachte* 'thought' (alongside *denken* 'think'), but *uns* 'us', *fünf* 'five'.[1] That [n] is weaker than [m] is evident in the intervocalic deletion of the former but not the latter in Portuguese, cf. MANU > *mão* 'hand' but FUMARE > *fumar* 'to smoke'.

In contrast to Foley and Lightner, Chen (1972 and elsewhere) found the universal correlation between preferential N-loss (and the distinctive nasalization that results) and place to be reversed in his sample of Chinese dialects: N-loss spreads progressively backwards from anterior labial [m] until [ŋ] is affected, as Chen's (1973b, 1974a) parametric formalization at 2 makes clear, where N-deletion spreads gradually from left to right:[2]

2 Chen $\underrightarrow{\text{m n ŋ}}$

However, whilst the order of individual nasal consonants along the parameter at 2 is supposedly universal, the parameter itself was not the only place-related pattern Chen uncovered. Chen (1972, 1973a) reports merger of all final N to [ŋ], according to the schema in figure 7.1, to be common. There is no indication as to how the two patterns might interact, nor any discussion of their (in)compatibility and relative frequency. Where N-merger is characteristic, Chen hypothesizes that N-deletion is only the end result of a gradual process in which merger of all nasal Codas to velar [ŋ] is a necessary precondition for N-deletion. Only after merger to [ŋ] is the nasal articulatorily reduced and then deleted, resulting in distinctive nasalization. Denasalization may follow.

Ruhlen (1973: 12) goes so far as to suggest that this model of [ŋ]-merger and deletion is universal. Should this be the case, then no universal parameter of N-deletion according to place of articulation can be formulated, since only one place, velar, survives before deletion. Tuttle (1991: 59) is less firm but claims nevertheless that all nasals tend to shift to velar place before effacement. However, the purported universality of the

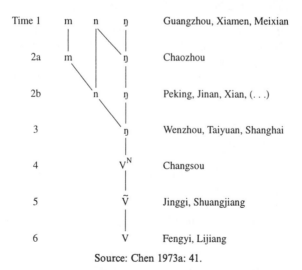

Source: Chen 1973a: 41.

Figure 7.1   Pattern of Merger and N-deletion

[ŋ]-merger model is easily countered by developments in my Northern Italian sample where N-deletion occurs without evidence of [ŋ]-merger; see section 7.1.2. In more telling fashion the N-merger hypothesis is quickly disproved by developments in the very sample of Chinese dialects Chen referred to when formulating his universal velarization parameter. As Entenman (1977) and Zee (1985) point out, Chen's representation of [ŋ]-merger and deletion is an inaccurate reflection of his own data: a number of dialects, e.g., Jinan, and Xian, that are purported to contrast /n/ and /ŋ/ at Time 2a/b in fact contrast /Ṽ/ (< */Vn/, */Vm/) and /Vŋ/ (< */Vŋ/). Ruhlen's suggestion of N-merger to [ŋ] before deletion in Old French is not corroborated and contradicts the more traditional view, e.g. Pope (1952), that all final N merged to [n] before effacement.

Hombert (1986, 1987), based on purported developments in Teke languages, agrees with Chen in suggesting that distinctive nasalization develops preferentially in the context /Vm/ before spreading to /Vn/. However, he makes no universalist claim about the development of /Vŋ/. Proto-Teke */ŋ/ is apparently lost everywhere in Hombert's Teke sample without any synchronic trace of vowel nasalization. This synchronic fact is interpreted diachronically by Hombert as simple deletion of */ŋ/ without vowel nasalization and hence an independent phenomenon not relevant to the development of distinctive nasalization. There seems no reason to accept Hombert's *ad hoc* separation of the velar nasal. One-step /Vŋ/ > /V/ is unlikely, and is contradicted by developmental patterns noted in closely related languages cited in a later study by Hombert and Puech (1989). In this non-Teke group which includes Shake and Bagiele, evidence of /VN/ > /Ṽ/ is limited to */Vŋ/ only, and indeed */Vn, Vm/ are as yet untouched by nasalization or N-deletion. One-step /Vŋ/ > /V/ also contravenes the suggested operation of the new V-NAS model which predicts the following sequence of events: [Vŋ] > [Ṽŋ] > [Ṽ] > [V]. Such sequencing is further supported by Ohala's (1975) observation that, of all nasal consonants, [ŋ] is phonetically most like [Ṽ]. Hence the frequently reported cross-linguistic alternation between /Ṽ/ and /Vŋ/, e.g. Vietnamese /bɔŋ/ < Fr. /põ/ 'bridge of a ship' (Greenlee and Ohala 1980). We conclude, therefore, that synchronic /V/ in Teke for earlier */Vŋ/ simply reflects denasalization of an intermediate /Ṽ/.

Hombert's Teke-based claim of relative ordering as /Vm/ ≫ /Vn/ is also not confirmed by developments in other Bantu languages closely related to Teke. In neighbouring Eastern Grassfields languages, distinctive nasalization (and subsequent denasalization) is reported to affect */Vn/ most commonly, and not */Vm/ or */Vŋ/ (see Hombert and Puech for details). Further contradiction of Hombert's parameter is found in the Manenguba (Bantu A.15) languages spoken close to Eastern Grassfields. Hedinger (1987) reports that, of four reconstructed nasals /*m, *n, *ɲ, *ŋ/, loss of the palatal */ɲ/ in morpheme-final position is by far the most frequent.

Disagreement amongst universalists regarding the effect of N place comes

as no surprise: conclusions have been arrived at using completely independent samples showing extreme variability in terms of size, quality and reliability. It remains true, however, that no single cross-linguistic pattern appears discernible: even a cursory glance at some of the cross-linguistic data cited by universalists when formulating their claims, as well as the additional evidence drawn from Eastern Grassfields and Manenguba, leads to unpredicted variation. The reasons for cross-linguistic divergence reported here are unknown, although our knowledge of the phonological history of many of the languages referred to is insufficient for a proper assessment of the accuracy of data and reconstructions. Patterning appears at this stage to be relatively random: Chen considers [ŋ] to be the strongest, whilst Lightner, and Foley (supported by Ohala) consider it to be the weakest. The picture is further complicated by the additional possibility of N-place merger, instead of any place parameter governing N-deletion, as has reportedly occurred in some Chinese dialects, and French.

Further investigation and more reliable data are required to establish whether this apparent randomness reflects interaction in individual languages with factors at present unassessed or unknown, e.g. vowel length distribution, or analogical change associated with consonant-place effects reported on other processes of sound change, e.g. intervocalic stop lenition, generalized depalatalization or delabialization processes and word-final consonant loss. If such interactions do exist, then we may go some way towards accounting for cross-linguistic variation in N-place effects.

7.1.2 Developments in Northern Italian

Historical developments already discussed in some detail in section 2.2.2.1 resulted in the appearance of a three-way place contrast amongst nasals in Northern Italian, i.e. bilabial /m/, dental /n/, and palatal /ɲ/. With the loss of final vowels, all three phonemic nasals could be found in word-final position:

3		BALNEU 'bath'	CANE 'dog'	FAME 'hunger'
	Stage 1	[banju]	[kaːne]	[faːme]
	Stage 2	/baɲ/	/kaːn/	/faːm/
	Imolese	[bɛ̃ːɲ]	[kɛ̃ː]	[fɛ̃ːm]
	Ravennate	[bʌ̃ːɲ]	[kʌ̃ː]	[fʌ̃ːm]
	Lughese	[baːɲ]	[kɛ̃ː]	[fɛ̃ːm]
	Bolognese	[baːɲ]	[kæŋ] (< *[kæ̃ɯ̃])	[faːm]
	Riminese[3]	[baːɲ]	[kɛːn]	[fɛːmə]
	Bergamese	[baːɲ]	[kaː] (< *[kãː])	[fam]
	Milanese	[baɲ]	[kãː]	[fam]
	Cairese	[baɲ]	[kaŋ] (< *[kãɯ̃])	[fam]
	Tavetschan	[bɔɲ]	[cawn]	[fɔm]

Comparison of the Northern Italian data at 3 shows that, in word-final position, distinctive nasalization has developed preferentially in the context of dental /n₁/. There is evidence that /Ṽ/ from /Vːn₁/ was or is a regular phenomenon in at least seven dialects. In four members of the sample (Milanese, Imolese, Ravennate and Lughese) /Ṽ/ (< /Vːn₁/) still survives. In Bolognese, Cairese and Bergamese evidence of regular /Ṽ/ (< /Vːn₁/) is now only historical, as a result of secondary glide hardening in the first two and secondary denasalization in the last.

In some Romagnol dialects, including Lughese and Ravennate, all with regular /Ṽː/ < Stage 2 /Vːn#/, /Ṽː/ < Stage 2 /Vːm#/ is reported in a few word-forms, e.g. Ra. and Lg. [fjõː] < FLUME 'river', but [lom] < LUME 'light'. According to Schürr (1956: 318), sporadic examples of final /m/-deletion found in many Romagnol dialects are relics of a previously regular process, to be reversed later by a counter-process of /m/-restitution introduced from neighbouring dialects where /m/ was subject to fortition rather than lenition (see section 7.2 for details). In a smaller number of Romagnol dialects, such as Faentino and Forlivese, restitution of /m/ appears to have been less extensive with regular loss of final /m/ after back vowels, e.g. FLUME 'river' > Fa. [fjõː], LUME 'light' > Fa. [lõː], but PRIMU 'first' > [prem].

Nowhere in the sample is loss of /ɲ/ reported, whilst the spread of strong contextual nasalization is reported slightly less frequently before /ɲ/ than before final /m/, e.g. Lg. [baːɲ] but [fɛ̃ːm] at 3.

Interaction between N place of articulation, vowel length and the development of distinctive nasalization is evident in the sample. The preservation of /ɲ/ and the low frequency of nasalization before it is not unexpected, given the strict fashion in which the Vowel Length Parameter (VLP) operates in Northern Italian; see section 4.1.3. All Stage 2 vowels before /ɲ/ were originally short, a historical fact that has conspired to block or delay the spread of nasalization and N-deletion. Similar restrictions apply in the context /Vn₂/ from Lat. /Vnn/, as seen in example 4. Unexpected vowel shortening before Latin /m/, as illustrated at 3 and discussed in detail in section 7.2, also has a blocking effect. The very restricted spread of contextual nasalization before /ɲ/, and similarly before /n₂/ in Romagnol, is linked to secondary vowel lengthening, illustrated at 3 and 4. Lengthening is evident in five members of the sample, all in or on the edge of Romagna. In more conservative Bolognese and Lughese newly lengthened vowels have as yet not been nasalized. Only in the most innovative dialects, Imolese and Ravennate, was marked nasalization reported by Schürr (1917). Developments in Riminese provide the missing link: lengthened but not normally nasalized in the early part of this century, these and other long vowels have since undergone nasalization, especially before coronal /n/, itself often reduced and difficult to perceive.

4   ANNU
Stage 2   /an/
             'year'
Imolese   [ɛːn]
Ravennate   [ʌːn]
Lughese   [aːn]
Bolognese   [aːn]
Riminese   [aːn] and today [ãːn] ~ [ãː[(n)]]
Bergamese   [a(ː)n]
Milanese   [an]
Cairese   [an]
Tavetschan   [ɔn]

The developments in non-final position are less extensive, but can be seen to correlate nevertheless with the changes noted in word-final context. Intervocalic N-deletion is of course not found in my Northern Italian sample, but the effect of N place of articulation on patterns of nasalization before intervocalic N correlates with patterns observed in word-final position: extensive synchronic and diachronic evidence of nasalization of all tonic vowels before /n_1/ is reported in at least five dialects (Im., Lg., Ra., Bo., Ca.), in contrast to very restricted low vowel nasalization before /m/ (< Lat. /m/ and /mm/), /ɲ/ and /n_2/ in two dialects only (Im., and Ra.). In preconsonantal position, I have no evidence in the sample of discernible synchronic differences according to N place of articulation, e.g. Im. [tɛ̃ːt] < TANTU 'so' (m.), [kẽːp] < CAMPU 'camp', [ɛ̃ːk(a)] < HANC HO(RAM) 'still'. However, medieval texts in Bergamese and closely related Bresciano show the omission of orthographic *n* to be much more frequent before voiceless dental stops and affricates than before any other place (Lorck 1893: 31, Gibellini 1981: 107–8).

Elsewhere in Northern Italy, loss of Stage 2 /m/, final or intervocalic, is rare, and loss of /ɲ/ and /n_2/ rarer still. In all such cases, the spread of distinctive nasalization is essentially restricted to marginal Franco-Provençal dialects, very few in number, along the western periphery of Northern Italy, cf. *AIS* V 928 FUMO, II 412 STAGNO, II 309 ANNO. Loss of all historical nasals in word-final position, regardless of place, is in any case normal in these same Franco-Provençal dialects. That deletion of /n_1/ occurs preferentially in Franco-Provençal can be inferred from developments in intervocalic position: only /n_1/ is effaced, in contrast to the conservation of /m/, /ɲ/ and /n_2/.

One can posit the following place of articulation parameter to account for patterns of nasalization and N-deletion in Northern Italian:

5 N-Place Parameter

n_1 m ɲ N:

$\underline{\qquad n_2 \qquad}_{\longrightarrow}$

It agrees with previously suggested universal parameters at 1 above only to the extent that coronal n is placed to the left of bilabial m. I have extended the parameter slightly by incorporating geminate nasal consonants (N:) as the least likely context for both the spread of nasalization and N-deletion. Evidence of vowel nasalization before N: is almost non-existent in Italy, being reported only in Tuscan where contextual nasalization is today utterly pervasive, e.g. Tuscan [lãːnã] and [kãnnã] in contrast to Sard. [lãː] < LANA 'wool', [kanna] < CANNA 'cane', Bo. [loŋna] < [lõw̃na] < LUNA 'moon' but [panna] < St. 2 /pena/ < PINNA 'fin'. Complete loss of N: is not reported in any of these varieties and is in any case considered not to be a one-step process, but to require intermediate degemination to N before ultimate effacement is possible, as discussed in section 7.3.

According to the parameter at 5, first the phonologization of vowel nasalization and then N-deletion in Northern Italian occur preferentially in the context of Stage 2 $/n_1/$, before spreading to other Stage 2 nasals. However, N place itself does not seem paramount in determining relative order along the parameter. Once again, the effect of the Vowel Length Parameter (VLP) is evident, since dental /n/ (< Lat. /n/, and /nn/) appears at both ends in both the most likely and least likely context of change. The two examples of /n/ can only be distinguished by contrastive vowel length differences, i.e. /Vːn/ (< Stage 1 [Vːn]) vs. /Vn/ (< Stage 1 [Vnn]). As predicted by the VLP, phonological processes of nasalization and N-deletion develop preferentially in the context of phonologically long vowels, i.e. /Vːn/ and not /Vn/.

Tuttle (1991: 59–62) looks at matters from the reverse perspective, and formulates a scale of strength of N place in Northern Italian according to a suggested degree of resistance to N-deletion and nasalization. He also includes velar [ŋ], although in our terms it cannot properly be compared, since it is only recent with quite a different history (see chapters 2 and 8 for details). His order of decreasing strength is: [m] ≫ [ɲ] ≫ [n] ≫ [ŋ] where m is strongest. Expressed in terms of relative weakness consistent with discussion in this chapter, the reversed order is: [ŋ] ≫ [n] ≫ [ɲ] ≫ [m] where [ŋ] is weakest. On closer examination, no Northern Italian data is cited to suggest that [ɲ] behaves differently from [m] in terms of nasalization effect or N-effacement. Instead, the ordering appears to be governed by the following phonetic differences: (1) m has marginally greater duration than [ɲ]; and (2) [m] has the most easily identifiable murmur of all nasal consonants. Although I also cite duration as critical in accounting for developments in Northern Italian, the reliability of the experimental

evidence referred to by Tuttle is doubtful. Duration figures cited are from 1891, and for all nasals appear excessively high when compared with the general pattern of results reported in recent years and given below in section 7.3 for a range of Romance varieties. The study by Malécot (1956) cited by Tuttle in support of relative identifiableness is of only limited value: only [m], [n] and [ŋ] were tested. [ɲ] was not included, and hence proper comparison is not possible.

7.1.3 N-deletion elsewhere in the Romance-speaking area

The pattern of preferential deletion of Latin simple /n/ in Northern Italy is repeated in many other Romance dialects. As in Northern Italian, in Catalan, Gascon, and Lengadocian, Latin /n/ is preferentially lost in secondary final position, as seen at 6:

6		Cat.	Gasc.	Leng.	
VINU	> [bīː] >	/bi/	/bi/	/bi/	'wine'
but *BANJU >		/baɲ/	/baɲ/	/ban/	'bath'
FUMU >		/fum/	/hym/	/fyn/	'smoke'
ANNU >		/aɲ/	/an/	/an/	'year'

In varieties of Sardinian and Corsican where intervocalic N-deletion is reported, only Latin /n/ is affected:[4]

7	Sard. [mãw̃]	< MANU	'hand'
but	[dom(m)u]	< DOMU	'house'
	Cors. [pãː(n)e]	< PANE	'bread'
	[fum(m)u]	< FUMU	'smoke'

In more radical Tuscan, intervocalic N-deletion more usually affects /n/, although /m/ may also be lost, e.g. [dõˈãːĩ] domani 'tomorrow', alongside [vĩɲɲã] vigna < *VINJA 'vineyard'.

In Portuguese, only Latin intervocalic /n/ is historically deleted, e.g. LANA 'wool' > lã, but lima < LIMA 'file', vinha < *VINJA < VINEA 'vineyard'. However, more recently /ɲ/, spelt nh, may be variably deoccluded in some Portuguese dialects, e.g. tenho [tẽɲu] and [tẽj̃u] 'I hold' (Lipski 1975: 75; Parkinson 1979: 44). Should weakening of Port. /ɲ/ go further to Ø, then we have some evidence to suggest that, with regard to N-deletion in Portuguese, the order of [m] and [ɲ] along the N-place parameter is reversed relative to the order posited at 5 for Northern Italian, i.e. Portuguese [n] ≫ [ɲ] ≫ [m].

There was apparently no place parameter governing the spread of N-deletion in the history of French. The traditional view amongst French historical linguists is that secondary final nasals, first [-m#], and then [-ɲ#], were dentalized before N-deletion occurred (Pope 1952). Alternatively, complete velarization preceded N loss (Ruhlen 1973, Straka 1955).

7.2 N-Fortition and the Story of /m/

Universalists have in the past focused exclusively on the effect of N place on the spread of nasalization and N-deletion. However, developments in my Northern Italian sample indicate that the effect of N place of articulation is not restricted to weakening processes such as N-deletion, but is also relevant to what might be called 'N-fortition', i.e. any process governed by N place that effectively blocks the spread of vowel nasalization before N. In accordance with the operation of the new V-NAS model, such a 'fortitive' process is predicted to make N less prone to effacement. The process of N-fortition, widespread in Northern Italian, is particularly evident in the context of bilabial /m/ (< Lat. /m/), and accounts for the particular ordering of /m/ as a less preferred context than /n₁/ along the Northern Italian N-place parameter.

Resistance to the spread of vowel nasalization and N-deletion can be increased in one of two interrelated ways: (1) phonological vowel shortening which, in accordance with the operation of the VLP in Northern Italian, prevents vowel nasalization, and subsequent N-deletion; and (2) secondary N-gemination which may follow vowel shortening as an independent chronological event.[5] Phonological vowel lengthening, which might favour nasalization processes, is effectively blocked before geminate nasals: in contrast to CVVC and CVC:, the sequence *CVVC: is phonotactically impermissible in Northern Italian, as elsewhere in the Romance-speaking area. The same pan-Romance phonotactic restriction against *CVVC: also operates as a phonologically sensitive ordering constraint. N-gemination is blocked after phonologically long vowels until the vowel has been shortened, i.e. CVVN > CVN > CVN:. There is no evidence, as has occasionally been suggested (cf. Repetti 1989 and Tuttle 1991), that N-gemination may have occurred in Northern Italian while vowels were still long, subsequently triggering immediate compensatory vowel shortening, i.e. CVVN > *CVVN: > CVN:. Conversely, secondary vowel lengthening is only permitted before historically long consonants which have been previously degeminated, i.e. CVN: > CVN > CVVN and never CVN: > *CVVN: > CVVN. Finally, gemination itself operates as an additional constraint on N-deletion: as noted previously reduction of N: to Ø requires an intermediate stage of degemination to simple N. One-step N: > Ø is not reported anywhere.

Secondary reduction of expected /V:/ before Stage 2 /m/ is noted in all sample dialects, and is found throughout much of Northern Italy, as at 8, and AIS II 215 LIMA. As a result of such phonological shortening, modern reflexes of Stage 2 /V:m/ and /Vm/ now coincide.

8		LIMA	FUMU	FAME	FLAMMA
		'file'	'smoke'	'hunger'	'flame'
	Stage 1	[liːma]	[fuːmu]	[faːme]	[flamma]
	Stage 2	/liːma/	/fuːm/	/faːm/	/flama/
but	Mi.	[lima]	[fym]	[fam]	[fjama]
	Bg.	[lema]	[fœm]	[fam]	[fjama]
	Im.[6]	[lema]	[fom]	[fɛ̃ːm]	[fjɛ̃ːma]
	Ta.	[liəmə][7]	[fem]	[fɔm]	[flɔma]
	Ca.	[lima]	[fym]	[fam]	[fjama]
	Bo.	[lemma]	[fomm]	[faːm][8]	[fjaːma]

Indeed, this process of conditioned shortening is well known to Italian dialectologists who have frequently noted that in many Northern Italian dialects the development of tonic vowels before Lat. /m/ corresponds to that of predictably short vowels in historically closed syllables, e.g. Tuttle (1991), Zörner (1985: 234–5) and Schürr (1956: 318–19). However, the geolinguistic spread of long vowel shortening before /m/ in Northern Italian should not be overstated: it is in general less than my sample suggests, cf. *AIS* II 215 LIMA, V 980 LAMA. Comparative evidence suggests that shortening has only recently been introduced from the west to Romagna where four sample members (Imolese, Lughese, Ravennate and Riminese) are spoken. In Romagnol varieties spoken immediately to the south of these, long vowel reflexes before /m/ survive, e.g. Cesenate [prəjma] < PRIMA 'first' (f.), Cesenatico [præjm] < PRIMU (see also *AIS* II 215 LIMA). And in some Romagnol varieties with evidence of vowel shortening, it is possible Stage 2 long vowels, in particular /aː/, were never reduced, rather than being relengthened later on. Modern reflexes of /aː/ before /m/ in Imolese correspond to those of /aː/ before Lat. /n/, where vowel length has always been stable, e.g. Im. [fɛ̃ːm] alongside [kɛ̃ː] < CANE 'dog' and [fjɛ̃ːma] < FLAMMA 'flame' alongside [lɛ̃ːna] < LANA 'wool'. Finally, sporadic traces of conditioned /m/-loss after historical long vowels still found in Ravennate and Riminese, e.g. [fjõː] < */fluːm/ < FLUME 'river' but [lom] < */luːm/ < LUME 'light', are also suggestive of a more general preservation of vowel length until recent times in that part of Romagna where sample members are found.

   In a small number of Northern Italian dialects vowel shortening before /m/ was later followed by regular secondary gemination of /m/, as in Bolognese [lemma] and [fomm] at 8. However, the extent of /m/-gemination in Northern Italy has been greatly exaggerated by Italianists such as Rohlfs (1966), Schürr (1919) and others who have confused the dialectal orthographic convention *mm* with [mː]. Orthographic geminates are traditionally used to mark a preceding short vowel, as Salvioni (1884: 157) explicitly notes: 'in milanese . . . ogni consonante lunga [ortografica] vi è pronunciata breve', and 'la vocale che precede questa consonante [lunga] è sempre

brevissima'. Traditional *limma* represents Mi. [lima] and not [limma] as has been suggested. The *AIS* shows Lat. M > [mm] to be restricted primarily to the Grisons and to small areas in and around Piedmont; see II 215 LIMA. However, Tuttle (1991: 48) and Malagoli (1930: 141) also report /m/-gemination to be frequent along the Appenine border with geminating Tuscany, hence typical [primmo] < PRIMU 'first', and [lumme] < LUME 'light'.

Elsewhere in Italy, gemination of /m/ is common, and particularly regular in Campania, Corsica and Sardinia, e.g. FUMU > Sard. [fummu], as well as [fummo] 'smoke' in some Tuscan dialects (see Rohlfs 1966, Melillo 1977 and *AIS* V 928 FUMO, 1015 FAME).

In a few Northern Italian dialects, where N-fortition is regular in the context of Lat. /m/, Latin /n/ may also be comparably affected – possibly by analogy – in certain restricted circumstances. Whilst there is little evidence in the sample or elsewhere in Northern Italy of secondary vowel shortening in the Stage 2 context /Vːn#/, analogical vowel shortening in the Stage 2 context /Vːna/ as before Stage 2 /Vːma/ is reported in some dialects. Traces of both are found in Tavetschan and other Romantsch dialects where unexpected but slightly inconsistent shortening of long vowels /iː, uː/ is recorded: VINU > [vin] 'wine' alongside [cawn] < CANE 'dog', and [ʃpinə] < SPINA 'thorn' but [ʎiːnə] < LUNA 'moon'. Once the vowel is shortened, nasalization is predictably blocked. Of the sample dialects, only Milanese shows fully this pattern in which all vowels regardless of height are affected before historically intervocalic /n/:

9

		LANA	LUNA	*LAMA	LIMA
		'wool'	'moon'	'blade'	'file'
	Stage 2	/laːna/	/luːna/	/laːma/	/liːma/
	Mi.	[lana]	[lyna]	[lama]	[lima]
cf.	Bg.	[laːna]	[lyːna]	[lama]	[lima]
	Im.	[lɛ̃ːna]	[lɔ̃ːna]	[lɛ̃ːma]	[lema]

The *AIS* confirms that such vowel shortening is most consistent in areas of Western Lombardy bordering Milan, and in parts of Lombard-speaking Ticino, and Novara (see *AIS* VI 1077 LANA, II 255 FARINA, II 361 LUNA).[9]

Gemination of intervocalic simple /n₁/ after vowel shortening, very rare in Northern Italy, is reported in a few Franco-Provençal dialects of the Valle d'Aosta, and neighbouring Piedmont. Here doubling of earlier /n/ is part of a secondary gemination of all simple consonants after synchronically short tonic vowels, e.g. Brusson (*AIS* pt.123) ['lœnna] < LUNA 'moon' (*AIS* II 361), [fɛ'rœnna] < FARINA 'flour' (*AIS* II 255). But even here, N-geminating varieties are unusual, and regular nasalization of long vowels and deletion of intervocalic /n/ is more typical in surrounding Franco-Provençal dialects (Walser 1937). In Bolognese, modern gemination of Stage 2 /n₂/ and /ɲ/ is recent and similarly tied to a more general secondary phenomenon affecting all consonants after synchronic short vowels:[10]

10 Bo. /pana/ [panna] < Stage 2 /pena/ < PINNA 'feather'
        /veɲa/ [veɲɲa] <   /viɲa/ < *VINJA 'vineyard'
        /tata/ [tatta] <   /teta/ < TITTA 'teat'
        /tar/   [tarː]   <   /tor/   < TURRE 'tower'
    but /lɛːna/ [lɛːna] <   /laːna/ < LANA   'wool'
        /paːna/ [paːna] <   /pana/ < PANNA 'cream'
        /pɛːl/ [pɛːl]   <   /pɛl/   < PELLE 'skin'

7.3 N Place, Distinctive Nasalization and N-Fortition in Northern Italy: Phonological and Phonetic Explanations for Interaction

There are plausible phonological and phonetic reasons why the phonologization of vowel nasalization and subsequent N-deletion in Northern Italian may occur preferentially in the context of /n/ and not /m/, and why the converse process of N-fortition may be favoured in the context of /m/, as shown by the modern Northern Italian reflexes of Stage 2 /kaːn/ and /faːm/ given previously at example 3.[11]

If we look first at patterns of N-deletion, it is evident that phonologically pertinent timing differences are relevant, as noted in section 7.2. We have no evidence anywhere of a one-step reduction of NN to Ø, in contrast to apparent N > Ø, e.g. Sard. [mãw̃] < MANU 'hand', but [kanna] < CANNA 'cane' and variable [lãːna] ~ [lãːĩã] ~ [lãːa] alongside stable [kãnnã] in Tuscan. From the phonological perspective, the difference can be accounted for by the respective formalizations of N and NN. Whilst simple consonants are linked to one timing slot, geminates are linked to two:

11

To date, I have not seen a diachronic or synchronic phonological rule posited for any language in which two related timing slots are eliminated simultaneously . Where historically geminate NN is completely lost today, as in French [ɑ̃ː] < [aːn] < OFr. /an/ < ANNU 'year', such loss is the result of a more gradual reduction in phonological timing, i.e. NN > N > Ø. The intermediate singleton N is synchronically recoverable in French itself in words like [an] < [anə] < St. 2 /ana/ < ANNA 'Anne'. Additional confirmation of this graduality is found in Corsican dialects which share the Sardinian pattern of intervocalic /n/-deletion. In a smaller number of these Corsican dialects, such loss coincides with an independent process of consonant degemination, e.g. [lãː] < LANA but [kana] < CANNA and [vaka] < VACCA 'cow'. From the phonetic perspective, the resistance shown by geminate NN is supported by the great phonetic length of such geminates, relative to

Table 7.1   Average Duration in Milliseconds of Nasals in Three Different Stress Positions in Four Romance Languages

a. /'V__V/	n	m	ɲ	ɲɲ	nn	mm	S
Spanish 1a	55.0	64.0					1
Spanish 1b	51.0	58.0					3
Spanish 2 LS	64.0	92.0	98.0				1
Spanish CS	41.0	55.0	64.0				1
Italian 1	63.5	86.5			150.0	176.0	4
Sardinian	70.0	118.0			163.0	160.0	4

b /V'__V/	n	m	ɲ	ɲɲ	nn	mm	S
Spanish 1a	56	73					1
Spanish 1b	74	81					3
Spanish 2 LS	48	66	69				1
Spanish CS	37	61	59				1
Italian 2	50	60		125			1
Sardinian	61	108		130	150	175	4

c /'V__#/	n	m	ɲ	S
Spanish 1a	80	97		1
Spanish 1b	61	82		3
Catalan	62	78	75	3

LS = laboratory speech, CS = continuous speech, S = number of speakers
Sources: Spanish 1a and b (Borzone and Signorini 1983); Spanish 2 (Ayuso 1991); Italian 1 (Sampson 1981); Italian 2 (Vagges et al. 1978); Sardinian (Contini 1987); Catalan (Recasens i Vives 1986).[12]

simple N, as confirmed by the comparative durational measurements for Romance languages given in table 7.1.

Whilst simple nasals, e.g. [n], [m] and [ɲ], are phonologically identical with respect to the timing tier, i.e. one skeletal slot each, regular phonetic differences in duration may provide the basis for N-place-related effects reported in Northern Italian. The figures in table 7.1 indicate that in all the Romance languages for which I have experimental data, coronal [n] is predictably shorter in phonetic duration than all other nasals across contexts. On the basis of precisely such a regular phonetic correlation in Romance, Tuttle (1991) has also suggested that preferential deletion of coronal [n] in Northern Italian is accounted for by its short duration, relative to other nasals. Loss of a comparatively short coronal [n] may be further

facilitated by continuous speech phenomena, as reported by Barry (1991) and Browman and Goldstein (1987: 17–18). They note that coronal segments, such as [n], show a far greater tendency than their labial and velar counterparts to be affected by assimilation and deletion in casual speech, e.g. /'mʌst bi/ > ['mʌsbi] 'must be'. Browman and Goldstein provide experimental phonetic evidence confirming the ease with which coronal gestures are overlapped by contiguous non-coronal gestures. As a result, coronality, even if present articulatorily, is perceptually masked, and complete articulatory loss may follow. The high velocity of tongue tip movement, compared to that of lips or tongue dorsum, may favour masking.

I have few figures for N length in other languages, but the correlation between place and length found in the Romance languages reported in table 7.1 finds at least partial, but apparently not universal, support in other languages. According to Umeda (1977: 848), [m] is substantially longer than [n] across contexts in American English, e.g. 'V__V [m] 70 ms., [n] 34 ms. But Orešnik and Pétursson (1977) report [n] to be slightly longer than [m] in Icelandic. On the other hand, it is possible that differences in N duration may provide some basis for cross-linguistic variation in the effect of place on N loss. Indeed in the case of Portuguese, Martins (1975) also found [m] (75 ms.) to be substantially longer in duration than [n] (47 ms.), across all contexts. Curiously enough, however, [ɲ] is found to be the shortest with an average duration of only 37 ms. This may account for the frequent reduction/ deocclusion today of [ɲ] to [j̃] in some varieties of Portuguese reported in section 7.1.3.

Chen (1973a: 50) appears to have been the first to suggest that phonetic duration differences could account for the preferential loss of /m, n/, in contrast to retention of /ŋ/, in Chinese dialects: he claims [ŋ] to be, on average, twice as long phonetically as either [m] or [n]. However, his hypothesis cannot be verified, since no duration figures of any kind are provided.

Other phonetic factors, independent of duration, appear to support the suggested relative ordering of nasals, at least with regard to n and m. Perceptual experiments involving VN syllables carried out by Malécot (1956), Nakata (1959) and Repp and Svastikula (1987), show [n] (and [ŋ]) to be substantially less salient perceptually than [m]. Listeners were found in all cases to be more easily able to identify [m] regardless of the acoustic cue provided, whether isolated murmur or formant transitions alone. And in a previously cited investigation of nasal sound pressure levels in Australian English, Clarke and Mackiewicz-Krassowska (1977) found levels to be significantly lower in vowels before /m/ than before /n, ŋ/, suggesting that vowels before bilabial nasals were relatively the least nasal.

Despite the possibility of phonetic explanations for the apparently lesser resistance of coronal [n] to the spread of N-deletion than other types of N, it is evident from the discussion in section 7.1.2 that operation of the Vowel

Length Parameter (VLP) has an overriding effect over N place in the development of distinctive nasalization in Northern Italian. /n/ appears at 12 to be both a more likely and a less likely context than /m/ for the spread of both deletion and nasalization phenomena:

12 /Vːn₁/ /Vːm/ /Vn₂/
    /kaːn/ /faːm/ /an/
    ⟶

The blocking effect of phonologically short vowels on the spread of vowel nasalization clearly also has an overriding secondary effect on N-deletion, regardless of place, as the development of Stage 2 /an/ and /kaːn/ in Northern Italian demonstrates. If we compare the data given previously at 3 and 4, we see that there is diachronic or synchronic evidence of a distinctively nasalized reflex of Stage 2 /kaːn/ in at least seven of the nine sample members. In contrast, listed reflexes of Stage 2 /an/ show no trace of N-deletion, and only a very limited distribution of phonologized vowel nasalization (see also section 4.1.2).

However, notwithstanding its primacy, operation of the VLP over time is itself not completely independent of the influence of N place. I have shown in section 7.2 that phonologically pertinent vowel length changes before N linked to specific places of articulation can interact over time with the operation of the VLP in Northern Italian to make the development of distinctive nasalization less likely, e.g. Stage 2 /Vːm/ > [Vm] (> [Vmm]), instead of potential [Vːm] > [Ṽːm] > [Ṽː]. Vowel-length reduction before /m/ which blocks nasalization (and thence also N-deletion) appears better placed than durational differences across N place in accounting for the more general retention of /m/ and preferential loss of /n₁/ found in the sample.

The effect of N place on patterns of distinctive nasalization and N-fortition in Northern Italian has its basis in a suggested inverse relationship – both phonological and phonetic – between vowel and N length: greater vowel length will correlate with lesser N length and vice versa. Hence we find in our sample long vowels can be followed by short nasals and long nasals can only be preceded by short vowels, i.e. [VːN], [VNː], but a sequence of long vowel + long nasal consonant is impermissible, i.e. *[VːNː]. This pattern is entirely consistent with the previously mentioned pan-Romance phonotactic constraint which permits CVːC or CVCː (and CVC) structures, but not *CVːCː.

From the phonetic perspective, place is reported by Lehiste (1976: 227) to have a predictable effect on consonant duration which, in turn, tends to correlate inversely with duration of the preceding vowel. According to Lehiste, vowel duration tends to be shortest before labials which tend to be longer than coronals and velars (see table 7.1 for duration of N).[13] The only figures available for relative V and N duration are average figures provided by Recasens i Vives (1986) for three Catalan speakers in the context VN#.

These are: V 75 ms. + [m] 78 ms. vs. V 87 ms. + [n] 62 ms. Whilst more experimental work clearly needs to be done, Recasens i Vives's very limited results provide some small, albeit tentative, confirmation of Lehiste's claim.

In a refinement of his earlier suggestion regarding interaction between N-place duration and N-deletion made in 1973, Chen (1975: 50) makes precisely the same suggestion that preferential loss in Chinese dialects of /n/ rather than /ŋ/ is the result of substantial differences in length relative to the preceding vowel. He reports /ŋ/ in /Vŋ/ to be four times longer than /V/, in contrast to same relative length of /V/ and /n/ in /Vn/. Unfortunately, once again, no other figures are provided.

Lower levels of intrinsic vowel duration before /m/ than before /n/ appear to be the basis for the phonological process of vowel shortening affecting Stage 2 /Vːm(a)/ in Northern Italian. Speakers of Northern Italian dialects, as those in other parts of Italy (Rohlfs 1966: 310–11), seem to have been particularly sensitive to phonetically determined vowel length differences before /m/ and /n/, leading apparently to language-specific phonologization of reduced V duration before /m/. Phonological reinterpretation has ensued, and expected Stage 2 /Vː/ now appears as /V/ before /m/, even in open syllables, e.g. Mi. ['lima] < Stage 2 /liːma/ < LIMA 'file'.

The naturalness of the vowel shortening properties of /m/ in Northern Italy is confirmed by the available cross-linguistic evidence. The same phenomenon is also reported to be normal in Old French (Fouché 1958). Elsewhere Rietveld and Frauenfelder (1987) measured vowel duration before /l, s, r/ and /m/, and found unexpected vowel shortening before [m] in Dutch. Perry (1990) also reports that secondary vowel lengthening found in other contexts was normally blocked before /m/ in Middle High German.

7.3.1 N-fortition and secondary gemination of /m/ in Bolognese

The suggested inverse phonetic relationship between vowel duration and the place of the following nasal consonant needs to be interpreted carefully. While interaction between vowel and consonant duration exists, there is no suggestion that the phonetic effect is so great that the phonologization of place-governed vowel shortening will trigger compensatory lengthening of the following N, i.e. one-step /VːN/ > /VNː/.[14] Any phonetic increase in N duration will simply not be sufficient to result in instantaneous rephonologization of short N as a long consonant. The phonological (and phonetic) shift in this case is simply too great and in any case all synchronic examples of post-tonic N-gemination in Northern Italian can be explained as the result of a much later and completely independent process.

Among the sample members, post-tonic gemination after short vowels is pervasive only in Bolognese, e.g. Bo. ['lemma] < ['lema] < LIMA 'file', alongside ['laːma] < *LAMA 'blade', ['paːna] < PANNA 'cream'. Confirmation of the intermediate stage of short vowel + short nasal consonant is found in

the existence of precisely this phase in the other members of the sample, evident in 8. That doubling of /m/ is very recent even in the Bolognese area can be inferred from its restricted geolinguistic spread around Bologna: it is to date found in the city itself and in rural dialects to the north and south of the city. Fieldwork on my part confirms it to be unknown to the east towards Imola (only 15 km from Bologna) and also absent in archaic rural Bolognese to the west, e.g. Monteveglio (Hajek 1994). In these areas we find ['lema]. It may be possible that onset of /m/-doubling may be dated around the start of the nineteenth century. Literary texts of the late eighteenth century still use single *m*, e.g. *semia* < SIMIA 'monkey', *prema* < PRIMA 'first', which are by the middle of the next century written as *semmia, premma*. All the comparative, structural and textual evidence suggests that vowel shortening before /m/ must have occurred many centuries earlier in Bolognese and most other Northern Italian dialects where it is known to occur.

Additional confirmation that /m/-gemination occurred independently of vowel shortening in Bolognese is provided by the evidence that it forms part of a much larger process of non-compensatory consonant gemination after all short tonic vowels, given above at 10 and repeated here at 15.

15 Bo. /pana/ [panna] < Stage 2 /pena/ < PINNA 'feather'
      /veɲa/ [veɲɲa] <   /viɲa/ < *VINJA 'vineyard'
      /tata/ [tatta] <   /teta/ < TITTA 'teat'
      /tar/ [tarː] <   /tor/ < TURRE 'tower'
  but /lɛːna/ [lɛːna] <   /laːna/ < LANA 'wool'
      /paːna/ [paːna] <   /pana/ < PANNA 'cream'
      /pɛːl/ [pɛːl] <   /pɛl/ < PELLE 'skin'

The phonetic basis for secondary gemination in Bolognese, although associated with short vowels, is in fact not as directly related to vowel length as discussion in this section might suggest. Instead, consonant gemination is triggered by an unusual but predictable fortis vs. lenis difference in Bolognese. Stressed long vowels are characterized by a lenis or lax articulation of both vowel and following consonant(s) which are never geminated. On the other hand, fortis or tense articulation is characteristic of short vowels and following consonants. This lenis vs. fortis distinction has been reported to occur in a handful of Emilian and possibly Romagnol dialects (e.g. Gaudenzi 1889, Uguzzoni 1971 and Schürr 1918). Increased articulatory tension is not apparently an inherent characteristic of short tonic vowels – a fact confirmed by the fact that it is not found in most other Northern Italian dialects with a vowel-length contrast. My own fieldwork on sample members confirms the absence of a lax-tense articulation contrast in sample members other than Bolognese. In other languages, such as English, long vowels are reportedly tense and short vowels lax (Clark and Yallop 1995: 32).

Experimental work by Uguzzoni (1971) on secondary geminates in the

more conservative Emilian dialect of Frignano provides some confirmation that length is in the first instance a secondary correlate of increased articulatory tension. Word-final consonants after short tonic vowels are articulatorily and perceptually long. However, she found a discrepancy in perceptual and articulatory length in intervocalic position. Although the very tense articulation of such consonants gives the perceptual impression of their being longer than their lax counterparts after long tonic vowels, articulatory measurements found them to be of the same duration. In more innovative Bolognese, the perceptual lengthening effect of a strong or tense articulation has led to reinterpretation of these tense consonants as articulatorily long, and subsequent regular gemination after short tonic vowels. Most sources on Bolognese, e.g. Mainoldi (1950, 1967), Coco (1970) and Vincenzi (1978), emphasize the length of these geminates, although they also frequently note their tense quality. Rizzi (1984) considers tenseness alone to be evident, denying the existence of consonant gemination in Bolognese. My own fieldwork – confirmed from casual observation by others of my recordings – finds length to be immediately perceptible, although for some speakers at least it is associated with a fortis articulation. The length of so-called post-tonic geminates is now statistically confirmed by experimental work (Hajek 1994, in press).

7.4 CONCLUSIONS

Examination of cross-linguistic evidence uncovers no strictly universal pattern of N-place effects on the spread of distinctive nasalization. Conflicting, possibly random patterning was found outside the Romance-speaking area. However, the range of data examined to date by universalists and myself is very limited, and further investigation of developments in other languages may show place-related changes to be more systematic than they presently appear. On the other hand, developments in Northern Italian seem to pattern in a regular and predictable fashion: Stage 2 $/n_1/$ is the most frequent locus for nasalization-related processes. Phonologically pertinent vowel length differences, however, are seen to override the effect of N place: $/n_1/$ and $/n_2/$ are placed at separate points along the suggested N-place parameter for Northern Italian. The difference can only be accounted for by the effect of phonological vowel-length differences on the spread of vowel nasalization and, therefore, on subsequent N-deletion. Vowel length also governs N-fortition in which the spread of distinctive nasalization becomes less likely, as the necessary conditions for its development are eliminated over time, particularly before bilabial /m/. I suggest that the Northern Italian place parameter as well as N-fortition phenomena ultimately have a phonetic basis in low-level temporal differences which favour loss of coronal [n], provided that the preceding tonic vowel is

phonologically long, but also in vowel shortening before bilabial nasals. Finally, the chronological interrelationship between long vowel shortening before Stage 2 /m/ and secondary gemination in Bolognese is examined. Vowel shortening does not trigger Compensatory Lengthening of following nasals. Instead, secondary gemination is a generalized post-tonic phenomenon associated with a fortis vs. lenis articulation of stressed vowels.

8

N-DELETION: ITS MANNER AND ITS MOTIVATION

8.1 INTRODUCTION

In this chapter the manner of, and suggested motivation for, N-deletion are considered in some detail. Universalists looking at the development of distinctive nasalization have generally focused on N-deletion as a simple one-step process, i.e. N > Ø, with only limited reference being made to possible intermediate steps of attenuation. Whilst focus in this study has also been on N > Ø, I suggested in section 1.2.1.1 that the complete loss of N is in reality better viewed as the final link of a longer chain of gradual reduction. The possible path of attrition is not unary: phonologists have suggested that different phonetic mechanisms may be employed, and many of these can be captured formally in autosegmental representation through manipulation of Feature Geometry. The ability of Feature Geometry (FG) to capture N-attrition and N-deletion is examined and evaluated here. The result is rather a mixed bag: the formalism appears as both too powerful – as previously suggested – but also too weak, unable to represent in an adequate fashion other types of change, e.g. temporal reduction.

The overriding motivation for N-deletion, most frequently reported in Coda position, is usually ascribed to a cross-linguistic tendency towards open CV\$ syllables, which favours the loss of syllable-final consonants, or more precisely consonants in Coda position. However, in Northern Italian at least, Coda-deletion of N does not operate independently: as will be seen, it interacts with and is triggered by vowel length and vowel nasalization. An analysis is also provided that attempts to unify the seemingly unrelated processes of N-loss reported in Northern Italy (e.g. TANTU 'so' > Bg. [taːt], but LANA 'wool' > Bg. [laːna]) and Central and Southern Italy (e.g. TANTU > Sard. [tantu], but LANA > [lãː]). I suggest that developments in both areas can be accounted for by the operation, albeit in slightly different circumstances, of the same sub-syllabic template.

8.1.1 *Feature Geometry and N-attrition*

The hypothesis that the phonologization of vowel nasalization is dependent on some phonological process of N-attenuation (or even deletion) preceding it, was tested in chapter 3, and found not to hold. No clear evidence of an ordering relationship between attenuation processes and vowel nasalization was reported, and I suggested that, according to context and type, they could occur in any order. Indeed, the only ordering restriction – on

both synchrony and diachrony – was one in which N-deletion is normally expected to be preceded by a phonological process of contextual nasalization in those contexts where nasal vowels surface or have previously surfaced.

Despite the apparent independence of vowel nasalization and attrition or reduction of N (i.e. any phonological process that results in the denasalization, temporal reduction or deconsonantization of N) the substantive issues of delimiting the range of possible N-attrition processes, as well as determining the relationship these may have with N-deletion, are important ones which require further investigation. Many processes of attenuation or reduction have already been mentioned, some in great detail, e.g. degemination (see section 3.4.2). Some of these, and others, are considered once more in this chapter.

Present-day formalism allows for the representation of the attenuation of N in different manners by manipulation of the skeletal and sub-skeletal structure. However, the capabilities of the formalism are in themselves no indication of what really occurs in languages, and require empirical verification. The formalism could quite plausibly be too weak for the purposes of capturing possible sound change as a phonological phenomenon, because it is unable to represent some processes of N-attrition. In other cases it may be too powerful because it allows the representation of phonological operations that may never occur either diachronically or synchronically. In chapter 3 strong criticism was made of attempts at manipulating phonological structures to satisfy theoretical approaches to the treatment of distinctive nasalization, e.g. Piggott's use of underspecification and floating [+nasal] to derive nasal vowels in French. Here we look specifically at a set of Feature Geometric operations.

Given the structure at 1, the manipulations at 2 arguably represent the most likely range of attenuation processes affecting N, which may lead ultimately to its complete loss. The phonetic and phonological ramifications of each such formal manipulation are discussed in the sections that follow.

1

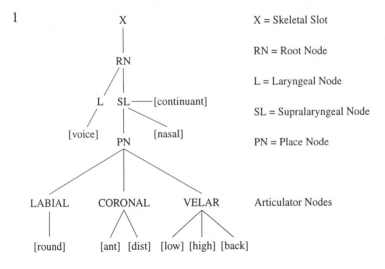

X = Skeletal Slot

RN = Root Node

L = Laryngeal Node

SL = Supralaryngeal Node

PN = Place Node

Articulator Nodes

2a deletion of skeletal slot
 b deletion of Root Node
 c deletion of Supralaryngeal Node
 d deletion of Place Node
 e voicing assimilation ([+voi] → [−voi] / __ [−voi])
 f manner assimilation ([−cont] → [+cont] / __ [+cont])
 g place shift (e.g. velarization)

8.1.2 *Skeletal slot deletion and temporal reduction*

Perhaps the simplest formal operation available to us is deletion of the skeletal slot as the first and only step in the reduction of N. Such a move will result in automatic loss of all that is dependent on it. Since the skeleton is a prosodic tier capturing phonological duration, skeletal slot deletion precludes by definition any process of sub-skeletal Compensatory Lengthening (CL) from adjacent segments since nothing remains to be filled. From the phonetic perspective, loss of the phonological timing slot is equivalent to the elimination of phonetic duration. The absence of phonetic timing means that all other phonetic characteristics (e.g. manner, place, voicing detail) previously associated with the slot cannot be instantiated and are, therefore, also lost.

Whilst N-deletion as a one-step process over time is formally convenient, it is inconsistent with the hypothesis made in section 1.2.1.1 that N-deletion is the end result of a gradual phonetic (and phonological) attrition of the original nasal stop. Certainly, it is true that universalist studies on the development of N have always focused on N-deletion. However, some phonologists have noted that some sort of phonetic 'weakening' of N is a necessary precondition for N-deletion. Chen (1972 and elsewhere), Pagliuca and Mowrey (1987), and Foley (1975, 1977) all specifically refer to some sort of weakened, but poorly defined, N, often transcribed as a raised [^{N}], which may then be completely lost, e.g. VN > $\tilde{\text{V}}$N > $\tilde{\text{V}}^N$ > $\tilde{\text{V}}$.

If reduction of non-geminate N to [^{N}] is found to be a phonologically significant process involving temporal reduction, then attempts to account for it should logically focus on the timing tier, i.e. the skeleton. There is some evidence that attrition of N, at least in some languages, manifests itself primarily as a reduction in the phonetic duration of N. In at least one dialect, Riminese, /n$_1$/ in word-final position is today so brief that, in the presence of marked contextual nasalization, it is often difficult to perceive, e.g. [karbõw̃^{n}] 'coal' < Stage 2 /karboːn/. Chen (1972: 114) and Schourup (1973: 112) also make reference to a similarly temporally reduced post-vocalic N in Chinese dialects and Hausa respectively. Experimental work confirms too that N may undergo substantial temporal reduction before voiceless stops, as reported in section 6.4.1.3. In English reduction may be so great that N is completely elided.

Reduction of duration may also be manifested through N-tapping or rhoticization of N. Evidence of this phenomenon is found in a number of different Romance-speaking areas, e.g. in some Franco-Provençal dialects [lyːɾa] from earlier [lȳːɾa] < [lȳːna] < LUNA 'moon' (Walser 1937). The phenomenon is an old one in Romanian dialects, and in many areas the vowel and tap are still nasalized (Avram 1990). In Northern Italian a similar phenomenon is also reported in some Ligurian dialects, with secondary denasalization within the last twenty to forty years (van den Bergh 1983). Continuing reduction of duration may lead to ultimate effacement, evident in the dialect of Novara di Sicilia, a long-standing Gallo-Italian colony in Sicily but historically very close to Ligurian. Here we find the following alternation: a light apical tap [ɾ̃ ~ ɾ] in lento speech and complete loss in allegro styles, e.g. [skarpᵊl'lĩːɾu] ~ [skarpᵊl'lẽːu] < *SCALPELLINU 'stonecutter' (Tropea 1966).

That N-tapping is fundamentally duration reduction and not manner change is confirmed by Elugbe (1978). He provides experimental (airflow and spectrographic) evidence demonstrating that the phonetic distinction between non-geminate [n] and short tapped [ɾ̃] found in many Edoid languages, e.g. Ghotuọ, is duration-based. Elugbe and Hombert (1975) provide additional experimental confirmation: native listeners were found to use duration as the primary perceptual correlate in order to distinguish between phonetically normal and short consonants. Elugbe (1989) also reports a three-way phonetic timing contrast in related Ọlọma and Ẹmhalhẹ, e.g. non-geminate [d], short [ḍ] and tapped [r]. Further, we note that tapped consonants in some Edoid languages are indeed the historical product of a temporal reduction of earlier short Ç (Elugbe 1989: 111–12). Such a change cannot be formally captured at present as a timing-related phenomenon along the skeletal tier. Moreover, autosegmental formalism is unable at present to represent what is in effect a three-way phonological length distinction as a timing-related phenomenon along the skeleton. A partial solution would be to attach phonetically non-geminate consonants like [n, d] to two skeletal slots in autosegmental representation, and short consonants to one. However, Edoid non-geminate consonants are not perceived as geminate, and are not treated as such by speakers. They are, in fact, associated with phonologically and phonetically non-geminate consonants in other languages by native and non-native speakers alike. In any case, tapped consonants would still have to be distinguished from their non-tapped counterparts by feature marking below the timing tier. Indeed, the shift of [n] to [ɾ̃] can normally only be dealt with as a non-temporal feature-changing process below the skeleton, i.e. [−continuant] > [+continuant], this being the only feature for which nasal stops and rhotic taps and flaps differ in standard feature specifications.

8.1.3 *Root-Node deletion, Supralaryngeal Node deletion and Compensatory Lengthening*

Deletion of the Root Node leaves the original skeletal slot in position, but devoid of all melodic, i.e. feature, content. The result is pseudo-temporal in effect since it is formally equivalent to segment deletion without loss of the skeletal slot. The formalism allows new material to be attached directly to the slot by a process of Compensatory Lengthening (CL), i.e. the spreading of a fully specified Root Node from an adjacent skeletal slot, as seen at 3. The spreading segment, previously associated to only one skeletal slot, is now long.

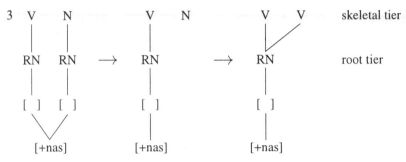

So-called Compensatory Lengthening (CL) of Root Nodes is now widely invoked in phonological analysis, and supported by an extensive literature, e.g. Wetzels and Sezer (1986), Hayes (1989), Goldsmith (1990) and Bickmore (1995). In synchronic analysis, CL is an elegant way of accounting for surface differences in length triggered by morphophonemic segment-deletion. Indeed, the derivation of length in surface nasal vowels from underlying short vowel plus N is frequently accounted for in precisely this fashion, e.g. French [bɔ̃ː] ← /bɔn/ 'good' (m. sg.) alongside [bɔn] ← /bɔn + ə/ (f. sg.). Specific examples of such treatments invoking CL to account for nasal vowel length include versions of the Coalescence and N-attenuation analyses (e.g. Hayes 1986b and Hualde 1989 respectively) of distinctive nasalization discussed in chapter 3.

CL also has wide currency in the treatment of sound change; see e.g. Wetzels and Sezer (1986), and Bickmore (1995) for numerous examples. It was noted in section 4.1.2 that most universalists are happy to assume that N-deletion also triggers compensatory lengthening of adjacent vowels, i.e. one-step [bɔn] > [bɔ̃ː]. However, I wish to reiterate the claim made in chapter 1 that the diachronic adequacy or necessity of the notion of CL has not been established. Significantly, from an empirical point of view, at no point in this study has there been any need to invoke CL to account for patterns of vowel lengthening reported in the sample. In each case, as already noted in sections 4.1.2, 4.1.3 and 6.4.1, operation of the Vowel Length Parameter precludes any need for CL in Northern Italian. The available

evidence suggested that a phonological process of vowel lengthening was always chronologically ordered before vowel nasalization and N-deletion in all contexts, i.e. VN > VːN > ṼːN > Ṽː, and not VN > Ṽː. The only possible exception to this, i.e. the development of VNFric sequences, is minor, and involves not CL but complete vocalization. There may be other cases in languages where one cannot establish vowel lengthening before N-loss over time. However, even here it is more plausible – diachronically and phonetically – to suggest a process of gradual vocalization of N to V, rather than positing at some point in time an empty skeletal slot somewhere in the grammar, and abrupt change from V to N or N to V (see section 8.1.4 below).

The empty Root-Node/Compensatory Lengthening account is for the purposes of describing sound change phonetically implausible, breaching as it does all the suggested constraints noted in section 1.3.1. First, the empty Root-Node stage contravenes the constraint that all posited stages of sound change should have a phonetic instantiation. Unfilled elements with no segmental content cannot satisfy this requirement. A Compensatory Lengthening account also breaches the requirement that in any shift from one segment to another purported sound change should be gradual, minimal and natural. That gradualness and naturalness are important characteristics of sound change is accepted by historical phonologists as fundamental and serves as an essential evaluatory metric (Picard 1995, Dressler 1971). A hypothesized sound change is more plausible the smaller the phonetic distance between input and output segments. Where the phonetic distance between segments is great, then necessary phonetically plausible intermediate stages of sound change need to be determined and posited. Dressler suggests for instance that simultaneous modification in manner and place of a segment is excessive and should not be accepted as plausible sound change. There indeed seems little reason why a change in place features should be accompanied by change in manner (and indeed major class) features or vice versa.

A simple example will suffice to demonstrate how such constraints allow us to evaluate in almost intuitive fashion the plausibility of a posited sound change of the type assumed by Compensatory Lengthening. Let us assume we are told of a posited one-step change [n] > [ɔ̃] in the absence of any other information and asked to evaluate such a shift. No mention is made of CL or any other detail. There seems little doubt we would conclude the change to be impossible: the distance between the two segments is simply too great from both phonetic and phonological perspectives. Yet, this is precisely the type of sound change predicted by a Compensatory Lengthening account of nasal vowel lengthening triggered by N-deletion. If the apparent shift from [n] to [ɔ̃] cannot be accounted for by other means, i.e. vowel lengthening ordered before N-deletion, and they are indeed found to be directly related, the process is one of gradual vocalization along the following

suggested trajectory: [n] > [m] > [w̥̃] > [w̃] > [ũ] > [õ] > [ɔ̃]. At no point along the path of change is any segment empty of root node or feature content. Each stage is pronounceable, minimal in degree of alteration and the relationship between any two segments in immediate sequence, therefore, satisfies naturalness requirements.

It should also be pointed out that all purported diachronic examples of CL cited in the literature are amenable to reinterpretation, and should be, as non-compensatory phenomena, e.g. the oft-cited Latin s-deletion phenomenon where earlier [kasnus] reputedly changed to [kaːnus] through CL (e.g. Hayes 1989, Bickmore 1995 and others). The logic adopted by phonologists to justify the use of CL to describe sound change is seriously flawed. In his discussion of Latin, two of Hayes's critical arguments in support of a CL account (and indeed CL in general) are that: (1) 'vowels typically do not lengthen before clusters', and (2), even if a pre-deletion lengthening rule were adopted, 'lengthening is not depicted as compensatory (that is, the lengthened vowel does not take up the time vacated by the /s/)' (1989: 261, n. 2). The first is empirically wrong: vowel lengthening before clusters and in closed syllables in general is widespread – it is reported in this study to occur in Northern Italian before N(C) and is just as frequent before all other clusters including /sC/, e.g. Bolognese [voːster] < VOSTRU 'your', [paːsta] < St. 2 /pasta/ < PASTA, [ɛːlt] < /alt/ < ALTU 'high'. As for the second, there is in diachrony (as opposed to morphophonemic alternations in synchrony) no logical reason why sound change should *a fortiori* require the preservation of a timing slot vacated by another segment. The second principle is circular, deriving not from historical data itself but from the CL analysis of synchronic data.

A partial alternative to Root-Node deletion is the elimination of only the Supralaryngeal Node directly dependent on the Root Node. This has the effect of preserving the pre-existing specification of major class features ([consonantal] and [sonorant]) inside the Root Node, as well as the Laryngeal Node, whilst eliminating specifications for place and continuance. In a similar process of empty node filling, the Supralaryngeal Node is refilled by automatic Compensatory Lengthening or spreading from an adjacent segment. In the case of the sequence VN, loss of N's Supralaryngeal Node and subsequent spreading of V's supralaryngeal node would lead to the attachment to N of V's [+continuant] and place features. The consequences of this formal manipulation are undesired and not supported by observed sound changes. Once again all the suggested plausibility constraints are breached, including the suggested separation of place and manner in gradual sound change. In the case of word-final /bɔn/, the result would be one-step shift to [bɔ̃β̃], i.e. from coronal nasal stop to an unknown nasalized bilabial tap. If front vowels are assumed to be coronal in place, /bem/ would presumably lead to [bẽɾ̃].

8.1.4 *Non-temporal reduction*

The phonetic reduction of N to Ø over time is not restricted to being a purely durational phenomenon. Nasal stops may also be affected in the first instance by non-temporal phonetic reduction or attenuation, only secondarily leading to temporal loss, e.g. N > F̃(ricative) > G̃(lide) > Ø. Non-temporal phonetic reduction may be phonologized and can, in many cases, be captured by autosegmental formalism. Different types of non-temporal reduction processes have been suggested by phonologists and these are discussed in the sections that follow.

Whilst some sort of non-temporal N-attenuation may precede N-deletion, it does not follow necessarily that N-deletion is the inevitable result of N-attenuation as is often assumed by universalists and other phonologists. If the gradual chain of changes leading to N-deletion is restricted, as I have suggested in section 1.2.1.1, to only those changes in which the segment is still nasalized, then processes of attenuation in which all trace of nasality is lost, but some segment preserved, must be excluded. Denasalization of N to C, discussed below in section 8.1.6, is one such case. Similarly excluded is N-weakening leading to complete vocalization, i.e. N > G̃ > Ṽ > V, rather than slot-deletion, i.e. N > G̃ > Ø. From the phonetic perspective, complete vocalization of VN to VV involves the gradual phonetic assimilation of N to V. Such assimilation is phonologized as a gradual feature-changing process that leads, as de Chene and Anderson (1979) and Stephen Anderson (1981) suggest, to reassignment from Coda to Nucleus of the preserved skeletal slot originally occupied by N within the syllable Rhyme.[1]

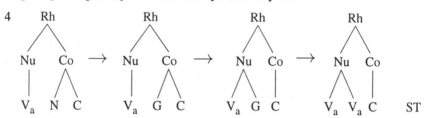

Rh = Rhyme   Nu = Nucleus   Co = Coda   ST = Skeletal Tier

The manner in which the Vowel Length Parameter appears to operate in my Northern Italian sample precludes in most, if not all, circumstances the need to posit complete vocalization: pre-nasal V must already be long before vowel nasalization develops. As a result, the nucleus, with long vowel, is already branching, and no further material can be brought into it. In these circumstances, N-reduction leads to complete deletion. The only exception to this observation may have been possible N-vocalization in historical N+Fricative clusters in some varieties of Northern Italian, although there is some historical and cross-dialectal evidence of vowel lengthening occurring even here before distinctive nasalization developed in this context.

8.1.5 *Deletion of the place node*

Trigo (1990: 13–14) argues that deletion of the place node, otherwise referred to as 'Oral Depletion', may be one manifestation of N-attenuation. Whilst developments in some Northern Italian dialects reported below are synchronically indicative of the loss over time of underlying place features, I do not accept Trigo's suggestions that loss of the underlying place node allows for placeless nasal consonants to surface synchronically, or that the absence of all place features is the result of a phonetic phenomenon of place deletion.

A poorly described but apparently placeless nasal, symbolized as [h̃], derived from an earlier */ŋ/ is reported by Trigo to occur in Aguaruna adjacent to vowels, e.g. [ãh̃ʌm] 'later', [sʌh̃ĩk] 'beads' and [sakãh̃ʌ̃] 'skeleton'. There is no evidence of nasal segments being phonetically placeless in any Northern Italian dialect and doubts exist as to the exact nature of [h̃]. Whilst I accept that segments may be underlyingly placeless, all segments are normally considered to surface with place features. Segments that are assumed to be underlyingly unspecified for place, such as /h/, typically obtain place features from adjacent segments by the time they surface. For example, [h] in [ha] (= [ạa]) is thought to share the place features of the following vowel [a].

Historical reconstruction of Aguaruna suggests too that the so-called placeless nasal [h̃] is in reality a nasalized velar glide [ɰ̃], the lenited result of an earlier */ŋ/. Velar place, or more precisely approximation of articulators in the velar region, would in any case be further favoured phonetically by velum lowering for nasalization, and dorsum raising in the articulation of adjacent high vowels.

It should also be pointed out that elimination of underlying place features does not, as Trigo implies, necessarily lead to N-reduction through automatic secondary changes in manner and major class features, i.e. [−continuant] → [+continuant], [+consonantal] → [−consonantal]. In some Northern Italian dialects, the synchronic reflex of Lat. /n/ appears to have lost underlying place features in secondary word-final position: it surfaces today in a phonetically predictable fashion agreeing with the identity of the preceding vowel, without any evidence of further reduction: palatal [ɲ] after palatal front vowels, and labial [m] after labialized/rounded back vowels, e.g. Alpine Lombard *greñ* < Stage 2 /graːn/ < GRANU 'grain', *viñ* < Stage 2 /viːn/ < VINU 'wine', *bom* < Stage 2 /bɔːn/ < BONU 'good' (Rohlfs 1966: 429; Tuttle 1991).

It is true that, synchronically, N place in such examples is fully predictable, hence not underlyingly specified but derivable by redundancy rules in Alpine Lombard and elsewhere. Diachronically, however, the present distribution of N place after vowels has an entirely different explanation. It is the result of simple rightward spread of labial and palatal place to a nasal consonant with

a pre-existing coronal articulation. The result in the first instance is a nasal consonant with doubly articulated place (labial-coronal, palatal-coronal, etc.). As already reported in section 7.3, gestures, especially coronal ones, are prone to masking. Even though coronality is still present in this initial phase, reduced perceptibility may lead to its eventual loss (Browman and Goldstein 1987). Confirmation of the suggestion of coronal susceptibility is confirmed by the total resistance of historical /m/ and /ɲ/ to vowel-conditioned place shift in those Northern Italian dialects where Latin /n/ has assimilated, e.g. PRIMU > St. 2 /priːm/ > [prem] ~ [prim] and not *[preɲ] ~ *[priɲ] 'first'.

Critically, at no point during this process of place assimilation is N place – at least at surface level – ever absent, contra Trigo. Cross-linguistically, contextual place overlap in nasals is widespread, e.g. English in # Manila, where [n#m], [ⁿm#m] and [m#m] can be found according to speech style. Similar place overlay resulting in doubly articulated nasals is widely reported in NC clusters, e.g. Cuban Spanish, Catalan and Arles Provençal (Coustenoble 1945). Doubly articulated nasal phonemes are also common in some parts of the world, e.g. labial-velar [ŋm] in African languages with complete closure at two points of articulation. In Vietnamese and some varieties of Provençal we find word-final [ŋᵝ] where complete velar closure is simultaneously accompanied by an unconditioned bilabial constriction which is nasalized but without lip-rounding or complete closure.

We conclude then that elimination of the place node has no triggering effect relating to the attenuation of N as Trigo predicts. Nasals subject to complete place shift remain full nasal consonants. Second, place-node deletion is not an appropriate sound change as it contravenes one suggested constraint on diachrony, i.e. that posited stages should be phonetically pronounceable (see section 1.3.1). Third, at no point over time do nasals involved in the sound change ever surface as placeless. Indeed, they are for at least part of the process doubly-articulated for place until a later simplification to a predictable one-place articulation. Therefore, the synchronic absence of underlying place features should be seen to involve a final reanalysis at an abstract level of grammar of what was diachronically a gradual and phonologized process of place assimilation.

8.1.6 Voicing assimilation and devoicing

Assimilatory devoicing of N before voiceless consonants may reduce the perceptual saliency of N. Without a compensatory increase in turbulent airflow through the nasal cavity, it is possible that the perceptually weakened N may then be deleted – as, it has been suggested, occurs before voiceless obstruents in English (see section 6.4.1.3 for details). However, I have already discussed in some detail in section 3.4.4 the alternative, possibly more widespread, effect of N-devoicing. The cited cross-linguistic evidence

(e.g. Sardinian, Old Norse and Toba Batak) points not to N-deletion, but to a strong tendency towards total assimilation with preservation of the skeletal slot, i.e. NC > ṆC > Cː, e.g. PENSARE > [peṇsare] > Sard. [pessare] 'to think'. The phonetic processes of contextual devoicing and subsequent denasalization may be phonologized and captured autosegmentally as at 5:

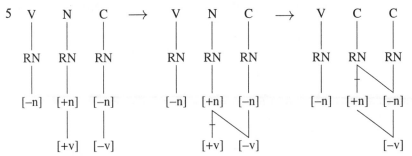

[n] = [nasal]   [v] = [voice]

Total N-to-C assimilation appears to be unrelated to the historical development of distinctive nasalization. In Sardinian there is a clear isogloss boundary between [pensare] and [pessare] in neighbouring dialects. In Contini's (1987) finely detailed phonetic atlas and companion description of Sardinian there is no evidence at all of any intermediate forms, such as [pẽṇsare] or [pẽssare], with any trace of nasalization. The absence of intermediate [pẽssare] is hardly surprising, given the strong cross-linguistic constraint against the appearance of CṼCː (where Cː is oral), already noted in section 3.4.4.

Devoicing of N may also occur as a regular phenomenon in word-final position.[2] Here, too, Hyman (1975a: 258) notes that devoicing occurs alongside the absence of any phonological process of vowel nasalization and leads to complete denasalization, and not deletion, of N, e.g. Fe'Fe' *[Vn] > [Vṇ] > [Vt].

8.1.7 Manner assimilation

Contextual manner assimilation, discussed in some detail in section 5.4.1.1, leads to the loss of oral closure in nasal stops. It is a cross-linguistically common process affecting nasals before fricatives, noted previously in Icelandic [dažsa] dansa as at 6:

6   N   F   N   F
      | | →   \ /
   [−cont]   [+cont]   [+cont]

Nasal stops may also undergo similar manner assimilation in intervocalic position. As noted in chapter 5, nasalized fricatives are inherently unstable, and prone to gliding and further reduction. Hence, the further reduction of

Tuscan /-n-/ to [ĩ], described by Giannelli and Savoia (1978) as a nasalized apicodental approximant, e.g. Tuscan [i pːãːnẽ] > [i pːãːĩẽ] *il pane* 'the bread'. Such reduction may have one of two consequences. First, if vowels are already predictably long, then N-weakening may lead ultimately to complete phonetic and phonological loss, as in Tusc. [i pːãːĩẽ] and optional [i pːãːẽ]. This clearly falls within the phonological definition of N-deletion as skeletal slot deletion. Alternatively, manner assimilation may lead, not to N-deletion, but to complete vocalization and preservation of the original skeletal slot. If vowels are originally short before N and the Nucleus non-branching, vocalization of N, with incorporation into the Nucleus, may occur. Stephen Anderson (1981: 516–17) suggests precisely such a scenario for Visperterminen German, e.g. [en] > [ẽi] *denken* [dẽixu] 'think', [in] > [ĩː] *finster* [fĩːʃter] 'dark'.

8.1.8 *Place shift and velarization*

Velarization is the most widely referred-to process of context-free place shift in the literature on distinctive nasalization processes. It has frequently been suggested, e.g. Ruhlen (1973), Chen (1972, 1973a, 1974), Cedergren and Sankoff (1975) and Trigo (1988, 1990), that N-velarization is a process of attenuation which favours N-deletion. The phonetic basis for the latter hypothesis is the reported acoustic and perceptual similarity between velar [ŋ] and [Ṽ], supported by cross-linguistic evidence of alternation between the two (Greenlee and Ohala 1980, Ohala and Ohala 1993). House (1957) found, in perceptual experiments involving synthetic speech, that listeners were more likely to confuse [ŋ] than either [m] or [n] with [Ṽ].

Previously in section 7.1.1 I discussed in limited detail Chen's claim that place differences amongst syllable-final nasal consonants are lost over time through velarization. Reduction to weak [ᴺ] and eventual complete loss follow, as seen in the model repeated at 7:

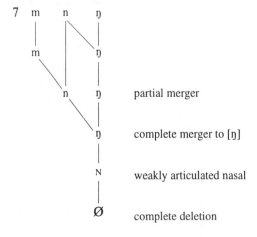

partial merger

complete merger to [ŋ]

weakly articulated nasal

complete deletion

There is little reason, however, to accept the premises underlying Chen's model at 7 above, that: (1) N-place shift always leads to complete velarization before loss; (2) velarization is some kind of weakening before loss; and (3) [ŋ] as weakening leads inevitably to complete N loss, rather than vocalization.

Given the nature of the model, the weakly articulated nasal should, by implication, be velar in place. However, on Chen's own admission, the weakly articulated [^{N}] has two variants, differing in place. Chen (1972: 114) notes both [^{n}] and [^{ŋ}] in his data, and gives a definition of each: [n] in [a^n] is 'weak and short and possibly articulated without tongue-tip touching [teeth ridge]', whilst [^{ŋ}] is an 'incomplete [ŋ]'. The first variant suggests that reduction without velarization is frequent in his sample.

Zee (1985) reports velarization not to be an inevitable manifestation of merger, and is critical of Chen's failure to report the frequent dentalization and more sporadic labialization of /ŋ/ found in many Chinese dialects. Word-final labialization of Lat. /n/, independent of contextual factors, is reported in some varieties of Spanish (Montes 1979; Yager 1989), and Northern Italian (Rohlfs 1966: 429), e.g. Piranese *pam* < PANE 'bread', *bem* < BENE 'well', *bom* < BONU 'good'. Zee (1979, 1981) found that in perceptual experiments using manipulated natural speech, N-place shift was to a large degree conditioned by adjacent vowel quality, e.g. [im] tended to [in]. However, the overall frequency of the shift [Vŋ] > [Vn] was reported to be far higher than that of its reverse [Vn] > [Vŋ], regardless of the quality of V.

That velarization is not an inevitable precursor of further weakening and loss is made evident by developments in those Chinese dialects studied by Chen where N loss is governed by Chen's own [m] ≫ [n] ≫ [ŋ] place parameter (see section 7.1.1). Here Chen (1975: 50) suggests that the resistance of final /ŋ/ to loss is due to its greater phonetic length relative to the preceding vowel in Chinese. Unfortunately, his claim cannot be assessed in the absence of other details or figures.

Finally, the reported acoustic and perceptual similarity between [ŋ] and [Ṽ] does not support the inference that velarization leads necessarily to N-deletion, as Chen suggests at 7. The phonetic similarity could plausibly favour skeletal slot preservation, with alternation between [ŋ] and [Ṽ], along a gradual continuum of change, i.e. [ŋ] > G̃ > Ṽ > V. The appearance of unetymological [ŋ] in Northern Italian dialects, discussed below in section 8.1.7.1, shows too that the continuum may also be reversed, i.e. V > Ṽ > G̃ > [ŋ].

In many Spanish dialects, synchronic [Ṽŋ$] and [Ṽː$] are frequently reported to alternate in place of earlier Lat. /V(ː)n/, e.g. [pãŋ] ~ [pãː] < Std Sp. /pan/ < PANE 'bread'. The traditional view, as expressed by Cedergren and Sankoff (1975) and Terrell (1975), is that velarization of /n/ is the first part of a natural process in which deletion follows, i.e. [n] > [ŋ] > Ø.[3]

However, there is some dispute as to the frequency of velarization, and its relationship, if any, with N-deletion in Spanish dialects. Uber (1984) hypothesizes that two independent processes, (1) [Vn] > [Vŋ] and (2) [Vn] > [Ṽ], co-exist as alternatives in some varieties of Spanish. Guitart (1982), noting occasional examples of glottalization, suggests that velariza-tion is part of a process of supralaryngeal restoration after /n/ loss and glottalization, operating as an alternative to complete deletion: [Vn$] > [Ṽ²] > [Ṽ] or [Ṽŋ]. More significant is Bjarkman's (1985: 5–7) claim that investigators have been confused by the perceptual similarity between [ŋ] and heavily nasalized vowels, and, in the absence of experimental verification, have mistakenly reported velarization instead of nasal vowels.

Detail is lacking, but it is clear that our understanding of developments in Spanish is confused. Further investigation is clearly required before any satisfactory conclusions about the relationship in Spanish dialects between velarization and [Ṽ] can be arrived at. However, it remains possible, following Bjarkman's observation and pending further examination, that velarization has led to gradual vocalization, rather than deletion, in Spanish dialects, i.e. [Vn$] > [Vŋ] > [Ṽŋ] > [ṼG̃] > [Ṽː], and not [Vŋ] > [Ṽŋ] > [Ṽ], as Cedergren and Sankoff (1975) and Terrell (1975) suggest. One additional hypothesis also requires further investigation: the appear-ance of final [ŋ] in Spanish dialects may be related to a process of nasalized glide hardening common in Northern Italy and discussed immediately below.

8.1.8.1 The development of [ŋ] in Northern Italian

The regular correspondence between Latin syllable-final /n/ and modern [ŋ] in Bolognese and Cairese, e.g. CANE 'dog' > Bo. [kæŋ], Ca. [kaŋ] and TANTU 'so' (m.) > Bo. [tæŋt], Ca. [taŋt], very easily leads to the conclusion that Latin /n/ was velarized in these dialects. However, examination of com-parative and historical data indicates such a correlation to be strictly superficial: modern [ŋ] in Bolognese and Cairese is the result of nasalized glide hardening that occurred some time after syllable-final /n/ was lost, i.e. [Ṽːn$] > [Ṽː$] > [VG̃$] > [Ṽŋ] > [Vŋ].[4]

Different factors support this conclusion. The vowel before word-final [ŋ] is characteristically short, e.g. Bo. [kæŋ], Ca. [kaŋ] < Stage 2 /kaːn/. However, were [ŋ] in these dialects to derive directly from Latin /n/ through simple place shift, the historical long vowel would be expected to remain, e.g. *[kæːŋ].[5] One could conceivably posit a rule of vowel shortening before [ŋ] < /n/. However, in Bolognese at least, such a rule does not correlate with the modern long reflex for all Stage 2 low vowels before other syllable-final nasals, e.g. Bo. [raːm] < Stage 2 /raːm/ < (AE)RAME 'copper', [baːɲ] < / baɲ/ < *BANJU 'bath', [aːn] < Stage 2 /an/ < ANNU 'year'.[6]

Descriptions of Bolognese from the nineteenth century on suggest that word-final hardening of [G̃] to [ŋ] is a very recent phenomenon. Ferrari

(1835) is explicit in his description of distinctive nasalization 'alla francese', i.e. [Ṽ$] without syllable-final [ŋ], and Coco (1970) notes that strong vowel nasalization is an increasingly archaic feature in modern Bolognese, typical of the oldest speakers, but now more normally replaced by generalized 'epenthesis' of [ŋ].

Further conclusive evidence against velarization of /n/ is provided by the appearance of 'epenthetic' [ŋ] before intervocalic /n/, e.g. Bo. [loŋna] < LUNA 'moon'. Nasalized diphthongal off-glides [w̃, j̃, ũ̯], represented since the nineteenth century in Bolognese orthography, were later hardened to [ŋ], e.g. LUNA 'moon' > [lõw̃na] *louna* > [loŋna], SPINA 'thorn' > [spẽj̃na] ~ [spẽũ̯na] *speina* > [speŋna].[7]

Coco's observations on the very recent occurrence of 'epenthesis' or glide-hardening in Bologna city is confirmed by my own fieldwork. Nasalized glides in all contexts (word-finally and before /-n-/) survive in rural varieties of Bolognese, especially amongst older speakers to the immediate west (Dozza [kæ̃ũ̯] 'dog', [lõw̃na]), to the south and to the east (Monteveglio [lõw̃na]). Here too younger speakers are beginning to consonantize.

Final confirmation of [G̃] > [ŋ] is found in the synchronic alternation in Cairese between diphthongal and 'epenthetic' forms, such as [lajna] ~ [lau̯na] ~ [laŋna] < LANA, [lywna] ~ [lyŋna] < LUNA.

Developments in Bolognese and Cairese indicate that, in Northern Italian at least, the appearance of velar [ŋ] is not linked to a process of N merger or any process of attenuation. Instead, the presence of [ŋ] reflects a counter-vailing tendency, not predicted by Chen (1972) and Ruhlen (1973), towards the hardening of nasalized glides in syllable-final position.

8.2 SYLLABLE STRUCTURE EFFECTS AS A RATIONALE FOR N-DELETION

Although the importance of syllable position was duly noted in chapter 6 when considering the effect of context on the spread of distinctive nasalization, I have refrained until now from discussing in detail the relationship between syllable structure and the sound changes of the sort examined in this study. I have so far concentrated on providing different phonetic and phonological explanations for N-attrition and deletion according to specific contexts, e.g. temporal reduction of N before voiceless stops, manner assimilation of N before fricatives, etc. However, the effect of syllable structure on N loss in Northern Italian, as in many other languages, is strongly evident.

It seems no accident that all cases of N-deletion in the Northern Italian sample, as elsewhere, are restricted to syllable-final or Coda position, as at 8a and 8b:

8a	CANE 'dog'	TANTU 'so' (m.)	LANA 'wool'	NASU 'nose'
St. 2	/kaːn$/	/tant$/	/laː$na/	/$naːz/
Bo.	[kæŋ]	[tænt]	[leːna]	[nɛːz]
Mi.	[kãː]	[tãːt]	[lana]	[naːz]
Bg.	[kaː]	[taːt]	[laːna]	[naːs]
Fr.	[ʃjẽː]	[tãː]	[lɛn]	[ne]

b

```
     Rh              Rh              Rh    Rh            Rh
    /  \            /  \             |     |           /  \
  Nu    Co        Nu    Co         Nu  On Nu        On  Nu  Co
  /\    |         |     /\         /\  |  |         |   /\  |
 k a    a    n   t a   n  t       l a  a  n   a     n   a a  z
```

I have already noted in a previous chapter that universalists are in agreement as to the cross-linguistic infrequency of syllable-initial N loss in V$NV sequences, and agree unanimously that such loss only occurs when syllable-final N in VN$ has already been affected.[8] Furthermore, preferential loss in syllable-final position is not restricted to N, but extends to all consonants (Escure 1977; Foley 1977; Hooper 1976). This universal pattern of preferential Coda-deletion is of course repeated in the Northern Italian sample: whilst Coda N loss is common, nowhere is N in syllable-onset position lost, whether word-initially or word-medially.

Phonologists such as Hooper (1976) and Foley (1977), recognizing the effect of syllable position on the ability of N and other consonants to resist weakening and loss, have suggested that preferential loss of Coda consonants is a function of the inherent weakness of syllable-final position. Such weakness derives from the frequently reported universal tendency towards open syllables, which favours the elimination over time of closed syllables: CVC$ > CV$.[9] The operation of this tendency over time is evident, for example, in Italian, a relatively conservative Romance dialect, where practically all final syllables are open as a result of the regular loss of Latin final consonants, e.g. SARTOR > It. *sarto* 'tailor', CANTATIS > *cantate* 'you sing' (pl.), DAT > *dà* 'gives'. Also, many languages restrict the permissible syllable types to open syllables, and no language has exclusively closed syllables.[10] Dogil and Luschützky (1989: 25–7) and Ohala and Kawasaki (1984: 115–19) provide numerous typological, structural and phonetic reasons why CV$ syllables should be cross-linguistically preferred to CVC$ syllables, and why sound change may be expected to affect C preferentially in VC$ rather than in CV$. Perceptual experiments show the junction between C and V to be more salient in CV$ than in VC$. Listeners are reported to place the perceptual centre of syllables at a point close to CV transitions. Further, the perception of C manner and place is also found to

be substantially better in CV$ than in VC$ syllables. Speakers are also reported to attempt to produce more precise, temporally better defined articulations at the CV interface.

Experimental evidence of articulatory asymmetry between Onset and Coda positions specifically with regard to nasal consonants is reported by Manuel (1991) and Fujimura and Lovins (1978) who show that velum position is lower in VN$ than in NV$ syllables. This articulatory asymmetry results in a substantially reduced acoustic demarcation between V and N in VN$ when compared to NV$. Manuel, like Fujimura and Lovins, suggests that this articulatory and acoustic asymmetry leads to the reduced perceptual saliency of other features of syllable-final N. As a result, listeners, faced also with the acoustic smearing of nasality across V and N, may mishear or not hear consonantal closure in the manner intended by the speaker, and may assume that N is weakened (assimilation) or absent (deletion). If they misinterpret or fail to perceive N, they may repeat the misperception or omission when speaking. This account of how syllable-final N can be assimilated or lost is of course consistent with the listener-oriented model of sound change adopted in this study.

Notwithstanding the attractions of the open syllable hypothesis, syllable-final position is only one, albeit major, factor in the process of N-deletion in Northern Italian. Any account will need to make reference to the significant interaction between N-deletion and other factors, such as vowel nasalization, and vowel length, as discussed in the following sections.

Further, whilst it is generally agreed that languages exhibit a tendency towards open syllables and, following this, that syllable-final consonants are inherently weak, these observations seem not to be strictly universal in application. I have already pointed out in section 6.3 that in Sardinian, and Corsican, Latin intervocalic /n/ is preferentially deleted in what is traditionally treated as syllable-initial position, whilst syllable-final /n/ is preserved untouched, e.g. LA$NA 'wool' > Sard. [lãː], but TAN$TA 'so' (f.) > Sard. [tan$ta].

Bichakjian (1981) and Entenman (1977: 86) both note that languages often display a countervailing tendency towards the elimination of open syllables with the creation of new closed syllables. Such a counter-tendency is apparent in Northern Italian where it manifests itself in one of three ways. The first and most widespread is through loss of final unstressed vowels, e.g. PANE 'bread' > Stage 2 /paːn$/. However, although final vowel loss is normal, newly closed syllables are themselves prone to a secondary process of Coda elimination, e.g. PANE > Stage 2 /paːn/ > Mi. [pãː], Bg. [paː]. The second is through secondary gemination of intervocalic consonants, typical in the sample only of Bolognese, e.g. LI$MA 'file' > Bo. [lem$ma] (cf. section 7.2). The third and final means is through consonantization of historical vowels through intermediate gliding, e.g. LUNA 'moon' > [lõw̃na] > Bo. [loŋna].[11] However, these facts notwithstanding, Jan Smith (1981: 41)

provides evidence that creation of open syllables is overall far more frequent than of closed. In a synchronic study of fast-speech phenomena in Venezuelan Spanish he found that 'an average of 88% of the reduction processes resulted in open syllables and 12% in closed syllables'. Further, 'only 7% of the syllables undergoing change involved a change from open to closed, while 44% involved a change from closed to open.'

8.2.1 *A syllable account of N-deletion in Northern and Southern Italian*

The syllable as a phonological entity was only accepted into generative formalism in the 1970s, e.g. Hooper (1976) and Hyman (1975b). At first, reference to the syllable was restricted to the syllable boundary ($), which hampered the ability of the formalism to deal with syllable-sensitive phenomena. With such limited means, it is not possible to express any relationship between word-final N-deletion in Northern Italian and intervocalic N-deletion in Sardinian and elsewhere in terms of syllable-final phenomena. In these circumstances, we are forced to conclude that Sardinian intervocalic N-deletion is a counter-example to the universalist hypothesis of preferential syllable-final loss.

However, in this section and the one that follows, I show how the current, more developed notion of the syllable allows us to treat the apparently contradictory manifestations of N-deletion in both Northern Italian and Sardinian as parts of the same unitary syllable-sensitive process. In section 8.2.1.1 I look first at developments in Northern Italian, and how these can be accounted for by the operation of a partially syllabic template. I then show how Sardinian N loss may be incorporated within the same framework.

8.2.1.1 N-deletion and the syllabic template in Northern Italian

Two factors have shown themselves to be crucial in the development of distinctive nasalization in tonic syllables in Northern Italian, these being: (1) vowel length, and (2) syllable structure. In chapter 4, and repeatedly in the chapters that follow it, evidence has been provided suggesting that a restricted version of the Vowel Length Parameter (VLP) operates in Northern Italian, as a result of which only phonologically long vowels before N may be phonologically nasalized. To satisfy this requirement, it was suggested that short vowels are lengthened first, even before NC clusters (see section 6.4.1). This vowel length constraint leads to an additional restriction on the spread of N-deletion: since short vowels cannot ordinarily be phonologically nasalized in Northern Italian, it follows, in line with the new V-NAS model given in section 3.3.1, that N-deletion will occur only after [V:] and not [V], e.g. Mi. [kɑ̃:] < Stage 2 /kaːn/ 'dog', but [an] < Stage 2 /an/ 'year'.

The extent of the influence of syllable structure on the spread of vowel nasalization and N-deletion was first detailed in the formulation of the two

contextual parameters discussed in chapter 6. Evidence of N-deletion in the Northern Italian sample is strictly limited to syllable-final or Coda position, as noted previously and shown in the examples at 8.

Vowel length and syllable structure combine to form a predictable syllabic template for N-deletion, as at 9. The result is a branching Rhyme with binary Nucleus, and N in Coda position, all attached to three skeletal slots specified as nasal.

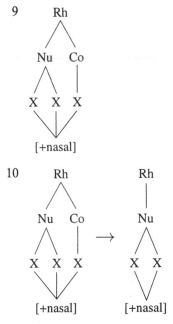

From the phonetic point of view, the syllabic template at 9 and its reduction at 10 follow from the results of experimental work cited in this study. In section 4.1.4 it was reported that the perception of contextual nasalization increases with greater vowel duration. In the presence of strong contextual nasalization, the perceptual salience of N, already inherently reduced in syllable-final position (Dogil and Luschütsky 1989; Ohala and Kawasaki 1984), is further reduced by the acoustic effect of greater velic opening reported by Manuel (1991). In these circumstances, the weakening and complete loss of N is not unexpected.

Phonological observations about the development of distinctive nasalization may be drawn from these phonetic facts. The phonologization of contextual nasalization occurs preferentially in the context of phonologically long vowels (see sections 4.1.2 and 4.1.3). At some point, after the template at 9 has been satisfied, the Coda is delinked, and all trace of N deleted.[12] Only a nasalized branching Nucleus remains, as at 10.[13] Sub-syllabic reduction as Coda deletion is entirely predictable from both phonetic and

phonological perspectives. First, N-deletion is a timing-related phenomenon that should be captured phonologically as such somewhere in the prosodic structure (see section 7.3.1). The preferential reduction and loss of the Coda, rather than of the Nucleus, follow from its reduced perceptual salience relative to other members of the syllable. Reduction of the Rhyme as elimination of the Nucleus is not possible: tonic nuclei are perceptually salient and are never lost in Northern Italian or in any language. Loss of sub-syllabic structure is sensitive to an additional constraint on the operation of the skeletal tier in Northern Italian: phonological reduction of the long nasalized nucleus to a single-slot short vowel is apparently not permitted , i.e. [Ṽ:(N)] > *[Ṽ(N)].

The syllabic template is relatively complex, since reference must be made to sub-syllabic structure, to the skeleton and to [+nasal]. Neither of the alternative templates at 11 would be sufficient.

11a

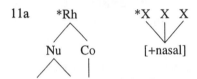

11a predicts that any and all segments in the Coda will be deleted. Whilst this may be true over the long term, the template in this form fails to refer to the important vowel nasalization constraint on N-deletion. Without reference to [+nasal] in the Rhyme, [aːn] and [ãːn], in contravention of the new V-NAS model, will be equally prone to N-deletion. But operation of the model in Northern Italian is confirmed by patterns of change uncovered: N, very stable in forms such as [aːn] is only lost in structures of the kind seen in [ãːn]. The skeletal template at 11b, without any reference to syllabic structure, also encompasses a false claim about the link between deletion processes and nasalization in Northern Italian. Unlike the structures at 9 and 11a, where the Coda is phonetically and, therefore, phonologically the weakest, it is not immediately evident from the structure at 11b which skeletal slot might be lost. As a result, we need first to specify in an *ad hoc* fashion automatic deletion at some place in the configuration. If deletion is rightmost, then [mãã] > *[mã], and [lãːna] > *[lãːa] are in theory possible. However, neither is reported in the sample. If deletion is leftmost, [mãã] > *[ãã], [pããn] > *[pãn] result, which are likewise unproven.

8.2.1.2 The syllabic template in Sardinian and Corsican

Whilst the pattern of N-deletion in paroxytones in Sardinian and Corsican may appear to be quite different to that found in Northern Italian, there are some similarities. One of these is the strict manner in which the VLP operates, at least in paroxytones: nasalization and deletion are reported only in the context [V:N], e.g. [mãw̃] < [maa$nu] < MA$NU 'hand', [lãː] < LA$NA 'wool',

but [tan$ta] < TAN$TA 'so' (f.), [lim$ba] < LIN$GUA 'tongue', [ka$na] < CAN$NA 'cane'. Although [n] in Sard. [tan$ta] is in weak syllable-final position, the absence of nasalization and subsequent N-deletion can be accounted for by the predictable shortness of the tonic vowel in closed syllables, which according to the VLP prevents the phonologization of contextual nasalization. With regard to observed differences in N-deletion patterns between Northern Italian and Sardinian, recent innovations in syllable theory allow them to be reconciled within the same syllabic template. In those dialects like Sardinian and Corsican, where only intervocalic Lat. /n/ is lost, /n/ in MA$NU would in traditional terms be considered to be syllable-initial and, therefore, strong. However, Kahn (1980), Amastae (1986) and Clements and Keyser (1983) have suggested that weakening and deletion processes affecting intervocalic consonants in English, Spanish and Danish are the result of the ambisyllabification of such consonants. By suggesting that intervocalic obstruents are simultaneously in Onset and Coda position, Amastae notes, for instance, that so-called ambisyllabification captures the generalization that all Coda obstruents are lenited in Spanish, e.g. *dado* > [daðo] > [dao] 'given', alongside *sed* > [seð] > [se] 'thirst'.

The same process of ambisyllabification appears to apply in Sardinian and Corsican: all intervocalic obstruents, and sonorants /l, n/, are subject to marked lenition, e.g. FOCU > ['fo:ɣu] 'fire'. However, /n/ is unique in being subject to the additional requirements that for ambisyllabification to occur the preceding stressed vowel must be both long and nasalized, i.e. N in MANU is not only syllable-initial in line with expectations, but is now also syllable-final as a result of Coda spreading from the first syllable, as at 12b. Intervocalic N now forms part of both syllables and finds itself in the weak Coda position of the first syllable.[14]

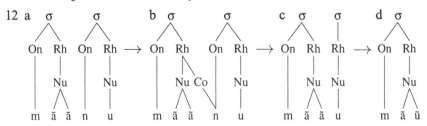

After ambisyllabification, all the necessary conditions for N-deletion in accordance with the syllabic template at 10 are satisfied, i.e. vowel length, vowel nasalization, and N in Coda position. Deletion of [-n-] follows. Disyllabic [mã:ũ] survives in Corsican and parts of Sardinia. In other areas, especially of Sardinia, a secondary process of syllable reduction eliminates Nucleus hiatus. Since all Nuclei are maximally binary, [ã:] is abbreviated, leading ultimately to [mãw̃], as at 12d. In contrast to the elimination in Sardinian and Corsican of [-n-], preservation of intervocalic Latin /n/ in Northern Italian dialects with nasalization before it, e.g. Im.

[lẽːna] < LANA 'wool', may now be accounted for by a failure to undergo ambisyllabification. There is some evidence of foot conditioning of ambi-syllabification in Sardinian and Corsican: effacement, common in paroxytones ('σσ) is not reported in proparoxytones ('σσσ) in Corsican and is relatively rare in Sardinian. Proparoxytonic vowel compression blocks nasalization spread, and is often phonologized as a short vowel, before leading to later secondary post-tonic C-gemination in some varieties, e.g. Corsican ['anema] ~ ['annema] < St. 1 /aːnima/ ANIMA 'spirit' and not *[ãːnema] ~ [ãːema].

The phonetic basis of ambisyllabification is yet to be fully determined, and there has been to date relatively little investigation of the matter. There is some evidence to suggest that ambisyllabificaton involves the phonologiza-tion of increased speed and decreased duration of articulation. Fujimura and Lovins (1978) note that the ambisyllabic tapping of intervocalic /t, d/ consonants in American English is characterized by rapid movement and temporal reduction. Connell (1991: 43), like others before him, reports a contrast between ambisyllabic and Onset-syllabified intervocalic consonants in the Lower Cross languages of Nigeria. In these languages, ambisyllabic consonants, including nasals, are typically tapped, i.e. reduced in duration. There may also be a reduced degree of articulator contact and further secondary reduction to approximants.

It comes as no surprise that Sardinian, and Corsican (and indeed Tuscan) show all the suggested phonetic correlates of ambisyllabification. They are marked precisely by rapid speed, very reduced articulator contact and segment duration – all of which leads to extreme lenition of intervocalic consonants, especially obstruents and coronal /n/, and widespread loss of such segments.

8.3 CONCLUSIONS

The evaluation of Feature Geometry manipulation in accounting for attenuation and deletion of N shows rather mixed results, confirming that in some cases, at least, the representation is too powerful. Seven suggested manipulations of Feature Geometry were evaluated. They are listed here briefly again:

13a deletion of skeletal slot
 b deletion of Root Node (and Compensatory Lengthening)
 c deletion of Supralaryngeal Node (and Compensatory Lengthening)
 d deletion of Place Node
 e voicing assimilation ([+voi] → [−voi] /__[−voi])
 f manner assimilation ([−cont] → [+cont] /__[+cont])
 g place shift (e.g. velarization)

Of these, only 13a leads unambiguously to the complete effacement of N. Alternatives 13b and 13c are rejected outright. 13f has attenuative

consequences, whilst 13d has none such *per se*. 13e has, but not necessarily towards N-deletion. And as a formal manipulation 13g does not in itself necessarily have such a consequence.

Deletion of the skeletal slot is a straightforward operation and perhaps the least controversial of all of them. N-deletion, cross-linguistically frequent, is defined phonologically as the loss of the skeletal slot originally attached to N, and phonetically as the elimination of all duration necessary for a phonetic instantiation previously associated with that slot. Whilst slot deletion is a simple formal operation, reduction of N to Ø is considered to be a gradual process over time. However, the alternative manipulations, viewed as having potential attenuative effect on N, performed variably, sometimes very poorly indeed. First, not all attenuation processes lead inevitably to N-deletion. Alternative pathways exist. Vocalization to V, or voicing assimilation and subsequent total assimilation to C may result. In the case of velarization, care must be taken to determine whether the appearance of [ŋ] in a language is the result of place shift from [m] and [n], or of glide hardening, as is clearly the case in Northern Italian dialects. In addition where place shift occurs, it is not necessarily to the velar position.

Whilst many types of suggested processes of assimilation can be represented formally and, therefore, be incorporated into the grammar, temporal reduction of N, reported in some languages and in some contexts, was found to present major problems for autosegmental formalism. Other suggested attenuation processes, e.g. Root-Node deletion and Place-Node loss, were not found to be necessary for, or appropriate to, the types of sound change reported in this study. In particular, Root-Node deletion and associated Compensatory Lengthening (CL) were found to be particularly unsatisfactory, breaching all evaluatory measures or constraints placed on the plausibility of posited sound change from one segment to another. The diachronic implausibility of such operations was compounded by their lack of descriptive necessity: no reference needs be made to them to account for any developments reported in the Northern Italian sample. Supralaryngeal Node deletion and refilling were similarly found to be inadequate and undesirable.

Finally, the effect of syllable structure on N-deletion in Northern Italian was considered in some detail. In accordance with earlier findings by other phonologists, syllable-final or Coda position was found to be the locus for preferential loss. Such loss is favoured by a cross-linguistic tendency towards open syllables and the phonetic evidence of reduced perceptual salience. However, syllable structure alone cannot account for N-deletion: vowel length and vowel nasalization also play crucial roles. These three factors combine to form a tonic syllable template that must be satisfied in Northern Italian before loss occurs. Finally, the notion of ambisyllabicity allows one to eliminate the apparent exceptionality of intervocalic N loss in Sardinian and elsewhere, so that developments in both Northern and Centro-Southern Italian can be seen to fall within the same syllable-related framework.

9

RESULTS AND CONCLUSIONS

9.1 INTRODUCTION

This study had a number of distinct but interrelated aims. The first was to determine the universal characteristics, if any, of the development of distinctive nasalization over time, and in so doing, to evaluate the frequently conflicting universalist claims made in the past. Second, I wished also to consider the relationship between phonetics and phonology, and the manner in which phonological phenomena are phonetically determined. Third, I examined the implications of patterns of sound change and of the phonetic explanations for them for the formal representation of phonological phenomena, e.g. syllable structure and Compensatory Lengthening. Particular attention was given to patterns of sound change found in Northern Italian.

With regard to the first issue, results indicate that the development of distinctive nasalization may be far more complex than previously considered by universalists. Many purportedly universal parameters are found not to be supported by cross-linguistic evidence. In these circumstances, the regular patterning of changes found in Northern Italian suggests that strong areo-genetic influence is at play.

On the other hand, it is possible, pending further investigation and elaboration, that some constraints on patterns of sound change, such as the new V-NAS model of distinctive nasalization, and the Vowel Length Parameter (VLP), may hold universally, at least where certain conditions are met.[1] That is, no clear counter-examples to them have yet been found. The new V-NAS model and the Vowel Length Parameter interact with the operation of other parameters, and place important constraints on the manner in which changes affecting VN manifest themselves.

As for the relationship between phonetics and phonology, it was possible in most cases to find phonetic explanations for observed phonological phenomena. Whilst many of the claims about the formal content of phonology can be considered to be phonetically plausible, e.g. contextual assimilation as feature-spreading, it was found that some formal operations, e.g. Compensatory Lengthening, did not appear to satisfy such a criterion, and were not appropriate to the description of the sound changes reported in this study.

9.2 DISTINCTIVE NASALIZATION AND UNIVERSAL PARAMETERS OF SOUND CHANGE

In the course of this work, I have considered in some detail the possible universal effect of a number of different factors on the development of the component parts of distinctive nasalization, i.e. vowel nasalization and N-deletion. These are listed briefly at 1:

1a vowel length   4.1.2–4.1.4
 b the presence or absence of tonic stress   4.2–4.2.3
 c the length of the stress foot   4.3–4.3.7
 d vowel height   5.1.1–5.4
 e front vs. back vowel quality   5.5
 f contextual position   6.1–6.4.1.3
 g N place of articulation   7.1.1–7.3.1

With the exceptions of vowel height and the front vs. back distinction, each listed factor was found to have a regular, discernible effect on the spread of phonological processes of nasalization and N-deletion in my Northern Italian sample. Different parameters were posited to capture factor-specific patterning in Northern Italian, and in many cases, elsewhere. Suggested parameters are listed together at 2:

2a Vowel Length Parameter   4.1.3

$$\underset{\longrightarrow}{\text{V:N VN}}$$

 b Extended Stress Parameter   4.2.2

$$\underset{\longrightarrow}{\text{'VN }^+\text{VN }^-\text{VN}}$$

 c Foot Parameter   4.3.4

$$\underset{\longrightarrow}{\text{'σ# 'σσ# 'σσσ#}}$$

 d Nasalization Contextual Parameter   6.1.2

V:n# VNFric VNStop V:nV VNStop Vn#
      [−v]   [+v]   VnV
                                   Vnn(V)
$\longrightarrow$

 e N-deletion Contextual Parameter   6.1.2

V:n# VNFric VNStop VNStop V:nV Vn# Vnn(V)
        [−v]   [+v]   VnV
$\longrightarrow$

 f N-Place Parameter   7.1.2

n_1 m ɲ N:
$$\underset{\longrightarrow}{\quad n_2 \quad}$$

The effect of relative vowel height and front vs. back vowel quality on the spread of distinctive nasalization was difficult to determine in my Northern Italian sample. Changes reported in other Northern Italian dialects were also too uncertain to allow for the positing of vowel height and quality parameters with any certainty. However, the examination of developments elsewhere did not demonstrate that vowel height or vowel quality had a single universally consistent effect on the spread of distinctive nasalization. As regards the six parameters listed at 2, the examination of developments outside Northern Italy uncovered numerous counter-examples to parameters 2d–f, disallowing any suggestion of their universal applicability. The possible universality of parameters 2a–c has yet to be repudiated. However, I have suggested that languages with prosodic structures different to those examined in this study may not demonstrate the same stress- and foot-related effects.[2] In such circumstances, the proposed universality of parameters 2a–c remains somewhat tentative.

9.2.1 *Areo-genetic bias in the Northern Italian sample*

Given that contextual position and place were not found to have a cross-linguistically uniform effect on the spread of vowel nasalization and N-deletion, the regular patterning of context and place effects in member dialects of my sample may be indicative of a strong areo-genetic bias. It is not clear to what extent such a bias is specific to Northern Italian, or whether the same pattern bias extends to other Romance varieties. However, with regard to contextual position, we note that Sardinian and other Centro-Southern dialects present preferential loss of intervocalic /n/ in contravention of the Northern Italian contextual parameter at 2e. Similarly, the N-place parameter reported for Northern Italian, and repeated at 2f, was also seen in section 7.1.3 to operate in many other, but not all, Romance dialects. On the other hand, in previous studies (e.g. Hajek 1988, 1991a) on the effect of nasality on vowel height changes in VN sequences, I found that areo-genetic bias could not account for the unexpected range of patterning types found in Northern Italian.

The effect of possible areo-genetic bias should not be allowed to invalidate the results of this study. Even in Maddieson's (1984) large-scale synchronic sample, in which all efforts are made to minimize areo-genetic interference, such influence is strongly evident, as reported by Janson (1991). Indeed it may be simply impossible to construct a bias-free language sample of any kind. Furthermore, since sound change is presumed in the first instance to have a phonetic basis, any areo-genetic patterning still requires phonetic explanation.

9.2.2 *The ramifications of non-universality*

The absence of a single universal effect of vowel height, front vs. back vowel quality, contextual position and N place of articulation on the spread of

distinctive nasalization was neither predicted nor properly evaluated by universalists such as Chen, Foley, and others. However, that these factors were found in this study to have a cross-linguistically variable effect is hardly surprising, given the frequently conflicting claims made by universalists.[3]

Despite cross-linguistic variability, factor-specific changes are not necessarily random. With regard to the vowel height effect, for instance, in some languages, e.g. Akan and Panamanian Spanish, high vowels favour the spread of distinctive nasalization (see section 5.1.5). In others, such as Teke, low vowels provide the preferential context (see section 5.1.3). Nowhere is there any cross-linguistic evidence of a totally *ad hoc* effect of vowel height on the spread of vowel nasalization and N-deletion, e.g. [iN] $\gg$ [aN] $\gg$ [yN] $\gg$ [œN] $\gg$ [uN] $\gg$ [oN] $\gg$ [eN]. That cross-linguistic evidence in favour of both high and low vowels could be found is consistent with the phonetic evidence in support of the preferential phonologization of both high vowel and low vowel nasalization.

A particular factor, such as vowel height, may present numerous perceptual cues (cf. sections 5.3.1 and 5.3.2), to listeners when they evaluate vowel nasalization. Experimental results suggest that such cues differ in effect, and may not be integrated in the same manner by all listeners. If different cues predominate across languages, then divergent cross-linguistic patterns of factor-specific sound change may result. The view expressed by Chen (1974a) and Foley (1977) that a single scale or parameter is sufficient to define and restrict the range of factor-specific sound change needs to be modified where factor-specific effects on distinctive nasalization were found to vary. Evidence of non-random variation in some cases suggests that not one but competing scales or parameters are sometimes needed to delimit language-like processes from the larger set of all logically possible processes.

In the case of vowel height influence on the spread of distinctive nasalization, it is possible that all changes may be accounted for by two scales, i.e. a high $\gg$ mid $\gg$ low parameter, and a low $\gg$ mid $\gg$ high parameter. Despite their contradictory nature, they may combine to exclude any random vowel height effect on distinctive nasalization.

In other cases, we may require a far larger number of parameters to account for non-random language-specific change. Previous examination of the effect of nasality on vowel height and quality changes (Hajek 1988, 1991a) showed that change in individual dialects fell within a range of competing but internally non-random patterns, i.e. centralization, raising, lowering, and anti-clockwise movement. It is as yet not fully determined why one pattern should be favoured in one dialect and not another, but reported vowel height changes of whatever type appear to be highly patterned in all the dialects examined.[4]

In situations where competing patterns of change are uncovered, these represent cross-linguistic tendencies, since no truly universal parameter can logically be formulated. As the number of parameters needed to account for

non-random change increases, it is clear that the organization of sound systems and of sound change is more complex than universalists working on distinctive nasalization have suggested. It is possible that the discovery of true universality, even in these cases, is not an impossible goal. At present discussion of sound change universals is markedly non-language-specific, i.e. universality is defined as 'in all languages X will occur'. The existence of competing tendencies suggests such overarching generality needs to be circumscribed. Each apparent cross-linguistic tendency may indeed be universal in an implicational sense, i.e. sound change A will always occur in languages with structural property C (or, as is more likely, with properties C, D . . .), sound change B will always occur in languages with structural property E (or properties E, F . . .). The task is to discover what these structural properties might be and how they come to be associated with specific sound change patterns. This matter has been little studied to date, although I have noted, for instance here and elsewhere (Hajek 1993b) that Romance dialects with intervocalic N-deletion are, for instance, all characterized by extremely marked lenition and elimination of intervocalic consonants (obstruents and sonorants) in general. The same pattern is not found in my Northern Italian sample where intervocalic N-deletion is unknown and intervocalic lenition is relatively restricted and much less pervasive.

The existence of competing patterns of sound change, not unexpected given the complexity of the speech signal available to the listener, has ramifications for the detailed reconstruction of the phonological history of a language. In a language in which earlier VN now appears regularly as Ṽ and in the absence of any other evidence, the linguist may be unable to establish the precise order of change with regard to a particular factor, e.g. vowel height. In contrast, discussion of the ordering relation between phonological processes of vowel nasalization and N-deletion indicates that where the linguist is faced with /V/ in language A and /VN/ in closely related language B, he or she should at least minimally reconstruct intermediate stages of contextual and distinctive nasalization, i.e. VN > ṼN > Ṽ > V. Reconstruction involving simple N-deletion, in the absence of some phonological process of vowel nasalization is, with a few well-defined exceptions, e.g. degemination, considered to be unlikely.

9.2.3 Ordering constraints and parametric interaction

In chapter 3 the interrelationship between vowel nasalization and N-deletion was examined in some detail. It was found that the presence or absence of the former operates as an important ordering constraint on N-deletion, i.e. in the context VN complete loss of N is typically preceded by some phonological process of vowel nasalization. This particular ordering relationship between vowel nasalization and N-deletion forms the basis of the new

V-NAS model of distinctive nasalization. Alternative analyses that called for the order of nasalization and N-deletion to be reversed or to be simultaneous were found to be contradicted by empirical examples of (1) phonologized long-distance nasalization, e.g. Malay [məŋãw̃ãl] 'to guard'; and (2) contrastive vowel nasalization without N-loss, e.g. Nendaz Valaisan /ãna/ < LANA 'wool' vs. /pana/ < PANNA 'cloth'.[5] The ordering constraint was found not to be restricted to the diachronic development of distinctive nasalization, but also to have clear implications for the synchronic derivation of surface [Ṽ] from underlying /VN/.

Furthermore, it was suggested in section 3.5.3 that so-called local nasalization (e.g. French [leɔ̃ː] léon 'lion', [oseɑ̃ː] océan 'ocean') and long-distance nasalization processes (e.g. Malay [məŋãw̃ãl] 'to guard') are not completely independent phenomena, as some have claimed. Instead, both can be subsumed under the new V-NAS model.

One surprising discovery in the course of this study has been the pervasive influence of the Vowel Length Parameter (VLP) on developments in Northern Italian. Whilst Hombert (1986, 1987) hypothesized that differences in vowel length had a universally predictable effect on the spread of distinctive nasalization, he gave no indication as to how vowel length might interact with and control the operation of other factor-specific parameters. In this study, it was shown in sections 4.1.1 and 4.1.2 that phonological differences in vowel length, i.e. V:N ≫ VN, affect the spread over time of distinctive nasalization processes in all languages considered to date. However, in Northern Italian and elsewhere, e.g. German dialects, the VLP is particularly restrictive: phonologization of contextual nasalization occurs only when the vowel is long, i.e. [Ṽ:N] but *[ṼN]. Given the new V-NAS model ordering constraint, N-deletion is, therefore, also restricted to [Ṽ:(N)]. Short [V] before N must be lengthened before it can be nasalized, i.e. [VN] > [V:N] > [Ṽ:N], e.g. ANNU 'year' > Stage 2 /an/ > Lg. [aːn] > Im. [ẽːn] > Fr. [ɑ̃ː].

Numerous experimental results cited in section 4.1.4 confirm that greater phonetic vowel duration leads to increased levels of perceived vowel nasalization. Although the reasons for such a relationship remain poorly understood, and need further investigation, the phonetic evidence suggests that the phonologization of nasalization is sensitive not only to phonologically pertinent differences in vowel length, but also to small phonetic differences, not normally considered to be phonologically relevant.

Whilst the interaction over time of all the posited parameters at 2 above is still to be fully ascertained, it is clear that durational differences – both phonological and phonetic – have a crucial effect, at least in Northern Italian. Of the six factors b–g listed at 1 above, interaction in some manner with vowel length/duration was evident in at least four, possibly five cases: (1) stress differences; (2) foot length; (3) context; (4) N place; and, if not directly, at least indirectly, (5) vowel height.

Typical of the overriding power of the VLP is the N-deletion contextual parameter given at 2e above and repeated for convenience at 3. Here, word-final position is both the most likely and one of the least likely contexts for deletion, distinguishable only by reference to vowel length.

3 Vːn# VNFric VNStop VNStop VːnV Vn# Vnn(V)

[−v]   [+v]   VnV

From the formal perspective, the sub-skeletal phenomenon of [+nasal] spreading, and its skeletal counterpart of slot deletion of N were both found to be heavily influenced by prosodic factors operating above the skeleton. Alongside vowel length considerations, syllable structure also plays an important role in distinctive nasalization phenomena. Syllable structure, vowel length and nasalization combine to form a sub-syllabic template that needs to be satisfied in Northern Italian before N-deletion occurs in tonic syllables. In addition, intervocalic /n/-deletion in dialects like Sardinian, which could at one stage not be treated as a syllable-final phenomenon, can now be seen to fall together with patterns of N-deletion in Northern Italian and elsewhere, by means of ambisyllabification. Whilst universalists have always been aware of the effect of syllable-structure (cf. section 6.1.1), relatively little attention has been paid to the effect of stress differences 2b, and none to the effect of foot length 2c. In both cases, it was suggested that the predictable effect of prosody on distinctive nasalization is derived from prosodically determined vowel duration effects, and the effect of these on the perception and phonologization of contextual nasalization.[6]

9.2.4 *Phonetics and phonology*

The non-random nature of sound change across languages is presumed to derive from the inherent constraints of the speech mechanism. Given the phonetic basis of sound change, phonetic explanations should be sought to account for them in the first instance. In sections 1.2.1 and 1.2.1.1 it was hypothesized that the mechanism of phonologization is to a significant degree perceptual in nature: the listener reinterprets phonetically determined distortion in the speech signal as intended by the speaker. In most cases, plausible phonetic explanations for observed changes could be found, e.g. temporal reduction of N before voiceless stops. Particular emphasis was given to the perceptual consequences of articulatorily determined coarticulation, e.g. the smearing effect of strong vowel nasalization on the perception of N. It was also seen that phonological structures, and claims that refer to them, often have a plausible phonetic basis. The phonological process of proparoxytonic vowel shortening found in many Northern Italian dialects is found to be the result of a phonetic process of compression that becomes more marked as the number of post-tonic syllables is increased. Similarly,

the frequently stated observation that N, like other consonants, is preferentially deleted in weak syllable-final position follows from the reduced perceptual salience of the Coda. By providing a concrete phonetic basis for phonological processes, and for the formalism necessary to present them, the abstract content of phonology and of the formalism is reduced.

9.2.5 *Sound change and the grammar*

The claim made in section 1.2 that sound change involves the gradual modification of low-level phonetic phenomena leading to phonologization is compatible with recent work on the interaction over time between sound change and grammar (e.g. John Harris 1989 and McMahon 1991). Phonologization results in the entry of such phenomena into the post-lexical component of the grammar as lexically abrupt, phonetically and phonologically gradient, language-specific phonetic rules. Over time, the nature of a sound change may alter radically as it percolates deeper into the grammar. Whilst still in the post-lexical component, it may become phonologically categorical, captured by binary rule. The boundary between gradient and categorical rules was observed to be blurred, and remains difficult to determine with precision, as is also the boundary between universal low-level and language-specific phonetic rules. A phonological rule, once categorical, may continue to move deeper into the grammar, and begin to show all the characteristics of the more abstract lexical component, e.g. lexical diffusion, and morphological conditioning. Ultimately, the sound change may become fully lexicalized and appear in the underlying representation. It was observed in chapter 3 that such a hypothesis needs to be modified slightly. Whilst the development of distinctive nasalization in Northern Italian is consistent with sound change as phonetically gradual and lexically abrupt in an initial phase, there is evidence that the results of such sound changes may move directly from the post-lexical component into the underlying representation without any trace of intermediate percolation through the lexical strata in the lexical component.

9.2.6 *Distinctive nasalization and the formalism*

The benefits of Autosegmental Phonology to phonological representation have been discussed by phonologists (e.g. Durand 1990, Goldsmith 1990), and were duly noted in section 1.3. Features are no longer randomly organized. Assimilation processes can now be seen as feature spreading, and not merely as coincidental feature changing. Segmental and suprasegmental content are easily separable, and very clearly organized in a hierarchical fashion. I have taken advantage of these innovations, and have been able, for instance, to make useful reference to the fine detail of

syllabic structure, and interaction between it and segmental phenomena, e.g. the syllabic template in section 8.2.1.1.

However, whilst I accept that the innovations of Autosegmental Phonology are often valuable, certain limitations were also noted: (1) autosegmental formalism has sometimes been used in an unconstrained manner in the description of distinctive nasalization; and (2) the full power of non-linear representation need not be invoked to account for the sound changes reported in this study. The formal power of non-linear representation in the description of sound change has prior to this study not been properly considered in any detail.

With reference to the first limitation, the Floating Nasal and N-attenuation analyses of distinctive nasalization, were found to be poorly motivated attempts to manipulate autosegmental representation, as discussed in sections 3.2 to 3.2.4. By attaching [nasal] directly to the Root Node, rather than the Supralaryngeal Node, they seek to reverse the ordering constraint inherent to the new V-NAS model, seen at 4. These analyses claim that elimination of N's non-nasal melodic content below the Root (N-attenuation), or even of the Root (Floating Nasal), allows for secondary relinking of [+nasal] to the preceding vowel. However, further investigation demonstrates that such analyses are empirically unsatisfactory from both diachronic and synchronic perspectives, and should be rejected.

4a V → Ṽ / __N

 b N → Ø / Ṽ__

Surprisingly, the inherent limitations of the traditional generative formalism fit in rather well with the diachronic and synchronic ordering constraint on phonological rules of nasalization and N-deletion suggested in this study. In a classical generative analysis, as exemplified at 4, it would no longer be possible to relate nasalization and deletion if their order was reversed. Where in a synchronic analysis N-deletion is posited without any preceding rule of nasalization to account for morphophonemic alternation of the sort in Catalan and Bergamese, e.g. Cat. *bo* 'good' (m.) vs. *bona* (f.), then this should be seen to be the result of a later denaturalizing reduction or telescoping of what was once a more complex process of contextual vowel nasalization and N-deletion.

With regard to the second limitation of excessive formal power, in chapters 3 and 8 the usefulness for diachronic description of a series of possible formal manipulations was examined in some detail. Whilst some manipulations were found to capture certain types of sound change, these changes did not trigger, as was suggested by some, N-attenuation, N-deletion or vowel nasalization. Other manipulations were found to be completely inappropriate to the description of sound change. Particular criticism was made of the formal mechanism of Compensatory Lengthening (CL) – involving either spreading of one Supralaryngeal Node to an adjacent

empty Root Node, or more commonly of one Root Node to an adjacent empty skeletal slot. The rarer first type was only briefly discussed in chapter 8, and immediately rejected given its undesirable consequences. The second type, most often referred to as CL in the literature, is now widely disseminated as a tool in synchronic and diachronic phonology, including analyses of distinctive nasalization. It is also rejected here. There is first no empirical need for it. Tonic vowels before N in Northern Italian need normally to be long before [+nasal] spreading and subsequent N-deletion are permitted.[7] This developmental constraint eliminates any need to refer to the formal mechanism of Compensatory Lengthening to account for the length of nasal vowels in Northern Italian. Secondary gemination phenomena in Bolognese, e.g. LIMA > Stage 2 /liːma/ > [lemma], was also found to be unrelated to CL. Evidence of non-compensatory lengthening in other contexts in Bolognese, as well as vowel shortening without consonant gemination in related dialects, e.g. Mi. [lima], suggest that secondary gemination of /m/ is more appropriately seen as chronologically separate from, and therefore not directly tied to, vowel shortening. Exceptionally, in some languages nasal vowel length may be derivable from complete vocalization of N to V in specific circumstances, e.g. VNFric > ṼF̃Fric > ṼG̃Fric > ṼːFric > Vːfric. However, such vocalization is the result of a very gradual process of assimilation as feature spreading, rather than any abrupt process of Compensatory Lengthening involving Root Node spreading to empty skeletal slot.

That abstract formal analyses, like CL and Floating Nasals, were found to be inappropriate for the description of sound change was not unexpected, since they breach the suggested sound change constraints listed in section 1.3.1 and repeated here: (1) all posited sound changes should have a plausible phonetic instantiation, and (2) in the shift from one segment to another changes should be gradual, minimal and natural. The purported one-step shift from /bɔn/ to /bɔ̃/ (Floating Nasal) or from /bɔn/ to /bɔ̃ː/ (CL) satisfies none of these. Instead, the evidence in this study suggests that such abstract operations with such dramatic consequences are more plausibly restricted to a later synchronic restructuring or telescoping of previously gradual diachronic phenomena.

9.2.7 Distinctive nasalization vs. fortition

Universalists have traditionally focused on VN as a locus for the spread of distinctive nasalization. In this study, however, it was observed that sound change in the context VN does not inevitably involve vowel nasalization and N-deletion. 'Fortitive' processes, with a countervailing effect on the spread of distinctive nasalization, were also examined and discussed in detail. In section 6.2 it was seen that whilst VN+Continuant clusters might provide the preferential context for the spread of distinctive nasalization in some

languages, in others the same process might be blocked in the same context by N gemination (e.g. TENUIT '(he) held' > It. *tenne*), or obstruentization of continuants (e.g. *VINJA 'vineyard' > Sard. *bindza*, INVITARE 'invite' > S. Calabrian *imbitare* > Sicilian *mmitare*). In section 7.2 specific N place of articulation effects resulting in the shortening of previously long vowels were found to block the spread of vowel nasalization, and hence N-deletion. In some Northern Italian dialects, e.g. Bolognese, phonological vowel shortening was followed at some later point in time by a process of N-gemination, e.g. LIMA 'file' > Bo. [lemma], rendering the spread of distinctive nasalization even less likely.

In Bolognese and Cairese, there was fortition of a slightly different sort: nasalized off-glides have undergone hardening to [ŋ] in syllable-final position, e.g. LUNA 'moon' > St. 2 /luːna/ > [lõw̃na] > Bo. [loŋna] (see section 8.1.8.1).

9.3 Directions for Future Research

There is still great scope for further research on the interrelationship between V and N over time, and the implications this might have for our understanding of sound change, the phonetic basis of phonology, and the nature of grammar.

Whilst the developments in Northern Italian are strongly suggestive of the non-random nature of the sound changes involved in the development of distinctive nasalization, they are not conclusive. Further cross-linguistic evaluation of reported patterning is clearly required. It has already been reported that some factors, e.g. vowel height, and contextual position, have no strictly universal effect on the spread of nasalization and N-deletion. Instead, competing non-random patterns of change were found for these factors. Additional investigation may require modification to parameters for which no counter-evidence has to date been reported. I have already noted that there are plausible phonetic reasons for which the suggested foot parameter may only be applicable to languages with left-headed feet. Notwithstanding the need for further cross-linguistic evaluation, it was noted in chapter 2 that our endeavours are hampered by difficulties in obtaining adequate diachronic data for the purposes of comparison. The reliability of previous large-scale studies by Chen of distinctive nasalization processes in Chinese dialects, already questioned by Zee (1985) and Entenman (1977), has been further put in doubt in this study, suggesting that developments in Chinese require careful re-examination.

In a similar vein, the strong criticisms made of Compensatory Lengthening suggest that the use of such a mechanism to account for purported historical lengthening phenomena in many other languages (see Hayes 1989 and Wetzels and Sezer 1986 for examples) is best avoided.

Many issues relating to the development of VN have been dealt with only in relatively little detail, or not at all, in this study. The emphasis here, as in earlier, universalist studies has been on developments affecting tonic VN sequences, in particular VN$. Despite discussion in chapter 4 of the effect of atonic position on the spread of distinctive nasalization, the lack of sufficient descriptive detail about atonic distinctive nasalization phenomena across languages hampers investigation. I have not touched at all on other issues, such as patterns of denasalization, and interaction between V and N in NV$ syllables, or on the effect of nasality on vowel height and quality changes. Preliminary results (Hajek 1988, 1991a) suggest that the interaction between nasality and changes in vowel height is more complicated than previously considered, and requires further, more detailed investigation. Notwithstanding the inevitable limitations of this study, the examination of sound change patterning, and of the possible phonetic basis for such patterning, is seen to be invaluable in providing insight into the nature of phonology and of phonological representation.

NOTES

Introduction

1 The term 'distinctive nasalization' is traditionally used to a describe vowels that are in surface contrast with oral vowels. Such a surface contrast is traditionally formalized in the following manner: /Ṽ/ vs. /V/. Whilst phonologists often use // to mark a surface (i.e. phonemic in structural analysis) contrast, in generative representation // is more readily used to mark underlying representation. Surface /Ṽ/ or better [Ṽ] is in the view of many generative phonologists normally derivable from an underlying /VN/ (cf. 3.1.1). For the sake of convenience, and in line with tradition, I will use /Ṽ/ to mark a surface contrast in vowel nasality. Reference to underlying structure will normally be made explicit.

1 Sound Change and Language Universals: Representations and Models of Change

1 The terms 'scale' and 'parameter' are used interchangeably to describe a series of related items or contexts. Note that the parameter at 1 may not be strictly universal. Chen (1973c: 189) reports the relative ordering of velars and dentals to be reversed in Cocopa, but see Foley (1977).
2 Chen (1972 and following) goes one step further by incorporating universal parameters of the type given above at 1 and 2 into metarules, rules that govern rules, formulated in an evolved generative style. Cf. Chen (1974a: 919–21) who formulates possible metarules to govern palatalization and distinctive nasalization across languages.
3 Cf. Foley's (1975; 1977) implausible reconstructions of Latin and Romance, the result of inadequate cross-linguistic comparison, and the explicit rejection of phoneticity and phonetic plausibility.
4 Their notion is not inconsistent with the more implicit attitude taken by other universalists, such as Schourup (1973) and Ruhlen (1973). Lightner (1970; 1973) takes a slightly more liberal attitude: although the end result is universal, i.e. /Ṽ$/ < /VN$/, there is divergence *en route* in implementation. The sense of *strict* or *absolute universal* differs somewhat in synchronic typology, i.e. 'all languages have property X'.
5 Strictly speaking, 'universal' in *universal tendency* is somewhat of a misnomer in this context, since it refers not to the degree of cross-linguistic adherence, but to the underlying cause for such a tendency being potentially manifest as a phonetically 'natural' phenomenon in all human languages due to the shared nature of the speech mechanism (Stampe 1969, Donegan and Stampe 1979, Ohala 1980a, b).
6 Some detail not directly relevant here has been omitted, e.g. vowel length and quality. French and Milanese may be taken as typifying the morphophonemic alternation between Ṽ and VN, e.g. Fr. *bon* [bɔ̃ː] 'good' (m.) v. *bonne* [bɔn] (f.), Mi. [būː] *bon* v. *bona* [bɔna] in contrast to the V–VN alternation found in Catalan *bo* v. *bona*, and Bergamese *bu* v. *buna*, and discussed in the text that follows.
7 From the structuralist point of view, this so called 'sound change' is innovation (change in allophonic rule), rather than true change (phonological restructuring); cf. Cravens (1988).
8 Note that Labov (1981) does consider sound change as Lexical Diffusion at onset to be possible in some cases. 'Exceptions' to Neogrammarian laws exist of course, but are treated as outside the scope of such laws and are subject to other mechanisms of change – sound substitutions, borrowings, analogical formations, etc. I hesitate somewhat in using the term 'Neogrammarian', since the Neogrammarian hypothesis is far more

complex than the adequate but extremely simplified characterization presented here and in recent phonological literature, e.g. Kiparsky (1988), John Harris (1989).

9 From the evidence in the literature, exceptions seem to be morphologically conditioned, e.g. Harris (1989: 40–1), as one might expect given the interplay between morphology and phonology in the lexical strata.

10 Gradient rules should of course be assigned gradient rather than binary values. However, given the obvious difficulties in establishing a scalar value (see Durand 1990: 190), phonologists conventionally tend not to do so for the sake of convenience, e.g. Keating (1985a). For similar reasons, I will follow convention and assign binary values, but where necessary state the rule to be language-specific. Given the blurred boundary between language-specific phonetic and categorical phonological, the use of binary values may not present a serious problem.

11 Exceptionally, the development of NJ shows some evidence of morphological conditioning in Latin prefixes *in-* and *con-*, e.g. CON+IUNGERE > Italian /kon+dʒundʒere/ ~ /kon+jundʒere/, Bolognese [kondzondzer] 'conjoin' in contrast to *VINJA > Italian [viɲɲa] 'vineyard', Bolognese [veɲɲa]. Alternatively, and more likely, the rare examples of Latin N + J in today's dialects are all affected by learned influence.

12 The Ohalan model cannot capture nor account for the substantial cross-linguistic differences in coarticulated vowel nasalization.

13 On one recent occasion, Ohala appears to have changed his stance by accepting that phonologization of contextual nasalization may occur in the absence of N-deletion. See Ohala and Solé (1991) for details. But more recently he appears to have returned to his earlier position (Ohala 1993).

14 Goldsmith (1990), Durand (1990) and van der Hulst and Smith (1982) provide general introductions to, and detailed descriptions of, Autosegmental Phonology, and the closely related sub-theories of Feature Geometry, and Syllable Theory.

15 I have for the sake of convenience grossly oversimplified the diagrammatic representation at the level of feature structure given at 10. Skeletal slot X may also variously be given as V, C, or N in the text for the sake of clarity.

16 Tonal autosegments, once delinked, may be saved by relinking: this is a characteristic of suprasegmental structures only. I have seen no compelling reason to believe that segmental features, such as [nasal] exhibit the the same capability, *contra* Piggott (1987; 1988a, b); cf. discussion in chapter 3.

17 This differs slightly from the possible range of assimilation phenomena discussed in section 1.1.2 which clearly can have some phonetic instantiation.

18 Chinantec is now known to contrast oral, nasal and mixed oral-nasal contour vowels. See Ladefoged and Maddieson (1990: 104–5) for spectrographic evidence. Acehnese may be an exception: alongside fully oral stops, it also contrasts lightly nasal and strongly nasal stops, distinguishable by relative amplitude of nasal airflow (Ladefoged and Maddieson 1986: 35).

19 The reader is referred to Entenman (1977), Farnetani (1979a, b), Laver (1980), Beddor (1983), van Reenen (1982a) and in particular to the chapters in Huffman and Krakow (1993) for detailed review and discussion of the phonetic characteristics of nasality.

20 Laver (1980) takes a very critical view of the importance given solely to velopharyngeal opening in studies of nasality.

2 The Data Base and Language Sampling: Methodological Issues and Background

1 The difference between Chomskyan and Greenbergian approaches to language universals extends much further than the number of languages in the sample. The former favours very abstract analysis below the surface of linguistic phenomena, whilst the latter concentrates on much less abstract analysis of surface phenomena. Comrie (1981, 1989: 5–10, 13–15) provides numerous arguments against the Chomskyan single-language approach to universals, and related problems of abstractness, and testability. With regard to sample size and abstractness, my own study finds itself somewhere in between the two endpoints. Whilst I concentrate on phenomena on or near the surface, and provide as concrete

accounts as possible for them, reference to more abstract structure below the surface, and its effect on surface structure, may also be made.

2 Pagliuca and Mowrey (1987) cite other errors in Maddieson's data base.

3 For the sake of convenience, all the dialects will be collectively labelled 'Northern Italian', despite the obvious geographical and linguistic misnomer with regard to Tavetschan, a Romantsch dialect spoken in the Swiss Grisons.

4 I follow, at least partially, Vincent (1988b: 26–7) who claims to abide by the more ancient and more modern traditions in not restricting the concept of 'Latin' to one particular variety of Latin of which there were arguably many, e.g. Classical, Low, Popular, Iberian, etc. However, it is true that in any discussion of the structure of Latin, whether phonological, morphological or syntactic, the fundamental reference point is usually what is called 'Classical Latin', 'the language of the educated classes of Rome in the period of Cicero and Caesar (first century BC)' (p. 27), since this Latin forms the basis of written Latin to this day.

5 However, no matter how tempting, there is no reason, without independent confirmation, to believe that orthographic representations such as *ca* must be interpreted as [ka], rather than [kaː], [kã] or [kãː]. The traditional view, e.g. Lorck (1893), is that the absence of orthographic *n* in words like *ca*, *pa* is used to mark distinctive nasalization in Old Bergamese.

6 Such a claim may be too strong, since it is possible that there is no synchronic trace of a previously extant stage (Hock 1986).

7 Of the sample members, we have extensive attestations of Milanese, Bolognese and Bergamese in the early medieval period. For Sursilvan (Tavetschan) and Romagnol (Imolese, Ravennate, Lughese, and Riminese) records are late medieval. We have only modern attestations of Cairese, but extensive medieval records of other Ligurian dialects.

8 In many Northern Italian dialects, such as Bolognese, evidence of regular vowel shortening can be found before nasal consonants, but is less extensive before non-nasals, e.g. [ˈɛːzen] < /aːzinu/ < ˈASINU where [ɛː] is identical to the historical long vowel reflex found in paroxytones, e.g. [ˈleːna] < /laːna/ < LANA, [ˈpɛːga] < /paːga/ < PACAT 'pays', whereas the long vowel in [ˈaːnum] (</animu/ < ANIMU 'spirit') is a very recent relengthening of a shortened vowel.

9 Antiquated Italian *speme* 'hope' (< Latin *spem* (acc.)) is a Latinism (Rohlfs 1966: 427). Dialectal Catalan 1st person *som* 'I am' is not directly from SUM but shows contamination by regular plural form *som* 'we are' < SUMUS.

10 I accept the traditional view of Portuguese philologists, e.g. Williams (1962: 92, 104), that Pt. *tão*, *quão* (and Sp. *tan*, *cuan*) are the result of final syllable apocopation of Lat. TANTU, QUANTU, as are *grão*, *são* (Sp. *gran*, *san*) of GRANDE and SANCTU, rather than the Spanish view, e.g. Pellegrini (1950: 209), that *tan*, *cuan* are reflexes of Lat. TAM, QUAM. In fact QUAM did survive in Old Spanish, Old Portuguese (and Old Italian), but only as *ca* with complete loss of final M.

11 Cf. Allen (1965: 30–1), Sturtevant (1940: 151–3), Tagliavini (1962: 78–9), Pisani (1952: 70), Fouché (1961: 650–1).

12 N and J are heterosyllabic, cf. Sard. [binˈdʒa], and open-syllable vowel lengthening cannot occur. See also Pensado (1989) for a similar analysis.

13 Lenition must be ordered historically before degemination, since newly degeminated voiceless stops are not lenited (Bruni 1984: 307–9; Rohlfs 1966: 323).

14 Saunders (1975, 1978) discusses in detail the rise of the new vowel length contrast, at least in Latin paroxytones, in Northern Italian; see also Pellegrini (1975: 71). The development of vowel length in Latin proparoxytones and oxytones demonstrates special characteristics, and is discussed in some detail in chapter 4.

15 Note that Stage 2 underlying and surface forms coincide in all cases. Reference in the text to one implies reference to its identical counterpart.

16 This vowel shortening before /n/ seems not to hold for all speakers. Beretta (1980: 19) reports vowels to be long before /n₁/. My own fieldwork confirms regular vowel length variation amongst Milanese speakers: one speaker shortened all vowels, another lengthened them, and the third, possibly through Italianization, presented a length contrast, e.g. [ˈpeːna] < P(O)ENA vs. [ˈpena] < PINNA. Similarly, the *AIS* reports speaker variation: Speaker 1's regular shortening before /n₁/ was only optional for Speaker 2; cf. VI 1071 LANA, and V 852 FONTANA.

17   There is a tendency to slight gemination after short vowels in very careful speech e.g.
     [kɐⁿna].
18   I was able to obtain reasonable copies of the original wax recordings of Romagnol dialects
     made by Schürr in 1914. Additional fieldwork was also carried out, and, with the slight
     exception of Riminese, despite the lengthy period between Schürr's recordings and new ones
     made in the late 1980s, there is a high degree of consistency. One explanation for this lies in
     the relative youth of his informants. Schürr's transcriptions are so unusually detailed that
     they have been somewhat simplified for use in this study.
19   On the basis of my own fieldwork with two Bolognese informants, Coco's (1970)
     description was found to be generally highly accurate. Dialect differentiation within
     Bologna is noticeable, but unusually seems to be motivated not by socio-economic factors
     as elsewhere in Northern Italy, but by geography, notwithstanding the small area (Trumper
     1977: 268–9, Minghè 1950). The dialect of one informant seemed to correspond almost
     totally with the dialect described by Coco (1970); the other showed slight differences,
     previously noted by Minghè (1950). One area of general difference with Coco (1970) is the
     distinction between front /æ/ and back /ɑ/, which Coco (1970) claims – contra Rizzi (1984),
     but supported by Trumper (1977: 268–9) – is increasingly archaic, and is lost as they merge
     to central /a/, e.g. BENE and BONU as /baŋ/ (phonetically [baŋ]) from intermediate [bæŋ] and
     [baŋ] respectively. Whilst [a] and [ɑ] seemed to be in fairly free variation, [æ] (< Latin
     E:, E, A) was much more frequent than [a], especially before nasals, and will be reported
     regularly in transcriptions, e.g. BENE > [bæŋ] and CANE > [kæŋ] (more rarely [baŋ], [kaŋ]),
     vs. BONU > [baŋ] ~ [bɑŋ].
20   Caduff (1952) seems reliable and was positively received on publication (Hall 1953).
     Schorta's (1946) recording of Tavetschan, of poor technical quality, was also obtained.

3   Distinctive Vowel Nasalization and Rule Ordering

1   Ruhlen (1973) takes the intermediate view that some surface nasal vowels in French are
    underlying nasal vowels and others are underlying /VN/ sequences. The former occur when
    morphophonological factors cannot be invoked, e.g. [õ] on 'one' (indef. pron.), in contrast
    to the latter, e.g. bonne (f.) [bɔn] ← UR /bɔnə/, and bon (m.) [bɔ̃] ← UR /bɔn/. But see
    Schane (1968: 48, n. 37) for criticisms of this view.
2   Synchronic alternation in French between surface [ʁ#] and medial [ʁn] is well-known, e.g.
    four 'oven', fournaise 'blaze'. Diachronically, the secondary word-final cluster /rn#/ was
    regularly simplified to /r/, e.g. FORNU > St. 2 /forn/ > Fr. [fuːʁ].
3   Chen (1972 and elsewhere) displays some confusion as to his view on the phonetic vs.
    phonological nature of nasalization and its place in the process of distinctive nasalization.
    Chen (1973a, 1974a, 1975), and Chen and Wang (1975) make it clear that the phonological
    process of vowel nasalization is subsequent to N-deletion, cf. 'the loss of the nasal ending
    with compensatory nasalization of the vocalic element' in Chen (1973a: 39), and '[the loss of
    nasals] nasalized the adjacent vocalic element' (Chen and Wang 1975: 272). Elsewhere,
    Chen (1973b: 226–7) decides that a phonological rule of vowel nasalization is ordered
    before N-deletion. However, Chen (1972: 12, 115–16) is completely unable to make up his
    mind. I will take as Chen's view, since it is the most frequently expressed, that vowels are
    phonetically nasalized before N. Only when N is lost is the phonetic nasalization
    phonologized or even lexicalized.
4   Recall that Hyman makes no distinction between gradient and categorical phonological
    rules, and considers a phonologized language-specific rule to be phonologically categorical.
5   Cf. Straka (1955: 270) and Reenen (1982a) on the integration of articulatory and perceptual
    factors in the development of distinctive nasalization.
6   Hyman (1975b: 172–3) is uncertain whether an absolute threshold exists beyond which all
    phonetic nasalization is phonologized, or whether phonologized nasalization is simply an
    enhancement or exaggeration. Presumably, the concept of absolute threshold is almost one
    of categorical distinction, whilst enhancement is one of relative degree.
7   However, care must of course be shown when evaluating perceptual evidence to determine
    degrees of nasality. Language-specific factors are well known to affect the perception of

phonetic phenomena; see Watson (1983) on voicing contrast, Terbeek and Harshman (1971) on vowel perception, and Berinstein (1979) on stress perception. Experimental research suggests that language-specific factors also affect the perception of nasality. Beddor and Strange (1982) found that linguistic experience affected the perception of vowel nasality by English and Hindi speakers. For speakers of Hindi, a language with distinctively nasalized vowels, nasal perception was categorical, whilst for speakers of English with only contextual nasalization, the oral-nasal distinction was more continuous in nature.

8   This is precisely the view taken for English by Cohn (1990): N-deletion is not preceded by a categorical rule of vowel nasalization.

9   The tilde itself is not necessarily a marker of vowel nasalization. It was generally used in medieval times as an orthographic abbreviation for N.

10   Trigo (1990) is indeed explicit that N-devoicing, the first step of total assimilation is an attenuation process and is in itself sufficient for the phonologization of vowel nasalization. But see section 8.1.6 for further discussion and criticism.

11   I am not referring to cases of spontaneous nasalization, in the absence, diachronic or synchronic, of N, e.g. Hindi [sãːp] < *sarpa* 'snake' (Ohala 1980a: 88). See also Ruhlen (1973) for other examples of distinctive nasalization without etymological N.

12   Rossi (1976) does not ordinarily mark vowel length. However, his experimental results (p. 211) indicate significantly greater vowel length in V$NV than in VN$.

13   Cf. *TP* 137 LAINE, 264 CHÊNE. *TP* provides additional evidence of near-minimal contrast in Valaisan, e.g. [lãːna] frequently contrasts with [(d)zaːna] < *[ʤalna] < GALBINA, *TP* 137, 394. See also discussion of *ALF* data below.

14   Transcription of forms given in the *ALF* has been simplified slightly.

15   Hasselrot (1937: 56, n. 1) is explicit as to the distribution of oral and nasal vowels before N: oral vowels appear before what were once geminate NN, and nasal vowels generally before historically simple N. Hering (1936) makes the same observation.

4   Universal Features of Vowel Nasalization and N-Deletion: The Effect of Vowel Length, Stress and the Foot

1   Rarely advocated is the opposing view that distinctive nasalization is non-componential, e.g. Entenman's (1977) 'All-or-Nothing Principle'. Suffice it to say that the evidence cited in the universalist literature, as well as the evidence presented in this study, strongly supports a gradualist view of the development of distinctive nasalization. An alternative but also rarely expressed view is the one taken by Bichakjian (1981) of gradual but language-specific non-parametric change. However, none of the data he presents, drawn primarily from Portuguese and French, is necessarily inconsistent with a universalist parametric analysis.

2   Whilst an autosegmental account is provided in 2, universalists did not normally discuss the formal representation of CL.

3   The distinction between long vowels (and diphthongs) and short vowels need not be underlying, only phonologically pertinent at some level. For example, whilst the distribution of vowel length in Standard Italian and in many other Italian dialects is predictable, e.g. long vowels in non-oxytonic open stressed syllables, and short vowels in oxytonic, closed and unstressed syllables, the difference makes itself felt elsewhere in the phonology, e.g. syllable weight and stress placement, *raddoppiamento sintattico*; see Vincent (1988a and c).

4   Exceptionally, [ɔ̃m] *homme* 'man' is nasalized.

5   In fact, of the purported short nasal vowels in Ndzindziu, diphthongal (i.e. long) vowels predominate, e.g. [C_1ĩɔ̃], [C_1oɔ̃]. In such circumstances, apparently short [C_1ɔ̃] and [C_1õ] may represent the temporal reduction of previously long nasal vowels.

6   On vowel length distribution, see Dalbera-Stefanaggi (1978: 23), and Wagner (1941).

7   The reduction of Stage 2 final atonic /Vn#/ syllables to [u] is typical of large areas of Piedmont and Northern Liguria; cf. Rohlfs (1966: 188–9), e.g. Piedmontese *frasu* < 'FRAXINU 'ash', *termu* < 'TERMINE 'term', *Stéu* < 'STEPHANU 'Stephen'.

8 Cf. Tuttle (1991) for numerous examples from Bergamese and other Northern dialects in support of Schourup's Tonic ≫ Atonic stress parameter.

9 Word-final atonic /^Vn#/ and pretonic /^Vnt/ are, of course, not fully comparable, since the latter may also be conditioned by other factors, e.g. cluster position. Unfortunately, however, for our purposes, Latin word-final atonic NT was very early simplified in Italy to /n/, e.g. 'CANTANT > Mi. *cantan*, Ital. *cantan(o)* 'they sing' (Rohlfs 1966: 434).

10 A few Ligurian dialects are known, for instance, to contrast long and short vowels in unstressed position; see Plomteux (1975) for details.

11 Cf. Swabian German ['maːgә̄] *Magen* 'stomach' (Schirmunski 1962: 387).

12 Gliding of tonic nasal vowels in Cairese and Bolognese is discussed in chapters 2 and 8. That unstressed nasal vowels can also undergo gliding is well-known in Portuguese, e.g. 'HOMINE > ['omẽj] ~ ['omẽ̞j]; see also Drenska (1989). Labial off-gliding of atonic [ә̃#] accounts for the unexpected synchronic result [u#] in Cairese. Labialization is supported by the unexpected appearance of orthographic final *m* in unstressed syllables in Old Ligurian texts from the thirteenth century, e.g. *rusem* alongside expected *rusen* from Latin (AE)'RUGIN(EM) 'rust'. Today in Ligurian /'ryzu/.

13 According to Fouché (1961: 785), N-deletion preceded loss of final /t/ in final /nt/ clusters.

14 For more details, see especially Fagan (1972), but also Williams (1962), Rohlfs (1970), and Contini (1987).

15 The items listed in 17 highlight the importance of position relative to the stressed vowel, rather than to the stressed syllable. Accordingly, the underlined sequences define the categories: tonic = 'V̲N̲V, pretonic = V̲N̲'V and post-tonic = 'VCV̲N̲V. Strictly speaking /n/ in LANA follows the tonic vowel but is not normally assigned to the tonic syllable in this category. Similarly, /n/ in CENARE precedes the tonic vowel, but is traditionally syllabified as onset of the tonic syllable.

16 [d] in modern *tendes* is the result of previously intervocalic voicing. Pre-obstruent [n] is the result of secondary epenthesis after a nasal vowel.

17 Gal. *canle* = ['kaɲle] < [kãɰ̃le] < *[kãːle].

18 The figures are averages of measurements given by Major (1981: 346, table 4) for one speaker for tokens *la, lala, lalala,* with different stress patterns.

19 The figures are averages of syllable measurements for three speakers provided by Major (1985: 261, Table 1) for the paroxytonic token *lalàla.*

20 For discussion and details of stress- and syllable-timing, see, for example, Fant et al. (1991a and b), Recasens (1991), Wiik (1991) and Roach (1982). The defining characteristics, if any, of stress- vs. syllable-timed languages remain hotly debated, e.g. Toledo (1989), Roach (1982), Vayra (1989), Dauer (1983).

21 Recasens (1991) suggests that in some languages, e.g. Spanish, Italian, post-tonic vowels are predictably phonetically longer than pretonic vowels. His claim is based on unreliable results, at least for Italian, skewed by phrase-final lengthening of post-tonic syllables, as Vayra (1989: 88–9) has already noted.

22 Unusually, French is thought to be right-headed (Fletcher 1991). However, the hypothesis of different syllable-compression cannot be tested because of the particular characteristics of stress-placement in this language, i.e. always phrase-final, and post-tonic syllables do not occur.

23 The geographical distribution of proparoxytonic shortening in Italy is not clear; see Rohlfs (1966) who fails to note its frequency in Northern Italian. The phenomenon is reported in all sample members, with slight variation. It is least extensive in Tavetschan. A historical tendency to shortening is also reported for French (Fouché 1958).

24 Whilst SUM also survives, it underwent frequent contamination by SUNT throughout Italy, e.g. Mi. [suːt] 'I am', Tusc. *son(o)*, Altamurese [sɔ] – [sɔnd] 'I am' – 'they are'. See Rohlfs (1968: 267–9).

25 IA for JAM already appears in Pompeian inscriptions (Väänänen 1967: 69). For exceptional cases of survival of a nasal consonant in final tonic position, see section 2.2.2.1.

26 Pre-pausal, i.e. tonic, position only.

27 It is also possible that consonant-final NOːN never underwent closed syllable shortening but retained its original long vowel, e.g. NOːN > /noːn/ > /nõːn/ > /nõː/. Modern reflexes with long vowels, e.g. French [nõː] and Ticinese [nuː], are consistent with this hypothesis.

28 See Rohlfs (1966: 24–5), Vincent (1988c) and section 4.3.6 below for more details on oxytonic shortening.
29 Absence of stop-lenition is indicative of semi-learned influence affecting the development of this word. Consonants undergo secondary gemination after tonic short vowels.
30 The figures are averages for /iː, eː, aː, oː, uː/ which are the only Tamil vowels to occur in all three foot types; see Balasubramanian (1981: 157).
31 The mora is a phonologically derived timing unit thought to give weight to syllables; see Hayes (1989) for further details.
32 Phonetic oxytonic lengthening has a phonological effect by blocking initial gemination in Italian, and Central and Southern Italian dialects, e.g. It. /pju + pane/ > [pju ppaːne] or [pjuː paːne] 'more bread'.
33 My experience of spoken Italian indicates open syllable glottalization in prepausal position is not infrequent. A correlation between glottalization and short vowels and vowel shortening is commonly reported, e.g. Chinese dialects (Chen 1972), Cayapo (Vayra 1989: 95), Yavapai (Thomas 1991), and Australian English 'hair' [heː] and optionally [heʔ].
34 Figures are for tokens /'da/, /'dada/, /'dadada/. Unfortunately, no indication of the regional origin of the speaker is provided, although it is known that this factor has a major impact on phonetic vowel length in Standard Italian; see Trumper et al. (1991), Nespor and Vogel (1979) and Vayra (1989).
35 This reduction in vowel duration (and length), also typical of other Central and Southern varieties of Italian, and which appears to be historically stable, is most evident when compared with regional varieties of Standard Italian, e.g. Genoese, in which antepenultimate vowels are perceptibly much longer.
36 See Mancini (1986) and Vincent (1988c) on Senigalliese, spoken in the Marches. See also Repetti (1989: 25–7), and Rohlfs (1966: 320–1) on the distribution of post-proparoxytonic gemination in Italy. Secondary post-tonic gemination should not be treated as compensatory – the phenomenon appears to be a relatively recent one affecting only some of those parts of Italy. In some areas it is the culmination of complete analogical spread. In others such as Bolognese lengthening is attributable to a regular fortis articulation of short vowels and following consonants (see chapter 8 for details).

5 Vowel Height, Vowel Quality and the Development of Distinctive Nasalization

1 More precisely, Hombert (1986, 1987) restricts his observation to a grosser distinction between open /a, e, o/ and close /i,u/, since his Teke data does not allow him to separate low /a/ from mid /e, o/.
2 Orthographic oN and uN are thought to represent [u]N and [y]N in early Old French; see Ruhlen (1979) for details.
3 Dispute is not limited to interpretation of the data, but extends to the data itself, e.g. Entenman (1977: 114, n. 1) who notes that modern text editors, frequently supporters of the vowel-height-related nasalization hypothesis, have tampered with texts by eliminating examples of VN–VC assonance which appear unexpectedly in later texts. Disagreement even extends to which oral-nasal pairs did and did not assonate in Old French; cf. Matte (1984) and Entenman (1977: 114–15).
4 Schourup (1973: 192) cites in passing developments in Breton, Korean, Thai and Kashubian as additional evidence of a low ≫ mid ≫ high VHP. However, Entenman (1977: 65–8, 110) rejects as unfounded the examples of Breton, Korean and Kashubian. The degree of contextual nasalization in Thai, however, has been described as inversely proportional to vowel height.
5 See section 6.1.2 for details.
6 The pattern of vowel lengthening seems to be governed by vowel height, as the secondary lengthening of the lower Stage 2 vowels /ɛ, ɔ/, but especially /a/ in Emilia-Romagna seems to suggest; cf. section 2.2.3.3, Coco (1970), Schürr (1919).

7 It should be pointed out that the Bonneval examples given by Tuttle (1991) at p. 49 are incorrect: short vowels have been inadvertently transcribed as long.

8 The number of dialects with preferential high vowel nasalization is probably far higher, but cannot be ascertained with the limited data available.

9 Foley's (1975: 201–2) suggested explanation for the VHP is typically abstract: the VHP is a manifestation of a vowel strength parameter, along which strength decreases with increasing vowel height. N-deletion is most likely after strong (low) vowels, and least likely after weak (high) vowels.

10 Vowel-height-related variation in levels of velic opening may also have an acoustico-perceptual explanation: low vowels appear to require much greater velic opening than high vowels to be perceived as nasal. See Ohala (1975) and section 5.3.1 below.

11 See Al-Bamerni (1983: 254, table 8, 279, table 9).

12 I consider only relative rather than absolute duration of nasalization, since the latter may plausibly be affected by vowel-height-related differences in absolute vowel length. Whether specific vowel-related differences in relative nasalization duration are perceptually important is of course another matter, for which we have no direct experimental evidence. Listeners' responsiveness to nasality is, however, well known to be sensitive to durational differences in general; cf. section 4.1.4.

13 Although there appears to be firmer perceptual evidence in favour of preferential high vowel nasalization.

14 See Maeda (1982, 1989) for detailed discussion of the acoustic effect of nasalization on individual vowel spectra. But Delattre (1970) claims that the acoustic impression of nasalization is maximized by certain pharyngeal configurations, which correlate most with those found in the articulation of low vowels. See Delattre (1965, 1968) for suggested different acoustic properties of low and high vowel nasality.

15 I make no reference to the results of Brito's (1975) perceptual experiments of distinctive nasalization in Brazilian Portuguese. Although they appear to support preferential distinctive nasalization of low vowels, they must be rejected as completely unreliable. Even Brito admits her results are strongly skewed by the effects of orthographic interference, predictable low vowel quality changes, and problems some listeners had in adequately symbolizing what they heard. In addition, Brito failed to take into account the effect of context on the production and perception of syllable-final N: the choice of tokens strongly favours the articulatory and perceptual absence of articulated N after /a/, and its presence after higher vowels.

16 The effect of central vowel quality is not considered here for a number of reasons: (1) non-low central vowels are absent in Latin, and generally in Northern Italian; (2) non-low central vowels were not included in the experimental research discussed below in section 5.4.1; and (3) non-low central nasal vowels are cross-linguistically rare (Maddieson 1984).

17 In his earlier works, Chen claims the frequency rate of /$\tilde{V}_1$/ relative to /V_1N/ is 18% for front vowels and 7% for back vowels. Figures for front and central vowels were lumped together. Later, Chen (1975) separated the categories, and extended the vowel quality parameter to front (21%) > central (14%) > back (7%). Note that Chen's category of central nasal vowels consisted almost exclusively (99.97%) of low /ã/.

18 On cross-linguistic and cross-generational differences in speech perception, see Watson (1983), Berinstein (1979), Terbeek and Harshman (1971) and Janson (1982).

6 Contextual Ordering of Distinctive Nasalization

1 Malécot's findings appear to be aberrant, and have not been confirmed by anyone else, or reported for any other language; cf. section 6.4.1.1.

2 Foley tends to keep discussion of syllable conditioning and cluster conditioning separate. But it follows from the syllable-position parameter at 2a that intervocalic N will only be deleted after N is lost in all clusters.

3 Schourup notes at p. 191 that preconsonantal N-deletion without loss of word-final N occurred in Germanic and Old English. However, he suggests they are unlikely

counter-examples because they 'are known only from written records . . . and are . . . highly questionable sources for information about a subtle feature like nasality.'

4 E.g. CE:NSOR ~ CE:SOR 'censor'. N+F was also prone to simplification to F. Any N-deletion was, I claim, preceded by vowel nasalization in line with the new V-NAS model. It has been suggested, e.g. Sturtevant (1940: 153–4), that the tendency towards N-deletion before fricatives in Latin was apparently blocked by the countervailing pressure of the written language.

5 Salodiano is an Eastern Lombard dialect spoken very close to Bergamese, e.g. Sal. and Bg. *ca* < CANE 'dog'. The same pattern of deletion is reported in other closely related dialects, e.g. Old Brescian (Bonelli and Contini 1935: 145), and synchronically in Alpine Lombard dialects to the north of Bergamo, often with residual evidence of nasalization (Merlo 1951).

6 The Catalan pattern is also found further north in Lengadocian Occitan (Wheeler 1988).

7 The presence of nasalization before voiced N+Stop clusters, and its absence before intervocalic /n/ in Milanese is exceptional, the result of a secondary process of shortening of expected long /Vː/ before surface /n/. The VLP then operates to block nasalization of short tonic vowels in open syllables, i.e. LANA > Stage 2 /laːna/ > Mi. [lana], but not *[lãna]. See sections 2.2.3.1 and 7.2 for more details of vowel-length conditioning in Milanese.

8 Exceptionally, Milanese appears to contravene the strict implicational hierarchy, since nasalization in the context Stage 2 /VːnV/ is blocked by secondary shortening.

9 Nasalization before N + voiced stop clusters, and of Stage 2 short vowels before /n/ (< Lat. /nn/), is restricted to /a/, but only after secondary lengthening; see table 6.1, examples at 6 and 7 above, as well as discussion in section 6.4.

10 Recall that N-deletion in clusters is optional in Milanese (Salvioni 1884, Nicoli 1983).

11 The situation is further complicated by the fact that only rarely did Lat. N in these clusters appear in a stressed syllable, e.g. 'CON+IUGE 'spouse', 'CON+REU > 'CORREU 'co-accused', 'IN+FIMU 'lowest'. I will assume for the moment that any changes were the same regardless of the presence or absence of stress in Northern Italian.

12 Most data are found variously in Pensado (1985, 1986, 1989). See also Rohlfs (1966: 415).

13 Pensado (1985: 54–5) argues against geminated [nnw] in Ibero-Romance, since there is no evidence of an expected [ɲ] < NN before earlier [w] in Spanish; cf. ANNU 'year' > *año*, but *MANUARIA > manera*, not *mañera*.

14 But see section 8.2.1.

15 On tonic vowel length see Dalbera-Stefanaggi (1978: 23). Dalbera-Stefanaggi (1989: 151–4) argues convincingly against French influence in Corsica as a possible source of nasalization and N-deletion. Amongst other things, the phenomena are more marked amongst older speakers, having the least contact with French, and are reported only in the most isolated and linguistically archaic zones of Corsica.

16 Corsican has been heavily Tuscanized since the medieval period. Strictly speaking, most of Sardinia forms a linguistic entity independent of Central and Southern Italy. However, geographically all these dialects are close, and linguistically they are very similar, relative to the dialects of Northern Italy.

17 On the extent of lenition in Sardinian, Tuscan and Corsican, see Contini (1987), Giannelli and Savoia (1978) and Dalbera-Stefanaggi (1978) respectively. The extent of lenition in these dialects is far greater than anything reported in Northern Italian in both range of consonants affected and context. Northern Italian lenition is now only a historical phenomenon restricted to word-medial position.

18 An attempt to relate developments in Northern and Centro-Southern Italian to the influence of syllable structure is made in section 8.2.1.2.

19 The unexpected simplification of /ns, nf/ clusters in Low German, alongside preservation of word-final /n#/, has frequently been ascribed to substrate influence; see Schirmunski (1962).

20 Cf. also discussion of VLP in precisely such contexts in section 7.3.

21 However, Locke (1983: 220) provides conflicting English child-language data from various sources where nasals appear to be deleted equally in preconsonantal, intervocalic and word-final position, e.g. [mĩ] *mean*, [õi] *only*, [õ] *don't*, [ɛ̃] *and*, [ə̃] *gonna*.

22 There is some debate as to whether Latin vowel lengthening before N+Fric precedes or follows distinctive nasalization in this context. Lightner (1973: 26) claims the former, but Tuttle (1991) supports the latter. There is no compelling evidence to reject the hypothesis of pre-deletion lengthening in Latin. On the other hand, I am willing to accept the possibility

that in some languages vowel lengthening is not a necessary pre-condition for the development of distinctive nasalization in the context of N+Fric clusters for reasons given below, and in sections 8.1.4 and 8.1.7. However, secondary vowel length in such cases must be seen as the result of a very gradual process of complete vocalization of earlier N, rather than as a truly compensatory phenomenon.

23 On the distinction between N-deletion and vocalization, see sections 1.2.1.1 and 8.1.4 for further details.

7 Historical Development of Nasal Consonants and the Effect of N Place on Distinctive Nasalization

1 As is evident from the English translations of the German glosses, pre-fricative N-deletion has extended to all places in (Old) English.

2 Sometimes Chen is vague about the need to distinguish between [m] and [n]; see Chen (1974a: 921) 'the phonological domain of nasalization extends . . . from the anterior /m, n/ to the back /ŋ/' and also Chen (1973c: 187). But see Chen (1974a: 918, fig. 8). The place of palatal [ɲ] along the parameter is not explicitly discussed by Chen, since it is historically a late secondary development.

3 All long vowel reflexes tend now to be regularly nasalized, especially before [n], e.g. [kẽːn].

4 Cf. Contini (1987) on Sardinian, and Dalbera-Stefanaggi (1989) on Corsican. Note that /ɲ/ has a relatively restricted geolinguistic distribution in Corsica and Sardinia. NJ more usually appears today as N+Obstruent cluster in nasalizing Sardinian and Corsican dialects, e.g. VINEA 'vineyard' > *VINJA > Sard. [bindza], [binza], [bindʒa], Corsican [binja].

5 I limit discussion here to the gemination of post-tonic nasal consonants in Latin paroxytones, e.g. FAME, LIMA. Gemination of nasals and other consonants in Latin proparoxytones, e.g. 'FEMINA 'woman' > ['femmina], is more generally foot-related. See sections 4.3.3 and 4.3.4 for more details.

6 Similar conditions in Lughese, Ravennate and Riminese, although with previously noted traces of conditioned /m/-loss after long vowels in the last two, e.g. [fjõː] < FLUME 'river'.

7 < [ʎema] as a result of depalatalization. [əm'premə] < PRIMA 'first' is more typical; cf. Caduff (1952: 49).

8 The reflex [aː] is the result of a secondary lengthening of short /a/ only, cf. [baːɲ] < */baɲ/ 'bath', [aːn] < */an/ 'year'. The phenomenon must be recent since reflexes do not coincide with those of historically long /aː/, e.g. [lɛːna] < */laːna/ 'wool', and [kæŋ] < */kaːn/ 'dog'.

9 It is important to distinguish between dialects that conserve historical /n/ as [n] in intervocalic position, and those dialects, mainly in Piedmont, that have synchronic [ŋ] in its place, e.g. LANA 'wool' > [la(ː)na] vs. [laŋa]. The regularly short vowel before velar [ŋ] is not related directly to open syllable vowel shortening as such, but is an independent phenomenon related to the appearance of [ŋ]; see section 8.1.8.1 for further details.

10 Gemination after /ɲ, n₂/ differs slightly in historical detail from that of /m/ in Bolognese: Stage 2 long vowels were shortened before /m/. But before /ɲ, n₁/ all reconstructed Stage 2 vowels are predictably short to begin with.

11 The same phonetic reasons do not of course explain why /m/, rather than /n/ provides the preferential context for the development of distinctive nasalization in other languages, as reported in section 7.1.1.

12 The sources provide no statistical analysis.

13 However, the tendency is presumably not universal: Orešnik and Pétursson (1977) report [n] to be slightly longer than [m] in Icelandic.

14 The formal representation of so-called Compensatory Lengthening is discussed and evaluated in some detail in chapter 8.

8 N-Deletion: Its Manner and Its Motivation

1 It is unfortunate that de Chene and Anderson (1979) and Anderson (1981) refer to this gradual process of complete vocalization at 4 as Compensatory Lengthening (CL). This is

best avoided, as it leads to confusion with the better-known CL as the process of Root Node deletion and filling described in section 8.1.3.

2 See Abercrombie (1967: 138) on the phonetics of final devoicing, and his account of it as a phonetic assimilation process to utterance-final silence.

3 Cf. Sankoff and Rousseau (1989: 9–10) and Guitart (1982: 67) for limited discussion of this model of development in Latin American Spanish.

4 Rohlfs (1966: 427–8) also believes that [ŋ] is restitutive in Northern Italian. For a detailed description and account of nasalized glide hardening to [ŋ] in Bolognese and Cairese, see Hajek (1991c).

5 Long vowels before [ŋ] are reported in isolated Emilian dialects located in the Appennines, some distance from and not in direct contact with Bolognese, e.g. Collagna [bõːŋ] < Stage 2 /bɔːn/ 'good', [põːnt] < Stage 2 /pɔnt/ 'bridge'. However, Malagoli (1943: 6, n. 2) notes that in neighbouring dialects, such a velar [ŋ] is barely heard, e.g. Nismozza [kãːⁿp], Ligonchio [pãːⁿ].

6 Cf. also the quality differences affecting Lat. /a(ː)/ before [ŋ] and other nasals, e.g. [kæŋ] vs. [aːn].

7 Nasalized glides may survive in more casual speech, e.g. citation form [loŋna], but also casual/rapid [lõw̃na]. An intermediate sound between a nasalized glide and a nasal stop is also reported by Hajek (1991c).

8 Cf. Schourup (1973: 191–2), Foley (1977: 60), Ruhlen (1973: 13), Lightner (1973: 29–31).

9 Cf. Hyman (1975b: 161–3), Jespersen (1922), Postal (1968), Schane (1972) and Lightner (1973). According to Lightner, this tendency is itself governed by two principles: (1) languages tend to display a 'maximal' opposition of one segment to the segments around it, and (2) word-final segments tend to be dropped. Given the example /bandem/ > [bãdẽ], word-medial /n/ is lost to create maximal distance between /a/ and /d/, whilst /m/ is lost because word-final. For arguments against the first principle, see Entenman (1977: 86). Open syllables are not exclusively obtained by syllable-final deletion. V-epenthesis will also suffice, e.g. CVC$ > CVCV.

10 Numerous examples of African languages with exclusively open syllables are found in Bendor-Samuel (1989).

11 Andersen (1988) and Werlen (1982) give details of the diffusion of glide hardening in Europe, including Romantsch, e.g. [rigva] < [rijva] < RIVA 'bank'.

12 I have simplified matters by omitting reference to possible intermediate steps of phonologized N-reduction. These steps are discussed in some detail in sections 8.1.3 to 8.1.8.

13 The template and deletion would presumably apply in an iterative fashion along the N-deletion contextual parameter.

14 Fujimura and Lovins (1978) and Watson (1992) note that the representation of ambisyllabification is problematic: the affected segment should be expected to show all the characteristics of (strong) Onset position, as well those of (weak) Coda position. This issue has not been properly addressed in phonological studies of ambisyllabification.

9 Results and Conclusions

1 In the case of the VLP, it would be expected to apply at least in languages in which differences in vowel length are phonologically pertinent.

2 All the languages cited with reference to stress- and foot-related effects on distinctive nasalization in chapter 4 seem to have left-headed feet. Languages with right-headed feet may present vowel- and syllable-compression effects that conflict with the ones reported in chapter 4, and that may quite plausibly have a completely different effect on both nasalization and N-deletion.

3 Cf., for instance, suggested N place of articulation parameters in section 7.1.1.

4 Overall, it should be noted that the appearance of some patterns appears to be favoured over others: centralization appeared in 40 per cent of the sample.

5   See sections 3.5 to 3.5.3 for more details and examples of vowel nasalization without N-deletion.
6   See, for instance, the influence of the VLP on the formulation of the syllabic template of N-deletion in section 8.2.1.
7   VNFric may represent an exception to the vowel lengthening constraint; see sections 6.4.1.1 and 8.1.7 for details. But see section 6.4 for evidence of preferential V-lengthening in the same context.

BIBLIOGRAPHY

ABBREVIATIONS

AGI	*Archivio glottologico italiano.*
AIS	*Atlante italo-svizzero* (Jaberg, Karl and Jud, Jakob, 1928–48. *Sprach- und Sachatlas Italiens und der Südschweiz*, Zöfingen: Ringier, 8 vols).
ALF	Gilliéron, Jules and Edmont, E., 1902–9. *Atlas linguistique de la France*, Paris.
CPJ	Cleft Palate Journal.
DDG	*Deutsche Dialektgeographie.*
Haskins SR	*Haskins Laboratories Status Report on Speech Research.*
ID	*L'Italia dialettale.*
JASA	*Journal of the Acoustical Society of America.*
JCL	*Journal of Chinese Linguistics.*
JIL	*Journal of Italian Linguistics.*
JL	*Journal of Linguistics.*
JPhon	*Journal of Phonetics.*
JSHD	*Journal of Speech and Hearing Disorders.*
JSHR	*Journal of Speech and Hearing Research.*
LeC	*Lingua e contesto.*
LIn	*Linguistic Inquiry.*
Nasálfest	Ferguson, Charles A., Hyman, Larry M., and Ohala, John J. (eds), 1975. *Nasálfest, Papers from a Symposium on Nasals and Nasalization*, Stanford: Language Universals Project, Department of Linguistics, Stanford University.
PCLS	*Papers of the Regional Meeting of the Chicago Linguistic Society.*
PICPhS	*Papers of the International Congress of Phonetic Sciences.*
RID	*Rivista italiana di dialettologia.*
RLiR	*Revue de linguistique romane.*
RomPh	*Romance Philology.*
TP	Gauchat, Louis, Jeanjaquet, Jules and Tappolet, Ernest, 1925. *Tableaux phonétiques des patois suisses romands*, Neuchâtel: Paul Attinger.
UCLA WPPh	*UCLA Working Papers in Phonetics.*
ZRPh	*Zeitschrift für Romanische Philologie.*

REFERENCES

Abercrombie, David, 1967. *Elements of General Phonetics*, Edinburgh: Edinburgh University Press.

Abramson, Arthur S., Nye, Patrick W., Henderson, Janette B. and Marshall, Charles W., 1981. 'Vowel height and the perception of consonantal nasality', *JASA*, 70: 329–39.

Accorsi, Maria Grazia (ed.), 1980. *Lotto Lotti, Rimedi per la sonn*, Bologna: Commissione per i Testi di Lingua.

Ahlborn, Gunnar, 1946. *Le patois de Ruffieux-en-Valromey, Ain,* Göteborg: Elanders.

Al-Bamerni, Ameen, 1983. *Oral, Velic and Laryngeal Coarticulation Across Languages*, D. Phil. dissertation, University of Oxford.

Ali, Latif H., 1982. 'Some observations on the nasal-fricative sequences in English', *JPhon*, 10: 315–23.

Ali, Latif H., 1984. 'On the domain of nasality in English'. In Wolfgang U. Dressler, John R. Rennison and Oskar E. Pfeiffer (eds), *Fifth International Phonology Conference, Discussion Papers*, Wiener Linguistische Gazette, Suppl. 3, 1–6.

Ali, Latif H., Gallagher, T., Goldstein, J. and Daniloff, R., 1971. 'Perception of coarticulated nasality', *JASA*, 49: 538–40.

Allen, W. Sidney, 1965. *Vox Latina: The Pronunciation of Classical Latin*, Cambridge: Cambridge University Press.

Amastae, Jon, 1986. 'A syllable-based analysis of Spanish spirantization'. In Osvaldo Jaeggli and Carmen Silva-Corvalán (eds), *Studies in Romance Linguistics*, Dordrecht: Foris, 3–21.

Andersen, Henning, 1973. 'Abductive and deductive change', *Language*, 49: 567–93.

Andersen, Henning, 1988. 'Center and periphery: Adoption, diffusion, and spread'. In Jacek Fisiak (ed.), *Historical Dialectology, Regional and Social*, Berlin: Mouton de Gruyter, 39–83.

Anderson, J. C. and Jones, C. (eds), 1974. *Historical Linguistics*, Amsterdam: North-Holland.

Anderson, Stephen R., 1975. 'On the interaction of phonological rules of various types', *JL*, 11: 39–62.

Anderson, Stephen R., 1981. 'Why phonology isn't "natural"', *LIn*, 12: 493–539.

Anderson, Stephen R., 1985. *Phonology in the Twentieth Century*, Chicago: University of Chicago Press.

Angiolini, Francesco, 1897. *Vocabolario milanese-italiano*, Turin: G.B. Paravia.

Archangeli, Diana and Pulleyblank, Douglas, 1994. *Grounded Phonology*, Cambridge, MA: MIT Press.

Arrighi, Cletto, 1896. *Dizionario milanese-italiano*, Milan: Ulrico Hoepli.

Ascoli, Graziadio I., 1873. 'Saggi ladini', *AGI*, 1: 1–556.

Ascoli, Graziadio I., 1882. 'L'Italia dialettale', *AGI*, 8: 98–128.

Avram, Andrei, 1990. *Nazalitatea şi rotacismul în limba română*, Bucharest: Editura Academiei Române.

Ayuso Machuca, María Jesús, 1991. 'Acoustic description of Spanish nasal consonants in continuous speech', *PICPhS*, 12, 2: 414–17.

Badía Margarit, Antonio M., 1951. *Gramática histórica catalana*, Barcelona: Noguer.

Badini, Bruna, 1972. *Lingua, dialetto e società ad Ozzano dell'Emilia*, tesi di laurea, University of Bologna.

Balasubramanian, T., 1981. 'Duration of vowels in Tamil', *JPhon*, 9: 151–61.

Baldassari, Tolmino, 1979. *Proposta per una grafia letteraria della lingua romagnola*, Ravenna: Longo.

Balducci, Sanzio, 1980. 'Il dialogo per il carnevale . . . in lingua rustica bolognese di Sebastiano Locatelli, 1636–1709', *Studi urbinati di storia, filosofia e letteratura, Università degli studi di Urbino, Supplemento linguistico*, 2/2: 177–232.

Barba, Katharina, 1982. *Deutsche Dialekte in Rumänien*, Wiesbaden: Franz Steiner.

Barry, Martin C., 1991. 'Temporal modelling of gestures in articulatory assimilation', *PICPhS*, 12, 4: 14–17.

Beddor, Patrice S., 1983. *Phonological and Phonetic Effects of Nasalization on Vowel Height*, Bloomington: Indiana University Linguistics Club.

Beddor, Patrice S., 1991. 'Reply to Keating, Pierrehumbert, and Rischel', *Phonetica*, 48: 263–5.

Beddor, Patrice S. and Strange, Winifred, 1982. 'Cross-language study of perception of the oral-nasal distinction', *JASA*, 71: 1551–1561.

Bell, Alan, 1978. 'Language samples'. In Joseph H. Greenberg, Charles A. Ferguson and Edith A. Moravcsik (eds), *Universals of Human Language, vol. 1: Method and Theory*, Stanford: Stanford University Press, 123–56.

Bell-Berti, Fredericka, 1993. 'Understanding velic motor control: Studies of segmental context'. In Marie K. Huffman and Rena A. Krakow (eds), *Nasals, Nasalization and the Velum*, San Diego: Academic Press, 63–85.

Bellosi, Giuseppe and Quondametteo, Gianni, 1979. *Le parlate dell'Emilia e della Romagna*, Florence: Edizioni del Riccio.

Bendor-Samuel, John (ed.), 1989. *The Niger-Congo Languages*, Lanham: University Press of America.

Benguerel, André-Pierre and Lafargue, André, 1981. 'Perception of vowel nasalization in French', *JPhon*, 9: 309–21.

Beretta, Claudio, 1980. *Contributo per una grammatica del milanese contemporaneo*, Milan: Virgilio.

Beretta, Claudio and Luzzi, Giovanni, 1982. *Letteratura milanese*, Milan: Libreria Meravigli.

Bergh, Herman van den, 1979. *Aspetti e particolarità dei dialetti liguri: dalla provincia di Savona all'intera regione ligure*, dissertation, Catholic University of Louvain.

Bergh, Herman van den, 1983. 'Aspetti fonetici rilevanti delle sottovarietà dialettali liguri: -N- e -R- intervocalici'. In Lorenzo Còveri and Diego Moreno (eds), *Studi di etnologia e dialettologia ligure in memoria di Hugo Plomteux*, Genoa: SAGEP Editrice, 63–74.

Berinstein, Ava E., 1979. 'A cross-linguistic study on the perception and production of stress', *UCLA WPPh*, 47: 1–59.

Bertinetto, Pier Marco and Loporcaro, Michele (eds), 1988. *Certamen Phonologicum*, Turin: Rosenberg and Sellier.

Bertinetto, Pier Marco, Kenstowicz, Michael and Loporcaro, Michele (eds), 1991. *Certamen Phonologicum II*, Turin: Rosenberg and Sellier.

Bhaldraithe, Tomás de, 1945. *The Irish of Cois Fhairrge, Co. Galway*, Dublin: Dublin Institute for Advanced Studies.

Bibeau, Gilles, 1975. *Introduction à la phonologie générative du français*, Montreal: Didier.

Bichakjian, Bernard H., 1981. 'Generative phonology, universals and the explanation of French and Portuguese nasalization'. In Bernard H. Bichakjian (ed.), *From Linguistics to Literature, Romance Studies Offered to Francis M. Rogers*, Amsterdam: John Benjamins, 1–44.

Bickmore, Lee S., 1995. 'Accounting for compensatory lengthening in the CV and moraic frameworks'. In Jacques Durand and Francis Katamba (eds), *Frontiers of Phonology*, London: Longman, 119–48.

Bjarkman, Peter Christian, 1985. 'Velar nasals and explanatory phonological accounts of Caribbean Spanish', *Proceedings of the Second Eastern States Conference on Linguistics*, 1–16.

Bjerrome, G., 1959. *Le patois de Bagnes (Valais)*, Stockholm: Almqvist and Wiksell.

Bladon, Anthony, 1986. 'Extending the search for a psychophysical basis for dynamic phonetic patterns'. Paper presented to the NATO Advanced Research Workshop on the Psychophysics of Speech Production, Utrecht, 1986.

Bloch, Jules, 1934. *L'Indo-Aryen du Veda aux temps modernes*, Paris: Adrien-Maisonneuve.

Bloomfield, Leonard, 1933. *Language*, New York: Holt.

Blumstein, Sheila E., 1991. 'The relation between phonetics and phonology', *Phonetica*, 48: 108–19.

Bonelli, Giuseppe and Contini, Gianfranco, 1935. 'Antichi testi bresciani', *ID*, 11: 115–51.

Borzone de Manrique, Ana María and Signorini, Angela, 1983. 'Segmental duration and rhythm in Spanish', *JPhon*, 11: 117–28.

Bothorel, André, 1982. *Etude phonétique et phonologique du breton parlé à Argol (Finistère-Sud)*, Lille: Atelier National Réproduction des Thèses, Université de Lille III.

Bottiglioni, Guio, 1919. *Fonologia del dialetto imolese*, Pisa: F. Mariotti.

Bouchard, Denis, 1983. 'Nasal vowels in French without underlying nasal vowels and without a rule of nasalization', *Cahiers linguistiques d'Ottawa*, 11: 29–57.

Bream, Carol, 1968. 'La nasalisation des voyelles orales suivies de consonnes nasales dans le français et l'anglais parlés au Canada'. In Pierre R. Léon (ed.), *Recherches sur la structure phonétique du français canadien*, Montreal: Marcel Didier, 100–18.

Breatnach, Risteard B., 1947. *The Irish of Ring, Co. Waterford*, Dublin: Dublin Institute for Advanced Studies.

Brito, Gêlda A., 1975. 'The perception of nasal vowels in Brazilian Portuguese: a pilot study', *Nasálfest*, 49–66.

Browman, Catherine P. and Goldstein, Louis, 1987. 'Tiers in articulatory phonology, with some implications for casual speech', *Haskins SR*, 92: 1–30.

Brown, Wella, 1984. *A Grammar of Modern Cornish*, Saltash: Kesva an Tavas Kernewek.

Bruck, Anthony, Fox, Robert A. and La Galy, Michael W. (eds), 1974. *Papers from the Parasession on Natural Phonology*, Chicago: Chicago Linguistic Society.

Bruni, Francesco, 1984. *L'italiano, elementi di storia della lingua e della cultura*, Turin: UTET.

Bruzzi Tantucci, Eugenia, 1962. *Il dialetto di Castiglione dei Pepoli*, Bologna: Poseidonia.

Buck, Carl Darling, 1933. *Comparative Grammar of Greek and Latin.* Chicago: Chicago University Press.

Burgess, Eunice and Ham, Patricia, 1968. 'Multilevel conditioning on phoneme variants in Apinayé', *Linguistics*, 41: 5–18.

Bybee, Joan L., 1988. 'The diachronic dimension in explanation'. In John A. Hawkins (ed.), *Explaining Language Universals*, Oxford: Basil Blackwell, 350–80.

Caduff, Léonard, 1952. *Essai sur la phonétique du parler rhétoroman de la Vallée de Tavetsch, Canton des Grisons – Suisse*, Bern: A. Francke.

Cagliari, Luiz Carlos, 1977. *An Experimental Study of Nasality with Particular Reference to Brazilian Portuguese*, Ph.D. dissertation, University of Edinburgh.

Camilli, A., 1965. *Pronuncia e grafia dell'italiano*, Florence: Sansoni.

Carrió i Font, M. and Ríos Mestre, A., 1991. 'A contrastive analysis of Spanish and Catalan rhythm', *PICPhS*, 12, 4: 246–9.

Carvalho, Joaquim de Brandão, 1989. 'Phonological conditions on Portuguese clitic placement: on syntactic evidence for stress and rhythmical patterns', *Linguistics*, 27: 405–36.

Casablanca, Carlos A., 1987. 'Perception de voyelles en contexte nasal dans l'espagnol parlé à Porto-Rico', *PICPhS*, 11, 2: 202–4.

Cedergren, Henrietta and Sankoff, David, 1975. 'Nasals: a sociolinguistic study of change in progress', *Nasálfest*, 67–80.

Chen, Matthew, 1970. 'Vowel length variation as a function of the voicing of the consonant environment', *Phonetica*, 21: 129–59.

Chen, Matthew, 1972. *Nasals and Nasalization in Chinese: Explorations in Phonological Universals*, Ph.D. dissertation, University of California, Berkeley.

Chen, Matthew, 1973a. 'Cross-dialectal comparison: a case study and some theoretical considerations', *JCL*, 1: 38–63.

Chen, Matthew, 1973b. 'On the formal expression of natural rules in phonology', *JL*, 9: 223–49.

Chen, Matthew, 1973c. 'Predictive power in phonological description', *Lingua*, 32: 173–91.

Chen, Matthew, 1974a. 'Metarules and universal constraints in phonological theory'. In Luigi Heilmann (ed.), *Proceedings of the Eleventh International Congress of Linguists*, Bologna: Il Mulino, vol. 2: 909–24.

Chen, Matthew, 1974b. 'Natural phonology from a diachronic viewpoint'. In Anthony Bruck, Robert A. Fox and Michael W. La Galy (eds), *Papers from the Parasession on Natural Phonology*, Chicago: Chicago Linguistics Society, 43–80.

Chen, Matthew, 1975. 'An areal study of nasalization in Chinese', *JCL*, 3: 16–59.

Chen, Matthew Y. and Wang, William S-Y., 1975. 'Sound change: Actuation and implementation', *Language*, 51: 255–81.

Chene, Brent E. de, 1985. *The Historical Phonology of Vowel Length*, New York: Garland Press.

Chene, Brent E. de and Anderson, Stephen R., 1979. 'Compensatory lengthening', *Language*, 55: 505–35.

Chomsky, Noam and Halle, Morris, 1968. *The Sound Pattern of English*, New York: Harper and Row.

Ciociola, Claudio, 1979. 'Un'antica lauda bergamasca', *Studi di filologia italiana*, 37: 33–87.

Ciociola, Claudio, 1986. 'Attestazioni antiche del bergamasco letterario', *Rivista di letteratura italiana*, 4: 141–73.

Clark, John and Yallop, Colin, 1995. *An Introduction to Phonetics and Phonology*, Oxford: Blackwell, 2nd edition.

Clarke, Wayne M. and Hardcastle, William J., 1982. 'Factors influencing the measurement of oral and nasal sound pressure level', *JPhon*, 10: 245–50.

Clarke, Wayne M. and Mackiewicz-Krassowska, Halina, 1977. 'Variation in the oral and nasal sound pressure level of vowels in changing phonetic contexts', *JPhon*, 5: 195–203.

Clements, George N. and Keyser, Samuel J., 1983. *CV Phonology, A Generative Theory of the Syllable*, Cambridge, MA: MIT Press.

Clumeck, Harold, 1971. 'Degrees of nasal coarticulation', *Monthly Internal Memorandum, Phonology Laboratory*, University of California, Berkeley.

Clumeck, Harold, 1975. 'A cross-linguistic investigation of vowel nasalization: an instrumental study', *Nasálfest*, 133–52.

Clumeck, Harold, 1976. 'Patterns of soft palate movements in six languages', *JPhon*, 4: 337–51.

Coco, Francesco, 1970. *Il dialetto di Bologna*, Bologna: Forni.

Coco, Francesco, 1971. 'Effetti della degeminazione consonantica nel dialetto bolognese', *Atti del Convegno del Centro per gli studi dialettali italiani*, Turin: Rattero, 152–67.

Cohen, Victor B., 1971. 'Foleyology', *PCLS*, 7: 316–22.

Cohn, Abigail, 1987. 'A survey of the feature [± nasal]', manuscript, UCLA, Los Angeles.

Cohn, Abigail, 1988. 'Phonetic rules of nasalization in French', *UCLA WPPh*, 69: 60–7.

Cohn, Abigail, 1990. 'Phonetic and phonological rules of nasalization', *UCLA WPPh*, 76: 1–224.

Cohn, Abigail, 1993. 'The status of nasalized continuants', In Marie K. Huffman and Rena A. Krakow (eds), *Nasals, Nasalization and the Velum*, San Diego: Academic Press, 329–67.

Comrie, Bernard, 1981. *Language Universals and Linguistic Typology*, Oxford: Basil Blackwell, 1st edition.

Comrie, Bernard, 1989. *Language Universals and Linguistic Typology*, Oxford: Basil Blackwell, 2nd edition.

Comrie, Bernard, 1993. 'Typology and reconstruction'. In Charles A. Jones (ed.), *Historical Linguistics, Problems and Perspectives*, London: Longman, 74–97.

Condax, I. B., Acson, V., Miki, C. C. and Sakoda, K. K., 1976. 'A technique for monitoring velic action by means of a photo-electric nasal probe: application to French', *JPhon*, 4: 173–81.

Connell, Bruce, 1989. 'Instrumental evidence for phonetically gradual sound change', *Work in Progress, Department of Linguistics, University of Edinburgh*, 22: 58–68.

Connell, Bruce, 1991. *Phonetic Aspects of Lower Cross Languages, and their Implications for Sound Change*, Ph. D. dissertation, University of Edinburgh.

Connell, Bruce and Hajek, John, 1991. 'Universals of nasal attrition', *PICPhS*, 12, 5: 106–09.

Contavalli, Paola, 1963. *Tra bolognese e imolese, saggio di dialettologia strutturale*, tesi di laurea, University of Bologna.

Contini, Michel, 1987. *Étude de géographie phonétique et de phonétique instrumentale du sarde*, 2 vols., *Texte, Atlas et Album Phonétique*, Alessandria: Edizioni dell'Orso.

Corell, Hans, 1936. 'Studien zur Dialektgeographie der ehemaligen Grafschaft Ziegenhain und benachbarter Gebietstelle', *DDG*, 7: 77–215.

Coustenoble, H. N., 1945. *La Phonétique du provençal moderne en Terre d'Arles*, Hertford: S. Austin & Sons.

Cravens, Thomas D., 1984. 'Intervocalic consonant weakening in a phonetic-based strength phonology: Foleyan hierarchies and the *Gorgia Toscana*', *Theoretical Linguistics*, 11: 269–310.

Cravens, Thomas D., 1988. 'Problems and solutions in diachronic phonology: Historical correspondences and phonological evolution'. In Pier Marco Bertinetto and Michele Loporcaro (eds), *Certamen Phonologicum*, Turin: Rosenberg and Sellier, 77–102.

Croft, William, 1990. *Typology and Universals*, Cambridge: Cambridge University Press.

Dalbera-Stefanaggi, Marie-José, 1978. *Langue corse, une approche linguistique*, Paris: Klincksieck.

Dalbera-Stefanaggi, Marie-José, 1989. 'La nasalisation en Corse', *RLiR*, 53: 145–58.

D'Andrade, Ernesto and Kihm, Alain, 1988. 'Fonologia autosegmental e nasais em português'. In *Actas do 4° Encontro da Associação Portuguesa de Linguística*, Lisbon, 51–60.

Dauer, R. M., 1983. 'Stress-timing and syllable-timing reanalyzed', *JPhon*, 11: 51–62.

De Búrca, Seán, 1958. *The Irish of Tourmakeady, Co. Mayo*, Dublin: Dublin Institute for Advanced Studies.

Delattre, Pierre, 1965. 'La nasalité vocalique en français et en anglais', *French Review*, 39: 92–109.

Delattre, Pierre, 1968. 'Divergences entre nasalités vocalique et consonantique', *Word*, 24: 64–72.

Delattre, Pierre, 1970. 'Rapports entre la physiologie et la chronologie de la nasalité distinctive'. In *Actes du Xe Congrès International des Linguistes*, Bucharest: Académie de la République Socialiste de Roumanie, 221–7.

Delattre, Pierre and Monnot, Michel, 1981. 'The role of duration in the identification of French nasal vowels'. In Pierre Delattre, *Studies in Comparative Phonetics*, Heidelberg: Julius Groos, 17–38.

Delmonte, Rodolfo, 1983. 'Le parlate romagnole di confine: analisi fonetica e fonologica', *LeC*, 6: 157–261.

D'Introno, Francesco, Ortiz, Judith and Sosa, Juan, 1989. 'On resyllabification in Spanish'. In Carl Kirschner and Janet DeCesaris (eds), *Studies in Romance Linguistics*, Amsterdam, John Benjamins, 97–114.

Dogil, Grzegorz and Luschütsky, Hans-Christian, 1989. *Notes on Sonority and Segmental Strength*, Saarbrücken: Phonetica Saraviensa 10.

Donegan, Patricia and Stampe, David, 1979. 'The study of natural phonology'. In Daniel A. Dinnsen (ed.), *Current Approaches to Phonological Theory*, Bloomington: Indiana University Press, 126–73.

Drenska, Margarita, 1989. 'Análise acústica das vogais nasais em Português e Búlgaro'. In *Actas do 4° Encontro da Associação Portuguesa de Linguística*, Lisbon, 139–65.

Dressler, Wolfgang U., 1971. 'Some constraints on phonological change', *PCLS*, 7: 340–9.

Dressler, Wolfgang U., 1974. 'Diachronic puzzles for natural phonology'. In Anthony Bruck, Robert A. Fox and Michael W. La Galy (eds), *Papers from the Parasession on Natural Phonology*, Chicago: Chicago Linguistic Society, 95–102.

Dressler, Wolfgang U., Luschützky, Hans C., Pfeiffer, Oskar E. and Rennison, John R. (eds), 1992. *Phonologica 1988*, Cambridge: Cambridge University Press.

Dryer, Matthew S., 1989. 'Large linguistic areas and language sampling', *Studies in Language*, 13: 257–92.

Duc, Jacqueline, 1988. *Le patois d'Allevard*, Grenoble: IVR.

Dunn, Joseph, 1930. *A Grammar of the Portuguese Language*, London: David Nutt.

Dupraz, J., 1975. *Le patois de Saxel, Haute Savoie, Dictionnaire*, Saxel: author.

Duraffour, A., 1932. 'Phénomènes généraux d'évolution phonétique dans les dialectes franco-provençaux étudiés d'après le parler de la commune de Vaux (Ain)', *RLiR*, 8: 1–280.

Durand, Jacques, 1977. 'French nasalization revisited', *Cahiers de linguistique théorique et appliquée*, 14: 23–33.

Durand, Jacques, 1988. 'Phénomènes de nasalité en français du Midi: phonologie de dépendence et sous-specification', *Recherches linguistiques*, 17: 29–54.

Durand, Jacques, 1990. *Generative and Non-Linear Phonology*, London: Longman.

Durand, Jacques and Katamba, Francis (eds), 1995. *Frontiers of Phonology*, London: Longman.

Einarsson, Stefán, 1949. *Icelandic Grammar, Texts, Glossary*, Baltimore: John Hopkins.

Elugbe, Ben Ohi, 1978. 'On the wider application of the term "tap"', *JPhon*, 6: 133–9.

Elugbe, Ben Ohi, 1989. *Comparative Edoid: Phonology and Lexicon*, Port Harcourt: University of Port Harcourt Press.

Elugbe, Ben Ohi and Hombert, Jean-Marie, 1975. 'Nasals in Ghotuo: /lenis/ or [short]?', *Nasálfest* 167–73.

Encrevé, Pierre, 1988. *La Liaison avec et sans enchaînement*, Paris: Seuil.

Entenman, George, 1977. *The Development of Nasal Vowels*, Texas Linguistic Forum, vol.7, Austin: Department of Linguistics, University of Texas at Austin.

Escure, Geneviève, 1977. 'Hierarchies and phonological weakening', *Lingua*, 43: 55–64.

Fagan, David, 1972. 'Some historical parallels with Galician-Portuguese nasalization', *Annali, Istituto Universitario Orientale, Sezione Romanza*, 14: 19–44.

Fant, Gunnar, Kruckenberg, Anita and Nord, Lennart, 1991a. 'Durational correlates of stress in Swedish, French and English', *JPhon*, 19: 351–65.

Fant, Gunnar, Kruckenberg, Anita and Nord, Lennart, 1991b. 'Language specific patterns of prosodic and segmental structures in Swedish, French and English', *PICPhS*, 12, 4: 118–21.

Farnetani, Edda, 1979a. 'Aerodinamica della nasalizzazione', *Rivista italiana di acustica*, 3: 5–21.

Farnetani, Edda, 1979b. 'Foni nasali e nasalizzazione', *Acta phoniatrica latina*, 1: 30–57.

Ferguson, Charles A., 1966. 'Assumptions about nasals: a sample study in phonological universals'. In Joseph H. Greenberg (ed.), *Universals of Language*, Cambridge, MA: MIT Press, 2nd edition, 53–60.

Ferguson, Charles A., 1975. 'Universal tendencies and "normal" nasality', *Nasálfest*, 175–96.

Ferguson, Charles A. and Chowdhury, Munier, 1965. 'The Phonemes of Bengali', *Language*, 36: 22–59.

Ferrari, Claudio Ermando, 1835. *Vocabolario bolognese-italiano colle voci francesi corrispondenti*, Bologna: Tipografia della Volpe, 2nd edition.

Fischer-Jørgensen, Eli, 1982. 'Segment duration in Danish words in dependency of higher level phonological units', *Annual Report of the Institute of Phonetics, University of Copenhagen*, 16: 137–89.

Fletcher, Janet, 1991. 'Rhythm and final lengthening in French', *JPhon*, 19: 193–212.

Flutre, L.-F., 1955. *Le parler picard de Mesnil-Martinsart (Somme)*, Geneva: Librairie Droz.

Foley, James, 1975. 'Nasalization as universal phonological process', *Nasálfest*, 197–212.

Foley, James, 1977. *Foundations of Theoretical Phonology*, Cambridge: Cambridge University Press.

Foresti, Fabio, 1983. *Annotazioni sul vocalismo tonico bolognese della fine del XVI secolo, da due commedie di G. C. Croce*, Bologna: CLUEB.

Foresti, Fabio, 1988. 'Italienisch: Areallinguistik V. Emilia-Romagna'. In Günter Holtus, Michael Metzeltin and Christian Schmitt (eds), *Lexikon der romanistischen Linguistik*, vol. 4: *Italienisch, Korsisch, Sardisch*, Tübingen: Max Niemeyer, 569–93.

Forner, Werner, 1988. 'Areallinguistik 1. Ligurien'. In Günter Holtus, Michael Metzeltin and Christian Schmitt (eds), *Lexikon der romanistischen Linguistik*, vol. 4: *Italienisch, Korsisch, Sardisch*, Tübingen: Max Niemeyer, 453–69.

Forner, Werner, 1989. 'La dialettologia ligure: risultati e prospettive'. In Günther Holtus, Michael Metzeltin and Max Pfister (eds), *La dialettologia italiana oggi*, Tübingen: Gunter Narr.

Fouché, Pierre, 1958. *Phonétique historique du français*, vol. 2: *Les Voyelles*, Paris: Klincksieck.

Fouché, Pierre, 1961. *Phonétique historique du français*, vol. 3: *Les Consonnes et Index Général*, Paris: Klincksieck.

Fowler, Carol A., 1981. 'A relationship between coarticulation and compensatory shortening', *Phonetica*, 38: 35–50.

Fowler, Carol A., 1986. 'Acoustic and articulatory evidence for consonant-vowel interactions'. Paper presented at the 112th Meeting of the Acoustical Society of America.

Friebertshäuser, Hans, 1961. *Sprache und Geschichte des nordwestlichen Althessen*, DDG, 46, Marburg: Elwert.

Froehlich, P., 1967. *Some Problems in the Morpho-phological Structure of Bolognese*, dissertation, University of Marília, São Paulo.

Fromkin, Victoria A., 1976. 'The interface between phonetics and phonology', *UCLA WPPh*, 31: 22–6.

Fudge, Erik, 1969. 'Syllables', *JL*, 3: 1–36.

Fudge, Erik, 1987. 'Branching structure within the syllable', *JL*, 23: 359–77.

Fujimura, Osamu, 1977. 'Recent findings on articulatory processes – velum and tongue movements as syllable features'. In R. Carre, R. Descout and M. Wajskop (eds), *Modèles articulatoires et phonétique/Articulatory Modeling and Phonetics*, Grenoble: Groupe de la Communication Parlée, 115–26.

Fujimura, Osamu and Lovins, Julie, 1978. 'Syllables as concatenative phonetic units'. In Alan Bell and Joan Bybee Hooper (eds), *Syllables and Segments*, Amsterdam: North-Holland, 107–20.

Fujimura, Osamu and Lovins, Julie, 1982. *Syllables as Concatenative Phonetic Units*, Bloomington: Indiana University Linguistics Club.

Galassi, Romeo and Trumper, John, 1975. 'Fonematica autonoma del ferrarese di Bondeno', *LeC*, 1: 63–132.

Gartner, Theodor, 1910. *Handbuch der rätoromanischen Sprache und Literatur*, Halle: Max Niemeyer.

Gaudenzi, Augusto, 1889. *I suoni, le forme e le parole dell'odierno dialetto della città di Bologna*, Turin: Ermanno Loescher.

Giannelli, Luciano and Savoia, Leonardo M., 1978. 'Indebolimento consonantico in Toscana, (I)', *RID*, 2: 23–58.

Giannelli, Luciano, Maraschio, Nicoletta, Poggi Salani, Teresa and Vedovelli, Massimo (eds), 1991. *Tra rinascimento e strutture attuali*, Turin: Rosenberg and Sellier.

Gibellini, Pietro, 1981. 'Primi appunti sulla "Masséra" di Galleazzo'. In Pietro Gibellini (ed.), *Folengo e dintorni*, Brescia: Grafo.

Gilliéron, Jules, 1880. *Patois de la commune de Vionnaz, Bas-Valais*, Paris: F. Vieweg.

Goldsmith, John A., 1990. *Autosegmental and Metrical Phonology*, Oxford: Basil Blackwell.

Gorra, Egidio, 1890. 'Fonetica del dialetto di Piacenza', *ZRPh*, 14: 133–58.

Grammont, M., 1892. 'Le Patois de la Franche-Montagne et en particulier de Damprichard (Franche-Comté)', Partie I, *Mémoires de la Société de Linguistique*, 7: 461–7.

Grammont, M., 1894. 'Le Patois de la Franche-Montagne et en particulier de Damprichard (Franche-Comté)', Partie II, *Mémoires de la Société de Linguistique*, 8: 52–90.

Grammont, M., 1898. 'Le Patois de la Franche-Montagne et en particulier de Damprichard (Franche-Comté)', Partie III, *Mémoires de la Société de Linguistique*, 10: 167–203, 290–323.

Greenberg, Joseph H., 1966. 'Synchronic and diachronic universals in phonology', *Language*, 42: 508–17.

Greenberg, Joseph H., 1978. 'Diachrony, synchrony and language universals'. In Joseph H. Greenberg, Charles A. Ferguson and Edith A. Moravcsik (eds), *Universals of Human Language*, vol. 1, *Method and Theory*, Stanford: Stanford University Press.

Greenberg, Joseph H., 1979. 'Rethinking linguistics diachronically', *Language*, 55: 275–90.

Greenberg, Joseph H., Ferguson, Charles A. and Moravcsik, Edith A. (eds), 1978. *Universals of Human Language*, vol.1: *Method and Theory*, Stanford: Stanford University Press.

Greenlee, Mel and Ohala, John H., 1980. 'Phonetically motivated parallels between child phonology and historical sound change', *Language Sciences*, 2: 283–308.

Guarisma, Gladys, 1978. *Etudes Voutes*, Paris: SELAF.

Guitart, Jorge, 1982. 'On Caribbean Spanish phonology and the motivation for language change'. In James P. Lantolf and Gregory B. Stone (eds), *Current Research in Romance Languages*, Bloomington: Indiana University Linguistics Club, 63–70.

Gussman, Edmund, 1980. *Explorations in Abstract Phonology*, Lublin: Uniwersytet Marii Curie-Sklodowskiej.

Hagège, Claude and Haudricourt, André, 1978. *La Phonologie panchronique*, Paris: Presses Universitaires de France.

Hagiwara, M. P. (ed.), 1977. *Studies in Romance Linguistics*, Rowley, MA: Newbury House.

Haiman, John, 1988. 'Rhaeto-Romance'. In Martin Harris and Nigel Vincent (eds), *The Romance Languages*, London: Croom Helm, 351–90.

Hajek, John, 1988. 'Observations on the effect of nasality on vowel height in Northern Italian'. Paper delivered to the Linguistic Association of Great Britain Spring Meeting, Durham, 21–23 March.

Hajek, John, 1991a. 'The effect of nasality on vowel height: the allophonic and phonological relationship in Romance', *Progress Reports from Oxford Phonetics*, 4: 23–8.

Hajek, John, 1991b. 'French and only French: A case study in universal parameters of nasalization'. Paper delivered to the History of the French Language *Journée d'Études*, Oxford, March 2.

Hajek, John, 1991c. 'The hardening of nasalized glides in Bolognese'. In Pier Marco Bertinetto, Michael Kenstowicz and Michele Loporcaro (eds), *Certamen Phonologicum II*, Turin: Rosenberg and Sellier, 259–78.

Hajek, John, 1991d. 'La nasalizzazione nel dialetto bolognese: tratti fonologici'. In Luciano Giannelli, Nicoletta Maraschio, Teresa Poggi Salani and Massimo Vedovelli (eds), *Tra rinascimento e strutture attuali*, Turin: Rosenberg and Sellier, 273–9.

Hajek, John, 1993a. 'Old French nasalization and universals of sound change', *Journal of French Language Studies*, 3: 145–64.

Hajek, John, 1993b. 'I dialetti italiani e la nasalizzazione vocalica: tratti "universali"'. In Ramón Lorenzo (ed.), *Actas do XIX Congreso Internacional de Lingüística e Filoloxía Románicas, Sección IV. Dialectoloxía e Xeografía Lingüística*, A Coruña: Fundación «Pedro Barrié de la Maza, Conde de Fenosa», 161–8.

Hajek, John, 1994. 'Phonological length and phonetic duration in Bolognese: are they related?'. In Roberto Togneri (ed.), *Proceedings of the Fifth Australian International Conference on Speech Science and Technology*, Perth: Uniprint, vol. 2: 656–61.

Hajek, John, in press. 'A first acoustic study of the interaction between vowel and consonant duration in Bolognese', *Rivista italiana di acustica*.

Hall, Robert A. Jr, 1950. 'Nasalization in Haitian Creole', *Modern Language Notes*, 65: 474–8.

Hall, Robert A. Jr, 1953. Review of Caduff (1952), *Language*, 29: 534–5.

Hall, Robert A. Jr, 1976. *Proto-Romance Phonology*, New York: Elsevier.

Hall, Robert A. Jr, 1978. 'The reconstruction of Proto-Romance'. In Reinhold Kontzi (ed.), *Zur Entstellung der romanischen Sprachen*, Darmstadt: Wissenschaftliche Buchgesellschaft, 216–44.

Halle, Morris and Vergnaud, Jean-Roger, 1981. 'Harmony processes'. In N. Klein and W. Levelt (eds), *Crossing the Boundaries in Linguistics: Studies Presented to Manfred Bierwisch*, Boston: D. Reidel, 1–22.

Harms, Robert T., 1968. *Introduction to Phonological Theory*, Englewood Cliffs, NJ: Prentice-Hall.

Harris, John A., 1989. 'Towards a lexical analysis of sound change in progress', *JL*, 25: 35–56.

Harris, Martin and Vincent, Nigel (eds), 1988. *The Romance Languages*, London: Croom Helm.

Harris-Northall, Raymond, 1990. *Weakening Processes in the History of Spanish Consonants*, London: Routledge.

Hasselrot, Bengt, 1937. *Étude sur les dialectes d'Ollon et du district d'Aigle, Vaud*, Uppsala: Appelbergs.

Hattori, Shirô, Yamamoto, Kengo and Fujimura, Osamu, 1958. 'Nasalization of vowels in relation to nasals', *JASA*, 30: 267–74.

Haudricourt, A. G., 1967. 'La langue lakkia', *Bulletin de la société de linguistique de Paris*, 62: 165–82.

Hawkins, John A., 1988. 'Explaining language universals'. In John A. Hawkins (ed.), *Explaining Language Universals*, Oxford: Basil Blackwell, 3–28.

Hayes, Bruce, 1986a. 'Assimilation as spreading in Toba Batak', *LIn*, 17: 467–99.

Hayes, Bruce, 1986b. 'Inalterability in CV phonology', *Language*, 62: 321–51.

Hayes, Bruce, 1989. 'Compensatory lengthening in moraic phonology', *LIn*, 20: 253–306.

Hedinger, Robert, 1987. *The Manenguba Languages, Bantu A.15, Mbo Cluster. of Cameroon*, London: School of Oriental and African Studies.

Herbert, Robert K., 1977. 'Phonetic analysis in phonological description: Prenasalized consonants and Meinhof's rule', *Lingua*, 43: 339–73.

Herbert, Robert K., 1986. *Language Universals, Markedness Theory and Natural Phonetic Processes*, Berlin: Mouton de Gruyter.

Hering, Werner, 1936. *Die Mundart von Bozel, Savoyen*, Leipzig: Robert Noske.

Hernández-Chaves, Eduardo, Vogel, Irene and Clumeck, Harold, 1975. 'Rules, constraints, and the simplicity criterion: an analysis based on the acquisition of nasals in Chicano Spanish', *Nasálfest*, 231–48.

Hess, Susan, 1988. 'Universals of nasalization: Development of nasal finals in Wenling', *UCLA WPPh*, 70: 70–118.

Hock, Hans-Henrich, 1986. *Principles of Historical Linguistics*, Berlin: Mouton de Gruyter.

Hockett, Charles F., 1965. 'Sound change', *Language*, 41: 185–204.

Hoequist, Charles Jr, 1983. 'Syllable duration in stress-, syllable- and mora-timed languages', *Phonetica*, 40: 202–37.

Hollein, Harry and Hollein, Patricia (eds), 1979. *Current Issues in the Phonetic Sciences*, 2 vols, Amsterdam: John Benjamins.

Holmer, Nils M., 1962. *The Dialects of County Clare*, Dublin: Royal Irish Academy.

Holtus, Günter, Metzeltin, Michael and Schmitt, Christian (eds), 1988. *Lexikon der romanistischen Linguistik*, vol. 4: *Italienisch, Korsisch, Sardisch*, Tübingen: Max Niemeyer.

Hombert, Jean-Marie, 1986. 'The development of nasalized vowels in the Teke language group, Bantu.' In Koen Bogers and Harry van der Hulst (eds), *The Phonological Representation of Suprasegmentals*, Dordrecht: Foris, 359–79.

Hombert, Jean-Marie, 1987. 'Phonetic conditioning for the development of nasalization in Teke', *PICPhS*, 11, 2: 273–6.

Hombert, Jean-Marie and Puech, G., 1989. 'The evolution of nasal consonants in Northwestern Bantu languages'. Paper presented to the Second Conference on Laboratory Phonology, University of Edinburgh, 30 June–3 July.

Hombert, Jean-Marie, Ohala, John J. and Ewan, William G., 1979. 'Phonetic explanations for the development of tones', *Language*, 55: 37–58.

Hooper, Joan B., 1976. *Introduction to Natural Generative Phonology*, New York: Academic Press.

Hooper, Joan B., 1977. 'Substantive evidence for linearity: Vowel length and nasality in English', *CLS*, 13: 152–64.

House, Arthur S., 1957. 'Analog studies of nasal consonants', *JSHD*, 22: 190–204.

House, Arthur S. and Stevens, Kenneth N., 1956. 'Analog studies of the nasalization of vowels', *JSHD*, 21: 218–32.

Hualde, José I., 1989. 'Delinking processes in Romance'. In Carl Kirschner and Janet DeCesaris (eds), *Studies in Romance Linguistics*, Amsterdam: John Benjamins, 177–93.

Huffman, Mary, 1990. 'Implementation of nasal: Timing and articulatory landmarks', *UCLA WPPh*, 75: 1–149.

Huffman, Marie K. and Krakow, Rena A. (eds), 1993. *Nasals, Nasalization, and the Velum*, San Diego: Academic Press.

Hulst, Harry van der and Smith, Norval (eds), 1982. 'An overview of autosegmental and metrical phonology'. In Harry van der Hulst and Norval Smith (eds), *The Structure of Phonological Representations, Part 1*, Dordrecht: Foris, 1–46.

Hulst, Harry van der and Smith, Norval (eds), 1988. *Features, Segmental Structure and Harmony Processes, Part 1*, Dordrecht: Foris.

Hunter, George G. and Pike, Eunice V., 1969. 'The phonology and tone Sandhi of Molinos Mixtec', *Linguistics*, 47: 24–50.

Hyman, Larry M., 1975a. 'Nasal states and nasal processes', *Nasálfest*, 249–64.

Hyman, Larry M., 1975b. *Phonology, Theory and Analysis*, New York: Holt, Rinehart. and Winston.

Jackson, Kenneth H., 1955. *Contributions to the Study of Manx Phonology*. Edinburgh: Nelson.

Jakobs, Heike and Wetzels, Leo, 1988. 'Early French lenition: a formal account of an integrated sound change'. In Harry van der Hulst and Norval Smith (eds), *Features, Segmental Structure and Harmony Processes, Part 1*, Dordrecht: Foris, 108–129.

Jakobson, Roman and Halle, Morris, 1956. *Fundamentals of Language*, The Hague: Mouton.

Janson, Tore, 1982. 'Sound change and perceptual compensation'. In J. Peter Maher, Allan R. Bomhard and E. F. Konrad Koerner (eds), *Papers from the Third International Conference on Historical Linguistics*, Amsterdam: John Benjamins, 119–27.

Janson, Tore, 1991. 'Comments on Maddieson: Investigating linguistic universals', *PICPhS*, 12, 1: 355–8.

Javkin, Hector R., 1979. 'Phonetic universals and phonological change', *Report of the Phonological Laboratory, Berkeley*, 4: 1–107.

Jespersen, O., 1922. *Language, Its Nature, Development and Origin*, London: Allen and Unwin.

Johnson, Wyn, 1987. 'Lexical levels in French phonology', *Linguistics*, 25: 889–913.

Jones, Charles A. (ed.), *Historical Linguistics, Problems and Perspectives*, London: Longman.

Kahn, Daniel, 1980. *Syllable-Based Generalizations in English Phonology*, New York: Garland Publishing.

Karunatilake, W. S., 1974. 'A phonological sketch of Ceylon Gypsy-Telugu', *Anthropological Linguistics*, 16: 420–4.

Karttunen, Frances, 1976. 'Nahuatl Nasals', *LIn*, 7: 380–3.

Kawasaki, H., 1986. 'Phonetic explanations for phonological universals: the case of distinctive vowel nasalization'. In John J. Ohala and Jeri Jaeger (eds), *Experimental Phonology*, New York: Academic Press, 81–103.

Keating, Patricia, 1985a. 'CV phonology, experimental phonetics and coarticulation', *UCLA WPPh*, 62: 1–13.

Keating, Patricia, 1985b. 'Universal phonetics and the organization of grammars', In Victoria A. Fromkin (ed.), *Phonetic Linguistics, Essays in Honour of Peter Ladefoged*, Orlando: Academic Press, 115–32.

Keating, Patricia, 1988. 'The phonology–phonetics interface'. In Frederick J. Newmeyer (ed.), *Linguistics: The Cambridge Survey*, vol. 1: *Linguistic Theory: Foundations*, Cambridge: Cambridge University Press, 281–302.

Keating, Patricia, 1991. 'On phonetics/phonology interaction', *Phonetica*, 48: 221–2.

Kelkar, Ashok K. and Trisal, Pran Nath, 1964. 'Kashmiri word phonology: a first sketch', *Anthropological Linguistics*, 6: 13–22.

Kenstowicz, Michael, 1994. *Phonology in Generative Grammar*, Oxford: Blackwell.

Kiparsky, Paul, 1982. 'From cyclic phonology to lexical phonology'. In Harry van der Hulst and Norval Smith (eds), *The Structure of Phonological Representations, Part 1*, Dordrecht: Foris, 131–77.

Kiparsky, Paul, 1985. 'Some consequences of lexical phonology', *Phonology Yearbook*, 2: 85–138.

Kiparsky, Paul, 1988. 'Phonological change'. In Frederick J. Newmeyer (ed.), *Linguistics: The Cambridge Survey*, vol. 1: *Linguistic Theory: Foundations*, Cambridge: Cambridge University Press, 363–415.

Kirschner, Carl and DeCesaris, Janet (eds), 1989. *Studies in Romance Linguistics*, Amsterdam: John Benjamins.

Klausenburger, Jürgen, 1976. 'Règles synchroniques et diachroniques en phonologie française'. In Marcel Boudreault and Frankwalt Möhren (eds), *Actes du XIIIe Congrès International de Linguistique et Philologie Romanes*, Québec: Les Presses de l'Université Laval, vol. 1: 155–67.

Koekoek, Byron, 1955. *Zur Phonologie der Wiener Mundart*, Beiträge zu Deutschen Philologie 6, Giessen: W. Schmitz.

Kontzi, Reinhold (ed.), 1978. *Zur Entstellung der romanischen Sprachen*, Darmstadt: Wissenschaftliche Buchgesellschaft.

Krakow, Rena A. and Beddor, Patrice S., 1991. 'Coarticulation and the perception of nasality', *PICPhS*, 12, 5: 38–41.

Labov, William, 1981. 'Resolving the Neogrammarian controversy', *Language*, 57: 267–308.

Ladefoged, Peter, 1982. *A Course in Phonetics*, 2nd Edition, New York: Harcourt Brace Jovanovich.

Ladefoged, Peter and Maddieson, Ian, 1986. 'Some of the sounds of the world's languages', *UCLA WPPh*, 64: 1–137.

Ladefoged, Peter and Maddieson, Ian, 1990. 'Vowels of the world's languages', *JPhon*, 18: 93–122.

Lahiri, Aditi and Jongman, Allard, 1990. 'Intermediate level of analysis: Features or segments', *JPhon*, 18: 435–43.

Lahiri, Aditi and Marslen-Wilson, William, 1991. 'The mental representation of lexical form: a phonological approach to the recognition lexicon', *Cognition*, 38: 245–94.

Landry, Francis, 1985. *Étude synchronique des voyelles nasales dans le parler de Pubnico-Ouest*, mémoire de maîtrise, University of Montreal, Montreal.

Lass, Roger, 1980. *Explaining Language Change*, Cambridge: Cambridge University Press.

Lass, Roger, 1984. *Phonology*, Cambridge: Cambridge University Press.

Laver, John, 1980. *The Phonetic Description of Voice Quality*, Cambridge: Cambridge University Press.

Lehiste, Ilse, 1972. 'Manner of articulation. Parallel processing and the perception of duration'. In M. A. A. Tatham (ed.), *Occasional Papers 13, Symposium on Temporal Aspects of Speech Production, 11–13 January 1972, University of Essex*, Colchester, 1–24.

Lehiste, Ilse, 1976. 'Suprasegmental features of speech'. In Norman J. Lass (ed.), *Contemporary Issues in Experimental Phonetics*, New York: Academic Press, 225–42.

Lejeune, Michel, 1947. *Traité de phonétique grecque*, Paris: Klincksieck.

Léon, Pierre R. (ed.), 1968. *Recherches sur la structure phonique du français canadien*, Montreal: Marcel Didier.

Leonard, Clifford S., 1980. 'Comparative Grammar'. In Rebecca Posner and John N. Green (eds), *Trends in Romance Linguistics and Philology*, vol. 1: *Romance Comparative and Historical Linguistics*, The Hague: Mouton, 23–41.

Lepelley, René, 1974. *Le parler normand du Val de Saire, Manche*, Caen: Musée de Normandie.

Lepschy, Giulio C., 1965. 'Una fonologia milanese del 1606: il *Prissian da Milan della parnonzia Milanesa*', *ID*, 28: 143–80.

Levin, Juliette, 1988. 'Constraints on rime-internal syllabification in French: Eliminating truncation rules'. In David Birdsong and Jean-Pierre Montreuil (eds), *Advances in Romance Linguistics*, Dordrecht: Foris, 253–73.

Liberman, Mark and Pierrehumbert, Janet B., 1984. 'Intonational invariance under changes in pitch range and length'. In M. Aronoff and R. Oehrle (eds), *Language, Sound, Structure*, Cambridge, MA: MIT Press, 157–233.

Lightner, Theodore M., 1970. 'Why and how does vowel nasalization take place?', *Papers in Linguistics*, 2: 179–226.

Lightner, Theodore M., 1973. 'Remarks on universals in phonology'. In Maurice Gross (ed.), *Natural Languages, Proceedings of the First International Conference*, The Hague: Mouton, 13–50.

Lindblom, Björn, 1990. 'On the notion of "Possible speech sound"', *JPhon*, 18: 135–52.

Lindblom, Björn, 1992. 'Phonetic content in phonology'. In Wolfgang U. Dressler, Hans C. Lusckütsky, Oskar E. Pfeiffer and John R. Rennison (eds), *Phonologica 1988*, Cambridge, Cambridge University Press, 181–96.

Lindblom, Björn and Rapp, K., 1973. 'Some temporal regularities of spoken Swedish', *Papers in Linguistics from the University of Stockholm*, 21: 1–59.

Linthorst, P., 1973. *Les Voyelles nasales du français*, Groningen.

Lintz, L. B. and Sherman, D., 1961. 'Phonetic elements and perception of nasality', *JSHR*, 4: 381–96.

Lipski, John M., 1975. 'Brazilian Portuguese vowel nasalization: Secondary aspects', *Canadian Journal of Linguistics*, 20: 59–77.

Locke, John L., 1983. *Phonological Acquisition and Change*, New York: Academic Press.

Loporcaro, Michele, 1988. *Grammatica storica del dialetto di Altamura*, Pisa: Giardini.

Lorck, J. Etienne, 1893. *Altbergamaskische Sprachdenkmäler, IX-XV Jahrhundert*, Halle: Max Niemeyer.

Loriot, Robert, 1952. 'Les caractères originaux du dialecte du val Tujetsch, Tavetsch, dans la famille des parlers sursilvains'. In *Mélanges de linguistique et de littérature romanes offerts à Mario Roques*, Paris: Didier, vol. 3: 112–38.

Lovins, Julie B., 1978. ' "Nasal reduction" in English syllable codas', *PCLS*, 14: 241–53.

Lubker, James, 1968. 'An electromyographic-cinefluorographic investigation of velar function during normal speech production', *CPJ*, 5: 1–18.

Lubker, J. and Moll, K. L., 1965. 'Simultaneous oral-nasal airflow measurements and cinefluorographic observations during speech production', *CPJ*, 2: 257–72.

McCarthy, John, 1988. 'Feature geometry and dependency: a review', *Phonetica*, 45: 84–108.

McCarthy, John, 1989. 'Guttural Phonology', manuscript, University of Massachusetts, Amherst.

McDonald, E. T. and Baker, H. K., 1951. 'An integration of research on clinical observation', *JSHD*, 16: 9–20.

McMahon, April M. S., 1991. 'Lexical phonology and sound change: the case of the Scottish vowel length rule', *JL*, 27: 29–53.

Mackiewicz-Krassowska, Halina, 1977. 'Nasality in Australian English', *Working Papers of the Speech and Language Research Centre*, Macquarie University, 27–40.

Maddieson, Ian, 1984. *Patterns of Sounds*, Cambridge: Cambridge University Press.

Maeda, Shinji, 1982. 'The role of the sinus cavities in the production of nasal vowels', Paper delivered at IEEE/ICASSP 82, Paris, May.

Maeda, Shinji, 1989. 'The distance between two nasal spectral peaks as an acoustic measure for vowel nasalization', *Recueil de publications et communications 1988 en traitement automatique de la parole*, part 2, Lannion: Centre National d'Études des Télécommunications, 275–304.

Maeda, Shinji, 1993. 'Acoustics of vowel nasalization and articulatory shifts in French nasal vowels'. In Marie K. Huffman and Rena A. Krakow (eds), *Nasals, Nasalization and The Velum*, San Diego: Academic Press, 147–67.

Mainoldi, Pietro, 1950. *Manuale dell'odierno dialetto bolognese*, Bologna: Mareggiani.

Mainoldi, Pietro, 1967. *Vocabolario del dialetto bolognese*, Bologna: Forni.

Major, Roy C., 1981. 'Stress-timing in Brazilian Portuguese', *JPhon*, 9: 343–51.

Major, Roy C., 1985. 'Stress and rhythm in Brazilian Portuguese', *Language*, 61: 259–82.

Malagoli, Giuseppe, 1910. 'Studi sui dialetti reggiani, Fonologia del dialetto di Novellara', *AGI*, 17: 29–197.

Malagoli, Giuseppe, 1930. 'Fonologia del dialetto di Lizzano in Belvedere, Appennino bolognese', *ID*, 6: 125–96.

Malagoli, Giuseppe, 1934. 'Studi sui dialetti reggiani, Fonologia del dialetto di Valèstra. Medio Appennino reggiano', *ID*, 10: 63–110.

Malagoli, Giuseppe, 1943. 'Intorno ai dialetti dell'alta montagna reggiana', *ID*, 19: 1–29.

Malécot, André, 1956. 'Acoustic cues for nasal consonants', *Language*, 32: 274–84.

Malécot, André, 1960. 'Vowel nasality as a distinctive feature in American English', *Language*, 36: 222–9.

Mancini, Anna Maria, 1986. 'Note sul dialetto di Senigallia', *Quaderni dell'Istituto di Linguistica dell'Università di Urbino*, 4: 195–248.

Manuel, Sharon, 1991. 'Some phonetic bases for the relative malleability of syllable-final versus syllable-initial consonants', *PICPhS*, 12, 5: 118–21.

Martin, Lothar, 1957. *Die Mundartlandschaft der Mittleren Fulda, Kreis Rotenburg und Hersfeld*, *DDG*, 44, Marburg: Elwert.

Martinet, André, 1955. *Économie des changements phonétiques*, Berne: Francke.

Martins, Maria Raquel Delgado, 1975. 'Vogais e consoantes do português: Estatística de ocorrência, duração e intensidade', *Boletim de Filologia*, 24: 1–11.

Massariello Merzagora, Giovanna, 1988. *Lombardia*, Pisa: Pacini.

Massengill, R. and Bryson, M., 1967. 'A study of velopharyngeal function as related to perceived nasality of vowels utilizing a cinefluorographic television monitor', *Folia Phoniatrica*, 19: 45–52.

Matte, Edouard Joseph, 1984. 'Réexamen de la doctrine traditionnelle sur les voyelles nasales du français', *RPh*, 38: 15–31.

Mayerthaler, Willi, 1982. 'Markiertheit in der Phonologie'. In Theo Vennemann (ed.), *Silben, Segmente, Akzente*, Tübingen: Niemeyer, 205–46.

Melillo, Armistizio Matteo, 1977. *Corsica*, Pisa: Pacini.

Merlo, Clemente, 1951. *Profilo fonetico dei dialetti della Valtellina*, Wiesbaden: Franz Steiner for the Akademie der Wissenschaften und der Literatur in Mainz.

Minghè, Gianna, 1950. *Caratteri e varietà dell'odierna parlata bolognese*, tesi di laurea, University of Bologna.

Mioni, Alberto M. and Trumper, John, 1977. 'Per un'analisi del «continuum» linguistico veneto'. In Raffaele Simone and Giulianella Ruggiero (eds), *Aspetti sociolinguistici dell'Italia contemporanea*, Rome: Bulzoni, vol.1: 329–72.

Moll, K., 1962. 'Velopharyngeal closure on vowels', *JSHR*, 5: 30–7.

Montes, José Joaquín, 1979. 'Un rasgo dialectal del occidente de Colombia: -n > -m'. In *Homenaje a Fernando Antonio Martínez*, Bogotá: Instituto Caro y Cuervo, 215–20.

Montreuil. Jean-Pierre, 1991. 'Effetti di località in gallo-italico'. In Giannelli et al. (eds), 281–8.

Morin, Yves-Charles, 1977. 'Nasalization and diphthongization in Marais Vendéen French'. In M. P. Hagiwara (ed.), *Studies in Romance Linguistics*, Rowley, MA: Newbury House, 125–144.

Morin, Yves-Charles, 1986. 'La loi de position ou de l'explication en phonologie historique', *Revue québécoise de linguistique*, 15: 199–232.

Nakata, K., 1959. 'Synthesis and perception of nasal consonants', *JASA*, 31: 661–6.

Narang, G. C. and Becker, Donald, 1971. 'Aspiration and nasalization in the generative phonology of Hindi-Urdu', *Language* 47: 646–67.

Nespor, Marina and Vogel, Irene, 1979. 'Clash avoidance in Italian', *LIn*, 10: 467–82.

Nespor, Marina and Vogel, Irene, 1986. *Prosodic Phonology*, Dordrecht: Foris.

Newmeyer, Frederick J. (ed.), 1988. *Linguistics: the Cambridge Survey*, vol.1: *Linguistic Theory: Foundations*, Cambridge: Cambridge University Press.

Nicoli, Franco, 1983. *Grammatica milanese*, Busto Arsizio: Bramante.

Nihalani, Paroo, 1974. 'An aerodynamic study of stops in Sindhi', *Phonetica*, 29: 193–224.

Nihalani, Paroo, 1991. 'Low level phonetic implementation rules: Evidence from Sindhi', *PICPhS*, 12, 2: 134–7.

Norman, Jerry, 1988. *Chinese*, Cambridge: Cambridge University Press.

Ohala, John J., 1971. 'The role of physiological and acoustic models in explaining the direction of sound change', *Project on Linguistic Analysis Reports*, 2nd series, 15: 25–40.

Ohala, John J., 1974a. 'Experimental historical phonology'. In J. C. Anderson and C. Jones (eds) vol. 2, *Historical Linguistics*, Amsterdam: North-Holland, 353–89.

Ohala, John J., 1974b. 'Phonetic explanation in phonology'. In Anthony Bruck, Robert A. Fox and Michael W. La Galy (eds), *Papers from the Parasession on Natural Phonology*, Chicago: Chicago Linguistics, 251–74.

Ohala, John J., 1975. 'Phonetic explanations for nasal sound patterns', *Nasálfest*, 289–316.

Ohala, John J., 1980a. 'The application of phonological universals in speech pathology'. In N. J. Lass (ed.), *Speech and Language: Advances in Basic Research and Practice*, vol. 3, New York: Academic Press, 75–97.

Ohala, John J., 1980b. 'Introduction to Symposium no. 1: Phonetic universals in phonological systems and their explanation', *PICPhS*, 9, 3: 181–5.

Ohala, John J., 1981. 'The listener as a source of sound change'. In C. S. Masek, L. A. Hendrick and M. F. Miller (eds), *Papers from the Parasession on Language and Behaviour*, Chicago: Chicago Linguistic Society, 178–203.

Ohala, John J., 1983. 'The phonological end justifies any means'. In S. Hattori and K. Inoue (eds), *Proceedings of the Thirteenth International Congress of Linguists*, Tokyo: Sanseido Shoten.

Ohala, John J., 1986. 'Phonological evidence for top-down processing in speech perception'. In Joseph S. Perkell and Dennis H. Klatt (eds), *Invariance and Variability in Speech Processes*, Hillsdale, NJ: Lawrence Erlbaum Associates, 386–97.

Ohala, John J., 1988. 'Sound change is drawn from a pool of synchronic variation', *Berkeley Cognitive Science Report* 53: 1–27. Also published in L. E. Breivik and E. H. Jahr (eds), *Language Change: Contributions to the Study of its Causes*, Berlin: Mouton de Gruyter, 173–98.

Ohala, John J., 1990a. *What's Cognitive, What's Not in Sound Change*, Duisburg: Linguistic Agency University of Duisburg, Series A, Paper No. 297.

Ohala, John J., 1990b. 'The phonetics and phonology of aspects of assimilation'. In John Kingston and Mary E. Beckman (eds), *Papers in Laboratory Phonology I, Between the Grammar and Physics of Speech*, Cambridge: Cambridge University Press, 258–75.

Ohala, John J., 1993. 'The phonetics of sound change'. In Charles A. Jones (ed.), *Historical Linguistics, Problems and Perspectives*, London: Longman, 237–78.

Ohala, John J. and Kawasaki, Haruko, 1984. 'Prosodic phonology and phonetics', *Phonology Yearbook*, 1: 113–27.

Ohala, John J. and Ohala, Manjari, 1993. 'The phonetics of nasal phonology: Theorems and data'. In Marie K. Huffman and Rena A. Krakow (eds), *Nasals, Nasalization and the Velum*, San Diego: Academic Press, 225–49.

Ohala, John J. and Solé, Maria Josep, 1991. 'Differentiating between phonetic and phonological processes: the case of nasalization', *PICPhS*, 12, 2: 110–13.

Ohala, Manjari, 1975. 'Nasals and nasalization in Hindi', *Nasálfest*, 317–32.

Ohala, Manjari, 1983. *Aspects of Hindi Phonology*, Delhi: Motilal Banarsidan.

Ohala, Manjari and Ohala, John J., 1991. 'Epenthetic nasals in the historical phonology of Hindi', *PICPhS*, 12, 3: 126–9.

Orešnik, Janez and Pétursson, Magnús, 1977. 'Quantity in Modern Icelandic', *Arkív för Nordisk Filologi*, 92: 155–71.

Pagliuca, William and Mowrey, Richard, 1987. 'Articulatory evolution'. In Anna Giacalone Ramat, Onofrio Carruba and Giuliano Bernini (eds), *Papers from the Seventh International Conference on Historical Linguistics*, Amsterdam: John Benjamins, 459–72.

Parker, Frank, 1977. 'Perceptual cues and phonological change', *JPhon*, 5: 97–106.

Parkinson, Stephen, 1979. *The Phonological Analysis of Nasal Vowels in Modern European Portuguese*, Ph.D. dissertation, University of Cambridge.

Parodi, E. G., 1902. 'Studj liguri, il dialetto di Genova dal secolo XVI ai nostri giorni', *AGI*, 16: 105–60, 333–65.

Parry, Margaret H., 1984. *The Dialect of Cairo Montenotte*, Ph.D. dissertation, University College of Wales, Aberystwyth.

Passy, P., 1890. *Étude sur les changements phonétiques*, Paris: Firmin-Didot.

Patterson, George, 1978. 'Vers une description d'un parler acadien', *Revue de l'Université de Moncton*, 2: 107–13.

Pavia, Luigi, 1928. *Sulla parlata milanese e suoi connessi*, Bergamo: author.

Pellegrini, Giovan Battista, 1950. *Grammatica storica spagnola*, Bari: Leonardo da Vinci.

Pellegrini, Giovan Battista, 1975. *Saggi di linguistica italiana*, Turin: Boringhieri.

Pellegrini, Giovan Battista, 1977. *Carta dei dialetti d'Italia*, text and map, Pisa: Pacini.

Pelliciardi, Ferdinando, 1977. *Grammatica del dialetto romagnolo: la lèngva dla mi tèra*, Imola: Galeati.

Pensado, Carmen, 1985. 'Nu̯ en gallego y portugués. Multiplicidad de tratamientos como consecuencia de la interacción de cambios fonéticos', *Verba*, 12: 31–60.

Pensado, Carmen, 1986. 'El contacto de sílabas como origen de las evoluciones de las secuencias de consonante + wau en romance', *Revista de filología románica*, 4: 73–110.

Pensado, Carmen, 1989. 'How do unnatural syllabifications arise? The case of consonant + glide in Vulgar Latin', *Folia Linguistica Historica*, 8: 115–42.

Perkins, Revere D., 1989. 'Statistical techniques for determining language sample size', *Studies in Language*, 13: 293–315.

Perry, Thomas A., 1990. 'German vowel and syllable contact'. In Jerold A. Edmondson, Crawford Fagin and Peter Mühlhäusler (eds), *Development and Diversity, Language Variation across Time and Space*, Arlington, University of Texas and Summer Institute of Linguistics, 95–114.

Petrovici, Emile, 1930. *De la nasalité en roumain*, Cluj: Insitutul de Arte Grafice 'Ardealul'.

Piagnoli, Agide, 1904. *Fonetica parmigiana*, Antonio Boselli (ed.), Turin: Tipografia Salesiana.

Picard, Marc, 1995. 'Issues in the glottalic theory of Indo-European: the comparative method, typology and naturalness', *Word*, 46: 225–35.

Pierrehumbert, Janet, 1991. 'The whole theory of sound structure', *Phonetica*, 48: 223–32.

Piggott, Glyn L., 1987. 'On the autonomy of the feature nasal', *CLS*, 23: 223–38.

Piggott, Glyn L., 1988a. 'A parametric approach to nasal harmony'. In Harry van der Hulst and Norval Smith (eds), *Features, Segmental Structure and Harmony Processes, Part 1*, Dordrecht: Foris, 131–67.

Piggott, Glyn L., 1988b. 'The parameters of nasalization', *McGill Working Papers in Linguistics*, 5: 128–77.

Pisani, Vittore, 1952. *Grammatica latina storica e comparativa*, Turin: Rosenberg and Sellier, 2nd edition.

Plangg, Guntram, 1985. 'Phonemstrukturen im Surselvischen, Tavetsch'. In Guntram Plangg and M. Iliescu (eds), *Akten der Theodor Gartner-Tagung, Rätoromanisch und Rumänisch in Vill/Innsbruck 1985*, Innsbruck: Institut für Romanistik der Leopold-Franzens-Universität, 105–21.

Plénat, Marc, 1985. 'Sur quelques aspects de la nasalisation en français standard', *Cahiers de grammaire*, 9: 139–62.

Plénat, Marc, 1987. 'On the structure of the rime in French', *Linguistics*, 25: 867–87.

Plomteux, Hugo, 1975. *I dialetti della Liguria orientale odierna, la val Graveglia*, 2 vols, Bologna: Pàtron.

Poggi, Luisa, 1934. *Il vocalismo nei dialetti emiliani da Bologna ad Imola*, tesi di laurea, University of Bologna, 1934–5.

Pope, Mildred K., 1952. *From Latin to Modern French with Especial Consideration of Anglo-Norman*, Manchester: Manchester University Press, 2nd edition.

Posner, Rebecca, 1961. *Consonantal Dissimilation in the Romance Languages*, Oxford: Basil Blackwell.

Posner, Rebecca, 1971. 'On synchronic and diachronic rules: French nasalization', *Lingua*, 27: 184–97.

Postal, P., 1968. *Aspects of Phonological Theory*, University Park, PA: University of Pennsylvania Press.

Pulleyblank, Douglas, 1995. 'Feature geometry and underspecification'. In Jacques Durand and Francis Katamba (eds), *Frontiers of Phonology*, London: Longman, 3–33.

Raphael, Lawrence J., Dorman M. F., Freeman, Frances and Tobin, Charles, 1975. 'Vowel and nasal duration as cues to voicing in word-final stop consonants: Spectrographic and perceptual studies', *JSHR*, 18: 389–400.

Razzi, Lucia Matelda, 1984. *Il dialetto di Salò*, Brescia: Grafo.

Recasens, Daniel, 1991. 'Timing in Catalan', *PICPhS*, 12, 4: 230–3.

Recasens i Vives, Daniel, 1996. *Estudis de fonètica experimental del català oriental central*, Montserrat: Abadia de Montserrat.

Reenen, Pieter Th. van, 1982a. *Phonetic Feature Definitions: Their Integration into Phonology and their Relation to Speech, a Case Study of the Feature Nasal*, Dordrecht: Foris.

Reenen, Pieter Th. van, 1982b. 'Voyelles nasales en ancien français non suivies de consonne nasale', *Rapports-Het Franse Boek*, 52: 132–43.

Reenen, Pieter Th. van, 1985. 'La fiabilité des données linguistiques, à propos de la formation des voyelles nasales en ancien français'. In Aina Moll (ed.), *Actes del XVIè Congrés Internacional de Lingüística i Filologia Romàniques*, Palma de Mallorca: Moll, vol. 2: 37–51.

Reenen, Pieter Th. van, 1987. 'La formation des voyelles nasales en ancien français d'après le témoignage des assonances'. In Brigitte Kampers-Manhe and Co Vet (eds), *Études de linguistique française offertes à Robert de Dardel*, Amsterdam: Rodopi, 127–41.

Repetti, Lori D., 1989. *The Bimoraic Norm of Tonic Syllables in Italo-Romance*, Ph.D. dissertation, University of California, Los Angeles.

Repp, Bruno H. and Svastikula, Katyanee, 1987. 'Perception of the [m]–[n] distinction in VC syllables', *Haskins SR*, 91: 157–75.

Reuse, Willem J. de, 1987. 'La phonologie du français de la région de Charleroi (Belgique et ses rapports avec le wallon)', *La Linguistique*, 23, 2 : 99–115.

Richter, Lutoslawa, 1987. 'Modelling of the Rhythmic Structure of Utterances in Polish', *Studia Phonetica Posnaniensa*, 1: 91–126.

Rietveld, A. C. M. and Frauenfelder, U. H., 1987. 'The effect of syllable structure on vowel duration', *PICPhS*, 11, 4: 28–31.

Rizzi, Elena, 1984. 'L'apofonia nel dialetto di Bologna: una proposta di analisi morfofonemica', *RID*, 8: 91–108.

Roach, Peter, 1982. 'On the distinction between "stress-timed" and "syllable-timed" languages'. In David Crystal (ed.), *Linguistic Controversies*, London: Edward Arnold, 73–9.

Robinson, C. D. W., 1984. *Phonologie du Gunu*, Paris: SELAF.

Rochet, Anne P.and Rochet, Bernard L., 1991. 'The effect of vowel height on patterns of assimilation nasality in French and English', *PICPhS*, 12, 3: 54–7.

Rochet, Bernard L., 1976. *The Formation and Evolution of the French Nasal Vowels*, Tübingen: Max Niemeyer.

Rohlfs, Gerhard, 1966. *Grammatica storica della lingua italiana e dei suoi dialetti*, vol. 1: *Fonetica*, Turin: Giulio Einaudi.

Rohlfs, Gerhard, 1968. *Grammatica storica della lingua italiana e dei suoi dialetti*, vol. 2: *Morfologia*, Turin: Giulio Einaudi.

Rohlfs, Gerhard, 1969. *Grammatica storica della lingua italiana e dei suoi dialetti*, vol. 3: *Sintassi e formazione delle parole*, Turin: Giulio Einaudi.

Rohlfs, Gerhard, 1970. *Le Gascon. Études de philologie pyrénéenne*, 2nd edition. Tübingen: Max Niemeyer.

Rossi, Mario, 1976. *Contributions à la méthodologie de l'analyse linguistique avec application à la description phonétique du parler de Rossano, Province de Massa, Italie*, Lille: Atelier National Réproduction des Thèses, Université de Lille III, vol. 1.

Rousselot, P.-J., 1924. *Principes de phonétique expérimentale*, 2nd edition. vol. 1. Paris: H. Didier.

Rubach, Jerzy, 1977. 'Nasalization in Polish', *JPhon*, 5: 17–25.

Rubach, Jerzy, 1985. 'Lexical phonology: Lexical and post-lexical derivations', *Phonology Yearbook*, 2: 157–72.

Ruhlen, Merritt, 1973. 'Nasal Vowels', *Working Papers on Language Universals*, 12: 1–36.

Ruhlen, Merritt, 1979. 'On the origin and evolution of French nasal vowels', *RomPh*, 32: 321–35.

Rupp, Theodor, 1963. *Lautlehre der Mundarten von Domat, Trin und Flem*, Zürich: author.

Sagey, Elizabeth, 1986. *The Representation of Features and Relations in Nonlinear Phonology*, Ph.D. dissertation, Massachusetts Institute of Technology, Cambridge, MA.

Saltarelli, Mario, 1983. 'The mora unit in Italian phonology', *Folia Linguistica*, 17: 7–24.

Salvioni, Carlo, 1884. *Fonetica del dialetto moderno della città di Milano*, Turin: Loescher.

Salvioni, Carlo, 1975. 'Fonetica e morfologia del dialetto milanese', *ID*, 38: 1–46.

Sampson, Rodney, 1981. 'Subphonemic length variation in Italian consonants', *Word*, 32: 35–44.

Sanga, Glauco, 1979. *Dialetto e folklore, Ricerca a Cigole*, Milan: Silvana.

Sanga, Glauco, 1987a. 'Fonetica storica del dialetto di Bergamo'. In Glauco Sanga (ed.), *Lingua e dialetti di Bergamo e delle valli*, Bergamo: Lubrina, vol. 1, 37–64.

Sanga, Glauco (ed.), 1987b. *Lingua e dialetti di Bergamo e delle valli*, 3 vols, Bergamo: Lubrina.

Sanga, Glauco, 1988a. 'La lunghezza vocalica nel milanese e la coscienza fonologica dei parlanti', *RPh*, 41: 290–7.

Sanga, Glauco, 1988b. 'Due Lombardie', *RID*, 12: 173–202.

Sanga, Glauco and Bernini, Giuliano, 1987. 'Fonologia del dialetto di Bergamo'. In Glauco Sanga (ed.), *Lingua e dialetti di Bergamo e delle valli*, Bergamo: Lubrina, vol. 1: 65–81.

Sankoff, David and Rousseau, Pascale, 1989. 'Statistical evidence for rule ordering', *Language Variation and Change*, 1: 1–18.

Saunders, Gladys E., 1975. *A Comparative Study of the Gallo-Italian Dialects*, Ph.D. dissertation, University of Michigan.

Saunders, Gladys E., 1978. 'Evolution of vowel length in Gallo-Italian', *General Linguistics*, 18: 14–27.

Saunders, Gladys E., 1979. 'Speculations on a contact-induced phonological change in Gallo-Italian'. In Harry Hollein and Patricia Hollein (eds), *Current Issues in the Phonetic Sciences*, Amsterdam: John Benjamins, 1139–47.

Schachter, Paul and Fromkin, Victoria, 1968. *A Phonology of Akan: Akuapem, Asante, Fante*, Los Angeles: University of California.

Schane, Sanford A., 1968. *French Phonology and Morphology*, Cambridge, MA: MIT Press.

Schane, Sanford A., 1972. 'Natural rules in phonology'. In Robert E. Stockwell and Ronald Macaulay (eds), *Linguistic Change and Generative Theory*, Bloomington: Indiana University Press, 199–229.

Schane, Sanford A., 1973a. *Generative Phonology*, Englewood Cliffs, NJ: Prentice-Hall.

Schane, Sanford A., 1973b. 'The treatment of phonological exceptions: the evidence from French'. In Braj B. Kachru, Robert B. Lees, Yakov Malkiel, Angelina Pietrangeli, and Sol Saporta (eds), *Issues in Linguistics, Papers in Honour of Henry and Renée Kahane*, Urbana: University of Illinois Press, 822–35.

Schein, Barry and Steriade, Donca, 1986. 'On geminates', *LIn*, 17: 691–744.

Schirmunski, Viktor M., 1962. *Deutsche Mundarten*, Berlin: Akademische-Verlag.

Schneider, Klaus Dieter, 1968. *Die Mundart von Ramosch*, Berlin: Philosophy Faculty, Free University of Berlin.

Schorta, Andrea, 1946. *Schweizer Dialekte in Text und Ton, Rätoromanische und rätolombardische Mundarten*, Frauenfeld: Huber.

Schourup, Lawrence C., 1973. 'A cross-language study of vowel nasalization', *Ohio State University Working Papers in Linguistics*, 15: 190–221.

Schüle, Rose Claire, 1963. *Inventaire lexicologique du parler de Nendaz, Valais*, Bern: A. Francke.

Schürr, Friedrich, 1917. *Romagnolische Mundarten. Sprachproben in phonetische Transkription auf Grund phonographischer Aufnahmen*, Sitzungsberichte der philosophisch-historische Klasse der Akademie der Wissenschaften, Vienna, vol. 181/2.

Schürr, Friedrich, 1918. *Romagnolische Dialektstudien I, Lautlehre alter Texte*, Sitzungsberichte der philosophisch-historische Klasse der Akademie der Wissenschaften, Vienna, vol. 187/4.

Schürr, Friedrich, 1919. *Romagnolische Dialektstudien II, Lautlehre lebender Mundarten*, Sitzungsberichte der philosophisch-historische Klasse der Akademie der Wissenschaften, Vienna, vol. 188/1.

Schürr, Friedrich, 1956. *Nuovi contributi allo studio dei dialetti romagnoli*, Milan: Istituto Lombardo di Scienze e Lettere.

Schürr, Friedrich, 1974. *La voce della Romagna, profilo linguistico-letterario*, Ravenna: Edizioni del Girasole.

Schwartz, Rudolf, 1939. *Die pfälsische Mundart der Deutschen in Illischestie (Bukowina)*, Borna: Robert Noske.

Selkirk, Elisabeth O., 1972. *The Phrase Phonology of English and French*, Ph.D. dissertation, Massachusetts Institute of Technology, Cambridge, MA.

Sievers, E., 1901. *Grundzüge der Phonetik*, Leipzig: Breitkopf and Härtel.

Simone, Raffaele and Vignuzzi, Ugo (eds), 1977. *Problemi della ricostruzione in linguistica*, Rome: Bulzoni.

Smith, Jan, 1981. 'Fast speech phenomena in Venezuelan Spanish', *Minnesota Papers in Linguistics and Philosophy of Language*, 7: 36–45.

Smith, Neilson V., 1973. *The Acquisition of Phonology, a Case Study*, Cambridge: Cambridge University Press.

Srivastav, Veneeta, 1989. 'The absence of ṼC[+voi] sequences in Hindi: The interaction of global constraints and rule application', *CLS*, 25: 420–33.

Srivastava, R. N., 1972. 'Whitney's interpretation of *anusvara* and Generative Phonology', *Indian Linguistics*, 33: 203–19.

Stampe, David, 1969. 'The acquisition of phonetic representation', *CLS*, 5: 443–54.

Steriade, Donca, 1988. 'Review article, Clements, G. N. and J. Keyser, *CV Phonology*', *Language*, 64: 118–29.

Stevens, Kenneth N., Fant, Gunnar and Hawkins, Sarah, 1987. 'Some acoustical and perceptual characteristics of nasal vowels'. In Robert Channon and Linda Shockey (eds), *In Honor of Ilse Lehiste*, Dordrecht: Foris, 241–54.

Straka, Georges, 1955. 'Remarques sue les voyelles nasales, leur origine et leur évolution en français', *RLiR*, 19: 245–74.

Sturtevant, Edgar H., 1940. *The Pronunciation of Greek and Latin*, Philadelphia, PA: University of Pennsylvania Press, 2nd edition.

Swiggers, Pierre, 1984. 'The relevance of autosegmental phonology for diachronic linguistics', *Folia Linguistica Historica*, 5: 305–11.

Szabo, Robert K., 1973. 'The proper underlying representation for nasalized vowels', *Glossa*, 7: 1–40.

Tagliavini, Carlo, 1962. *Fonetica e morfologia storica del latino*, Bologna: Pàtron, 3rd edition.

Taylor, John R. and Uys, Johan Z., 1988. 'Notes on the Afrikaans vowel system', *Leuvense Bijdragen*, 77: 129–49.

Tekavčić, Pavao, 1972. *Grammatica storica dell'italiano*, vol. 1: *Fonematica*, Bologna: Il Mulino.

Tekavčić, Pavao, 1985. 'Problemi, esperienze, prospettive nelle ricerche di linguistica istroromanza'. In Ana María Cano González (ed.), *Homenaje a Alvaro Galmés de Fuentes*, Madrid: Editorial Gredos, vol. 1: 299–315.

Terbeek, Dale and Harshman, Richard, 1971. 'Cross-language differences in the perception of natural vowel sounds', *UCLA WPPh*, 19: 26–38.

Terrell, Tracy, 1975. 'La nasal implosiva y final en el español de Cuba', *Anuario de Letras*, 13: 257–71.

Thinnes, Norbert, 1981. *Untersuchungen zur Variation nasaler Vokale*, Wiesbaden: Franz Steiner.

Thomas, Kimberley D., 1991. 'Vowel length and pitch in Yavapai', *UCLA WPPh*, 78: 87–96.

Tinelli, Henri, 1974. 'Generative and creolization processes: nasality in Haitian Creole', *Lingua*, 33: 343–66.

Tiraboschi, Antonio, 1873. *Vocabolario dei dialetti bergamaschi antichi e moderni*, Bergamo: Fratelli Bolis, 2nd edition.

Tiraboschi, Antonio, 1879. *Appendici al vocabolario dei dialetti bergamaschi*, Bergamo: Fratelli Bolis.

Toja, Gianluigi, 1954. *La lingua della poesia bolognese del secolo XIII*, Berlin: Akademie-Verlag.

Toledo, Guillermo Andrés, 1989. 'Organización temporal del español I: compresión silábica en la palabra', *Hispanic Linguistics*, 2: 209–28.

Tolstoya, N. I., 1981. *The Panjabi Language*, translated by G. L. Campbell, London: Routledge and Kegan Paul.

Tomasoni, Piera, 1984. 'Ritornando a un'antica passione bergamasca', *Studi di filologia italiana*, 62: 59–107.

Tranel, Bernard, 1981. *Concreteness in Generative Phonology*, Berkeley: University of California Press.

Tranel, Bernard, 1991. 'CVC light syllables, geminates and moraic theory', *Phonology*, 8: 291–302.

Trauzzi, Alberto, 1901. 'Introduzione sulla fonetica e sulla morfologia del dialetto'. In Gaspare Ungarelli (ed.), *Vocabolario del dialetto di Bologna, con un'introduzione del prof. Alberto Trauzzi sulla fonetica e sulla morfologia,* Bologna, xiii–xli.

Trigo, Rosario Lorenza Ferre, 1988. *On the Phonological Behaviour of Nasal Glides*, Ph.D. dissertation, Massachusetts Institute of Technology, Cambridge, MA.

Trigo, Rosario Lorenza Ferre, 1990. 'On vowel nasalization and denasalization', manuscript, University of Boston.

Trigo, Rosario Lorenza Ferre, 1991. 'On pharynx–larynx interactions', *Phonology*, 8: 113–36.

Trommelen, Mieke, 1984. *The Syllable in Dutch with Special Reference to Diminutive Formation*, Dordrecht: Foris.

Tropea, Giovanni, 1966. 'Effetti di simbiosi linguistica nelle parlate gallo-italiche di Aidone, Nicosia e Novara di Sicilia', *Bollettino dell'Atlante Linguistico Italiano* Nuova serie, 13/14: 3–50.

Trumper, John, 1977. 'Ricostruzione nell'Italia settentrionale: sistemi consonantici, considerazioni sociolinguistiche nella diacronia'. In Raffaele Simone and Ugo Vignuzzi (eds), *Problemi della ricostruzione in linguistica*, Rome: Bulzoni, 259–310.

Trumper, John, Romito, Luigi and Maddalon, Marta, 1991. 'Double consonants, isochrony, and *raddoppiamento sintattico*: Some reflections'. In Pier Marco Bertinetto, Michael Kenstowicz and Michele Loporcaro (eds), *Certamen Phonologicum II*, Turin: Rosenberg and Sellier, 329–60.

Tuttle, Edward F., 1991. 'Nasalization in Northern Italy: Syllabic constraints and strength scales as developmental parameters', *Rivista di linguistica*. 3: 23–92.

Uber, Diane Ringer, 1984. 'Phonological implications of the perception of -s and -n in Puerto Rican Spanish'. In Philip Baldi (ed.), *Papers of the Twelfth Linguistic Symposium on Romance Linguistics*. Amsterdam: John Benjamins, 287–99.

Uguzzoni, Arianna, 1971. 'Quantità fonetica e quantità fonematica nell'area dialettale frignanese', *ID*, 34: 115–36.

Uguzzoni, Arianna, 1975. 'Appunti sulla evoluzione del sistema vocalico di un dialetto frignanese', *ID*, 38: 41–76.

Umeda, Noriko, 1977. 'Consonant duration in American English', *JASA*, 61: 846–58.

Väänänen, Veikko, 1967. *Introduction au latin vulgaire*, 2nd edition. Paris: Klincksieck.

Vagges, J., Ferrero, E., Magno Caldognetto, E. and Lavagnoli, C., 1978. 'Some acoustic characteristics of Italian consonants', *JIL*, 3: 69–85.

Valdman, Albert, 1970. 'Nasalization in Creole French', *PICPhS*, 6: 967–70.

Valdman, Albert, 1974. 'Long vowels and underlying postvocalic /r/ in Creole French'. In R. Joe Campbell, Mark G. Goldin and Mary Clayton Wang (eds), *Linguistic Studies in Romance Languages*, Washington DC: Georgetown University Press.

Valdman, Albert, 1977. 'On the structure and origin of Creole French'. In M. P. Hagiwara (ed.), *Studies in Romance Linguistics*, Rowley, MA: Newbury House, 278–301.

Vayra, Mario, 1989. 'Slittamenti timbrici e variazioni di durata nel vocalismo dell'italiano standard', *Quaderni del Laboratorio di Linguistica*, 3: 73–101.

Vayra, Mario, 1991. 'Appunti su un fenomeno di "centralizzazione" nel vocalismo dell'italiano standard'. In Giannelli et al. (eds), 195–212.

Vayra, Mario, Avesani, Cinzia and Fowler, Carol A., 1984. 'Patterns of temporal compression in spoken Italian', *PICPhS*, 10: 541–6.

Vincent, Nigel, 1978. 'Is sound change teleological?'. In Jacek Fisiak (ed.), *Recent Developments in Historical Linguistics*, The Hague: Mouton, 409–30.

Vincent, Nigel, 1988a. 'Italian'. In Martin Harris and Nigel Vincent (eds), *The Romance Languages*, London: Croom Helm, 279–313.

Vincent, Nigel, 1988b. 'Latin'. In Martin Harris and Nigel Vincent (eds), *The Romance Languages*, London: Croom Helm, 26–78.

Vincent, Nigel, 1988c. 'Non-linear phonology in diachronic perspective: Stress and word-structure in Latin and Italian'. In Pier Marco Bertinetto and Michele Loporcaro (eds), *Certamen Phonologicum*, Turin: Rosenberg and Sellier, 421–32.

Vincenzi, Giuseppe Carlo, 1978. 'Italiano e dialetti'. In E. T. Saronne (ed.), *Capire la linguistica*, Bologna: CLUEB, 185–244.

Vogel, Irene, 1975. 'Nasals and nasal assimilation patterns in the acquisition of Chicano Spanish', *Papers and Reports on Child Language Development*, 10: 201–14.

Vogel, Irene, 1982. *La sillaba come unità fonologica*, Bologna: Zanichelli.

Votre, Sebastião-J., 1981. 'Phonological and syntactic aspects of denasalization in spoken Brazilian Portuguese'. In David Sankoff and Henrietta Cedergren (eds), *Variation Omnibus*, Edmonton: Linguistic Research Inc., 97–103.

Vriendt, S. de and Goyvaerts, Didier L., 1989. 'Assimilation and Sandhi in Brussels', *Leuvense Bijdragen* 78: 1–93.

Wagner, Max Leopold, 1941. *Historische Lautlehre der Sardischen*, Beiheft 93 zur *Zeitschrift für Romanische Philologie*, Halle: Max Niemeyer.

Walser, Werner, 1937. *Zur Charakteristik der Mundart des Aosta-Tales*, Aarau: H. R. Sauerländer.

Wang, William, 1969. 'Competing changes as a cause of residue', *Language*, 45: 9–25.

Warren, Donald, Dalston, Rodger and Mayo, Robert, 1993. 'Aerodynamics of nasalization'. In Marie K. Huffman and Rena A. Krakow (eds), *Nasals, Nasalization and the Velum*, San Diego: Academic Press, 119–46

Watson, Ian M. C., 1983. 'Cues to the voicing contrast: A survey', *Cambridge Papers in Phonetics and Experimental Linguistics*, 2.

Watson, Ian M. C., 1991. 'Phonological change in French: Conceptions and representations'. Paper presented at the History of the French Language *Journée d'Études*, Oxford, 2 March.

Watson, Ian M. C., 1992. *Phonologization and Phonetic Processes*, Unpublished manuscript: University of Oxford.

Werlen, Iwar, 1982. 'Velarisierung, Gutturalisierung in den deutschen Dialekten'. In Werner Besch, Ulrich Knoop, Wolfgang Putschke and Herbert Ernst Wiegand (eds), *Dialektologie*, Berlin: Walter de Gruyter, vol. 2: 1130–6.

Wetzels, W. Leo, 1987. 'The timing of latent consonants in Modern French'. In Carol Neidle and Rafael A. Núñez Cedeño (eds), *Studies in Romance Languages*, Dordrecht: Foris, 283–317.

Wetzels, Leo and Sezer, Engin (eds), 1986. *Studies in Compensatory Lengthening*, Dordrecht: Foris.

Whalen, D. S. and Beddor, Patrice S., 1989. 'Connections between nasality and vowel duration and height: Elucidation of the Eastern Algonquian intrusive nasal', *Language*, 65: 457–86.

Wheeler, Max W., 1988. 'Occitan'. In Martin Harris and Nigel Vincent (eds), *The Romance Languages*, London: Croom Helm, 246–78.

Wiik, Kalevi, 1991. 'On a third type of speech rhythm: Foot timing', *PICPhS*, 12, 3: 298–301.

Williams, Edwin B., 1962. *From Latin to Portuguese*, Philadelphia, PA: University of Pennsylvania Press.

Witucki, Jeannette, 1974. 'The vowels of Chamorro'. *Papers in Philippine Linguistics*, 6: 55–74.

Yager, Kent, 1989. 'La -m bilabial en posición final absoluta en el español hablado en Mérida, Yucatán, México', *Nueva Revista de Filología Hispánica*, 37: 83–94.

Yegorova, R. P., 1977. *The Sindhi Language*, Moscow: Nauka.

Zee, Eric, 1979. 'Effect of vowel quality on perception of nasals in noise', *UCLA WPPh*, 45: 130–49.

Zee, Eric, 1981. 'Effect of vowel quality on perception of post-vocalic nasal consonants in noise', *JPhon*, 9: 35–48.

Zee, Eric, 1985. 'Sound change in syllable-final nasal consonants in Chinese', *JCL*, 13: 291–330.

Zörner, Lotte, 1985. 'Fonetica storica del piacentino presentata in base ai dialetti di Travo e di Groppallo', *Studi mediolatini e volgari*, 31: 205–46.

Zue, Victor W. and Sia, Eng-Beng, 1982. 'Nasal articulation in homorganic clusters in American English', *Working Papers of the MIT Research Laboratory of Electronics*, 1: 9–17.

INDEXES

LANGUAGES

AUTHORS

LATIN WORDS

Universals of Sound Change
in Nasalization

Publications of the Philological Society, 31